The Coming Free

Sometimes, the valley was filled with tears,
But I kept trudging on through the lonely years.
Sometimes, the road was hot with sun,
But I had to keep on till my work was done:
I *had* to keep on! No stopping for me—
I was the seed of the coming Free.
I nourished the dream that nothing could smother
Deep in my breast—the Negro mother.
I had only hope then, but now through you,

Dark ones of today, my dreams must come true:
All you dark children in the world out there,
Remember my sweat, my pain, my despair.
Remember my years, heavy with sorrow—
And make of those years a torch for tomorrow.
Make of my past a road to the light
Out of the darkness, the ignorance, the night.

from *The Negro Mother* by Langston Hughes

The Coming Free

DAVID RUBEL

FOREWORD BY

JOHN LEWIS

London, New York, Munich,
Melbourne, and Delhi

Project Editor   Anja Schmidt
Art Director   Dirk Kaufman
Editorial Assistant   Michelle Kasper
Designer   Jeremy Canceko
Design Assistance   Mark Johnson Davies
DTP Coordinator   Milos Orlovic
Production Manager   Ivor Parker
Project Director   Sharon Lucas
Creative Director   Tina Vaughan
Publisher   Carl Raymond

Agincourt Press
President   David Rubel
Senior Image Editor   Julia Rubel
Senior Image Researcher   Erika Rubel
Copy Editor   Laura Jorstad

For photo credits, see pp. 302–303.

Published in the United States in 2005 by
DK Publishing, Inc.
375 Hudson Street,
New York, New York 10014

Published in Great Britain in 2005 by
Dorling Kindersley Limited
80 Strand, London WC2R 0RL

05 06 07 08 09 10 9 8 7 6 5 4 3 2 1

A catalog record for this book is available from
the Library of Congress.

A CIP catalogue record for this book is available from
the British Library (UK)

ISBN: 0-7566-0728-0 (Hardcover)
UK ISBN: 1 4053 1053 7

Color reproduction by
GRB Editrice, Italy
Printed and bound in China by
Leo Paper Group

Discover more at
www.dk.com

Martin Luther King Jr. kneels in prayer before
being led off to jail in Selma, Alabama, in February
1965. At the time, King was leading a Southern
Christian Leadership Conference campaign in
Selma to gain African Americans the right to vote.

CONTENTS

Foreword: Forever Coming Free

It's been a long and continuing struggle to make our country what Abraham Lincoln called "a more perfect union." Fifty years have passed since the first days of the Montgomery bus boycott and the lynching of Emmett Till. Forty years have passed since that Bloody Sunday in Selma, Alabama, and the passage of the Voting Rights Act. Gone are the legal barriers of segregation, but our freedom as a nation has not yet been won. We have come a great distance, but we still have much further to go before we lay down the burden of race in America. And if we are to fulfill the true destiny of this nation, then that struggle must continue.

The founders of this great nation challenged us all with a unique mission. They asked us to use all of our imagination and all of our creative power to build a nation on the potency and the fragility of ideas, and then they made the ideals of liberty and justice the cornerstone of this system. They left us with some fundamental guidance—the U.S. Constitution and the Bill of Rights—and they outlined how those ideals could be shaped into a governmental framework, but the rest is up to us. As a nation and as a people we must live those ideals to make them real. So it is the mandate of every American—every member of Congress or local school board, every U.S. president or sitting judge, every business owner or community activist, every student and average citizen—we all must confirm and reconfirm our commitment to those ideals every day to make that dream a reality.

Freedom is not a state; it is not a plateau or a mountaintop to rest upon. Freedom is an act. It is a series of conscious choices that lead successively to a continually more enlightened society. Freedom is forever coming; we are forever coming free. And every act we make as American citizens, every policy of government, every tactic of business, every step we take collectively and individually affects our ability to meet our mandate. In the civil rights movement we used to say that our struggle was not for a month, a season, or a year. We knew that ours was the struggle of a lifetime and that each generation had to do its part to build what we called in the movement the "beloved community," a nation at peace with itself.

Consider those two words: *beloved* and *community*. *Beloved* means not hateful, not violent, not uncaring, not unkind. And *community* means not separated, not polarized, not locked in struggle. The most pressing challenge in our society today is defined by the methods we use to defend the dignity of humankind. But too often we are focused on accumulating the trappings of a comfortable life.

John Lewis in Atlanta in July 1965, two years into his chairmanship of the Student Nonviolent Coordinating Committee (SNCC).

The men, women, and children depicted in this book put aside the comfort of their own lives to get involved with the problems of others. They knew that if they wanted a free and just society, they could not wait for someone else to create that society. They knew they had to be the change that they were seeking. They knew they had to do their part, to get out there and push and pull to bring this society forward.

As a young child, I tasted the bitter fruits of racism, and I didn't like it. I saw those signs that said WHITE MEN, COLORED MEN, WHITE WOMEN, COLORED WOMEN, WHITE WAITING, and COLORED WAITING. I heard about the nightriders of the Ku Klux Klan. I knew the brutality of the Jim Crow codes of tradition and law that ruled the American South.

I used to ask my mother, my father, and my grandparents, my great-grandparents, "Why segregation?! Why racial discrimination?"

And they would say, "That's the way it is. Don't get in trouble. Don't get in the way."

But when I was fifteen years old, I heard the voice of Martin Luther King Jr. on an old radio, and it sounded like he was talking directly to me. He talked about ordinary men and women with extraordinary vision who decided to take a stand. At that moment,

I knew that I could strike a blow against racial discrimination. I decided I would get in the way. I decided I would get in trouble. But it was good trouble; it was necessary trouble.

As American citizens and citizens of the world, we must be maladjusted to the problems and conditions of today. We have to find a way to dramatize our issues. And we have to get in the way. We just have to get in the way and make our voices heard. We have an obligation, a mission, and a mandate to do our part. We have a mandate from the Spirit of History to follow in the footsteps of those brave and courageous men and women who fought to make a difference.

The Coming Free is a testimony to the struggle to enhance the dignity and worth of every human being. This pictorial history is not just the history of African Americans, but the history of all America. It serves as an important reminder to all who read it of the sacrifices one generation made for the cause of civil rights. It serves as a reminder of the sacrifices we may have to make again, if we do not value the freedom we have already won. It serves as a reminder of the sacrifice required to answer the call of justice.

Enjoy this book. Read the text, study the photographs, and look deeply into the faces of a determined people, ordinary men

On Bloody Sunday—March 7, 1965—civil rights demonstrators began a march from Selma, Alabama, to Montgomery, the state capital. At the Selma city limits, the marchers were beaten into retreat by state troopers. In this photograph, John Lewis (center, wearing a light coat) tries to ward off their blows.

and women with extraordinary vision who brought about a nonviolent revolution under the rule of law, a revolution of values, a revolution of ideas. And let it inspire you to go out and find a way to get in the way. Let it inspire you to make some contribution to humanity. You have a mission and a mandate from the founders of this nation and all of those who came before who struggled and died for your freedom. Go out and win some victory for humanity, and let the spirit of this nation's history, let the spirit of the modern-day civil rights movement be your guide.

John Lewis

Rep. John Lewis

LEFT: **A view of the August 1963** March on Washington from inside the Lincoln Memorial. TOP: **John Lewis delivers** his controversial speech at the March on Washington. RIGHT: **In February 2004, Lewis,** now a congressman from Georgia, recounts his Bloody Sunday experiences to Ohio senator Mike Dewine as they walk across the Edmund Pettus Bridge in Selma, Alabama, the scene of the 1965 attack.

PART I
NOT SLAVE, NOT FREE

The Civil War made a shambles of the American South, overthrowing its political leadership and demolishing the better part of its economic infrastructure. On a more personal level, former Confederate soldiers returned home to find that whatever wealth they had once possessed was largely gone—either expropriated by Confederate tax collectors, plundered by foraging soldiers, or destroyed by Union armies bent on wrecking the South's ability to make war. Despite Ulysses S. Grant's graciousness to Robert E. Lee at Appomattox, there was no doubt which side had won the war. Thus the era of Reconstruction began.

As a consequence of the war, the slaves were freed, but what does one do with more than four million people deprived of the only economic system they have ever known? What does one do with those people, suddenly thrust into a depressed economy with no skills, no assets, and no support structures? The modern civil rights movement of the 1950s and 1960s is sometimes called the Second Reconstruction because the first one failed so miserably to provide satisfactory answers to these questions.

Under Ulysses S. Grant and William Tecumseh Sherman, the Union army waged "total war" during late 1864 and early 1865, methodically disemboweling the southern economy. A northern photographer who journeyed to Charleston to record the ceremonial flag raising at Fort Sumter on April 14, 1865, took this photograph of central Charleston, through which Sherman's army had passed two months earlier.

The New Slavery 1864–1907

Perhaps the best place to begin this story is in Atlanta during the fall of 1864. Union general William T. Sherman's capture of that city in September and his subsequent March to the Sea made it clear to anyone paying attention that the Confederacy was doomed. Pres. Abraham Lincoln's November 1864 reelection, until then much in doubt, became assured, and planning began in earnest for the collapse of the Confederacy. Most of the debate in Congress involved the terms under which the rebellious South would be reintegrated into the Union. Considering the war's unprecedented carnage, President Lincoln's policy was rather lenient. With the exception of the top Confederate leaders, he proposed pardoning all southerners who took an oath of loyalty to the Union.

Furthermore, once 10 percent of a state's voters had taken such an oath, they could elect a new state government and seek readmission to the Union. Because most Republicans in Congress favored a higher bar, preferring a 50 percent standard, the debate continued, and it was ongoing on April 14, 1865, when Lincoln was shot by John Wilkes Booth and Andrew Johnson became president.

This Civil War–era ambrotype shows an unidentified Union private in 1864. Soldiers often purchased these inexpensive photographs as keepsakes for loved ones.

With Congress out of session for the next eight months, Johnson was able to do as he pleased. So, beginning in late May 1865, he launched the brief era of presidential Reconstruction with a series of proclamations that allowed southerners to establish new state governments under even more lenient terms than Lincoln had contemplated. The new legislatures were required to repudiate slavery, secession, and the Confederate war debt; otherwise, no conditions were placed on them.

Johnson further promised to lift federal military rule in all complying states and permit them to send delegations to Congress. Given these easy terms, it wasn't long before nearly every former Confederate state met them.

The practical consequences of this laissez-faire policy became apparent in early December 1865, when the Thirty-ninth Congress (elected with Lincoln in November 1864) convened its first session. The Johnson-authorized state governments sent representatives as well, and among those presenting credentials were such notorious former rebels as Alexander Stephens of Georgia, who had been vice president of the Confederacy. Northern Republicans were outraged, and, led by Pennsylvania congressman Thaddeus Stevens, they blocked the seating of the southerners. Stevens's faction, known as the Radical Republicans, didn't yet control a majority in either house—the real power still lay with Republican moderates—but a combination of southern arrogance and presidential intransigence quickly carried the moderates (along with the bulk of the northern electorate) into the Radical camp.

THE BLACK CODES

Meanwhile, on December 18, 1865, Secretary of State William H. Seward, a holdover from the Lincoln administration, announced that the required number of states had ratified the

This poster offered rewards for the three conspirators in the Lincoln assassination still at large. It was one of the first "wanted" posters to use photographs of the fugitives being sought.

Thirteenth Amendment. Thus, slavery was abolished in the United States, but what of the former slaves? The Thirty-eighth Congress had chosen to treat the freed people as wards of the state, and just before passing out of existence in March 1865, it had created the Freedmen's Bureau to meet their immediate needs. Yet this approach did not last.

Although the Freedmen's Bureau was generally helpful to the former slaves—who appreciated its efforts to feed, shelter, and educate them—it was never properly funded and often failed to meet its own goals. Moreover, white southerners loathed the bureau and opposed its activities from the start. They had another plan in mind for shaping the new black labor force—

which they enunciated in the Black Codes, a collection of laws passed by the Johnson-authorized state governments during late 1865 and early 1866. Although specific regulations varied from state to state, the Black Codes were universally designed, in the words of one observer, to "restore all of slavery but its name." They denied freed people the right to vote, restricted their movement, outlawed their ownership of land, excluded them from certain jobs, made them subject to a separate and much more severe penal code, and prohibited their possession of firearms. This last condition made southern blacks especially vulnerable to the white paramilitary groups then forming.

Although southern whites insisted that the Black Codes were necessary to prevent social chaos in the wake of emancipation, most congressional moderates saw them for what they were, an arrogant effort to reimpose white mastery over the daily lives of blacks. Despite the December 1865 credentials fight, most congressmen had to this point remained hopeful of compromising with the president on a new and more balanced Reconstruction policy. When Johnson remained stubbornly committed to his own ideas, however, even after the imposition of the Black Codes, their patience finally expired.

"By early 1866," historian Eric Foner has written, "moderates had concluded that equality before the law—enforced, if necessary, by national authority—had become an inevitable consequence of emancipation and a condition for restoring the South to full participation in the Union." This principle became the basis for the

Andrew Johnson
1808–1875

Andrew Johnson was a staunch Democrat from the mountains of eastern Tennessee, where his core constituents were yeoman farmers. Like those people, he resented the preeminence of the southern planter aristocracy. When Tennessee left the Union in June 1861, Johnson became the only U.S. senator from a seceding state to remain loyal. It wasn't because he opposed slavery. Johnson was a slaveholder himself and an inveterate racist who loved the South and its traditions. He just hated the plantation owners more.

As president, Johnson assumed that, without federal intervention, yeomen would naturally displace the planters who had led the South into rebellion. This assumption proved to be groundless. Yet even when the old elite resumed its place of power, Johnson refused to reconsider the wisdom of his Reconstruction program.

Civil Rights Act of 1866, which defined all people born in the United States as national citizens and specified the rights to which each was entitled, regardless of his race. These included the rights to make contracts, bring lawsuits, and enjoy the "full and equal benefit of all laws and proceedings for the security of person and property." Never before had the federal government defined the rights of citizenship in statute law, and the act marked a substantial shift in federal–state

relations. Previously, states had been the primary definers and protectors of citizens' rights.

Congress acted so boldly because more was at stake than the rights of the freed people. Although the North had won the war, it was beginning to seem under presidential

Former slaves read Bibles in this postwar photograph of a refugee-camp-*cum*-school set up by the Freedmen's Bureau in Arlington, Virginia.

Reconstruction that the South was winning the peace, and this was an outcome no northern politician could tolerate.

Blinded by his emotions, President Johnson failed to recognize the situation and therefore blundered badly. He despised the Civil Rights Act because it offended both his deeply held racism and his states' rights belief that the federal government had no business defining the individual rights of citizens. So he vetoed the bill, permanently poisoning his relationship with the Republican moderates, who enacted it anyway. The Civil Rights Act of 1866 thus became the first major piece of legislation ever passed over a presidential veto.

THE FOURTEENTH AMENDMENT

Yet the incensed Republicans still weren't satisfied. Unwilling to entrust the principle of equal protection to shifting congressional majorities, they decided to write it into the Constitution as the Fourteenth Amendment, passed in June 1866 and later revered as the law's most powerful bulwark of minority rights. Before the amendment could be ratified, however, it became the central issue in the unusually exciting 1866 midterm elections. Eager for support, President Johnson toured the nation, campaigning vigorously for congressional candidates

associated with his National Union party. (These were mostly Democrats who had backed his lenient approach to Reconstruction and opposed ratification of the Fourteenth Amendment.) Meanwhile, Republicans defended the amendment, emphasizing that only its ratification could prevent the Confederacy from rising again in the South.

The outcome was a Republican landslide and, more importantly, a strong mandate for the Radicals, who gained veto-proof majorities in both houses of Congress. At Johnson's urging, all of the southern legislatures (with the notable exception of Tennessee) responded during the winter of 1866–1867 with rejections of the Fourteenth Amendment, but the gestures were meaningless. The Republican moderates, still enraged by Johnson's pigheadedness, had already thrown in with the Radicals, and on March 2, 1867, the day before the Thirty-ninth Congress adjourned, they began the era of congressional Reconstruction by passing, over another of Johnson's vetoes, the Reconstruction Act of 1867. This law returned the South to military occupation, creating five districts and placing each under the control of a military governor.

Blanche K. Bruce of Mississippi was one of sixteen blacks to serve in Congress during Reconstruction. He served in the U.S. Senate from 1875 until 1881.

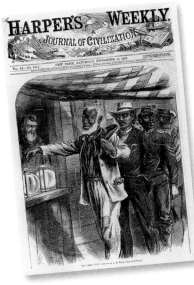

This cover of the November 16, 1867, issue of *Harper's Weekly* shows blacks voting for the first time.

The act also made ratification of the Fourteenth Amendment a prerequisite for readmission to the Union and required the establishment of new state governments based on the principle of universal manhood suffrage. In other words, it gave African Americans the right to vote.

Once in place, the federal troops began compiling lists of eligible voters. Following the dictates of the legislation, they included blacks while excluding most whites because of their former allegiance to the Confederacy. The result was, predictably, black-dominated Republican majorities in nearly every southern state. When subsequently given the opportunity to vote, these new electorates enthusiastically ratified the Fourteenth Amendment and also put into office the first generation of African-American public servants.

INTERRACIAL DEMOCRACY

These new politicians came from the emerging black middle class, made up primarily of artisans who had been free before the war but also including Union army veterans and literate slave ministers. They served locally as sheriffs, judges, and city councilmen; on the state and county level as legislators and commissioners; and federally as congressmen and senators. Most pressed diligently for elimination of the southern caste system and what they called the "uplift" of their race, but equally important was their mere existence, which gave fresh hope to the freed people that one day comparable economic and social gains might match their already astounding political progress.

During the late 1860s and early 1870s, genuine interracial democracy indeed developed in the South, yet it didn't flourish there. Federal laws had clearly established the rights of African Americans, and federal troops had been sent to protect those rights, but the national government's ability to impose its will on recalcitrant states and counties has always been more valued in theory than in practice.

The murderous antagonism of so many whites was too much for the fragile interracial governments to bear, and it

This wood engraving from the January 27, 1872, issue of *Harper's Weekly* shows three members of the Ku Klux Klan from Mississippi wearing the disguises in which they were captured.

The Ku Klux Klan

The original Ku Klux Klan was founded in Pulaski, Tennessee, in 1866 as a fraternal organization. Its first members were Confederate veterans who wanted to keep alive the camaraderie they had enjoyed during the war years. Quickly, however, the Klan became a rallying point for white opposition to emancipation, and in 1867, former Confederate lieutenant general Nathan Bedford Forrest transformed the group into a terrorist organization strong enough to challenge the Radical Republican rule of Tennessee governor William G. Brownlow.

The Klan soon spread to other Black Belt states, deriving its strength from the refusal of southern whites to accept citizenship for blacks. The more blacks voted and held office, the crazier whites got, fueling horrific violence. Favorite KKK targets included white Republican leaders and blacks who asserted their rights.

forced them to seek even more help from Washington. Ulysses S. Grant, who succeeded Andrew Johnson as president in March 1869, was initially responsive. Not the racist Johnson had been, he made the suppression of white violence against southern blacks a central purpose of his administration. For example, in October 1871, six months after Congress passed the Ku Klux Klan Act empowering the president to declare martial law in terrorized communities, Grant used the

new legislation to federalize South Carolina, where the Klan had been mobilizing to prevent African Americans from voting in the upcoming state elections.

Over the long term, however, Grant's aggressive deployment of troops failed to restrain white southerners, who continued to use violence to destabilize local Republican governments. The southerners understood that, sooner or later, northern resolve would have to weaken, and of course it did. In the aftermath of the financial panic of 1873 (brought on by unbridled postwar speculation), the country entered a deep depression, during which Grant and his political allies craved political stability. Because such stability could never be achieved while the status of the southern Negro remained a national issue, the question of what to do with the freed people once again came before the nation. This time, the answer was not so kind.

Already, passage of the May 1872 Amnesty Act had restored the political rights of hundreds of thousands of white Democrats, returning them to the voter rolls and precipitating the defeat of several Republican administrations. As a result, federal civil rights laws became nearly impossible to enforce in those states, and when violence surged again during the mid-1870s, Grant declined to intervene. The date usually given for the end of Reconstruction is 1877, when the last federal troops were removed from the South; however, it was the resurgence of the southern Democratic party in 1872 and 1873 that made this outcome inevitable.

THE 1876 PRESIDENTIAL ELECTION

By 1876, white Democrats had retaken control of nearly every former Confederate state. Just three—

This cartoon from the May 12, 1880, issue of *Puck* ridicules the "strong" government of Ulysses S. Grant, caricatured here as a carpetbagger. In an adjoining panel, however, current president Rutherford B. Hayes is attacked for being too weak.

> ## "The whole public are tired of these annual autumnal outbreaks in the South."
>
> PRES. ULYSSES S. GRANT ON THE ELECTION-TIME VIOLENCE

Florida, Louisiana, and South Carolina—remained in Republican hands, and Republicans held these states only tenuously.

In the 1876 presidential election, Democrat Samuel J. Tilden won the popular vote by more than a quarter million ballots. The New York governor also led in the electoral college, 184–165, but twenty votes remained in question. One of these belonged to an Oregon elector whose job as a U.S. postmaster disqualified him under the Constitution. The rest belonged to the states of Florida, Louisiana, and South Carolina, each of which produced two sets of returns, one filed by the Democrats and the other by the Republicans. After some delay and consternation, Congress appointed a fifteen-member commission, made up of eight Republicans and seven Democrats, to resolve the disputed points. In each case, the commission voted along party lines for Republican candidate Rutherford B. Hayes.

Once this pattern became clear, southerners began threatening a filibuster that would have blocked completion of the

THE "STRONG" GOVERNMENT 1869–1877.

Sharecropping

The former slaves who submitted themselves to sharecropping did so because it was one of the few ways in which they could sustain themselves and their families without capital. To be a sharecropper required nothing. The landowners provided them with land, tools, seed, fertilizer, and a shack in which their families could live. Landowners also supplied on credit (at vastly inflated rates) other necessities of life, such as food and clothing. In exchange, they claimed from one-half to two-thirds of the resulting crop (or more, if they cheated, which many did).

All family members were put to work. Typically, the men plowed while the women and children hoed and harvested. Because their labor was often essential, the children of sharecroppers rarely attended school. In 1900, less than one-quarter of sharecropper children between the ages of five and nine were receiving any formal education.

electoral count. This threat was never carried out, however, because the Republicans made a deal. In exchange for accepting Hayes as president, the southerners were promised a number of concessions, including the immediate withdrawal of all federal troops from the South. For the record, the southerners also promised to respect the rights of the freed people, although they were never held accountable for this last undertaking.

Once restored to power, the South's white ruling class set about erasing whatever gains blacks had made during congressional Reconstruction. The economic reenslavement of African Americans took some time, however, because first their political rights had to be suppressed. In 1865 and 1866, the Johnson-authorized state governments had accomplished this simply by passing discriminatory laws, but the ratification of the Fifteenth Amendment in 1870 now precluded race-based disfranchisement. Therefore, other strategies had to be developed and implemented. The most effective of these were the gerrymandering of voting districts, indirectly discriminatory voting qualifications such as the literacy test and the poll tax, and massive election fraud.

In Mississippi, for example, a constitutional convention was called in 1890 for the explicit purpose of eliminating the black vote. According to the terms of the literacy test it adopted, a Mississippi voter must "be able to read any section of the Constitution of the United States, or he shall be able to understand the same when read to him, or give a reasonable interpretation thereof." The catch was that the assessment of an applicant's literacy was left up to the judgment of

A boy drives an ox-drawn cart through Thomasville, Georgia, during the late 1880s.

the white county registrars—who, as one might expect, rejected nearly all black applicants while passing nearly all whites. As a result, black registration in Mississippi dropped from 190,000 in 1890 to just 8,000 in 1892, and when the federal government declined to challenge the practice, other states adopted similar measures.

THE NEW ECONOMIC SLAVERY

In the meantime, most southern states returned to the strategy of the Black Codes—that is, the legal manipulation of African-American behavior—backed up, as always, by the threat of violence. Their primary goal was to restore discipline and predictability to the southern agricultural workforce. New statutes that would have been impossible to enact while blacks remained a potent political force now became law all over the South. Some limited the economic options of plantation laborers in order to bind them more closely to the land. Others sought to remove black children from their families and transfer them to the control of white landowners for court-ordered "apprenticeships." Still others required blacks to sign annual labor contracts or face arrest for vagrancy. It was believed that nothing less than the survival of the plantation elite depended on the South's ability to resume production of cotton using gang labor of the sort common under slavery.

With neither land of their own nor the skills necessary to succeed in an urban economy, most freed people had no choice but to remain agricultural laborers. Still, they resisted wage labor and refused to work in gangs. Instead, they reached an accommodation with the plantation owners: They would work portions of the old plantation land themselves—that is, without a white overseer—and split the harvest with the landowner. This system, called sharecropping, seemed fair enough in theory, but in practice it quickly became another efficient means of black exploitation. Many sharecroppers kept as little as one-third of their harvests, and by the time that the white landowners deducted the costs of supplies provided on credit, there was often nothing left. In fact, plantation accounting was such that no matter what the actual costs of the advanced supplies, sharecroppers usually found themselves in debt to the landowner and therefore unable to leave. As late as 1910, five decades after emancipation, only one-quarter of black farmers in the South owned the land they worked.

Meanwhile, the region's social order was also transformed. During Reconstruction, blacks and whites had tended to keep to their own institutions, but this separation was a matter of choice and custom, not law, and its specifics varied from place to place. After 1877, however, whites throughout the South began treating racial segregation, which had never been rigidly observed, as a long-standing southern "folkway" —a revisionist assertion that they used to justify a succession of Jim Crow laws further restricting black behavior. The first of these, enacted in Tennessee in 1881, required railroads to provide separate coaches for black and white passengers. Louisiana passed a similar law in 1890, providing for "equal but separate accommodations for the white and colored races" on its trains.

PLESSY V. FERGUSON

In 1891, a group of well-to-do New Orleans blacks organized to fight what was happening to them. Creating the Citizens' Committee to Test the Constitutionality of the Separate Car Law, they raised money, obtained legal counsel, and searched for a suitable plaintiff of mixed blood to demonstrate the law's arbitrariness. (The South's "one-drop" rule held that anyone with Negro blood was a Negro, no matter what the amount

A rear view of a Pullman "Tryphosa" lounge car. This all-wood, eight-section car, built at the Pullman Car Works in June 1890, was similar to stock that the East Louisiana Railway would have operated.

Jim Crow Laws

In 1828, a struggling white entertainer named Thomas Dartmouth "Daddy" Rice began performing a new dance to an old slave song he had recently learned. "Come listen all you galls and boys/I'm going to sing a little song/My name is Jim Crow/Weel about and turn about and do jis so/Eb'ry time I weel about I jump Jim Crow," the lyrics went.

One of the first whites to wear blackface, Rice enjoyed such great success with the number that Jim Crow eventually became a stock character (along with Jim Dandy and Zip Coon) in the minstrel shows that dominated American popular entertainment during the mid–nineteenth century. Gradually, the name also became a racial epithet, considered about as harsh as *darky* or *coon* but much less offensive than *nigger*.

A caricatured African-American banjo player of the sort made famous by Jim Crow minstrel shows.

or the actual color of his skin.) The man the committee found was thirty-year-old Homer A. Plessy, a Creole shoemaker so light-skinned that he could easily pass for white. On June 7, 1892, Plessy bought a first-class ticket and boarded a train of the East Louisiana Railway, seating himself in a car reserved for whites. By the committee's prearrangement with the railroad, which objected to the cost of the extra segregated cars, the conductor asked Plessy his race. "Colored," Plessy replied, and when he refused the conductor's request that he move, he was arrested.

Plessy's case first came to trial in the Criminal District Court for the Parish of New Orleans, where Judge John H. Ferguson ruled that the Separate Car Act was indeed constitutional. When Ferguson's decision was upheld by the Louisiana Supreme Court, Plessy appealed to the U.S. Supreme Court, where his white lawyer, Albion W. Tourgée, argued that Louisiana's law violated the Fourteenth Amendment because it denied Plessy equal protection. Unfortunately, by a decisive 7–1 vote, the Court disagreed, holding in *Plessy v. Ferguson* (1896) that "merely a

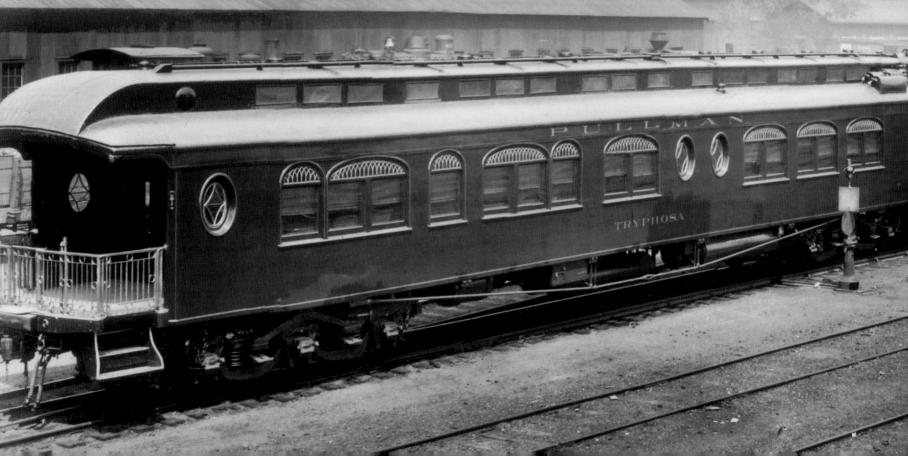

In 1895, Ida B. Wells married Chicago lawyer Ferdinand L. Barnett even though Susan B. Anthony advised her against the union, telling Wells that she possessed a "special call for special work."

A large crowd gathers in 1893 to watch the lynching of a black man accused of murdering a three-year-old white girl.

Ida B. Wells and the Antilynching Crusade

No one knows for certain how many African Americans were lynched between 1880 and 1920, when the grisly practice was at its height, but probably about three thousand were hanged, shot, burned alive, or tortured to death in order to establish and preserve white supremacy in the South.

Given the total population of about ten million blacks in 1920, the probability of any one Negro being lynched was rather remote. But the terror of lynching lay more in its threat than in its execution. Lynching intimidated blacks and excited whites *not* because it was common, but because it could be perpetrated at any moment without fear of punishment.

Lynchings in the South were typically carried out by "respectable" citizens, whose actions were supported by police and defended zealously by local politicians. Police officers released victims into the custody of the lynch mob, and the only regret commonly expressed by southern politicians was that they weren't able to take part personally.

The most common justification for lynching was the allegation of rape, a highly emotional charge that southern whites used to disguise the harsh political logic of their lawlessness. "There is only one crime that warrants lynching," South Carolina governor Benjamin R. "Pitchfork Ben" Tillman declared, "and Governor as I am, I would lead a mob to lynch the negro who ravishes a white woman."

White southerners generally defended the practice of lynching fiercely. For example, when Ida B. Wells began attacking it in 1892, she was forced to leave the South under threat of death.

Born into slavery in northern Mississippi, Wells attended Rust University, where she had studied to become a teacher. (Rust was one of many schools for freed people founded in the South by northern missionaries after the Civil War.) Unfortunately, a yellow fever epidemic in 1878 killed both of her parents, forcing her to leave school to care for her six younger siblings. Using what she had learned at Rust, Wells found teaching jobs in small, rural schools and later in nearby Memphis.

Although her low wages barely sustained her, the fact that she was a teacher bestowed a measure of middle-class respectability, which she used to insinuate herself into Memphis's bustling black social life. Discovering that she preferred journalism to teaching, Wells soon began writing articles for a local black newspaper. In 1891, she became part-owner and editor of the *Memphis Free Speech*.

On March 9, 1892, Calvin McDowell, Thomas Moss, and Will Stewart were taken from the Memphis city jail and lynched. These three prosperous African Americans had jointly owned a grocery store that had been competing successfully with a neighboring white store. Resentful of their success, their white neighbor had begun feuding with them, and over time the dispute escalated from street brawls to the shooting of three sheriff's deputies by armed men guarding the People's Grocery Company.

On May 21, 1892, an unsigned editorial in the *Free Speech* denounced the lynchings as murder. "Nobody in this section of the country believes the old threadbare lie that Negro men rape white women," Wells wrote anonymously. The *Memphis Evening Scimitar* responded with its own editorial, urging that the author of the *Free Speech* article (assumed to be a man) be tied to a stake and castrated. Wells's male business partner fled the city, and Wells herself, lecturing in New York City, chose not to return home.

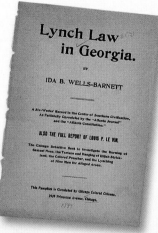

An 1893 pamphlet by Ida B. Wells titled *Lynch Law in Georgia*.

Because the lynchings of McDowell, Moss, and Stewart had followed unquestionably from a business rivalry rather than a rape, Wells began looking into the circumstances of other lynchings and came to the conclusion that the practice was fundamentally a means of keeping blacks in their economic place. Her research led to the publication in 1895 of *A Red Record*, which used statistical analysis to show that charges of rape occurred in less than a third of all lynchings—and even in those cases, Wells argued, the accusations were usually fictitious.

Wells's efforts changed many minds, both within the United States and overseas, where her European lecture tours generated broad sympathy. Even so, the political reality in America remained largely unaffected. In 1906, Pres. Theodore Roosevelt told Congress (against the pleadings of Booker T. Washington) that "the greatest existing cause of lynching is the perpetuation, especially by black men, of the hideous crime of rape." Not until the Great Migration of the late 1910s, when black workers began leaving the South in large numbers, did southern whites begin to curb the practice in order to keep their labor force at home.

legal distinction" between the two races did not suffice to infringe either the Thirteenth or Fourteenth Amendment.

According to the majority opinion, written by Justice Henry Billings Brown of Michigan, "We consider the underlying fallacy of the plaintiff's argument to consist in the assumption that the enforced separation of the two races stamps the colored race with a badge of inferiority. If this be so, it is not by reason of anything found in the act, but solely because the colored race chooses to put that construction upon it.…The argument also assumes that social prejudice may be overcome by legislation.…Legislation is powerless to eradicate racial instincts or to abolish distinctions based on physical difference, and the attempt to do so can only result in accentuating the differences of the present situation. If the civil and political rights of both races be equal, one cannot be inferior to the other civilly or politically. If one race be inferior to the other socially, the Constitution of the United States cannot put them on the same plane."

In other words, the Court ruled that racial separation did not necessarily imply inferior circumstances for blacks. If such circumstances resulted, Brown argued, they were the creation not of the law but of individual citizens, whose prejudice the Court was not empowered to regulate. From this reasoning arose the "separate-but-equal" standard that was to dominate civil rights law for the next sixty years. It also produced the less well-known but equally important "state-action" doctrine. According to this theory, the prohibitions of the Fourteenth Amendment applied only when the state itself sanctioned the discrimination. Private prejudice, therefore, existed beyond the law's reach.

The lone dissenter was Justice John Marshall Harlan of Kentucky, who issued a memorable rejoinder. The Separate Car Act had little to do with equality, Harlan pointed out, because

Booker T. Washington
1856–1915

Booker Taliaferro Washington was born into squalor in western Virginia, the son of a white man whose name he never knew. He was educated at the Hampton Normal and Industrial Institute, where he encountered the man who would become his mentor, Samuel Chapman Armstrong. The son of missionaries, Armstrong had commanded black troops as a Union brigadier and after the Civil War became an agent of the Freedmen's Bureau. Placed in charge of a large camp of freed people in Hampton, Virginia, he founded the Hampton Institute in 1868 to educate them.

Washington taught at Hampton for two years after his graduation before moving to Tuskegee, Alabama, in 1881 to head the new Tuskegee Institute there. A state-supported normal school, Tuskegee was founded as the result of a political deal between white Democrats and black Republicans. It amounted to little more than a few tumbledown shacks, but working with patience and vigor, Washington was able to transform the campus into a showcase of more than one hundred buildings made of pristine red bricks fired by the students themselves.

A brick and some nails manufactured by Tuskegee students.

Although by self-definition an educator, Washington was more importantly a power broker of the first order and the focal point of race relations in America from his Atlanta Compromise speech in 1895 until his death twenty years later. Not until the emergence of Martin Luther King Jr. two generations after that would an African-American leader command similar influence and respect from both wealthy white northerners and illiterate southern blacks.

> "In the North the Negro can spend a dollar but not earn it, while in the South he can earn a dollar but cannot spend it."

BOOKER T. WASHINGTON

"everyone knows that the statute in question had its origin in the purpose, not so much to exclude white persons from railroad cars occupied by blacks, as to exclude colored people from coaches occupied by or assigned to white persons."

Once a slaveholder himself, Harlan saw clearly the inequities of the new pseudoslavery. "Our Constitution is color-blind and neither knows nor tolerates classes among its citizens," he thundered, but to no avail. The *Plessy* decision correctly identified the emerging national consensus on race and won widespread popular approval. Whatever support for black civil rights had once existed in the North, the southern attitude toward Reconstruction had now come to dominate: Radical Reconstruction had been a terrible mistake and was best forgotten. Much better to leave the matter of race relations up to the individual states, most Americans believed. Meanwhile, emboldened by the *Plessy* decision, those same states quickly enacted new rounds of segregationist legislation.

ACCOMMODATIONISM

One of the first civil rights exercised by freed slaves in the aftermath of the Civil War was the freedom to move about the country. Most stayed within a few days' journey of their homes, searching for lost friends and relatives, but they traveled far enough to realize that

an obvious way to escape exploitation was to leave the South entirely. Yet where could they go and still find food and shelter? Agricultural laborers with neither skills nor education had no more place in the North in 1896 than they had in 1866. Moving there was hardly an option.

So, after *Plessy* made clear the hopelessness of their legal situation, many southern blacks looked elsewhere for relief and found accommodationism, a strategy that accepted the diminished political status of blacks and urged them to concentrate instead on economic advancement. Its chief proponent was Booker T. Washington, president of the Tuskegee Institute. Middle-class accommodationists such as Washington believed that political agitation was both futile and needlessly dangerous. It was much more prudent, they thought, for African Americans to forgo, at least temporarily, their political rights in favor of material self-improvement and the cultivation of white goodwill. The resulting gains in economic status would eventually allow them to claim the same citizenship rights exercised by whites. Or at least that was the plan.

Washington delivered the most famous statement of this doctrine before a predominantly white audience at the Cotton States and International Exposition held in Atlanta in September 1895. The speech, which came to be known as the Atlanta Compromise, proposed that blacks and whites replace political conflict with economic cooperation. Specifically, Washington offered a deal that he believed would accommodate both sides. In exchange for justice from whites, Washington said, blacks would concede two important points: First, they would admit that Radical

An undated photograph of Director of Agricultural Research George Washington Carver with students in his Tuskegee Institute laboratory.

Reconstruction had been a mistake because of its emphasis on political rights rather than the development of economic skills. Second, they would give up all demands for "social equality." Although Washington didn't clarify what he meant by this last phrase, most whites took it to mean a general endorsement of segregation.

For Washington, economic status represented the thin end of a wedge that blacks could use to force their way into white civil society. If blacks became, through patience and hard labor, more valuable cogs in the southern economy, then whites would have to respect them and treat them fairly—or so Washington believed. If not, what was the alternative? Washington could see no more likely course. "The opportunity to earn a dollar in a factory just now," he told his Atlanta audience, "is worth infinitely more than the opportunity to spend a dollar in an opera house."

Hailed by members of both races, the speech made Washington the preeminent voice of black

America for the next two decades. Some opposition was expressed. A small but vocal group of well-educated blacks complained that the Atlanta Compromise was no compromise at all because southern whites conceded nothing. Yet their arguments proved easy for Washington to dismiss at a time when many influential northern philanthropists were rushing to embrace accommodationism, because Washington's ideas complemented their own racial agendas so well.

Men such as Collis P. Huntington of the Central Pacific Railroad, William H. Baldwin of the Southern Railway, and Andrew Carnegie of Carnegie Steel had no interest in supporting equality for blacks because they accepted as self-evident the "scientific" evidence presented at the time—derived from studies of cranial size, for example—that blacks were intellectually inferior to whites. These men also accepted segregation and disfranchisement as necessary and appropriate measures. Yet they gave large amounts of

Tuskegee students lay brick on campus during the 1890s as part of their industrial education.

Industrial Education

In Booker T. Washington's view, the only way that southern blacks could get ahead was through industrial education. As the term was understood at the time, it had nothing to do with preparing students for factory jobs, which were largely off limits to blacks until the 1940s. Instead, *industrial education* meant the teaching of basic agricultural and mechanical skills. It also meant teaching students how to be industrious.

At Tuskegee, as at the Hampton Institute, all of the students were expected to perform manual labor about the school—cooking, cleaning, farming, building, and so on. This requirement helped Washington construct and maintain Tuskegee's facilities. It also allowed poor students to work their way through school.

For the vast majority of blacks, education higher than this was pointless, Washington felt, and his white donors agreed. Only a small group of black critics thought otherwise—pointing out that, with Washington's complicity, whites were using industrial education to eviscerate higher learning for blacks. "I do not believe in the higher education of the darky," Georgia governor Allen D. Candler opined in 1901. "He should be taught the trades, but when he is taught the fine arts he gets educated above his station and it makes him unhappy."

Washington angrily rejected the claim that industrial education placed a ceiling on black achievement, but most of his white benefactors saw it precisely that way. At a time when money for black education was scarce, Washington's fund-raising prowess and attractive ideology ensured that whenever public and private funds were made available, his type of schooling would receive a disproportionate share. As a result, a dual system of instruction emerged, with whites receiving superior educations and blacks inferior ones.

Populism

Even during the increasingly oppressive conditions of the 1880s and 1890s, persevering blacks in some southern states continued to vote in large numbers. This phenomenon was made possible by the disaffection of poor white farmers, who felt similarly exploited and whose votes held the Democratic power structure in check.

During the 1870s and 1880s, most of these farmers had joined cooperative movements such as the Grange and the Farmers' Alliances for the social and economic support they offered. By the late 1880s, however, these organizations had evolved into political juggernauts pressing for farmers' rights.

Recognizing that blacks were their natural political allies, the southern populists began aggressively courting the African-American vote, which still resided primarily in local Republican parties. In North Carolina, one such coalition chased Democrats from office in 1894 and then used its new power to rewrite the state's election laws, making voting simpler and ensuring that all ballots would be counted fairly. These reforms, in turn, permitted the election of a thousand blacks to public office.

Of course, such a happy interlude couldn't last. During the run-up to statewide elections in 1898, the Democratic party in North Carolina manipulated latent racial tensions to break up the governing interracial coalition. For example, warning that a great horde of ignorant Negroes was about to overrun the state, Democratic newspapers headlined spurious accounts of black men raping white women and otherwise incited the populace.

In North Carolina's largest city, Wilmington, the 1898 election was nothing short of a coup. Armed Democrats took to the streets, seizing public buildings and forcing the mayor, the police chief, and members of the city council to resign before banishing them from town. Democratic vigilantes also expelled prominent blacks and burned the offices of the *Wilmington Record*, the state's only black daily newspaper.

North Carolina's Republican governor pleaded with Pres. William McKinley, also a Republican, to send federal troops to Wilmington to protect the city's Republican voters. Yet McKinley refused, confirming northern tolerance of white supremacy in the South.

White vigilantes pose in front of the wrecked offices of the *Wilmington Record* following the November 10, 1898, race riot there.

"Things came to such a pass," W. E. B. Du Bois recalled much later, "that when any Negro complained or advocated a course of action, he was silenced with the remark that Mr. Washington did not agree with this. Naturally, the bumptious, irritated young black intelligentsia of the day declared: 'I don't give a damn what Booker Washington thinks! This is what I think, and *I have a right to think.*'"

THE NIAGARA MOVEMENT

In 1903, Du Bois, then a professor of economics and history at Atlanta University, published a now classic collection of essays titled *The Souls of Black Folk.* In "Of Mr. Booker T. Washington and Others," he chastised Washington for abandoning black political rights and dismissed accommodationism as the surest way to impose, not eliminate, black subjugation. Du Bois's blistering rhetoric galvanized the growing opposition to Washington, and in July 1905 he joined twenty-eight other influential African Americans at Niagara Falls to promote "organized, determined and aggressive action on the part of men who believe in Negro freedom and growth." Among those joining Du Bois were William Monroe Trotter, editor of the *Boston Guardian*, the most avidly anti-Washington of the nation's black newspapers; St. Paul criminal defense attorney Frederick McGhee, who had been born a slave in Mississippi; Dr. Charles E. Bentley of Chicago; Clement Morgan, a Boston lawyer who had been a classmate of Du Bois at Harvard; Harry C. Smith, editor of the *Cleveland Gazette*; and Alonzo F. Herndon, another former slave who had parlayed a small barbershop into the Atlanta Life Insurance Company.

The Declaration of Principles that these men prepared during their three-day meeting made their opposition to accommodationism unmistakably clear. Their core demand was "the abolition of all caste distinctions based simply on race and color." In their tactics as well, they set themselves apart from Washington with a

money to Washington because they saw his emphasis on industrial education as the only workable solution to the South's race problem, which they believed to be fundamentally a labor problem. What the South obviously needed was a permanent underclass of semiskilled black workers. In their view, Washington's program would create just that.

Booker T. Washington, of course, did not share these views. To the contrary, his desire to uplift his race was indisputably sincere. Yet accommodationism failed to serve the African-American community well; in the decade after 1895, the economic and political circumstances of

blacks continued to deteriorate, and whatever gains they achieved through self-help and hard work were more than negated by the escalating discrimination and violence practiced against them. After 1900, in particular, Washington's assertions of racial progress began to sound increasingly hollow and naive. With regard to voting, for example, he said that he would accept literacy tests and other voting qualifications as long as they were applied evenhandedly. Yet everyone, including Washington himself, knew they wouldn't be. Mostly, he discounted the importance of voting, yet his views also had the effect of endorsing white hypocrisy.

promise "to complain loudly and insistently" because "persistent manly agitation is the way to liberty."

Statements such as these widened the split that already existed between Du Bois and Washington and made their interaction, especially on a personal level, exceedingly bitter. Washington understood intellectually that Du Bois's advocacy of agitation was reasonable, if perhaps unwise, but he could never get beyond his own negative emotional

THE NIAGARA MOVEMENT

Enclosed will be found a copy of the Constitution of the Niagara Movement, the declaration of principles, and an explanation of its objects. If, after reading these, you are willing to be enrolled as a member, please detach the slip below, sign it and mail it to
W. E. B. Du Bois, General Secretary,
ATLANTA UNIVERSITY, Atlanta, Ga.

I have read the constitution and address and being in substantial agreement with the same hereby enroll myself as a member of the Niagara Movement.

(Date)
(Address)

A Niagara Movement membership form from the Howard University archives.

reaction to the strident tone of Du Bois's criticism. Rather than responding constructively to the Niagara challenge, Washington instead focused on suppressing it.

Adopting Du Bois's tone himself, Washington belittled the Niagara Movement, calling its members an unrepresentative clique of intellectuals who understood little about the lives of ordinary blacks. Du Bois responded that, as usual, Washington was missing the point. Higher education was necessary for black leaders, Du Bois argued, because only scholar-thinkers could effectively shepherd the unlettered black masses. From this logic emerged Du Bois's idea of the Talented Tenth, an elite group of college-educated urban blacks numbering about one-tenth of the total African-American population, who could lead the race to the promised land of racial equality.

Not surprisingly, Washington prevailed in this encounter. His personal prestige and productive relationships with important whites (among them Pres. Theodore Roosevelt) made blacks

W. E. B. Du Bois
1868–1963

William Edward Burghardt Du Bois was born in Great Barrington, Massachusetts, into a family that had been free for a hundred years. Unlike the impoverished rustic Booker T. Washington, Du Bois began his life near the top of the black world. He grew up as an urban intellectual, attended Fisk University in Nashville, and later became the first African American to obtain a doctorate from Harvard. "The honor, I assure you," he later quipped, "was Harvard's."

While Washington displayed a seemingly limitless capacity for absorbing insult, the prickly Du Bois couldn't bear the pain of racial injustice. He used his formidable erudition as a bulwark against the hurt but couldn't ever make it stop. No doubt it spurred him on, yet it also made his personality quite difficult for others to endure.

reluctant to cast off his leadership. Meanwhile, the Niagara Movement foundered, unable to raise enough funds for its own administration, much less the litigation strategy it had endorsed. Within two years, it was penniless and essentially defunct. Washington had won. Yet the movement's ideas persisted.

Founding members of the Niagara Movement pose in a Niagara Falls photography studio during their 1905 conference. They were forced to lodge on the Canadian side of the falls because every American hotel had a whites-only policy.

Separate But Not Equal

1908–1951

At first glance, the racial violence that consumed Springfield, Illinois, on the night of August 14, 1908, was nothing new. The first decade of the twentieth century had been an especially harrowing time for African Americans, who found slight relief in accommodationism and none at all in the Niagara Movement, which quickly came and went. Meanwhile, the number of lynchings spiked, and race riots seemed to become endemic.

William English Walling (above) and his *Independent* article on the 1908 Springfield, Illinois, race riot (right).

According to newspaper reports published afterward, the proximate cause of the riot was the alleged rape of a white woman by a black man. As was often the case, however, this charge served merely to excuse the release of built-up social pressure caused by changing economic and demographic circumstances. Although Springfield's population was only 10 percent black at the time of the riot, that number had been increasing rapidly, creating unwelcome competition for both unskilled jobs and low-income housing. "Lincoln freed you, we'll show you where you belong," the rampaging whites shouted as they lynched ten Negroes and stampeded two thousand more out of town.

When racial violence broke out in Mobile or Macon or elsewhere in the South, it was usually ignored by whites. However, because this riot had taken place in Springfield, the capital of a supposedly enlightened northern state, it attracted national attention, including that of socialist journalist William English Walling, who traveled himself to Springfield to discover the riot's cause. What Walling found was that the race problem in the United States was entering a new and crucial phase. On September 3, he published his findings in *The Independent*. His article, titled "Race War in the North," clearly identified the riot's cause as race hatred and also contained a call to action: "Either the spirit of the abolitionists, of Lincoln and [Elijah P.] Lovejoy, must be revived and we must come to treat the negro on a plane of absolute political and social equality, or [James K.] Vardaman and [Benjamin] Tillman will soon have transferred their race war to the North."

Returning to New York City, Walling decided that he would found a new organization of "fair-minded whites and intelligent blacks," whose goal would be the development of a new activist approach to the problem of race relations.

THE CALL

Recruiting whites proved easy. The first decade of the twentieth century was the height of the Progressive movement in America, when well-to-do urban reformers set themselves energetically to the task of ridding the United States of its economic disparities and social ills. Energized by a supremely optimistic faith in the future, Progressives sought evolutionary rather than revolutionary change. The political pressure that

During the 1930s, this large banner was flown from a window at NAACP headquarters in New York City (at 69 Fifth Avenue) every time a black man was lynched. The hope was that public awareness would inspire reform.

This photograph shows the exterior of Harry Loper's Cafe on South Fifth Street in Springfield, where some African Americans sought refuge during the 1908 riot.

they generated cleaned up the meatpacking industry, reined in the trusts, encouraged the settlement house movement, and dismantled several corrupt urban political machines. Until Walling began his pontificating, however, racial discrimination had not yet emerged as a significant Progressive issue.

Walling's first recruit was settlement house pioneer Mary White Ovington, a fellow socialist who read Walling's article in *The Independent*. Several weeks later, Ovington noticed that Walling was speaking on Russian politics at Cooper Union. Remembering the article, she decided to attend. During the course of his lecture, Walling pointed out that the race situation in America was far worse in some respects than anything in tsarist Russia. Afterward, Ovington introduced herself and pressed Walling, who was something of a procrastinator, to move forward with his idea for an interracial organization. Walling finally agreed to hold a meeting at his West Thirty-ninth Street apartment in early January 1909.

Oswald Garrison Villard was the son of Fanny Garrison Villard, herself a social reformer of note.

The meeting was attended by Ovington and social worker Henry Moskowitz. Another friend of Walling, muckraker Charles Edward Russell, was invited but couldn't attend. Two decisions were made. First, the group scheduled the beginning of its public campaign to coincide with the upcoming celebration of Lincoln's Birthday. Second, it resolved to recruit Oswald Garrison Villard as its fifth member.

The grandson of abolitionist William Lloyd Garrison, Villard had already received from his father, railroad magnate Henry Villard, a large inheritance that included both the *New York Evening Post* and *The Nation*. Oswald Villard was already familiar with the race issue, having supported Booker T. Washington before lately coming to question Washington's persistent optimism in the face of the deteriorating Negro situation. The invitation to join Walling's group therefore came at a propitious time, and Villard accepted it immediately. His first assignment was to polish the "call" that Walling had drafted as an invitation to the group's first event.

"Villard was an egocentric man of limited personal warmth," historian David Levering Lewis has written, "but he tended to express himself in writing with passion and generosity. Reeling off the mounting outrages against the race of Africans in America, in the North as well as the South, he infused 'The Call' with righteous wrath." The result was both instructive and influential.

"If Mr. Lincoln could revisit this country he would be disheartened by the nation's failure [to assure each citizen equality of opportunity]," Villard wrote. "In many States Lincoln would find justice enforced, if at all, by judges elected by one element in a community to pass upon the liberty and lives of another. He would see the black men and women, for whose freedom a hundred thousand soldiers gave their lives, set apart in trains, in which they pay first-class fares for third-class service,…while State after State declines to do its elementary duty in preparing the negro through education for the best exercise of citizenship." The document ended with a summons to "all the believers in democracy to join in a national

A man was lynched from this tree in Springfield, Illinois, during the August 1908 race riot there.

The Crisis

Two weeks after the closing of the 1910 NCAN conference, Du Bois became director of research and publicity for the new NAACP. This position combined several diverse responsibilities, but, much to Villard's displeasure, Du Bois concentrated on only one: his editorship of the association's monthly magazine, *The Crisis*.

The first issue appeared in November 1910 with a print run of one thousand. Within a year, however, its circulation jumped to sixteen thousand, and by 1919, it topped one hundred thousand, or twice the NAACP membership.

The fact that Du Bois tended to use *The Crisis* as his personal soapbox further irritated Villard. To his regret, the magazine's pages were often filled with attacks on white philanthropists, black ministers, and anyone else who failed to measure up to Du Bois's meticulous standards.

According to David Levering Lewis, when *The Crisis* "wasn't hurling thunderbolts," it "dripped acid." For example, when a white mob at the University of Missouri murdered a black janitor, Du Bois praised the institution for its course in "applied lynching."

The first issue of *The Crisis*, published in November 1910.

W. E. B. Du Bois at his desk in the offices of *The Crisis* during his first year as its editor.

conference for the discussion of present evils, the voicing of protests, and the renewal of the struggle for civil and political safety."

Meanwhile, building on his success with Villard, Walling accelerated his recruiting efforts, and soon the Committee on the Status of the Negro had swelled to fifteen people, three of whom were black. Too large now to continue gathering in Walling's apartment, the group shifted its meetings to the Liberal Club on East Nineteenth Street. By this time, the middle of March, plans were already under way for a National Negro Conference to be held on Monday, May 31, and Tuesday, June 1, at the Charity Organization Society hall off Astor Place. Significantly, Booker T. Washington was not among those contemplated as speakers, yet the list did include W. E. B. Du Bois, whom Charles Edward Russell had recently brought into the group.

THE FOUNDING OF THE NAACP

"The high-ceilinged auditorium of the Charity Organization hall was filled to capacity with a distinguished audience keenly aware of the

history about to be made," David Levering Lewis has explained. "The three hundred or so men and women in the hall included experienced social uplifters, affluent dabblers in reform, descendants of abolitionists,

> "This government cannot exist half slave and half free any better today than it could in 1861."
>
> OSWALD GARRISON VILLARD IN "THE CALL"

public-minded academics, and suffragists—with women comprising nearly one-third of those in attendance."

The first day's morning program consisted of speeches by three Columbia social scientists and one Cornell neurologist disputing the conventional wisdom that blacks were biologically inferior to whites. (Contemporary polygenetic thought held that there were several human species, with Africans making up an inferior order unrelated to whites.) A rare interracial lunch followed, and later that day Du Bois delivered a speech titled "Politics and Industry." Asserting that

disfranchisement had relegated blacks to second-class citizenship, he argued that economic advancement could not be achieved until political rights had been restored—and not the other way around, as Booker Washington would have it.

In the span of an evening, these angry words transformed what had been a rather genteel Monday into a raucous Tuesday.

As Du Bois himself explained in a journal account that he wrote, "The black mass oved forward and stretched out their hands to take charge. It was their problem. They must name the condition." Led by William Monroe Trotter and Ida B. Wells-Barnett, the black delegates strongly disputed the suggestion made by a white attendee that there could be "too much racial agitation." They also moved amendment after amendment to the charter of the National Committee for the Advancement of the Negro (NCAN), which was being created to carry on the conference's work. With Walling in the chair, the meeting nearly fell apart, but once Villard replaced him, the delegates settled down and got to work. Even so, it was nearly midnight before the conference adjourned.

Afterward, a Committee of Forty was established under Villard to appoint the NCAN board, choose its officers, raise money, hire staff, and so on. At this point, Villard moved to bring Washington into the group, believing that it needed his credibility. To make the invitation more palatable, he marginalized agitators such as Trotter and Wells-Barnett, and he would have displaced Du Bois, too, if that had been within his power. Even so, Washington kept his distance and used the Tuskegee Machine, as his political operation was known, to depress interest in the group.

Washington's opposition made Villard's job all the more difficult. "Yet," David Levering Lewis has concluded, "because Villard prided himself on never failing in a cause to which he had publicly committed himself and because Du Bois believed that the fate of his people hung in the balance, these two imperious men exerted themselves through editorials, public addresses, and personal suasion to solidify their respective bases." In May 1910, they staged the organization's second conference, out of which came the retooled National Association for the Advancement of Colored People (NAACP), the nation's oldest extant civil rights organization.

THE PINK FRANKLIN CASE

Shaping an effective interracial organization was especially difficult because there were no applicable historical precedents for its leaders to follow. Although most NAACP members were black and blacks were well represented on its board of directors, the organization's top officers were white, as was most of its professional staff. Furthermore, because all of the board meetings were held at the association's headquarters in New York City, they were poorly attended, ceding even more authority to the white officers.

For several years, Villard carried the NAACP almost single-handedly. Serving simultaneously as president, chairman, and treasurer, he used his own funds to meet frequent cash shortfalls and provided the association with free office space in his *Evening Post* building. He also encouraged the development of what would become the NAACP's most important contribution to African-American civil rights: its emphasis on litigation, which the Niagara Movement had contemplated but never been able to fund.

This still from D. W. Griffith's *The Birth of a Nation* shows Klansmen surrounding their black prisoner, played by a white actor in blackface.

During the summer of 1910, a warrant was issued in South Carolina for the arrest of an illiterate black farmhand named Pink Franklin. He was wanted under a peonage statute that forced debtors into servitude until their debts were repaid. Even though the peonage law had already been declared unconstitutional, two white officers were assigned to execute the warrant. During the middle of the night—while Franklin, his wife, and son all lay asleep in their bed—the policemen crawled into Franklin's home through an open window. Waking to find white strangers in his bedroom, Franklin began shooting at them. The policemen returned the gunfire. All four adults were injured. Later, when one of the white officers died from his wounds, Franklin and his wife were both charged with murder. After narrowly escaping a lynch mob, they were brought to trial. Their black lawyers, arguing self-defense, won an acquittal for Mrs. Franklin, but Pink was sentenced to death.

OVERLEAF: **The body** of a black lynching victim is burned by an Omaha, Nebraska, mob in 1919.

An original poster for *The Birth of a Nation.*

The Birth of a Nation

D. W. Griffith's epic film *The Birth of a Nation*, released in 1915, was Hollywood's first great artistic and technical triumph. It delighted critics and held audiences spellbound. Everyone who was anyone had to see it, even Woodrow Wilson, who arranged a special screening at the White House.

The plot for Griffith's film came from *The Clansman*, a 1905 novel written by southern evangelist Thomas Dixon Jr. After attending a stage performance of *Uncle Tom's Cabin* in 1901, Dixon had vowed to publish a rejoinder that told the "truth" about slavery and Reconstruction. In fact, he wrote two such books, publishing *The Leopard's Spots* in 1902 and *The Clansman* three years later.

Dixon's striking depiction of blacks as sexual menaces and white southerners (especially women) as innocent victims of northern arrogance came through quite strongly in Griffith's work. "It is like writing history with lightning," Wilson exclaimed after viewing the film. "And my only regret is that it is all so terribly true."

An outraged NAACP organized picket lines outside theaters to protest the film's extreme racism and petitioned government officials to have it banned, all to no avail. However, these efforts did generate so much publicity that NAACP membership soared. By the end of 1916, the organization had 8,785 members in 71 branches, 68 in the North and 3 in the South.

To James Weldon Johnson
in the war in
friendship & admiration
of J. E. Spingarn

Joel E. Spingarn
1875–1939

Wealthy enough to do as he pleased, Joel Elias Spingarn taught comparative literature at Columbia University from 1899 until 1911, when he resigned to protest the autocratic behavior of university president Nicholas Murray Butler. Spingarn especially despised Butler's lack of respect for the principle of academic freedom.

Being a close friend of Du Bois, Spingarn threw himself instead into the work of the NAACP. In 1912, he began to make lecture tours on behalf of the new organization and energetically expanded its reach beyond the Northeast, which had previously been the extent of its influence. Later, when Villard finally tired completely of Du Bois and resigned in 1914, Spingarn became chairman of the NAACP board and served the association in various capacities until his death in 1939.

After South Carolina's highest court and the U.S. Supreme Court both upheld the guilty verdict, Villard became involved in the case. He even wrote to Booker T. Washington, asking for help: "I am wondering if we could not get the President [William Howard Taft] to take an interest in the case. A word from Mr. [Theodore] Roosevelt would help, of course. You yourself may have certain lines of action among white and colored people which could be quickly put into effect and might at least cause the commutation of the sentence." Acting on Villard's request, Washington asked several South Carolinians

to intercede. These men weren't able to arrange Franklin's freedom, but they did persuade the governor to reduce his sentence from death to life imprisonment.

Although the NAACP could take some solace in having helped to save Franklin's life, the result wasn't all that Villard and his associates— specifically, Joel Spingarn and his lawyer brother Arthur—had hoped for. Eager for better results in the future, the Spingarns, with Villard's blessing, began planning a much more focused NAACP legal campaign.

THE GREAT MIGRATION

During its first decade of existence, the NAACP lost many more battles than it won, yet its unapologetic efforts on behalf of blacks inspired many thousands to become dues-paying members. Another impetus to join was provided by World War I, which produced within the

A soldier who lost his leg during World War I takes part in this March 1919 parade of the Thirty-sixth Colored Infantry in New York City.

black middle class a widespread optimism that the United States would finally make itself, in Pres. Woodrow Wilson's words, "safe for democracy." Even the dour Du Bois became swept up in the jingoistic fervor. Using *The Crisis* as his mouthpiece, he urged African Americans to enlist in large numbers and otherwise rally behind the war effort. Responding to this call and the overall national mood, many blacks did, joining the Allied Expeditionary Force and seeing combat in France.

The outbreak of World War I also produced a predictable spike in demand for munitions at the same time that the fighting cut off America's traditional source of new labor: European immigrants. The result was an acute labor shortage, especially in the North and Midwest. Forced to look elsewhere for workers, factory owners who had previously excluded blacks now began hiring them in large numbers. Some even sent recruiters down to the South, offering train fare to anyone willing to take a job. Because these assembly-line positions often paid two to three times what blacks were making at home, many jumped at the chance, and thus began the Great Migration.

The term *Great Migration*, however, is something of a misnomer, at least statistically. Between 1890 and 1910, about two hundred thousand of the South's ten million blacks left for the North. It's hard to know precisely how many more migrated between 1914 and 1919, but a good estimate is about three hundred thousand—still a pittance compared with the number that remained.

Yet even this small number represented a profound shift in long-standing social patterns. The transition strongly affected the lives of the black emigrants, of course, but it also impacted whites, who were forced to adapt to a new and growing presence in their midst.

Equally important were the overseas experiences of black veterans, who had seen and done enough in France to to put the lie to southern claims that racial separation was "natural." The Russian Revolution of 1917 also suggested that, in the modern world at least, even the most extreme social reversal was possible. Black veterans thus returned from France optimistic, with a personal confidence bred of battle and a determination to make Wilson's rhetoric of self-determination real for themselves and their race.

The Silent March

The spark that ignited the July 2, 1917, race riot in East St. Louis, Illinois, was the decision by the Aluminum Ore Company to hire black workers to break up a strike called by white employees. In response, gangs of whites roamed the streets of the city, attacking Negroes. Hundreds were maimed, and at least thirty-nine were killed. Some were shot, some burned, and others hanged from telephone poles. Meanwhile, police officers exchanged pleasantries with the lynchers.

Although the East St. Louis riot was especially severe, its causes were not atypical. Thousands of southern blacks had recently moved into the city,

Silent protesters parade in New York City against the East St. Louis race riot. They marched "without uttering one word or making a single gesticulation," the *New York Age* reported.

looking for work and threatening the economic well-being of East St. Louis's anxious working-class whites. Racial prejudice was merely a lubricant.

Aghast at what was happening, the leaders of the NAACP organized a July 28 march in New York City to protest not only the East St. Louis bloodbath but also recent lynchings in Waco and Memphis. The participants conducted the parade in complete silence, except for the muffled beat of some drums.

Although they must have suspected as much, what the veterans discovered upon their return was that the wartime atmosphere of cooperation and tolerance had been merely expedient; now that the danger had passed, the surging ambition of blacks would no longer be tolerated. According to Benjamin Mays—then a twenty-four-year-old student, later the president of Morehouse College—"Negro soldiers were told, 'Take off those uniforms and act like a nigger should.'"

Those who obeyed were left alone; those who resisted were subjected to all manner of violence until they submitted. In one case, whites offended at the sight of a black man in uniform lynched him. Overall, the lynching rate, which had been in decline, more than doubled as a wave of race riots broke over the nation.

Notable among the twenty-five race riots that took place during the summer of 1919 was one in Longview, Texas, in which a white mob burned black homes and businesses. During the war, the NAACP's recruiting efforts in Texas had been particularly successful. By 1919, the state organization could boast of more than seven thousand members in thirty-nine branches, making it the NAACP leader in both categories. Soon after the Longview riot, however, Texas's

attorney general subpoenaed the records of the Austin branch so that he could evaluate its right to conduct business in Texas. NAACP executive secretary John R. Shillady, who was white, traveled to Austin to meet the challenge.

Outside his hotel, in broad daylight, Shillady was beaten by three men, one of whom was a

"We return. We return from fighting. We return fighting."

W. E. B. DU BOIS IN THE MAY 1919 ISSUE OF *THE CRISIS*

county judge. "The main object of this man's visit was to sow discontent among the Negroes," the judge told the newspapers afterward, "and I thought it was my duty to stop him. And we not only stopped him but have gotten him out of the community." None of Shillady's attackers was

ever arrested; instead, the incident became famous throughout the South as an example of how best to deal with the NAACP. Almost overnight, the substantial gains made by the organization during World War I were rolled back, and most of its southern branches were forced to close.

Another important contributing factor was the renaissance of the Ku Klux Klan. President Grant's stern enforcement of the 1871 Klan Act had, by 1872, suppressed the group, if not white violence. But, encouraged by "lost cause" sentimentalism, enthusiasm for the Klan began to grow again around the turn of the century, and the group was formally resurrected in 1915.

The second incarnation of the Klan fed so well on the patriotism of the war years that, by the early 1920s, it claimed more than three million

James Weldon Johnson
1871–1938

James Weldon Johnson became the NAACP's first full-time field secretary in 1916. Like W. E. B. Du Bois, he was an intellectual virtuoso, but with an even greater range of talents. After his graduation from Atlanta University in 1894, Johnson returned home to Jacksonville, Florida, where he taught high school while studying to become a lawyer. He also wrote poetry, founded a newspaper, and became part of a successful songwriting team with his brother, composer John Rosamond Johnson. Among their creations was "Lift Every Voice and Sing," which became the official song of the NAACP.

Moving to New York City in 1901, the Johnson brothers (along with Bob Cole) wrote hits for the Broadway stage and, as a favor to Booker T. Washington, "You're All Right, Teddy," Pres. Theodore Roosevelt's 1904 campaign song. In appreciation, Roosevelt appointed the multilingual Johnson to a U.S. consulship in Venezuela in 1906.

As the NAACP's first field secretary and (from 1920) its first black executive secretary, Johnson made his highest priority the organization of African Americans in the South, where nine out of ten blacks still lived. Undertaking a series of speaking tours, he left branches in his wake from Richmond all the way down to Tampa Bay. During one of those lectures in Atlanta, he encountered a young insurance agent named Walter White, whom he immediately hired for the national staff. White eventually succeeded Johnson in 1929.

members nationwide. Most of these came from two large groups: lower-middle-class whites threatened economically by immigration and religious fundamentalists made anxious by modernism and the national drift away from small-town Protestant values. The new Klan was therefore far different from the 1860s version, which had been concentrated in the rural South. The 1920s Klan was primarily an urban phenomenon, and its political influence was as likely to be felt in Indiana and Oregon as in Alabama or Mississippi. Klansmen were still racists, however, and—though much less so—still prone to violence.

THE UNIA

Meanwhile, many blacks during the 1920s devoted themselves to a new form of nationalism being promoted by Marcus Garvey through his Universal Negro Improvement Association (UNIA). In the North, where Garvey's movement first caught on, job discrimination was pervasive, blacks were being isolated into ghettos, and the sense of promise that had inspired the Great Migration was already fast collapsing. There seemed no safe place to go, except perhaps back to Africa.

Garvey, of course, did not invent black nationalism. The idea that African Americans should separate from whites and form their own republic was as old as the United States and had enjoyed an especially strong run during the 1820s, when the American Colonization Society founded Monrovia (later Liberia) on the western coast of Africa as a depository for freed slaves. What Garvey offered was a twist on the back-to-Africa doctrine that didn't actually involve leaving America.

According to Garvey, the core problem was European imperialism. In the world, he pointed out, there were currently four hundred million people of African descent. If all of these people

Leaders of the revived Ku Klux Klan stage a march down Pennsylvania Avenue in Washington, D.C., in September 1926.

A UNIA medal

rallied together, they could liberate Africa, by force if necessary, from the yoke of white colonialism—which would, in turn, dramatically improve the status of Negroes living elsewhere, including the United States. "Make Africa a first-rate power, a first-rate nation," Garvey declared in a September 1920 speech, "and if you live in Georgia, if you live in Mississippi, if you live in Texas, as a black man I will dare them to lynch you, because you are an African citizen and you will have a great army and a great navy to protect your rights."

With the NAACP in decline and the Klan on the rise, American blacks wielded so little political power at this time that the UNIA's program of unity, pride, and entrepreneurship seemed to many their best hope. As a result, Garvey became the leader of the first truly *mass* African-American movement. No one knew its actual size—least of all Garvey, who boasted of two million followers one day and six million the next. Du Bois, who despised Garvey and ridiculed his claims, estimated UNIA membership at no more than eighty thousand. Even so, Garvey's organization still dwarfed the NAACP.

With respect to financial resources, there also appeared to be little comparison. During the summer of 1919, Garvey had founded the Black Star Line Steamship Corporation and begun offering stock in the company. Nearly a hundred thousand shares were sold, producing more than enough capital to underwrite all of Garvey's operations.

Some of the funds were used to purchase three ships: a merchantman, an excursion boat, and a yacht. There was also talk of adding a fourth ship, a transatlantic steamer that could be used to open up trade with western Africa. The Liberians, Garvey thought, would make excellent trading partners. Other than landlocked Ethiopia, Liberia was the only

African nation to have escaped white colonization, and its ruling class conveniently spoke English. The Liberians, however, viewed Garvey as a potential political threat and chose to align themselves instead with the Firestone Rubber Company.

Setbacks for Garvey came on other fronts as well. The flagship merchantman of the Black Star Line turned out to be unseaworthy, and Garvey's lack of business experience, combined with his profound administrative incompetence, bankrupted the company. By early 1922, there was no money left to pay the UNIA's bloated staff, and Garvey, along with three other Black Star Line officials, was indicted on charges of fraud.

The UNIA sponsored annual parades in Harlem. By the time this one was held in August 1930, however, Garvey was living in exile, membership had dwindled, and the organization was near collapse.

Marcus Garvey

1887–1940

A native of Jamaica, Marcus Garvey founded the Universal Negro Improvement Association in a Kingston hotel room in 1914 after spending several years on the Continent. Receiving little attention at home, he moved in March 1916 to Harlem, where he continued to be ignored for another two years until the UNIA finally caught on near the end of World War I.

In 1923, with several of his black rivals aiding in his prosecution, Garvey was convicted of mail fraud and sentenced to five years in prison. A series of appeals kept him out of jail for two years, but he was finally forced to enter the Atlanta penitentiary in 1925.

He served only two years before Pres. Calvin Coolidge commuted his sentence in 1927 with the understanding that Garvey would be immediately deported back to Jamaica. The UNIA leader never set foot in the United States again.

Marcus Garvey's fancy dress and penchant for elaborate titles seemed to many an unintended caricature of the pomp of the British empire.

"It is tempting to portray Garveyism as an escapist fantasy, a pathetic expression of black political naivete, or a popular fad of a type all too common in the 1920s—when millions of Americans, whites and blacks, donned exotic hats and robes to become Masons, Elks, Oddfellows, and Shriners," historian Adam Fairclough has observed. "Garveyism, however, was more than a superficial phenomenon of a shallow decade; contemporaries took it very seriously indeed." The government of Great Britain, for instance, feared that Garveyism might destabilize its colonial empires in Africa and the Caribbean, while the U.S. government worried that a black mass movement at home could threaten white supremacy. Such fears were unrealistic because Garvey was too much the buffoon and too little the messiah; nevertheless, both governments were happy when he was jailed.

THE SCOTTSBORO BOYS

The 1930s was another difficult decade for blacks, and this time for whites as well. Unemployment and homelessness caused by the Great Depression broke down American family structures and loosened the social ties that bound communities together. Some of the uprooted people moved to shantytowns on the outskirts of cities in which they had once occupied middle-class homes; others took to the road, lurching back and forth across the country, escaping adverse climates and seeking out seasonal work. Typically, these "hoboes" traveled alone or in pairs, but occasionally they gathered together in larger groups—sometimes for a night, sometimes for several days—huddling together for warmth and talking together for the company it offered.

Two such groups met aboard a Memphis-bound freight train as it passed through the hill country of northern Alabama on the afternoon of March 25, 1931. One group, made up of four white boys, had just boarded the train. The other, comprised of four black youths, was already on board. Just which side started the brawl was never resolved, but it probably began with an exchange of racial slurs that quickly escalated into rock throwing—which, in turn, drew the attention of five more young blacks also aboard the train. The substantially reinforced black group then threw off three of the whites and would have evicted the fourth had the train not suddenly picked up speed.

Bruised and humiliated, the ejected whites set off for the nearest police station to file a complaint, claiming the attack had been unprovoked. At Paint Rock, Alabama, a Jackson County sheriff's posse searched the train's forty-two cars, finding nine blacks ranging in age from thirteen to

Eight of the Scottsboro Boys await trial in an Alabama jail cell.

twenty-one, the fourth white boy, and two young white women. After twenty minutes of standing around, blinking in the bright sun, the two girls, twenty-one-year-old Victoria Price and seventeen-year-old Ruby Bates, told Deputy Sheriff Charlie Latham that they had been raped by the Negroes, who were then arrested and taken to the county jail in Scottsboro. Less than two weeks later, the first trial began.

Defendant Ozzie Powell testifies in the Scottsboro case at the courthouse in Decatur. He eventually received a twenty-year sentence.

Accusers Victoria Price (left) and Ruby Bates in a photograph taken in Scottsboro, Alabama, in January 1932.

All of the trials were concluded within four days. All produced convictions and sentences of death by electrocution, with one exception. That was the case of thirteen-year-old Roy Wright, which ended in a mistrial. Eleven jurors voted for death, but one held out for life imprisonment. The prosecution's cases had rested entirely on the unsubstantiated testimony of Price and Bates. Price, an occasional prostitute, had been arrested just two months earlier for adultery, but the juries chose to believe her anyway. (These were composed entirely of white men because, in Alabama, women were exempted from jury duty and blacks were simply excluded.) When Judge Alfred E. Hawkins pronounced his death sentences, local whites celebrated outside the courthouse to the accompaniment of a raucous brass band.

In the South, the Scottsboro trials were considered remarkably fair given the "unspeakable" nature of the crime committed. Yet in the North, people were appalled at the haste of the proceedings, the obvious bias of the judge, and the shortcomings of the boys' lawyers, who were given little time to prepare and were hardly competent anyway. Most inflammatory was the fact that the available forensic evidence clearly pointed to the boys' innocence. The Scottsboro doctors who examined Price and Bates after the alleged rapes found neither bruising nor bleeding to substantiate their claims. Instead, they found only "nonmotile" semen, which corroborated defense testimony that both women had had sex with boyfriends two nights before. No semen was found on any of the defendants' clothes.

As public interest in the case grew, *Scottsboro* became a byword for racial injustice. Yet it was the American Communist party (CPUSA), and not the NAACP, that made the Scottsboro case famous. Walter White, James Weldon Johnson's successor as executive secretary of the NAACP, initially shied away from the case because it was too "tangled and ugly," he thought. The NAACP preferred nice middle-class defendants it could hold up as rallying points for racial pride. The illiterate, proletarian Scottsboro boys were hardly that. On the other hand, their low-class status made them excellent symbols for the Communists, who cast them as classic victims of capitalistic exploitation.

Not long after their trials, the Scottsboro boys were visited in jail by two lawyers from the Communist-controlled International Labor Defense (ILD). Both were Jewish New Yorkers who brought with them candy and an offer of help. They asked for permission to handle the boys' appeal, which was granted. At this point, Walter White withdrew from the case entirely, refusing to allow his strongly anticommunist organization to become involved with "that outfit of lunatics."

Once firmly in control of the Scottsboro case, the Communists began an international publicity campaign to apply pressure and build support. Communist front organizations hosted mass meetings, organized protest marches, launched petition drives, and courted sympathetic celebrities, including Albert Einstein and Theodore Dreiser. Because of these efforts,

the Scottsboro case became a leading news story of the 1930s, especially after the Supreme Court vacated all eight convictions in November 1932. The reason was that the boys' counsel had been so inept as to constitute a violation of their due process rights under the Fourteenth Amendment.

But Alabama wasn't ready to give up. The state ordered new trials, which began in March 1933 in Decatur, the seat of neighboring Morgan County, under the gavel of Judge James E. Horton. This time, the boys were defended by Samuel S. Leibowitz, one of the most respected criminal defense attorneys in the country, whom the ILD had recruited. Haywood Patterson's was the first case to be retried.

Leibowitz was aided by the testimony of a surprise witness, Ruby Bates, who recanted her Scottsboro testimony and admitted that no rape had occurred. Price, however, stuck to her story, and Patterson was again found guilty. Then, shockingly, Judge Horton set aside the verdict on the grounds that Price's uncorroborated testimony was contradicted by the physical evidence.

A fireman on the train ridden by the Scottsboro boys testifies at one of their trials using a scale model to support his recollections.

Black and white members of the Communist party at a March 1930 meeting in Washington, D.C. The CPUSA was the only political party at the time to promote racial equality and oppose white supremacy.

Once Horton's superiors recovered their composure, they persuaded the judge to recuse himself, and the trials went on, including a third one for Patterson. The new judge, William Washington Callahan, produced the desired results swiftly, and again the convictions were appealed. This time, in *Norris v. Alabama*, Leibowitz argued the unfairness of the all-white jury system. As the Court's April 1935 ruling established, no black had served on a jury in either Jackson or Morgan County "within the memory of witnesses who had lived there all their lives." Therefore, the prosecution of the Scottsboro boys had been unconstitutional because the defendants had been denied a jury of their peers. The state of Alabama would have to try again.

It did, dropping the charges against four of the defendants but trying Patterson for a fourth time, Clarence Norris for a third, and three others for a second. More guilty verdicts followed, and these held. Norris received the only death sentence, later commuted to life imprisonment.

Charlie Weems, the first to be paroled, obtained his release in 1943; Andy Wright, the last, was set free in 1950.

Communist involvement in the Scottsboro case ended on a somewhat tawdry note in October 1934, when two bumbling ILD lawyers were caught trying to bribe Price into recanting her testimony as well. A furious Leibowitz, who was not a Communist himself, cut all ties with the CPUSA; henceforth his work was funded by an interracial coalition set up with the help of a relieved NAACP. Nevertheless, as NAACP chief counsel Charles Hamilton Houston acknowledged, the Communists' "uncompromising resistance to southern prejudice set a new standard for agitation for equality."

THE BROTHERHOOD OF SLEEPING CAR PORTERS

Another consequence of the economic insecurity that plagued 1930s America was the huge surge in union membership. Until the Great Depression, the nation's labor movement was dominated by

This menial foundry work was typical of the jobs to which black factory workers were confined during the 1930s.

Howard University students picket the 1934 National Crime Conference in Washington, D.C., protesting the conference leaders' decision not to consider lynching a national crime.

the craft unions, which organized workers according to their skill rather than their industry. This allowed unions to cherry-pick the highest-paid workers with the strongest bargaining positions and leave the unskilled workers to fend for themselves. Because most black workers were unskilled, few were unionized. The American Federation of Labor (AFL) either relegated them to second-tier segregated unions or else excluded them entirely. Even after Pres. Franklin Roosevelt made collective bargaining a focus of his New Deal, AFL craft unions continued to block unionization of workers in the mass production industries.

Finally, in 1935, United Mine Workers president John L. Lewis persuaded several other progressive union leaders to break away from the AFL and form their own umbrella group, later named the Congress of Industrial Organizations (CIO). Under Lewis's leadership (and with a great deal of help from the Communists), the CIO organized the automobile, steel, and rubber industries. In doing so, its staff routinely unionized blacks and whites interracially.

The case of the Pullman porters fit neither model. The business of the Pullman Palace Car Company, founded in 1867, was to build and operate sleeping and dining cars for the nation's railroads. To attend to the needs of its primarily upscale white clientele, the Pullman Company hired more than ten thousand porters, all of them black. Because the ideal Pullman porter was both attentive and obedient, the company employed many former house slaves, who already knew how to serve and defer to whites. As the decades passed, however, the job of Pullman

porter rose sharply in black esteem and became highly prized among members of the college-educated middle class.

Although porters were forced to endure difficult working conditions, such as hundred-hour workweeks and sleeping three hours at a time inside Pullman car bathrooms, the job was so much better than others available to blacks—such as domestic service, manual labor, and sharecropping—that competition was fierce. Along with postal workers and longshoremen, the Pullman porters were the aristocrats of black labor. Their stable work and relatively high wages allowed them to buy homes, send their children to college, and become pillars of their communities.

Some porters were dissatisfied, however, and in June 1925, a number of them living in Harlem approached A. Philip Randolph about forming a union. (An outsider such as Randolph was needed because the notoriously antiunion Pullman Company fired any porter it discovered to be dabbling in unionism.) Although he had written often in *The Messenger* of the need for black workers to organize, Randolph was reluctant to commit because his earlier attempts at labor organizing had been failures. He offered initially only to write and publish a series of articles in *The Messenger* describing the porters' working conditions. In educating himself, however, Randolph became so enraged that he changed his mind and accepted the porters' offer.

That August, he presided over the first meeting of the new Brotherhood of Sleeping Car Porters (BSCP). Randolph's work, which proceeded slowly, was made even more difficult by the antagonism of black ministers and newspaper publishers, who spoke with one voice that of the

Pullman Company, the largest employer of African Americans in the country. It had long been Pullman policy to buy goodwill within the black community by making regular donations to black churches and placing large ads in black-owned newspapers. Now the company reaped the benefits of this wise investment.

Ignoring the vitriol as best he could, Randolph first organized the porters who lived in and around New York City. Then, raising the necessary funds from white socialists, he traveled to Chicago, where the Pullman Company was headquartered and the most porters lived. After personally leading an organizing drive there, he crisscrossed the

A. Philip Randolph
1889–1979

In 1911, a young and eager Asa Philip Randolph moved from his home in Crescent City, Florida, to New York City. He worked by day as an employment agent and at night attended City College, where he studied political economy and avidly read Marx. Unlike Du Bois, who focused on the black elite, Randolph devoted himself to the black working class, whom he saw as a more likely agent of change.

Yet Randolph didn't receive his true political awakening until the later 1910s, when the outbreak of World War I and the advent of revolutionary upheaval in Europe persuaded him to become a socialist.

In 1917, with his partner Chandler Owen, Randolph founded *The Messenger*, a journal of radical opinion that took on Booker T. Washington and W. E. B. Du Bois as readily as it did Woodrow Wilson. *The Messenger*'s purpose was to encourage working-class unity, but it gradually became apparent to Randolph that the audience for his highly intellectual critiques was far from blue collar.

For the rest of his life, Randolph struggled with this problem. Even after he turned to union organizing and became the most important civil rights leader ever to emerge from the labor movement, he remained somewhat handicapped by his regal bearing and carefully articulated speech, which kept members of his working-class following at a distance.

country, unionizing porters as he went and financing his expenses with the passing of a hat. Membership grew steadily, and by the end of 1926, the BSCP had locals in almost every major city. Two years after that, Randolph felt sufficiently confident to call a strike vote, which the BSCP's 4,623 members approved overwhelmingly.

Randolph had concluded that threatening a strike was the only way to bring Pullman to the negotiating table. Yet he also wanted to avoid a direct confrontation. His plan was to use the strike vote to push the federal government into declaring a transportation emergency—which would, in turn, force the Pullman Company into mediation. Unfortunately, Randolph miscalculated. Even with the help of several well-placed politicians, black and white, he was unable to persuade the National Mediation Board to declare an emergency. Fearful of the consequences of acting without governmental support, he backed down and "postponed" the strike just hours before it was scheduled to begin.

10 Reasons WHY EVERY PORTER SHOULD JOIN AND SUPPORT THE **BROTHERHOOD** of SLEEPING CAR PORTERS Train, Chair Car, Coach Porters & Attendants AN INTERNATIONAL UNION Affiliated with the A. F. of L. and ATTEND ORGANIZATION MEETINGS EVERY WEDNESDAY 2:30 P.M. 217 WEST 125th STREET (Room 201) New York 27, N. Y. MO 2-5090 - 1 Spend Some Time In Our Recreation Center

This leaflet recruited members for Randolph's Brotherhood of Sleeping Car Porters.

Union morale suffered a near-fatal blow, especially after the 1929 stock market crash caused many members to reconsider the wisdom of risking their jobs for the sake of the union. Porters deserted the BSCP in droves, and the resulting dues hemorrhage forced the closure of every local office, including the New York headquarters. The end seemed near, but somehow Randolph and his chief lieutenant, Milton P. Webster, held the union together long enough for its circumstances to change.

Thanks to some skillful lobbying by Randolph, the Railway Labor Act of 1934 specifically protected the organizing rights of Pullman porters, and in 1935 the BSCP finally forced its way into a reluctant AFL, becoming the first black union to receive a charter. Even so, two more years passed before the Pullman Company exhausted its delaying tactics and signed a contract with Randolph's union. Immediately, the porters received increases in pay, decreases in their workweeks, and a reduction in the number of miles they had to travel.

A MARCH ON WASHINGTON
Winning this epic twelve-year battle with Pullman made Randolph a national figure, with prestige far exceeding that due his otherwise small union. For the most part, Randolph used

A Pullman porter at Union Station in Chicago in 1943.

The Detroit Race Riot

During World War II, the city of Detroit, the fourth largest in the United States, became the world's leading producer of military goods. The Big Three automakers converted many of their existing assembly lines to tank and jeep production, while the federal government financed the construction of new plants in and around the city to meet other equally pressing needs.

As during World War I, the ensuing labor shortage attracted blacks from the South, who boosted Detroit's African-American population by 40 percent. Overcrowding followed, made much worse by the city's strict (albeit unofficial) housing segregation.

On June 19, 1943, the *Detroit Free Press* printed an editorial emphasizing the "pressing" need for adequate housing. The next day, a warm and muggy Sunday, several fights broke out between white and black teenagers at the crowded Belle Isle amusement park. Later that night, as crowds jammed the bridge to the mainland, the violence escalated, and a mob of five thousand whites gathered to attack blacks as they came off the bridge. From there, the riot spread inland until the mayor was forced to call in six thousand federal troops. Even then, order wasn't fully restored until Thursday, June 24. Meanwhile, twenty-five blacks were killed and nearly seven hundred injured.

The NAACP published this pamphlet written by Walter White and Thurgood Marshall in July 1943.

A mob stops a streetcar carrying blacks in Detroit during the June 1943 race riot.

survey showed that of 29,215 workers recently hired by ten New York State defense contractors, only 142 were black—and these ten employers were from the racially tolerant end of the spectrum.

After listening to President Roosevelt deliver his December 1940 "arsenal of democracy" radio address, Randolph decided to act—or, rather, to pressure the federal government into acting for him. His means would be "an 'all-out' thundering march on Washington" that would "shake up white America," protesting not only job discrimination but also segregation in the armed forces. To manage the event, Randolph created the Negroes' Committee to March on Washington for Equal Participation in National Defense, later known as the March on Washington Movement (MOWM). The group was staffed primarily by BSCP officials, who used porters to spread the word. Randolph began by calling for ten thousand blacks to take part.

The march—scheduled for July 1, 1941—irked Franklin Roosevelt, who was generally sympathetic to the cause of black civil rights yet resented the staging of any mass protest outside his own front door. To persuade Randolph to call the march off, he sent his wife, Eleanor, along with two other prominent liberals, New York City mayor Fiorello La Guardia and National Youth Administration director Aubrey Williams.

When the BSCP president refused their entreaties, Roosevelt took the obvious next step and invited Randolph to the White House.

The meeting took place on June 16. Randolph wanted a commitment from Roosevelt to end the job discrimination, and, receiving mostly charm instead, he again refused to call off the march. Buses were scheduled, special trains chartered, and other arrangements made. Then, on June 25, FDR signed Executive Order 8802, which stated that "there shall be no discrimination in the employment of workers in defense industries and in government because of race, creed, color, or national origin." The order also created a Fair Employment Practices Committee (FEPC) to monitor compliance, investigate complaints, and recommend

Three black servicemen sit atop a jeep in Guam in 1945. Most uniformed Negroes were assigned to labor details.

this influence to promote the cause of black workers within the labor movement, but he also spoke out on civil rights.

As the U.S. economy rallied after 1939, Randolph noticed that nearly all of the new defense jobs were going to whites. A government

The Mitchell Case

During World War II, because of all the personnel movements to and from military bases in the South, interstate transportation became an important focus of NAACP litigation. The most important case, *Mitchell v. U.S.* (1941), involved African-American congressman Arthur Mitchell, who had bought a Pullman car ticket in Chicago for a trip to Hot Springs, Arkansas. When Mitchell's train left Memphis, however, the conductor moved him to a blacks-only coach in deference to Arkansas's segregation law.

Mitchell complained to the Interstate Commerce Commission (ICC) that the railroad had violated the Interstate Commerce Act of 1887, which made it illegal for interstate carriers to subject passengers "to any undue or unreasonable prejudice or disadvantage in any respect whatsoever." The unsympathetic ICC agreed that the comforts of the segregated car were no match for those of the Pullman, but it denied that the difference was "undue or unreasonable." The Supreme Court held otherwise, ruling unanimously in Mitchell's favor. Its decision, though, applied only to interstate carriers.

The segregated bus station in Durham, North Carolina, photographed in May 1940.

appropriate action. No mention was made of ending segregation in the military, but Randolph was satisfied with the half loaf he was offered and, in return, called off the march.

Some MOWM organizers, notably Bayard Rustin, criticized Randolph for accepting less than the movement's full demands, and, according to Roi Ottley in *The New Republic*, "the masses of Negroes were bewildered by the sudden turn of events. Nothing tangible had been gained, they felt." Indeed, business owners resisted the FEPC, and because the committee had no power to enforce its recommendations, job discrimination continued, ameliorated only by the growing need for workers of all races. In the short term, therefore, the decision to cancel the march cost Randolph a fair measure of his prestige. Yet as time passed, the importance of what he had achieved became clear: The federal government had for the first time in memory admitted publicly that the nation had a problem with race.

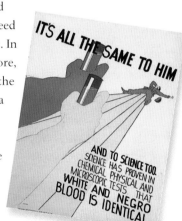

This 1943 NAACP poster attacks segregated blood drives by citing recent scientific evidence that black and white blood is identical.

ANOTHER DISAPPOINTMENT

In many respects, the black experience during World War II mirrored the course of events during the Great War a generation earlier. For example, the years between 1941 and 1945 saw another significant migration of African Americans from the rural South to the industrial North. With the total number of emigrants exceeding 1.5 million, railroads put on special trains to meet the need. From Mississippi alone, three hundred thousand blacks traveled to Chicago and Detroit, where the desperate demand for workers had finally opened the doors of industry to unskilled black labor.

Likewise, within the military, African Americans fought bravely in segregated regiments, as they had during World War I, yet remained painfully aware that they were defending overseas a concept of democracy denied them at home. At the end of the war, another generation of black veterans returned to America—nearly a million in all, eager for change and unwilling to accept a prewar caste system that they no longer considered inevitable. Again, they were met with repression and violence.

Medgar Evers was one of those veterans who believed that his combat service in France and Germany had earned him the right to vote. So, on July 2, 1946, the future Mississippi field secretary for the NAACP celebrated his twenty-first birthday by leading a group of fellow veterans to the Newton County courthouse in Decatur, Mississippi, to take part in that day's Democratic party primary. When Evers and his friends reached the courthouse, however, "some fifteen or twenty armed white men surged in behind us, men I had grown up with and played with," Evers recalled. "We stood there for a minute. We were bluffing. We knew we weren't going to get by this mob." After a brief standoff, Evers and his friends retreated, followed by a black Ford in which "a guy leaned out with a shotgun, keeping a bead on us all the time."

The All-White Primary

After Reconstruction, southern legislators developed a number of ruses to evade the Fifteenth Amendment's ban on racially discriminatory election laws. The most popular were voter qualifications, such as the poll tax and the literacy test, which could easily be manipulated to exclude blacks. An even bolder strategy was the all-white primary.

In the South, where Democrats faced little opposition, the party primary was usually the only contest that mattered. Therefore, if blacks could be excluded from that, it wouldn't matter whether they voted in meaningless general elections.

The justification offered was that political parties were private institutions and therefore not subject to the Fifteenth Amendment. Believing this reasoning to be spurious, the NAACP brought suit in Texas, where the state legislature had passed a law in 1923 barring blacks from party primaries.

The case was decided in 1927, when the Supreme Court ruled unanimously for the NAACP but on extraneous technical grounds. Texas then passed a slightly amended law, and the NAACP again brought suit.

Once more, the Supreme Court declared the all-white primary unconstitutional, this time on Fifteenth Amendment grounds. The closeness of the 5–4 vote, however, and the decision's extremely narrow grounds encouraged Texas to try a third time.

Meanwhile, two local lawyers not associated with the NAACP took control of the litigation, and in *Grovey v. Townsend* (1935), they lost decisively. In their brief, they had emphasized the crucial importance of party primaries in one-party states, but the Court proved reluctant to accept this argument because it would have meant overturning a large body of established law. Instead, the justices hid behind the "state-action" doctrine and held that the internal workings of the Democratic party were none of the Court's business.

In 1941, however, the Court held in *U.S. v. Classic*, a case involving the rigging of a Democratic congressional primary in Louisiana, that, because the Democratic primary was indeed the only election that mattered in Louisiana, it had to be subject to federal law. This decision encouraged the NAACP to file suit again, and in 1944 the Court's decision in *Smith v. Allwright* clearly prohibited all discriminatory primaries.

In June 1944, African-American voters in Atlanta register to vote in the upcoming July 4 Georgia Democratic primary. They were encouraged by recent primaries in Florida and Alabama, during which Negro voters were able to cast ballots without incident.

That election was the first statewide primary in Mississippi since the 1944 Supreme Court decision in *Smith v. Allwright* abolishing the all-white primary. Drawing national attention, it pitted incumbent senator Theodore Bilbo against several moderate challengers. An ardent white supremacist, Bilbo had a fanatical following among poor whites, and his campaign energized these voters by focusing on the threat to white rule posed by *Smith v. Allwright*. At each campaign stop, he urged supporters to prevent blacks from going to the polls. The state's newspapers agreed. "Don't attempt to vote in the Democratic primaries anywhere in Mississippi on July 2nd," the *Jackson Daily News* warned black readers. "Staying away from the polls on that date will be the best way to prevent unhealthy and unhappy results."

Bilbo won easily, and although some critics did manage to pressure the Senate into holding hearings in Jackson a few weeks later, these initially seemed pointless. The five-man subcommittee was controlled by three Democrats, all southerners, who refused to subpoena any black witnesses. Their reasoning was that few African Americans would volunteer to testify because doing so would surely subject them to white reprisals. To the senators' dismay, nearly two hundred people volunteered anyway.

For eighty years now, violence and intimidation had persuaded African Americans to suppress their deep human needs for hope,

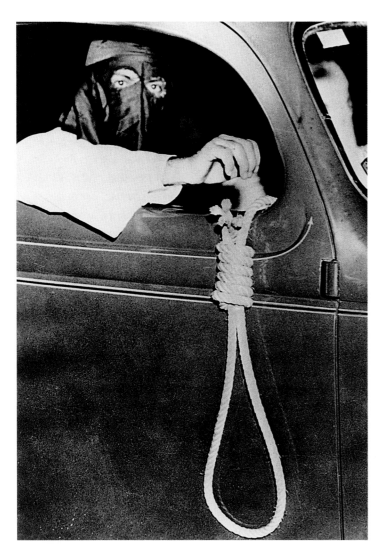

The night before the 1939 Florida Democratic primary, members of the Ku Klux Klan stage an automobile parade through the Negro section of Miami. Black voters were warned graphically to stay away from the polls.

fairness, and respect. As would become increasingly clear, however, this calculus was changing. The threat from whites remained as constant as ever, yet the emotional need among blacks for justice was growing—soon to reach a point at which it couldn't be denied, no matter the consequences.

Sadly, such risk-taking in 1946 still accomplished little. "You know, I am sure," subcommittee chairman Allen Ellender of Louisiana berated one witness, "that only white folks should vote in the Democratic primaries." Not surprisingly, the subcommittee's final report reflected this attitude—concluding that, because blacks in Mississippi would have been deprived of their Fifteenth Amendment rights "regardless of who the senatorial candidates may have been and what they may have said," Bilbo's campaign was not in any meaningful way at fault. The fact that Mississippi's whites

had made a mockery of the right to vote in their state was found to be outside the specific charge of the subcommittee and therefore was not addressed.

> "The best way to keep the nigger from voting is to see him the night before election."
>
> SEN. THEODORE BILBO DURING THE 1946 PRIMARY CAMPAIGN

THE BLINDING OF ISAAC WOODARD

The disfranchisement experienced by Evers changed his life and led eventually, if indirectly, to his assassination two decades later. Other black veterans didn't have to wait nearly so long for the gruesomeness of their fates to become apparent.

On the afternoon of February 12, 1946, Sgt. Isaac Woodard, a decorated Pacific veteran, was discharged honorably from the U.S. Army at Camp Gordon, Georgia. Right away, he boarded a bus for his home in South Carolina, sitting down in the back next to a white veteran with whom he'd become friendly during their long trip back aboard the same troop transport. Before leaving the bus station, however, the driver asked the white soldier to leave Woodard and move to the front of the bus. Woodard's resentment at this was later exacerbated when he asked the driver to make a rest stop, and the driver replied, "Hell, no," leading to an argument. "Dammit, you've got to talk to me like a man," Woodard demanded.

At Batesburg, South Carolina, the bus driver informed police chief Lynwood Shull that Woodard had been causing trouble, and Shull routinely arrested him. On their way to jail, however, along a dark and deserted street, Woodard began struggling with

Isaac Woodard poses with his mother for this undated photograph. It appeared originally in the *Amsterdam News*, the most widely read black newspaper in Harlem and one of the most influential in the country.

Shull, who later claimed that Woodard had been resisting arrest. Woodard countered that he reached for the policeman's blackjack only after Shull began slugging him with it. In either case, Shull blinded the sergeant with several quick blows to the eyes. Woodard was just sixty miles from home and the joy of seeing his wife and child again when he permanently lost his sight. Although Shull was later brought to trial in federal court, he was acquitted in just twenty-eight minutes. "Few in the courtroom knew, or seemed to care," *The Nation* reported, "that this was the first civil-rights case ever heard in South Carolina."

Seven months after Woodard's blinding, NAACP executive secretary Walter White led a delegation from the National Emergency Committee Against Mob Violence to meet with Pres. Harry Truman at the White House. White offered Truman several harrowing tales of violence against black veterans, but the president was most deeply moved by Woodard's story. "My God," he exclaimed. "I had no idea it was as terrible as that! We've got to do something!"

This postwar suburban paradise, like most housing developments built for the millions of returning World War II veterans, excluded blacks.

Restrictive Covenants

The racial violence that shook Chicago in July 1919 greatly disturbed the city's white political establishment, which decided in its aftermath that only strict racial segregation could keep the urban peace. Therefore, during the 1920s, Chicago's realtors began using restrictive covenants to prevent white home buyers from reselling or renting their property to blacks.

Although the Supreme Court had already struck down municipal ordinances that zoned for race, the restrictive covenant was allowed to stand because it was a private transaction. As a result, by 1944, 90 percent of all Chicago housing deeds contained restrictive covenants, as did the deeds for many of the new housing units being constructed for veterans all over the Northeast.

By 1948, however, the Supreme Court was finally ready to act. Ruling in *Shelley v. Kraemer*, it held that restrictive covenants, while themselves constitutional, could never be enforced in court. Two private parties could agree to discriminate, and a judge could do nothing to stop this. But should one of those parties decide to ignore a restrictive covenant, the other one couldn't sue to have it enforced. The reason was that the court would then become a party to the discrimination, thus invoking the state-action doctrine and violating the Fourteenth Amendment ban on state-sanctioned discrimination.

The president initially suggested a congressional inquiry, but when White pointed out that southern senators and representatives would surely block it, Truman settled instead on an investigation of his own created by executive order. The next day, he sent a note to Attorney General Tom Clark, a Texan whom Truman would later appoint to the Supreme Court. "I know you have been looking into the...

lynchings," the president wrote, "but...it is going to take something more than the handling of each individual case after it happens—it is going to require the inauguration of some sort of policy to prevent such happenings." The formation of the President's Commission on Civil Rights was announced on December 5, 1946.

In creating such a commission, Truman was running a substantial political risk. His 1948 reelection campaign was little more than a year away, and the conventional wisdom was that he couldn't retain the presidency without holding the Solid South. Yet Truman never flinched in following his civil rights initiative through to its logical conclusion. Democratic leaders implored him to back off, but he flatly refused. "My forebears were Confederates," he snapped. "Every factor and influence in my background—and in my wife's for that matter—would foster the personal belief that you are right. But my very stomach turned over when I learned that Negro soldiers, just back from overseas, were being dumped out of Army trucks in Mississippi and beaten. Whatever my inclinations as a native of Missouri might have been, as President I know this is bad. I shall fight to end evils like this."

Of course, there was also political advantage to be gained from supporting African-American civil rights. Examining the results of the 1944 presidential election, Truman would have found that a popular-vote shift of 5 percent or less would have reversed the results in twenty-eight states.

Dixiecrats hang President Truman in effigy from a Birmingham balcony.

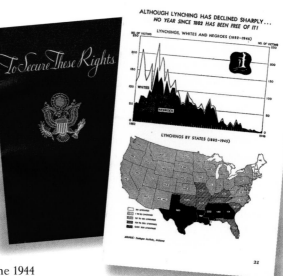

A lynching graphic from *To Secure These Rights*, which introduced into popular usage the phrase *civil rights*. Previously, Americans had spoken of "the Negro question."

In twelve of those, the black vote exceeded the margin needed to shift the result.

TO SECURE THESE RIGHTS

The President's Commission on Civil Rights issued its final report in October 1947. Titled *To Secure These Rights*, the document called for federal antilynching legislation, federal protection of voting rights, abolition of the poll tax, a fair-employment law, vigorous FBI enforcement of existing civil rights laws, the establishment of a permanent Civil Rights Commission, and the eradication of segregation from all areas of American life, especially the armed forces. Greeting the report enthusiastically, Truman declared, "I want you to know that not only have you done a good job but you have done what I wanted you to."

The southern reaction was predictably antagonistic. "If that report is carried out," one Baptist minister from Jacksonville warned the president, "you won't be elected dogcatcher in 1948." Undaunted, Truman sent a special message to Congress in February, endorsing the commission's report and asking for swift passage of those recommendations under congressional jurisdiction. For his own part, he issued an executive order in July desegregating the armed forces. Thus, the political battle lines were drawn.

The Democratic national convention met that same July in Philadelphia. As hot as the temperature was outside the hall, it was even hotter within the platform committee, where a group of delegates led by Minneapolis mayor Hubert H. Humphrey was pushing hard for a strong civil rights plank that many southern delegates found odious. When the platform committee ultimately decided to accept the Humphrey plank, the Alabama and Mississippi delegations walked out. A few days later, these and other rebellious southern Democrats met in Birmingham to form the States' Rights (Dixiecrat) party and nominate South Carolina governor J. Strom Thurmond for president.

True to their word, the Dixiecrats took four states out of the Democratic column in November, but these defections weren't enough to stop Truman, who narrowly defeated Republican Thomas E. Dewey in one of American history's most thrilling presidential elections.

In the end, the president was saved by a strong African-American turnout that helped him slip past Dewey in California, Illinois, and Ohio. Overall, Truman received about two-thirds of the black vote, much of which had been thought to belong to Progressive party nominee Henry A. Wallace.

So Truman was reelected—but without a mandate and, ironically, without much support in Congress. His persistent attacks on the "do-nothing" Eightieth Congress had produced a Democratic landslide and returned control of both houses to his party. Yet the mood of the country was turning sharply conservative, and Congress was following suit. As a result, the president's Fair Deal program, featuring national health insurance and guaranteed full employment, languished, as did his civil rights initiatives.

Campaign memorabilia from Strom Thurmond's 1948 presidential run.

South Carolina governor J. Strom Thurmond delivers a speech to the Texas House of Representatives during his 1948 Dixiecrat presidential campaign.

Two young Ku Klux Klan members flank their order's grand dragon during a July 1948 initiation ceremony in Atlanta.

PART II
BREAKING FREE

Imagine the tunnel of an old aqueduct blocked by a cave-in so that its water ceases to flow. Any competent engineer assigned to the task would clear this obstruction by methodically removing the collapsed bricks and stones, one by one. African Americans living during the mid–twentieth century faced a similar situation. Because of *Plessy v. Ferguson*, their legal rights were blocked. So they developed a similar solution. A cadre of black lawyers began methodically clearing the legal bricks and stones. By the early 1950s, their work was nearly done—a cause for rejoicing, yet also the most dangerous part of the job because of the pressure that had been building up for years behind the blockage.

In a blocked aqueduct, as debris is removed, the mass of the last few bricks and stones eventually becomes insufficient to withstand the pressure of the water that has built up behind the obstruction. Sooner or later, the water breaches the barrier and carries away everything in its path—including, perhaps, the unwary engineer. This is also the danger one finds in overturning social orders. The force of release can be as destructive as it is cleansing.

Members of the 101st Airborne Division escort black students home after a day of classes at recently integrated Central High School in Little Rock, Arkansas.

The Fight for Equal Education 1952–1955

In the fall of 1924, Charles Hamilton Houston began teaching at the Howard University Law School. Houston had sought a position at Howard because it was the most influential black law school in the country, having trained three-quarters of all Negro attorneys then practicing in the United States. With a bachelor's degree from Amherst and a doctorate from Harvard, Houston could have taught nearly anywhere, but he chose Howard because he wanted to revolutionize the way African Americans practiced law.

Fourth graders at St. Martin School in Washington, D.C., dash for the playground at recess in September 1954. The District of Columbia joined four states in acting to end school segregation immediately after the May 1954 *Brown* decision. Other states, however, resisted.

At its core, America's ideological heritage clearly endorsed the freedom and equality being sought by blacks. Indeed, the hope that the country's laws could one day be made to reflect its ideals sustained many generations of African Americans, even during the worst of times. Yet black lawyers during the early twentieth century typically viewed their profession as a business, rather than as a calling, and rarely took

part in the struggle for civil rights. Houston was determined to change that.

Serving in the army during World War I, the relatively privileged Houston experienced extreme racism firsthand, and after his return from France, he decided to become a lawyer so that he could fight back. In the fall of 1919, Houston entered the Harvard Law School, where two mentors, Roscoe Pound and Felix

Frankfurter, provided him with the intellectual framework he needed to channel his anger into something more productive.

Pound was a leading advocate of the new sociological jurisprudence, which held that lawyers needed to move beyond abstract notions of justice to consider current social conditions. The usefulness of legal precedents such as *Plessy v. Ferguson* had always been that they settled questions of interpretation and made enforcement of the law much more predictable. Yet Pound argued that evolving social circumstances changed people's ideas of what was just, and judges needed to respond accordingly. If this meant reversing precedents, Pound said, so be it.

From Frankfurter, whom Franklin Roosevelt appointed to the Supreme Court in 1939, Houston learned to view lawyers as social engineers. It was the attorney's job, in Frankfurter's view, to envision a just society and then use his legal tools to build it. Houston carried Frankfurter's activism with him to Howard, where he told his students, "A lawyer is either a social engineer, or he's a parasite on society."

In 1927, Houston headed up a major survey of Negro attorneys in the United States. One of the study's key findings was that most black lawyers were poorly trained, which hardly surprised Houston. Even at Howard, the students were part-timers, the classes were taught at night, and the strength of the curriculum was dubious. As a result, the school lacked even the most basic accreditation.

Another finding was that there simply weren't enough black lawyers, especially in the South,

> ## "A lawyer is either a social engineer, or he's a parasite on society."
>
> CHARLES HAMILTON HOUSTON

where only 487 practiced. In some southern states, the ratio of black citizens to black lawyers exceeded two hundred thousand to one. The scarcity of African-American lawyers particularly bothered Houston because, as he pointed out, "Experience has proved that the average white lawyer, especially in the South, cannot be relied upon to wage an uncompromising fight for equal rights for Negroes."

Once Houston became vice dean at Howard in 1929, he moved quickly to remake the school into an institution capable of turning out highly skilled lawyers dedicated to the fight for racial equality. Phasing out the night program, he extended the academic year, overhauled the curriculum, and began visiting undergraduate colleges to recruit the best students. Within two years, both the American Bar Association and the Association of American Law Schools accredited Howard, whose curriculum became so challenging that only one-quarter of the class that entered with Thurgood Marshall in 1930 graduated with him in 1933.

The new curriculum emphasized Houston's philosophical commitment to social engineering. According to Edward P. Lovett, an early student of Houston's and later a member of his Washington law firm, "In all our classes, whether it was equity or contracts or pleadings, stress was placed on learning what our rights were under the Constitution and statutes—our rights as worded and regardless of how they had been interpreted to that time. Charlie's view was that we had to get the courts to change—and that we could and should no longer depend upon high-powered white lawyers to represent us in that effort."

Charles Hamilton Houston
• 1895–1950

Charles Hamilton Houston's father, William, was also an attorney, having attended Howard Law School as a night student. But the son's motivation to become a lawyer had little to do with his father's career, which was entirely commercial. Instead, Charles Houston's motivation came from his work as a judge advocate during World War I, when he was forced to prosecute black soldiers for crimes they had probably not committed.

"I made up my mind," he later explained, "that I would never get caught again without knowing something about my rights; that if luck was with me, and I got through this war, I would study law and use my time fighting for men who could not strike back."

Howard University was founded in 1867 by Oliver O. Howard, a former Union general then serving as head of the Freedmen's Bureau. This row house in downtown Washington, D.C., was the campus of the university's law school when Houston was dean.

NAACP executive secretary Walter White (left) poses with members of his legal team (left to right): Houston, James G. Tyson, Leon A. Ransom, and Edward P. Lovett. Tyson and Lovett both studied under Houston at Howard.

THE NAACP'S LEGAL STRATEGY

"The problem of the twentieth century," W. E. B. Du Bois famously wrote in *The Souls of Black Folk* (1903), "is the problem of the color line." The task that the founders of the NAACP set for themselves six years later was to eradicate that line however they could.

By the early 1930s, a consensus had emerged that judicial means would be the most effective. In retrospect, one can easily see why: The NAACP was an elite organization with powerful intellectual roots but little mass following. A litigation strategy suited its strengths perfectly while minimizing its weaknesses. Early in the century, Du Bois had envisioned a cadre of urban scholar-thinkers leading the black freedom struggle—the Talented Tenth, he called them. Now it appeared that this vanguard would be comprised of lawyers, trained by Houston at Howard.

At first, Houston merely made his staff and students available to help NAACP lawyers write briefs and prepare oral arguments. But as he became more involved, he grew increasingly critical of the association's haphazard, overly reactive legal strategy. Typically, the NAACP would become involved in cases after they had begun to draw national attention, with little thought given to the influence they might have on future litigation. Houston instead wanted to bring cases,

developed by the NAACP itself, that would undermine, step by step, the legal basis for racial discrimination. He was therefore pleased when, in 1929, the NAACP became involved with the American Fund for Public Service, better known as the Garland Fund.

Fund founder Charles Garland was a twenty-one-year-old Harvard undergraduate in 1922 when his father died and left him eight hundred thousand dollars. Concluding that it would be improper to accept money he had done nothing to earn, Garland instead used the money to set up a fund for liberal and radical causes. Because he had no interest in administering the fund himself, he turned it over to a group of left-leaning activists—among them James Weldon Johnson, who took a leave from his job as NAACP executive secretary to head the fund. Soon, Johnson engineered a one-hundred-thousand-dollar grant to pay for a massive new NAACP litigation campaign. An initial payment of eight thousand dollars financed the preliminary legal research.

The task of finding someone to carry out this research fell to Arthur Spingarn, head of the NAACP's national legal committee. Spingarn asked fellow committee member Felix Frankfurter for advice, and Frankfurter suggested that Spingarn talk with Houston. Houston then recommended Nathan Ross Margold, a white lawyer who had been a class behind Houston at Harvard.

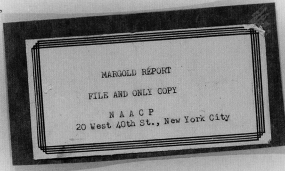

The cover of the original 1931 Margold Report from the archives of the NAACP, which are now preserved in the Library of Congress.

In October 1930, Spingarn hired Margold to identify the lawsuits to bring and the defendants to be served. Seven months later, Margold delivered a 218-page report.

THE MARGOLD REPORT

Since 1896, the constitutionality of Jim Crow had rested on the separate-but-equal doctrine enunciated in *Plessy*. In that decision, the Court had held that segregation, if applied evenhandedly, was constitutional because separation of the races was not inherently discriminatory.

James Weldon Johnson had wanted to concentrate the NAACP's challenge to *Plessy* on the "equal" side of the doctrine, targeting education in particular. Because conditions at black public schools in the South

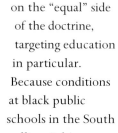

An NAACP membership pin from the middle of the twentieth century.

were so appalling, Johnson thought, it would be easy to show that they were unequal to those at white schools. Judges would then be required under the Fourteenth Amendment to order equalization, which few school districts could afford. Unable to meet the prohibitive cost of creating a truly equal dual system, districts would be forced to accept integration, which was the NAACP's ultimate goal.

Margold rejected this strategy for several reasons. For one, his research uncovered technical problems that made it difficult to determine which governmental entities to sue and what relief to ask for. Also, the task of proving inequality in court was trickier than Johnson had supposed. The plaintiffs would have to introduce complicated data about when schools were built, what facilities they contained, how well they were maintained, and so on—and even then, a victory would apply only to the specific school district being sued, not to other districts or to segregation generally, which would remain legal if facilities were somehow equalized.

On the other hand, Margold argued, the "separate" side of separate-but-equal provided a much more direct path to reversal. The experience of blacks since 1896 had demonstrated, Margold went on, that segregation *in practice* was indeed inherently discriminatory because nothing approaching equality had ever been realized. "We have a case," he wrote, "of segregation irremediably coupled with discrimination."

The Margold Report was well received, and the NAACP board would likely have moved ahead with its recommendations had not the Garland Fund grant disappeared into the rubble of the 1929 stock market crash. The simultaneous strain that the Great

Depression was placing on American society made the early 1930s seem a less than opportune time to begin a controversial legal campaign. Most African Americans still doubted the viability of a legal challenge to Jim Crow, and none doubted the reprisals that would surely visit anyone who became involved in such an effort. Given these circumstances, it was decided to shelve the Margold Report until the situation improved. Three and a half years passed before Houston recommended to the NAACP board in October 1934 that it revive the idea of a legal campaign.

Like that of James Weldon Johnson before him, Houston's thinking was strongly drawn to the field of education. He regularly toured the South, documenting with a sixteen-millimeter movie camera the flagrant disparities between the brick-

and-mortar buildings in which white students went to school and the dingy tarpaper shacks where black students were taught. Houston also examined the corresponding gap between black and white teachers' salaries. In Baltimore, for instance, the salary paid to a black elementary school teacher in 1930 was, on average, 57 percent of that paid to a comparable white teacher. This was a legal vulnerability that Houston knew could be exploited.

Demonstrating the inferiority of black schools could be procedurally complex, but proving the inequality of teachers' salaries required only the presentation of easily obtainable pay records. Equalization suits also had the added benefit of bringing money into the black community and into the coffers of the NAACP through donations from teachers with a direct financial interest in the litigation.

Students line up in front of a segregated school in Greene County, Georgia, in November 1941. (INSET) An interior view of another dilapidated school for black children in the South.

After the NAACP board decided to back Houston's proposal, Executive Secretary Walter White went to work on Houston to persuade him to lead the effort personally. Several months later, Houston agreed and announced that he would be taking a leave from Howard at the spring term to move to New York City and become the NAACP's first chief counsel.

SALARY EQUALIZATION CASES

Houston's legal strategy turned out to be valid, and with some effort he was able to establish a precedent that upheld the principle of salary equalization. However, there was a problem with the salary litigation: As Margold had warned, the equalization orders that Houston obtained applied only to the specific school districts being sued. Therefore, the NAACP faced the tedious task of suing districts individually to force compliance on a case-by-case basis. Such an approach was highly impractical, and the work was made even harder by the school boards' delays and retaliation against plaintiffs.

In Virginia, for example, a suit was brought in state court in late 1938 on behalf of black teachers in the Norfolk school district. While the judge issued postponement after postponement, the contract of the plaintiff, Aline Black, came up for

renewal. Because teachers in Virginia lacked tenure, the school board was able to withhold a new contract, thus depriving Black of her job. This made her unsuitable as a plaintiff because, no longer receiving a salary, she couldn't benefit from the equalization being sought. As a result, the Norfolk teachers had to start again with a new plaintiff and a new lawsuit.

It was also a rule of thumb that the deeper south one went, the less effective salary litigation became. Cases in Alabama and Florida failed entirely, and new obstructionist strategies, such as "merit-pay" systems that always seemed to pay whites more than blacks, made it more difficult to prove the existence of inequality to reluctant judges. By the early 1940s, with most of the major cities addressed, there seemed little point in pursuing smaller rural districts, and salary litigation began to decline. Meanwhile, the NAACP became involved in another type of litigation.

The dual school systems run by the southern states included black elementary schools, black secondary schools, and black colleges, but no black professional schools or graduate programs. Not much demand existed, and scholarships to out-of-state institutions were made available when necessary. It was Houston's contention, however, that sending students out of state failed

Thurgood Marshall during court proceedings in the *Murray* case. Donald Murray himself is seated in the center, flanked by another lawyer (probably Charles Hamilton Houston).

to satisfy each state's obligation to offer equal educational opportunities to all of its students.

He decided to start his initiative with law schools because judges were lawyers and could be expected to recognize the unfairness of forcing black students to train out of state, thus depriving them of expert instruction in state laws and invaluable local contacts. If Houston won this argument, he believed, it could lead to ever-broadening precedents that could, in turn, be applied to undergraduate, secondary, and even elementary education. For help, he turned to his former student Thurgood Marshall.

THE UNIVERSITY CASES

Marshall, a native of Baltimore, had always resented the fact that he had been excluded from the University of Maryland and forced to attend law school out of state (even if that law school had been Howard). After his graduation in 1933, he returned to Baltimore, opened a practice, and almost immediately began investigating the possibility of challenging segregation at the University of Maryland Law School.

He would have filed suit as early as January 1934 if only he had found a suitable plaintiff. Nine months later, he found Donald Murray.

The son of a prominent African-American family in Baltimore, Murray was, like Houston, an Amherst College graduate. In January 1935, already represented by Houston and Marshall, he applied for admission to the University of Maryland Law School and was rejected because he was black. Murray subsequently filed suit.

The first hearing in *Murray v. Pearson* took place in June 1935 in Baltimore City Court before Judge Eugene O'Dunne, who heard testimony from Murray, university president Raymond A. Pearson, the dean of the law school, and several state officials. The lead counsel for Maryland, Asst. Attorney General Charles T. LeViness, was simply overmatched. He tried to defend the university's segregation policy by citing *Plessy*, but his argument, which might have been accepted a decade earlier, now seemed foolish. Judge O'Dunne himself pointed out that Murray wasn't challenging Maryland's right to establish a segregated system, only the inequality of the system it *had* established—an inequality that *Plessy* specifically prohibited.

Later, when LeViness moved for an adjournment, O'Dunne instructed Marshall to object and then ruled from the bench that President Pearson admit Murray to the University of Maryland Law

School in September. The state appealed the case, but O'Dunne's decision was upheld.

Marshall savored the victory; however, because he had put so much effort into it, he found that the rest of his practice was floundering. Eventually, his growing financial problems forced him to seek help from Houston. In September 1936, he proposed that the NAACP begin paying him a monthly retainer of $150. By return mail, Houston replied that the NAACP made regular monthly payments only to members of its national staff. However, Houston continued, he would talk to Walter White about hiring Marshall "for six months if that interests you."

Accepting even a temporary staff job, Houston warned, would mean giving up his private practice and having to start again from scratch. But Marshall, who had no desire ever to return to civil litigation, seized the opportunity. A month later, he moved to New York City, where he spent two years working with Houston until his mentor returned to private practice in mid-1938. Marshall was just thirty years old when he became the most important Negro lawyer in the United States.

HEMAN SWEATT APPLIES TO LAW SCHOOL

As the NAACP's new chief counsel, Marshall gradually wound down the salary litigation and, with the help of an expanding legal staff, brought new exclusion suits of ever-expanding reach. The most important of these involved a Houston mail carrier named Heman Marion Sweatt, known to his friends as Bill. Angered by a postal service policy that prevented blacks from becoming clerks (and thus supervisors), Sweatt brought a legal complaint against the postmaster general, and the experience left him wanting to become a lawyer. At the time, there were 7,701 white lawyers in Texas and only 23 black ones.

A 1934 college graduate, Sweatt applied for admission to the all-white University of Texas Law School in February 1946. After his rejection on racial grounds, he sued for admission to the school, located in Austin. After a hearing in June 1946, the presiding Travis County

Mr. and Mrs. Heman Sweatt standing on the front steps of the Supreme Court in 1948.

Thurgood Marshall
• 1908–1993

According to family tradition, Thurgood Marshall's Congo-born great-great-grandfather was brought to America as a boy slave and grew up to be "one mean man." By Marshall's account, his ancestor's owner couldn't get him to do anything and finally told him, "You're too ornery to keep and too ornery to sell to a white man." So the master offered to set his slave free "if you'll get out of the town and county and state."

The great-great-grandson was not nearly so ornery. In fact, he was famous for being able to relieve tense situations with a joviality that offset Houston's severity and aloofness. His first secretary, Lucille Ward, told *Collier's* in 1952, "I haven't seen him in a long time, but I bet he still needs a haircut, his pants pressed, and hasn't yet learned how to spell 'separate.' And I bet he still speaks in court like the man who wrote the grammar book and yet commits felonious assault on the king's English in private."

judge, following the logic of *Murray*, gave the state six months to establish a colored law school or else admit Sweat to UT. The state responded by renting a few rooms in Houston and hiring two black lawyers to teach classes there. In December, the Travis County court reviewed these actions and, according to historian Richard Kluger, "found that the makeshift arrangement in Houston provided substantial equality to the

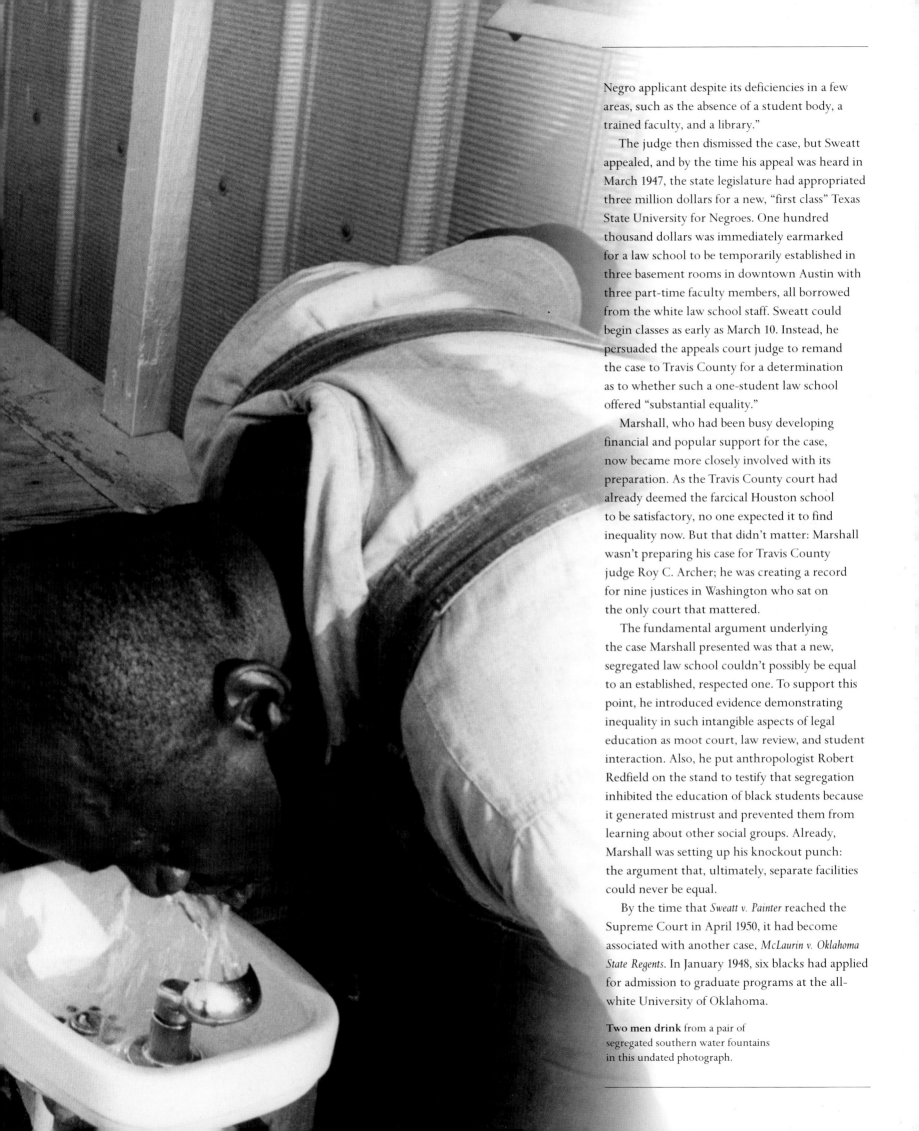

Negro applicant despite its deficiencies in a few areas, such as the absence of a student body, a trained faculty, and a library."

The judge then dismissed the case, but Sweatt appealed, and by the time his appeal was heard in March 1947, the state legislature had appropriated three million dollars for a new, "first class" Texas State University for Negroes. One hundred thousand dollars was immediately earmarked for a law school to be temporarily established in three basement rooms in downtown Austin with three part-time faculty members, all borrowed from the white law school staff. Sweatt could begin classes as early as March 10. Instead, he persuaded the appeals court judge to remand the case to Travis County for a determination as to whether such a one-student law school offered "substantial equality."

Marshall, who had been busy developing financial and popular support for the case, now became more closely involved with its preparation. As the Travis County court had already deemed the farcical Houston school to be satisfactory, no one expected it to find inequality now. But that didn't matter: Marshall wasn't preparing his case for Travis County judge Roy C. Archer; he was creating a record for nine justices in Washington who sat on the only court that mattered.

The fundamental argument underlying the case Marshall presented was that a new, segregated law school couldn't possibly be equal to an established, respected one. To support this point, he introduced evidence demonstrating inequality in such intangible aspects of legal education as moot court, law review, and student interaction. Also, he put anthropologist Robert Redfield on the stand to testify that segregation inhibited the education of black students because it generated mistrust and prevented them from learning about other social groups. Already, Marshall was setting up his knockout punch: the argument that, ultimately, separate facilities could never be equal.

By the time that *Sweatt v. Painter* reached the Supreme Court in April 1950, it had become associated with another case, *McLaurin v. Oklahoma State Regents*. In January 1948, six blacks had applied for admission to graduate programs at the all-white University of Oklahoma.

Two men drink from a pair of segregated southern water fountains in this undated photograph.

The regents' subsequent decision to deny them admission without creating separate programs for them put the university in an untenable legal position. One of the rejected applicants, sixty-eight-year-old George W. McLaurin, already had a graduate degree in education but wanted a doctorate. Backed by the NAACP, he sued the regents in federal court. The case was heard in August 1948 before a special three-judge panel of the sort authorized by the Judiciary Act of 1937 to hear cases relating to the constitutionality of state laws and fast-track appeals. McLaurin won easily and obtained a court order directing his admission to the university.

When McLaurin arrived on campus, however, he found that special arrangement had been made for him: The four courses for which he had registered were rescheduled to meet in a classroom with a small anteroom, in which he was required to sit, separated from the rest of the class at a desk

George McLaurin sits in the anteroom to which he was initially confined at the University of Oklahoma.

The six Negroes who applied for admission to the University of Oklahoma in 1948 were (from left to right) Mauderie Hancock Wilson, George McLaurin, James Bond, Mozeal A. Dillon, Ivor Tatum, and Helen Holmes. Of the six cases, Marshall chose McLaurin's because, at age sixty-eight, McLaurin could not plausibly be portrayed as a sexual threat.

marked RESERVED FOR COLORED. In the library, he was also assigned an isolated desk in the mezzanine, and in the cafeteria, he was ordered to eat by himself at a different hour than the rest of the students. Such "required isolation from all other students," Marshall complained to the court, created

"a mental discomfiture, which makes concentration and study difficult, if not impossible," and scarred McLaurin "with a badge of inferiority [the exact phrase from *Plessy*] which affects his relationship, both to his fellow students and to his professors." When the special district court rejected this argument, Marshall took advantage of the unique terms of the Judiciary Act and appealed its decision directly to the Supreme Court, where oral arguments were scheduled for April 4, 1950, the same day that *Sweatt* would be heard.

Most southern retail businesses provided separate services for blacks and whites unless, like this laundry company, they excluded Negroes altogether.

THE IMPLICATIONS FOR *PLESSY*

In November 1949, Marshall assigned Robert Carter, his chief assistant at the now well-staffed NAACP Legal Defense Fund (LDF), to supervise the preparations for *Sweatt*. Meanwhile, Erwin Griswold, dean of the Harvard Law School and one of the NAACP's favorite expert witnesses, offered Marshall some advice. Griswold knew that some of the justices were worried about southern claims that desegregation would lead to race riots, the possibility of which had even been mentioned in the State of Texas's brief on *Sweatt*. Therefore, he counseled Marshall to deny explicitly that these graduate-level cases had any relation to undergraduate, secondary, or elementary education. Limiting the scope of the remedy being sought, Griswold argued, would ensure a victory, while losing on the larger issue of *Plessy* would be "a serious set-

back, which might take a generation or more to overcome."

Marshall chose to ignore Griswold's advice and went ahead with his original plan to put the question of segregation's constitutionality to the justices as directly as he could, while characterizing the risk of violence as small and irrelevant.

The possibility of overturning *Plessy* pervaded the Court's deliberations with regard to *Sweatt*. In a letter written soon after the oral arguments, Justice Robert Jackson acknowledged that *Sweatt* and *McLaurin* "show pretty conclusively that the segregation system is breaking down of its own weight and that a little time will end it in nearly all States." Oklahoma, he continued, had tried to "save face by preserving... a sort of token separation which seems to gratify the one race and chafe the other, more for its symbolism than for any real advantage or disadvantage."

In an uncirculated memo, Justice Tom Clark wrestled more poignantly with *Plessy*: "We need no modern psychologist to tell us that 'enforced separation of the two races *does* stamp the colored race with a badge of inferiority,' contrary to *Plessy v. Ferguson*. My question, then, is 'how' to reverse, not 'whether' or 'why.'" On the other hand, Clark strongly expressed his "fear that a flat overruling of the *Plessy* case would cause subversion or even defiance of our mandates in many communities."

> "We need no modern psychologist to tell us that 'enforced separation of the two races *does* stamp the colored race with a badge of inferiority.'"
>
> JUSTICE TOM CLARK

"How will I vote when the swimming pool and grammar school cases arise?" he concluded. "I do not know; that is irrelevant. Should they arise tomorrow I would vote to deny certiorari or dismiss the appeal, so that we would not be compelled to decide the issues."

NAACP LDF

The NAACP Legal Defense and Educational Fund, Inc., was created in 1939 to take advantage of new laws granting tax-exempt status to nonprofit organizations that didn't have lobbying as a principal activity. Because the NAACP itself lobbied the government often, Walter White set up the Legal Defense Fund as a separate entity so that contributors could make tax-deductible donations.

At the outset, the LDF staff was merely Thurgood Marshall and a secretary. Eventually, Marshall was able to hire a few part-time legal assistants, and he trained some of the NAACP secretaries in routine legal office work, but it wasn't until 1945 that he hired another staff lawyer to help him with the courtroom work.

Thurgood Marshall (center) poses with members of his NAACP Legal Defense Fund staff in this undated photograph.

(Clark later circulated a much more restrained version of his memo.)

The decisions in *Sweatt* and *McLaurin* were handed down on June 5, with Chief Justice Fred Vinson authoring the unanimous opinions. Both were brief, cautious, and explicitly limited to the field of graduate education. Marshall had tried to force a reversal of *Plessy*, but the justices wouldn't bite.

"Broader issues have been urged for our consideration," Vinson declared, "but we adhere to the principle of deciding constitutional questions only in the context of the particular case before the Court."

The *Sweatt* opinion was straightforward: Even though the new Negro law school had become serviceable in the three years since it was created for Sweatt, it could not yet be considered

The Color Line

The separate-but-equal doctrine extended to sports as well. Until the late 1940s, major league baseball was played by whites only, with black players relegated to separate Negro leagues.

In 1943, when Branch Rickey joined the Brooklyn Dodgers, he became general manager of a team firmly in decline. One of the most imaginative executives in baseball history, Rickey knew that he would have to find a new source of talent. Already, he had invented the farm system, under which major league teams used minor league affiliates to develop young players; now he devised an even bolder scheme to repopulate the Dodger roster.

Rickey ordered his scouts to begin searching for Negro talent. He told them he wanted to start a new Negro league team, the Brown Dodgers, but this was a ruse. All along, he intended to sign the first black ballplayer to a major league contract.

Jackie Robinson was playing for the Kansas City Monarchs of the Negro American League in 1945, when Rickey invited him to New York. After revealing his plan, Rickey engaged Robinson in role playing, showering the twenty-six-year-old with racial slurs to learn whether he could control himself. "Mr. Rickey, do you want a ballplayer who's afraid to fight back?" Robinson ultimately demanded. "I want a ballplayer with guts enough not to fight back," Rickey replied. In October, he signed Robinson to a Dodgers contract.

Robinson spent the 1946 season playing for the Montreal Royals, the Dodgers' top farm team, before debuting for Brooklyn on April 15, 1947. The first baseman went hitless that day and endured an early slump (likely a result of the intense pressure he was under) but recovered to bat .297 and win the Rookie of the Year award.

In 1948, Roy Campanella, star catcher for the Baltimore Elite Giants, joined Robinson on the Dodgers, while Newark Eagles power hitter Larry Doby broke the color barrier in the American League. From that point on, no major league club could afford to ignore Negro talent and still remain competitive.

LEFT: **Robinson's Dodgers** cap and jersey.
BELOW: **Robinson signs** autographs for some fans.

This 1950 pamphlet, published by the *Pittsburgh Courier*, contained the complete texts of the Supreme Court decisions in the *Sweatt* and *McLaurin* cases, as well as the *Henderson* case, in which the Court outlawed segregated railway dining cars.

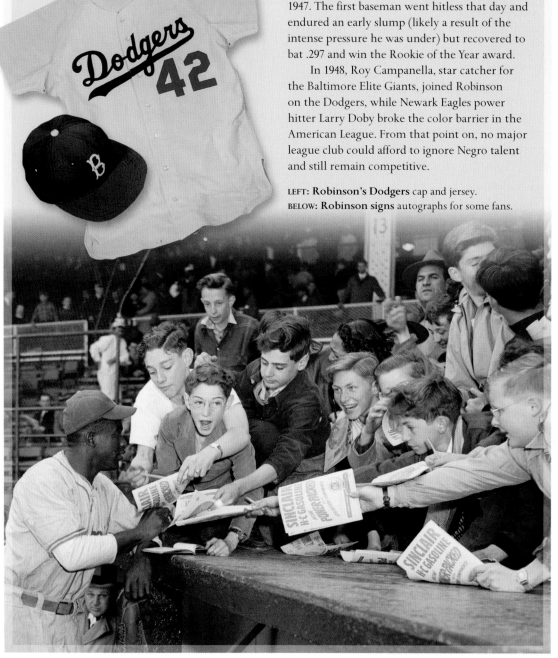

"substantially equal" to the all-white school. There were, of course, differences in physical facilities, Vinson wrote, but "what is more important, the University of Texas Law School possesses to a far greater degree those qualities which are incapable of objective measurement but which make for greatness in a law school. Such qualities, to name but a few, include reputation of the faculty, experience of the administration, position and influence of the alumni, standing in the community, traditions and prestige. It is difficult to believe that one who had a free choice between these law schools would consider the question close."

The Court then ordered the admission of Sweatt to the University of Texas Law School on the grounds that the Negro law school established by the state failed to offer an equal educational opportunity. *Plessy* was sidestepped, as it was also in the *McLaurin* case. Marshall had done his best to frame those facts to emphasize the role of segregation—after all, McLaurin had been given use of exactly the same educational facilities— but the Court merely voided the restrictions placed upon him and went no farther, refusing to follow its own logic to the conclusion that all restrictions imposed by segregation adversely affected black students at all levels of schooling.

The Summerton Grade School in Clarendon County, South Carolina, in a photograph taken for insurance purposes during the early 1940s. This school was specifically cited in the NAACP brief for *Briggs v. Elliott*.

Braving the real threat of economic and physical retaliation, black parents in several segregated states filed lawsuits after 1945 challenging the fairness of the dual system. Among these was a group of parents from Clarendon County, South Carolina, led by the Rev. J. A. DeLaine and Levi Pearson, who began pressing the county in 1947 to provide school buses for black students, as it already did for whites.

The facts of the case were typical for the Deep South: Clarendon County spent an average of $179 per white child and $43 per black child. White teachers were paid about three times as much as blacks. The dilapidated black schools had no lunchrooms, no gymnasiums, and only outdoor toilets. Yet in other ways—economic and social ways—the oppression in Clarendon was much worse than elsewhere. According to Richard Kluger, "If you had set out to find the place in America in the year 1947 where life among black folk had changed least since the end of slavery, Clarendon County is where you might have come."

As Clark's memo had indicated, the Court simply wasn't ready to overturn *Plessy*.

The narrow decisions left Marshall with another important choice: Should he bank his winnings now, as Griswold had suggested, or go for the big payoff? Bringing more pressure to bear on *Plessy* might finally force the Court to reverse it. However, such an effort might also fail and produce a harmful backlash, leading to a decision that reaffirmed the legality of segregation and condemned African Americans to another generation of Jim Crow. The stakes were as high as they could be when Marshall placed his bet.

THE STIGMA OF INFERIORITY

As a region, the South had always lagged behind the rest of the nation in funding for public education. However, as imperfect as its public

> "You could drive through Clarendon County, as I often did…, and see these awful-looking little wooden shacks in the country that were the Negro schools."
>
> FEDERAL APPEALS COURT JUDGE J. WATIES WARING

schools for whites were, its black schools were incomparably worse. In 1950, for example, the state of Mississippi spent $122.93 on each of its white elementary school students and only $32.55 per black pupil.

The Liberty Hill Colored School in Clarendon County, South Carolina, in an insurance photograph taken during the early 1940s. Liberty Hill was another specific focus of the *Briggs v. Elliott* litigation.

Clark's Doll Test

Footnote 11 in the *Brown* decision specifically cited a report Kenneth B. Clark had prepared for the 1950 Midcentury White House Conference on Children and Youth. The paper, "Effect of Prejudice and Discrimination on Personality Development," described a doll test that Clark and his wife, Mamie Phipps, had used to study "the extent of consciousness of skin color" in black children between three and seven years old. The children were shown four dolls, all made from the same mold and dressed alike, but their skin colors were different: Two were white, and two were black. Then Clark asked the children a series of questions, including:

- "Show me the doll that you like best."
- "Show me the doll that is the nice doll."
- "Show me the doll that looks bad."
- "Show me the doll that is most like you."

According to Clark, "The most disturbing question— and the one that really made me, even as a scientist, upset—was the final question: 'Now show me the doll that's most like you.' Many of the children became emotionally upset when they had to identify the doll they had rejected. These children saw themselves as inferior, and they accepted the inferiority as part of reality."

ABOVE: **A data sheet** from one of Clark's doll tests. RIGHT: **Dr. Clark gives** the doll test in 1947 to a young black child.

After a year without results, the protest escalated in 1948 into a federal lawsuit, prepared with the help of Howard-trained South Carolina lawyer Harold R. Boulware and the local NAACP. It was titled *Briggs v. Elliott*, after lead plaintiffs Harry and Liza Briggs. Immediately, Mrs. Briggs lost her job as a motel maid and Mr. Briggs was fired from his job as a gas station attendant. Other blacks suffered similar reprisals, but the lawsuit continued.

The case finally came to trial in May 1951 before another special three-judge court composed of George B. Timmerman, J. Waties Waring, and John J. Parker. Timmerman was an unabashed white supremacist, Waring was one of the few defenders of the Negro on the southern bench, and Parker was fair-minded, if unimaginative. Thurgood Marshall argued the case personally. The disparities in Clarendon County were so obvious that obtaining an equalization order would be easy, but Marshall wasn't going after equalization any longer. Now he wanted integration.

Able to see what was coming, the white political establishment of South Carolina realized that the state couldn't get away much longer with grossly underfunding its black schools. Therefore,

in early 1951, Gov. James F. Byrnes, who had pledged during his 1950 campaign to close the public schools rather than integrate them, persuaded the state legislature to enact South Carolina's first sales tax for the purpose of underwriting a bond issue that would fund equalization, estimated to cost at least forty million dollars.

The bond issue was still in the news when the *Briggs* trial began, and before any witnesses were called, the lawyer for Clarendon County, former Charleston district attorney Robert McCormick Figg Jr., read a statement acknowledging the inequality in Clarendon County's schools and stating that the school board would not oppose a court order directing it to eliminate existing inequalities through the construction of new facilities for its black students.

Figg's concession shortened the trial to just two days, obviating the need for Marshall to document the inequality of the facilities. That left the social science witnesses, the most important of whom was psychologist Kenneth B. Clark. The NAACP had earlier brought Clark to Clarendon County to conduct his doll test, which measured the self-esteem of Negro children. The results, consistent with those Clark had obtained

elsewhere, demonstrated that segregation stamped black children with a stigma of inferiority that undermined their self-esteem.

A month later, Parker ruled as expected. His majority opinion, joined by Timmerman, ordered Clarendon County to equalize its facilities but refused to restrict segregation in any way. Its review of Supreme Court decisions emphasized that the separate-but-equal doctrine remained in effect and called it "a late day" to challenge the constitutionality of segregation when the practice had been in place for "more than three-quarters of a century." Waring dissented, noting the persuasiveness of the social science evidence and concluding, "Segregation is per se inequality."

THE FIVE FACES OF *BROWN*

When *Briggs* reached the Supreme Court in December 1952, it was combined with three similar school segregation cases—*Belton v. Gebhart*, a Delaware case that had resulted in a state court integration order; *Davis v. County School Board of Prince Edward County*, which originated in a student strike led by a sixteen-year-old Moton High School junior; and a Kansas case, *Brown v. Board of Education of Topeka*. Every day, seven-year-old Linda

Black Support for Segregation

"For decades," black journalist Carl T. Rowan wrote in late 1953, "the southern Negro who could afford college usually trained to teach. That was the only profession where he could be sure of a job; segregation was his guarantee. And because teaching was open to Negroes while other professions were closed, the Negro teacher became a leader, a spokesman; his social status in his community was much higher than that of the white teacher in the white community. What could one expect the Negro teacher to do when segregation, the institution that made all this possible, was threatened?"

In fact, many blacks opposed integration. Teachers who had been thrilled with the NAACP's equalization lawsuits were concerned about losing their jobs. Others worried about the psychological damage hostile white teachers in integrated schools might inflict on vulnerable black children. "The elementary school age is one in which youngsters are deeply impressed," one black social worker warned. "They need a pat on the back when they do something well. So I think it better that they have Negro teachers who are likely to be sympathetic to them. It would crush the souls of the little darlings to have them taught by someone who despised them because of their color."

A crowded classroom in one of the South's better-equipped black schools, shown in a photograph taken during the 1940s.

Third-grader Linda Brown (inset) walks with her six-year-old sister, Terry Lynn, along the railroad tracks separating their house from the all-black Monroe Elementary School, which both girls attended.

Brown had to cross the tracks of a railroad switching yard in order to reach the bus stop for her segregated school on the other side of town. It wasn't the worst situation a black student had to endure, but Linda's father, Oliver Brown, couldn't bear any risk to his daughter when there was a perfectly good school within easy walking distance, albeit one for white children only.

In June 1951, NAACP lawyers Carter and Jack Greenberg, a white veteran who had attended Columbia Law after the war, argued the first round of *Brown* before a three-judge panel in Topeka. Because the physical-plant inequalities in Kansas were much less extreme than those in the South, more emphasis was placed on the psychological testimony. Under Greenberg's cross-examination, expert witness Hugh Speer, chairman of the education department at the University of Missouri–Kansas City, connected the theory of *Sweatt* and *McLaurin* to elementary education. "If the colored children are denied

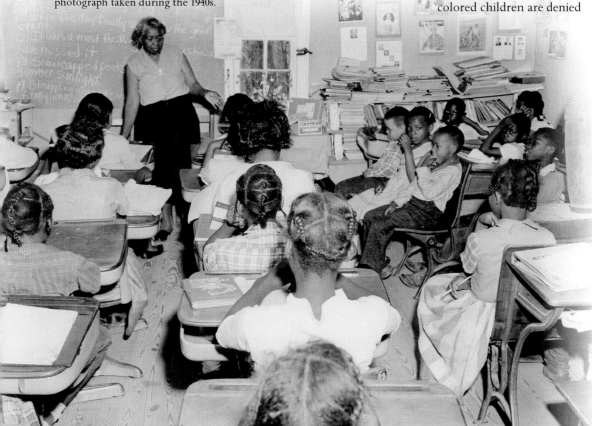

the experience in school of associating with white children who make up about 90 percent of our national society," Speer testified, "then their curriculum is being greatly curtailed." In that sense, he concluded, no curriculum could be equal under segregation.

Presenting the panel's unanimous opinion, Judge Walter Huxman ruled that, because the segregated facilities were substantially equal, the Topeka school board had not violated *Plessy*, which was still the law of the land. However, the panel did make an important "finding of fact," asserting that segregation indeed "has a detrimental effect upon the colored children" and that "the impact is greater when it has the sanction of law." Huxman would explain later that he had "wrapped up the decision in such a way that the Supreme Court could no longer duck [*Plessy*]."

By the time *Brown* reached the Supreme Court, the federal government had also weighed in. The denial of civil rights to African Americans, it said, was embarrassing the United States around the world, especially in Africa, and disrupting international relations. In an amicus brief filed

Spectators wait in line outside the Supreme Court to hear oral arguments in the *Brown* case.

with the Court, the outgoing Truman administration complained that "racial discrimination furnishes grist for the Communist propaganda mills, and it raises doubts even among friendly nations as to the intensity of our devotion to the democratic faith." When the Eisenhower administration took office in January 1953, it filed its own amicus brief, also asking the Court to outlaw segregation.

Meanwhile, the South was bringing pressure of its own. Grand Dragon Bill Hendrix of the Southern Knights of the Ku Klux Klan declared that an "American Confederate army" would march in rebellion if the Court overturned *Plessy*, and even moderate southern newspapers

This photograph from October 1952 shows Pres. Dwight D. Eisenhower chatting with attorney John W. Davis, who was the lead counsel opposing the NAACP in the *Brown* case.

predicted that an integration order would empower the Klan and other hate groups. The NAACP tried to dismiss such talk as "a not-so-subtle attempt to intimidate the Court," arguing that most southerners were ready for integration and would obey the law. Integration was certainly taking hold in Delaware, NAACP spokesmen pointed out—but South Carolina was another matter, and the justices were obviously concerned. Already, the South had ignored several Court rulings banning segregation in interstate travel, and more extreme disobedience had to be contemplated.

THE LANDMARK DECISION

The first case heard on December 9, 1952, was *Brown*, argued by Robert Carter, who presented the NAACP's underlying argument: School segregation was unconstitutional because it violated the Fourteenth Amendment's equal protection clause. Later that day, Marshall argued *Briggs*, during which he presented the bulk of the controversial social science evidence. At the time, Marshall had won 13 of his 15 Supreme Court cases, but he was going up against another titan, 1924 Democratic presidential nominee John W. Davis, who had argued more than 250 cases before the Court, more than any other twentieth-century lawyer.

In a contemporary letter to a fellow attorney in South Carolina, Davis wrote of Clark's evidence, "I can only say that if that sort of 'guff' can move any court, 'God save the state!'"

The three days of hearings were inconclusive. A majority of justices was already poised to overturn *Plessy*, but the Court was fractured and poorly led by Chief Justice Vinson, who was personally reluctant to reverse *Plessy*. Unable to reach a consensus, the Court ordered more argument during the 1953 term on the intention of the framers of the Fourteenth Amendment with regard to public education. The real purpose was to give the justices more time to sway one another, but an unexpected event changed the dynamic of the Court entirely: Fred Vinson died of a heart attack in September 1953, and California governor Earl Warren became the new chief justice.

Because the politician in Warren understood the impact that overruling *Plessy* would have on the country, he made unanimity his primary goal. The chief obstacle was Justice Stanley Reed, who relinquished his stated intention to dissent only after Warren promised to seek a gradual rather than immediate remedy.

As it turned out, this commitment to gradualism held an otherwise shaky Court together, but there would be a price to pay for the justices' lack of nerve.

By custom, the Court announced its decisions on Mondays but never revealed which decisions would be coming down, so plaintiffs were rarely present. This was the case on May 17, 1954, when *Brown* was the fourth opinion delivered.

present place in American life throughout the nation. Only in this way can it be determined if segregation in public school deprives these plaintiffs of the equal protection of the laws."

"Does segregation of children in public schools solely on the basis of race, even though the physical facilities and other 'tangible' factors may be equal, deprive the children of the minority group of equal educational

"Can all this be ended by a Supreme Court ruling? If so, how? Will there be chaos? Fighting in the streets?"

JOURNALIST CARL T. ROWAN

News bulletins interrupted radio shows and stopped the presses of afternoon newspapers across the country. Explicitly noting the persuasiveness of the sociological evidence, the Court decided the case in the NAACP's favor.

The text of the *Brown* decision was rather modest and its language restrained, but its significance was clear. In previous cases, Warren pointed out, the Court had not found it necessary to determine whether *Plessy* "should be held inapplicable to public education," but now "that question is directly presented."

Describing education as "perhaps the most important function of state and local governments," Warren wrote that the Court "cannot turn the clock back to 1868 when the [Fourteenth] Amendment was adopted, or even to 1896 when *Plessy v. Ferguson* was written." Instead, "we must consider public education in the full light of its full development and its

opportunities?" Warren went on. "We believe that it does.…We conclude that in the field of public education the doctrine of 'separate but equal' has no place. Separate educational facilities are inherently unequal."

Then Warren temporized: "Because these are class actions, because of the wide applicability of this decision, and because of the great variety of local conditions, the formulation of decrees in these cases presented problems of considerable complexity." Thousands of schools and millions of students in twenty-one states and the District of Columbia were affected. Therefore, instead of setting a deadline for compliance, the justices gave the South a year of grace. The Court declared segregation in public education illegal, but it delayed implementation of the decision until it could hear arguments during the next term on how and when enforcement orders should be issued.

The Warren Court

Earl Warren was appointed chief justice of the Supreme Court in 1953. He retired in 1969. During the intervening sixteen years, he presided over one of the most important periods in Court history, during which much of American constitutional law was rewritten.

In this work, Warren was unquestionably the leader. With *Brown*, he transformed a sharply divided Court into a symbolically unanimous one. "Those behind the 'Impeach Earl Warren' movement," historian Bernard Schwartz has written, "were correct in considering him the primary mover in the Warren Court's jurisprudence."

While his predecessors had stressed the importance of property rights, Warren focused on personal rights instead. This emphasis led to decisions that barred the use of illegally seized evidence in trials and established a constitutional right to privacy.

The Warren Court in 1953. Front row (from left to right): Felix Frankfurter, Hugo Black, Earl Warren, Stanley Reed, William O. Douglas. Back row (from left to right): Tom Clark, Robert H. Jackson, Harold Burton, Sherman Minton.

RIGHT: **Students at Russell High School** in Atlanta gather around a radio shortly after noon to hear the news that the Supreme Court has ruled school segregation unconstitutional.
BELOW: **The front page** of the May 17, 1954, edition of the *Philadelphia Bulletin*.

Black and white students line up near the end of the 1954–1955 academic year at a newly integrated school in Washington, D.C.

THE SOUTHERN BACKLASH

Once the euphoria passed, Marshall remained cautiously optimistic. "I don't believe that legislatures will buck the Supreme Court," he told the press. "I think Governors Byrnes and [Herman] Talmadge [of Georgia] are speaking for themselves [when they say they will close the public schools]. The people in the South will follow the law. They are as law-abiding as anybody else." At a meeting held in Atlanta a week later, southern leaders of the NAACP predicted privately that the border states would comply without much resistance and that white opposition would be concentrated primarily in

Justice William O. Douglas wrote this May 11, 1954, memo to Earl Warren, complimenting the chief justice on the *Brown* opinion.

Supreme Court of the United States

Memorandum

May 11, 1954

Dear Chief Justice

I do not think I would change a single word in the memoranda you gave me the wrong. The two draft opinion meet my idea exactly. You have done a beautiful job. As ever WOD

Mississippi and the Black Belt counties of Georgia and Alabama. Their assessment, it turned out, was unduly optimistic.

The first indications of the white South's ferocious backlash came from political leaders who trashed the decision in the press. A number of congressmen stated flatly that their states would defy the Supreme Court and continue to segregate public schools. "The South will not abide by or obey this legislative decision by a political court," Sen. James O. Eastland of Mississippi declared in one of his more polite statements.

By the time that the Court issued its implementation decision (known as *Brown II*) on May 31, 1955, the moment for compliance had long passed. The NAACP brief had argued strongly for immediate relief, but the justices retained their cautious approach and ordered integration using the intentionally vague phrase *with all deliberate speed*. The task of devising specific remedies was left up to the federal district court judges, who were instructed to proceed on a case-by-case basis. Most southerners considered the decision a great victory.

Using hindsight, some historians have argued that the Court missed an important opportunity when it failed to include with *Brown I* an implementation decree requiring immediate compliance. Citing the statements of many southern moderates, who urged compliance immediately after the decision, these historians have contended that such a decree would have changed the course of the debate by denying the opposition time to organize. This argument, however, presumes that such an order was possible, which it likely was not. Had Warren insisted on immediate compliance, the consensus on the Court would have been broken, and the voicing of dissenting opinions would have produced much the same result.

Brown's rather limited practical effect has also made it the object of disparagement from left-leaning scholars. It wasn't the Court that forced the South to integrate, some have argued,

> "We conclude that in the field of public education the doctrine of 'separate but equal' has no place. Separate educational facilities are inherently unequal."
>
> FROM THE *BROWN* DECISION

but the mass political movement that rose up in *Brown*'s wake. The *Brown* decisions, they say, demonstrate the folly of any political litigation strategy. Much more influential, in their view, were the mass-action programs originated by the Communist party and further developed by the Congress of Industrial Organizations.

The fact that nearly a decade passed before even token integration was achieved in many

states—and fifteen years before Mississippi took *Brown* seriously—supports this claim. But for all its deficiencies, the Court's decision in *Brown* was probably the most important turning point in the struggle for black civil rights because it let African Americans know that at least one branch of the government was on their side. After *Brown*, in the words of one California civil rights leader, "Black folks in Richmond saw the light and really began to believe they could break through." In time, the *Brown* decisions also compelled a reluctant Pres. Dwight D. Eisenhower to employ federal force against Jim Crow in the South.

Black students arrive at Clinton High School in Clinton, Tennessee, on December 4, 1956. Violence erupted in the town less than a week after desegregation of the high school in August 1956 and continued on into December.

The Murder of Emmett Till

1955

In the wake of the *Brown* decision, public opinion polls showed that, overwhelmingly, southern whites believed miscegenation (sexual intercourse between whites and blacks) and intermarriage to be the ultimate goals of integration. This conviction was so pervasive that, even now, it's simple to trace the emotional connections that were made: Desegregation meant race mixing, race mixing meant miscegenation, and the threat of miscegenation meant that some blacks would have to suffer in order to keep the rest in their place.

There were, of course, southern moderates in 1954—men such as Big Jim Folsom of Alabama, who spent the summer campaigning successfully for governor—but they said little and did less when it came to race that year, ceding the debate to the hard-liners, who were quick to seize the initiative.

"Generations of Southerners yet unborn will cherish our memory because they will realize that the fight we now wage will have preserved for them their untainted racial heritage, their culture, and the institutions of the Anglo-Saxon race," Mississippi senator James O. Eastland told a gathering of fellow firebrands shortly after the *Brown* decision was handed down. "We of the South have seen the tides rise before. We know what it is to fight. We will carry the fight to victory."

About the same time that Eastland made his speech, the NAACP instructed its branches in segregated states to begin the process of forcing desegregation through the courts. Initially, this meant collecting signatures for petitions that would be presented to the local school boards. Unfortunately, this petitioning turned out to be a serious tactical misstep.

The responsibility for the violence and oppression that *Brown* engendered rests ultimately with those who carried it out. As suggested earlier, however, the justices of the Supreme Court bear some responsibility for first delaying desegregation and then evading the burden of implementing it. This burden fell instead on the parents of black schoolchildren, who were forced to file suits in federal court on a case-by-case basis and thus expose themselves to reprisals.

The NAACP also erred. Focused as tightly as it was on reversing *Plessy*, the organization gave insufficient thought to the remedy and grossly underestimated the depth and ferocity of the white resistance. Despite Thurgood Marshall's reassuring assertions to the contrary, the South was most certainly not ready for integration.

THE CITIZENS' COUNCILS

Leading the resistance were the urban, middle-class Citizens' Councils, known as the "white-collar Klan." The first of these groups was formed in Indianola, Mississippi, in July 1954 by Robert "Tut" Patterson, a thirty-two-year-old plantation manager who had once been captain of the Mississippi State football team. Directly inspired by Judge Tom P. Brady's *Black Monday*, Patterson's movement quickly grew, spreading throughout Mississippi and seven other states. By 1956, it boasted 250,000 members, with 60,000 in Mississippi alone.

As Dan Wakefield observed in an October 1955 *Nation* article, "The Citizens' Councils that have grown up in the South since the United States Supreme Court decision on school integration are composed of 'respectable' gentlemen and ladies (there is now an auxiliary) who are dedicated to depriving the Negro of his civil rights by means of the latest, most up-to-date methods....Attorneys, bankers, planters, mayors, former local chamber of commerce presidents, and assorted school officials are among the civil leaders who have joined to help 'Tut' Patterson hold back the flood. Just how they are going about it is rather vague, at least in official

Robert Patterson, founder of the Citizens' Councils, in 1956.

Black Monday

Robert Patterson supplied the organizational energy behind the Citizens' Council movement, but not its intellectual muscle, which came from fellow Mississippian Tom P. Brady, a circuit court judge in Brookhaven. In a speech delivered to the Sons of the American Revolution in Greenwood and later to the founding Citizens' Council in Indianola, Brady offered a detailed legal attack on the "socialistic" *Brown* decision, which he placed within the context of American history and black–white relations, both interpreted from a distinctly southern point of view. The speech was so well received that

Brady expanded it into a ninety-two-page booklet published in 1955 and distributed throughout the South by the Association of Citizens' Councils of Mississippi.

According to Brady, civil rights organizations such as the NAACP were part of an international Communist conspiracy to destroy white supremacy and had to be resisted. "If the result of the [*Brown*] decision will be harmful to the bulk of the people of this country, will be calculated to foster those forces which seek this country's destruction, then to fail to resist the decision is morally wrong and the man who fails to condemn it and do all that he can to see that it is reversed is not a patriotic American."

BLACK MONDAY

SEGREGATION OR AMALGAMATION ...AMERICA HAS ITS CHOICE

BY TOM P. BRADY

"The social, economic, and the religious preferences of the Negro remain close to the caterpillar and the cockroach."

TOM P. BRADY IN *BLACK MONDAY*

White demonstrators hold up anti-integration signs in response to the *Brown* decision.

A **Saturday afternoon** in 1942 in the Negro section of Belzoni, Mississippi, captured by Farm Security Administration photographer Marion Post Wolcott. INSET: **Belzoni's main street** on that same Saturday afternoon.

council announcements. It was first reported that the councils, although definitely opposed to violence, would keep the land pure by 'economic pressure.' The idea of 'economic pressure' drew many bad press clippings, however, and now 'Tut' Patterson says there is no such thing."

Of course, Patterson was dissembling. In Yazoo City, Mississippi, for example, the local Citizens' Council took out a full-page newspaper ad listing the names of the fifty-three Negroes who had signed the desegregation petition circulated by the local NAACP branch. Their names also appeared on placards posted in store windows and in surrounding cotton fields. Those signers who worked for white people were immediately fired from their jobs, while those who owned their own businesses suffered boycotts and, even worse, loss of access to their suppliers. (One grocer, for instance, had to close his store because his distributors cut him off.) Once the severity of these consequences became apparent, all but two of the signers removed their names from the petition, but they didn't get their jobs or stores back. Meanwhile, membership in the Yazoo City NAACP plummeted, while membership in the local Citizens' Council ballooned from 16 to 1,500.

The Citizens' Councils also attacked the NAACP directly. Working with contacts in state government, they engineered new laws prohibiting state employees from advocating integration—forcing teachers, for example, to choose between NAACP membership and their jobs. At the same time, a number of states unearthed long-forgotten laws that required the NAACP to file membership lists with the state government. The list turned over in Louisiana was then published by the Citizens' Councils, inviting more retribution. As a result, NAACP membership in Louisiana fell from 13,190 in 1955 to 1,698 in 1956, and the number of branches plunged from 65 to 7 during the same period. When the Alabama NAACP refused to hand over its list, it was held in contempt of court and barred from operating anywhere in the state. The interdiction lasted eight years.

THE HORROR OF MISSISSIPPI

In Mississippi, indisputably the most racist southern state, the situation was even worse. A state law still on the books in 1955 made it illegal to produce or circulate printed matter advocating either social equality or intermarriage between blacks and whites. The penalty was a five-hundred-dollar fine and six months in jail. Extralegal sanctions, of course, were much more severe, and they applied to other forms of civil rights agitation as well.

George W. Lee was a fifty-two-year-old printing shop owner in the Delta town of Belzoni. He was also a local NAACP leader active in voter registration efforts. In 1954, only twenty-two thousand African Americans were registered to vote in Mississippi, about 4 percent of those eligible. In fourteen counties, six of which had black majority populations, there were no registered blacks at all. In Forrest County, a minister with two degrees from Columbia University failed twice to pass the voter literacy test. When asked for an explanation, the county registrar said that the minister's membership in the NAACP made him unfit to vote.

On the night of May 7, 1955, Lee was driving in Belzoni when several whites in a convertible pulled up alongside him. They fired several shotgun

A large crowd of mourners at the funeral of murdered civil rights activist George W. Lee in May 1955.

blasts into his car, which then swerved and crashed into a shack. Although the gunfire tore away much of his lower face and jaw, Lee still managed to pull himself out of the wreckage. Two black taxi drivers came to his aid, but Lee died on the way to the hospital. When the Humphreys County coroner listed the cause of his death as a car accident, the new NAACP field secretary for Mississippi, Medgar Evers, called on Gov. Hugh White to send state investigators to Belzoni, but White refused, explaining that as a matter of policy he never responded to NAACP requests.

Rep. Charles Diggs Jr. of Detroit, one of only three blacks in the Eighty-fourth Congress and the first ever from Michigan, pressured the FBI into conducting an inquiry. But the federal investigation was perfunctory, no charges were ever filed, and the handling of the case merely demonstrated to most whites that the lynching of blacks in Mississippi was still permissible.

On the afternoon of Saturday, August 13, 1955, sixty-three-year-old Lamar Smith got into an argument with some white men outside the busy Brookhaven, Mississippi, courthouse (where Tom Brady sometimes presided). Smith was another black voter registration activist, and he was likely arguing with the men about his civil rights. Soon, one of them pulled out a gun and shot Smith in full public view. The county sheriff saw a man leaving the scene covered in blood but didn't stop him. Three whites were eventually arrested for the crime but later set free when no one, black or white, could be found who was willing to testify against them.

Just seven days after Smith's murder, fourteen-year-old Emmett Till boarded a train in Chicago to visit some relatives in the Magnolia State. His subsequent lynching can be seen simply as a extension of the racial violence that had already consumed Smith and Lee, but such a characterization wouldn't explain why *Emmett Till* became a household name and *Lamar Smith* didn't. What made Till's case so different was that it involved not merely race but sex as well.

A year earlier, in *Black Monday*, Tom Brady had asserted that *Brown*'s encouragement of miscegenation

Medgar Evers
1925–1963

Medgar Evers attended Alcorn State College on the GI Bill and, after his graduation, took a job with T. R. M. Howard's Magnolia Mutual Insurance Company, selling policies door to door in the Delta. The job was an apprenticeship for his life's work.

Feeling guilty about selling insurance to people who could barely afford to feed themselves, Evers began using his job as a cover for political organizing work, talking up the NAACP and the mass meetings being held by his boss, Dr. Howard, in Mound Bayou, Mississippi.

In 1953, Evers volunteered to become a plaintiff in a university case and subsequently applied to the University of Mississippi Law School, which brought him to the attention of the national NAACP. In December 1954, the organization hired him as its first full-time field secretary in Mississippi.

Emmett Till's Family

Mamie Carthan's family left Mississippi for Chicago in January 1924, when she was two years old. In October 1940, when she was eighteen, she married Louis Till. Nine months later, their only child, Emmett, was born.

Sadly, Mamie and Louis never got along very well, and they were separated in 1942. A year later, Louis was drafted and sent overseas. In 1945, the War Department sent Mamie a letter informing her, with no further explanation, that her husband had been executed in Italy because of "willful misconduct." During the early 1950s, Mamie met and married a second husband, Gene "Pink" Bradley, but this marriage also failed within two years.

In many ways, Emmett Till was a typical American adolescent of the mid-1950s. He grew up in a solidly middle-class neighborhood on Chicago's South Side, where segregation had allowed black-owned businesses to thrive.

He ate bologna sandwiches, drank Kool-Aid, and liked to dance to the new rock 'n' roll music, especially the recordings of the Moonglows, the Coasters, the Flamingos, and the Spaniels.

Although his elementary school was all black, as was the Illinois Central coach on which he traveled down to Mississippi, his experiences in the North in no way prepared Till for segregation as it was then practiced in the South.

Emmett Till and his mother, Mamie Till Bradley, in a 1950 photograph.

---

would ultimately lead to racial violence. His description of the triggering event proved shrewdly accurate. "The fulminate which will discharge the blast," Brady wrote, "will be the young negro schoolboy....The supercilious, glib young negro, who has sojourned in Chicago or New York and who considers the counsel of his elders archaic, will perform an obscene act, or make an obscene remark,...upon some white girl." And that is fairly close to what happened.

Twenty-one-year-old Carolyn Bryant in a 1955 photograph. She and her husband, Roy, couldn't afford a car and lived with their two young children in two small rooms at the back of their store.

THE WOLF WHISTLE

The tiny Leflore County hamlet of Money, less than an hour's drive from Belzoni, straddles the road from Greenwood, the county seat, to nowhere in particular. Its geographic existence was justified in 1955 by the presence of several stores, one of which was Bryant's Grocery and Meat Market, run by twenty-four-year-old Roy Bryant and his pretty twenty-one-year-old wife, Carolyn. Roy was also a part-time truck driver. When Roy was away, Carolyn minded the store, whose clientele was mostly black sharecroppers and their families.

On the evening of Wednesday, August 24, Emmett Till and some of his cousins borrowed the '41 Ford belonging to Till's great-uncle Mose Wright and drove the three miles from Wright's cabin into Money. Nicknamed "Bobo" or simply "Bo," Till was a chubby kid whose cockiness compensated for a slight stammer caused by a childhood bout with polio.

Hanging out in front of the Bryants' store, Till mingled with the other black teens and began bragging about a girlfriend he had back in Chicago who was white and whose picture he carried in his wallet. (Till's mother, Mamie Till

Bradley, was never able to explain whose picture this might have been, except to suggest the unlikely possibility that it was a promotional photo of Hedy Lamarr that came with the wallet.) According to one of Till's cousins, Emmett's bluff was eventually called. "You talk pretty big, Bo," a local boy said. "There's a pretty little [white] woman in the store. Since you know how to handle white girls, let's see you go in and get a date with her." Full of bravado, Till walked into the store.

As with many details of the Till case, it's difficult to be certain what happened next, but Carolyn Bryant's testimony at the subsequent murder trial seems at least as credible as any of the secondhand accounts. According to her testimony, Till came into the store about eight o'clock to buy some candy. She gave him the chewing gum he wanted and then held out her hand for the money—at which point, she claimed, "he caught my hand in a strong grip and said, 'How about a date, baby?'" Bryant then pulled her hand loose and headed for the living quarters at the rear of the store, where her sister-in-law was caring for her two young children. But, she continued, Till cut her off and put his hands around her waist, telling her not to be afraid because he'd been "with white women before." At this point, according to Bryant, "another Negro came in and dragged him out of the store by his arm." Even then, not realizing the significance of what he had done, the exuberant eighth grader chirped, "Bye, baby," and, according to some accounts, wolf-whistled at Carolyn Bryant.

Quickly, Till's Mississippi cousins hustled him into the Ford and drove him away. Whatever Till had actually done, it was clear to all that he had dangerously transgressed the strict rules of racial conduct in Mississippi. That night, there was talk of getting him out of town on the next train, but when nothing happened on either Thursday or Friday, the tension eased, and the incident became just a good story.

Nothing happened to Till on Thursday because Roy Bryant was away, hauling shrimp from Louisiana to Texas, and when he returned just before daybreak on Friday, his wife chose not to tell him about the incident. He found out later from talk around the store on Friday afternoon.

At this point, Roy Bryant had a choice. He could have done nothing, but that, he was sure, would have marked him as a coward in the estimation of his peers, so he decided to pay Till a visit.

Having no car of his own, he enlisted the help of his half brother J. W. Milam, a thirty-six-year-old plantation overseer in nearby Tallahatchie County. Six feet two and 235 pounds, Milam was known around the region as a man who could "handle Negroes better than anybody."

THE KNOCK ON THE DOOR

About two o'clock in the morning on Sunday, August 28, Bryant and Milam knocked loudly on the door of Mose Wright's unpainted, three-room cabin and said they wanted "the boy who done the talkin'." A frightened Wright led them to the room where Till was sleeping. Bryant told Wright to turn on the lights, but none were functional, so Milam used his powerful five-cell flashlight to illuminate Till's face. "You the nigger who did the talkin'?" Milam asked. "Yeah," Till replied. "Don't say 'Yeah' to me," snapped Milam. "I'll blow your head off."

Milam then told Till to get dressed because they were taking him outside. Wright begged Bryant and Milam merely to whip Till, explaining that he was only a boy from up north who didn't know how to behave around southern whites.

Wright's wife, Elizabeth, offered the white men money, but Milam simply turned around and said, "How old are you, preacher?" "Sixty-four," Wright answered. "If you cause any trouble," Milam continued, "you'll never live to be sixty-five."

The principal account of how Milam and Bryant came to murder Till first appeared in William Bradford Huie's January 1956 *Look* article, "The Shocking Story of Approved Killing in Mississippi." A white journalist from Alabama, Huie is often credited with originating "checkbook journalism" because he paid Milam and Bryant four thousand dollars for their story. (The rules against double jeopardy, or being tried twice for the same crime, had made them, by that time, legally invulnerable.) According to Huie's article, the two men didn't initially intend to murder Till, only to scare him. But, they said, Till's refusal to repent or beg for mercy compelled them to kill him.

"What else could we do?" Milam told Huie. "He was hopeless. I'm no bully; I never hurt a nigger in my life. I like niggers in their place. I know how to work 'em. But I just decided it was time a few people got put on notice." Till was beaten, shot through the head,

> "As long as I live and I can do anything about it, niggers are gonna stay in their place. Nigger's ain't gonna vote where I live. If they did, they'd control the government."
>
> J. W. MILAM, QUOTED IN "THE SHOCKING STORY OF APPROVED KILLING IN MISSISSIPPI"

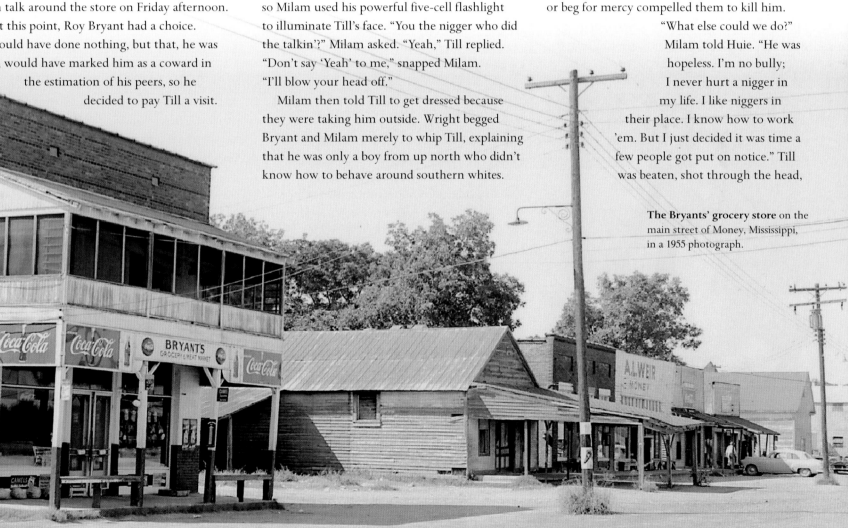

The Bryants' grocery store on the main street of Money, Mississippi, in a 1955 photograph.

> "Have you ever sent a loved son on vacation and had him returned to you in a pine box, so horribly battered and water logged that someone needs to tell you this sickening sight is your son—lynched?"
>
> MAMIE TILL BRADLEY TO REPORTERS

Mose Wright, photographed in a bedroom of his home, holds up some clothing belonging to his murdered grandnephew, Emmett Till.

and then dumped into the Tallahatchie River. His mangled body—forehead crushed, an eye gouged out—was weighted down with a seventy-pound cotton-gin fan tied to his neck with barbed wire.

There are several major holes and improbabilities in Huie's account, not the least of which is Milam's characterization of Till as impudent and arrogant throughout. However brash the Chicagoan may have been, it's inconceivable that a fourteen-year-old boy (or anyone else) could have been thrust into such a situation and not have felt deeply threatened. Yet Milam and Bryant's story was accepted in its entirety by white southerners because it fit their collective racial ideology. Similarly, a baseless

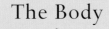

This ring originally belonged to Louis Till, whose army service record was leaked to the press in October 1955. He had been executed for committing rape and murder.

rumor that Till's penis had been cut off and stuffed into his mouth was accepted by many African Americans at the time because it literalized their own experience of white brutality. In this way, the Till case swiftly took on a significance in American life that went well beyond its mostly confused and hidden facts.

Obeying Milam, an initially intimidated Wright didn't report the abduction until the next morning, when Leflore County sheriff George Smith began the usual search of bridge foundations, riverbanks, and other places where lynching victims typically turned up. On Monday, with Till still missing, Smith arrested Milam and Bryant on kidnapping charges. Two days later, Till's body

was discovered by a teenager fishing at Pecan Point in Tallahatchie County. The bloated corpse was so badly deformed and decomposed that Wright identified his grandnephew only by the signet ring on his finger. It had belonged to Till's late father, Louis, and bore the initials L.T. The next day, the charges against Milam and Bryant were changed to murder.

THE PUBLIC REACTION

At first, it seemed as though justice might be done. Governor White ordered District Attorney Gerald Chatham to "fully prosecute" Milam and Bryant, and he appointed a capable special prosecutor, former FBI agent Robert B. Smith, to assist Chatham, who was slowed by high blood pressure. Meanwhile, the defendants were having difficulty finding lawyers to represent them, and newspaper editorials were trumpeting public outrage at the brutality of the crime.

As national attention grew, however, so did the inflammatory nature of the attacks being leveled at Mississippi and its racial status quo. Six months earlier, Roy Wilkins had taken over the NAACP following the death of Walter White, and in a statement quoted in newspapers throughout the nation on September 1, Wilkins said, "It would appear from this lynching that the state of Mississippi has decided to maintain white supremacy by murdering children. The killers of the boy felt free to lynch him because there is in the entire state no restraining influence of decency, not in the state capital, among the daily newspapers, the clergy nor any segment of the so-called better citizens."

The Body

Tallahatchie County sheriff H. C. Strider wanted to bury Till's body as quickly as possible in Mississippi, but Emmett's mother insisted that his corpse be returned to Chicago. Strider reluctantly agreed but had the mortician sign an order that the casket not be opened.

When the remains arrived in Chicago, Mamie Till Bradley disregarded the order and had the casket opened so that she could be sure that her son was dead and not hiding out in Mississippi. Horrified by what she saw, she ordered an open-casket funeral so that, in her famous words, "everybody can see what they did to my boy."

Over the next three days, between fifty and one hundred thousand people filed past Till's body, many fainting or leaving the funeral chapel in tears. Then, on September 15, the black weekly *Jet* published photographs of Till's mutilated corpse so that all black America could see it.

Mamie Till Bradley faints at the sight of her son's casket, which arrived from Mississippi at the Illinois Central Terminal in Chicago on September 2.

Condemnations such as this quickly caused proud Mississippians to close ranks. As early as September 2, the *Jackson Daily News* editorialized that "the NAACP is trying its best to inflame the nation against the South in general and Mississippi in particular." Four days later, the editor of the *Greenwood Morning Star* wrote, "Justice in the Till case appeared certain of being carried out by the court had the outsiders not interfered. Now there are rumors that the whole thing was a plant by the NAACP and sympathy is swinging to the side of the accused." Suddenly, five prominent Delta defense lawyers agreed to take the case pro bono, and a defense fund of ten thousand dollars was raised to meet expenses.

Because Till's body had been found in Tallahatchie County, the case was transferred there, and the trial held in Sumner, the county seat. Although the population of Tallahatchie County was two-thirds black, there were no black voters because Sheriff H. C. Strider refused to accept poll-tax payments from black residents.

On September 3, Sheriff Strider told reporters that he didn't think the corpse found in the river was Till's. "The body we took from the river looked more like that of a grown man instead of a young boy," Strider said. "It was also more decomposed than it should have been after that short stay in the water." According to the sheriff, Till was probably still alive and hiding out.

THE TRIAL BEGINS

By the time the trial began on Monday, September 19, Sumner was overrun with more than a hundred reporters, many from the national press, including camera crews from all the national television networks. Twenty-one-year-old David Halberstam, just out of Harvard and covering the trial for a small Mississippi daily, later called it "the first great media event of the civil rights movement."

District Attorney Gerald Chatham pauses to think during the Till murder trial. The cotton-gin fan in front of Chatham's table was used to weigh down Till's body in the Tallahatchie River.

Inside the segregated courtroom, it seemed as though the circus had come to town. The defendants' wives and children were allowed to sit with them, and the Milam and Bryant youngsters, none older than four, put on a show, noisily playing cowboy and peekaboo throughout the lengthy voir dire. Meanwhile, Strider's armed deputies patrolled the courthouse, patting down everyone who entered and keeping blacks and whites as separate as possible. "I have received over 150 threatening letters, and I don't intend to be shot," the sheriff explained to the press. "If there is any shooting, we would rather be doing it."

The jury pool consisted of 120 people, all white and all male. District Attorney Chatham did his best to achieve impartiality, but the task was impossible. All he could reasonably do was challenge those members of the jury pool who were either related to the defendants, had

This **1956 membership flyer** used the Till murder to promote the NAACP. Overall, as a result of Till's death, contributions to the NAACP reached record levels that year.

contributed to their defense fund, or would admit to having already made up their minds. Even so, enough potential jurors failed to meet this standard that the selection process went on until Tuesday morning, when Chatham asked for a recess because he had just learned of several possible new witnesses.

The new witnesses were a surprise to Chatham because Sheriff Strider had never investigated the crime, other than to claim he was pursuing evidence that "the killing might have been planned and plotted by the NAACP." The new witnesses were instead uncovered by black reporters working closely with leaders of the state NAACP, including Medgar Evers and Amzie Moore.

According to Evers's wife, Myrlie, "He and Amzie Moore and a few others dressed as sharecroppers and went to the plantations to ask people about the murderers." Evers and Moore

turned up several witnesses, but two of the most important disappeared and couldn't be found before the trial resumed on Wednesday. (Some accounts suggest that these men were held in jails outside the county by sympathetic policemen who didn't want them to testify.)

THE SURPRISE WITNESSES

It was generally understood in Mississippi that testifying against a white man in court was, for a black man, a crime punishable by death. Therefore, it remained an open question as to whether any blacks would dare testify. This question was answered in the affirmative when the prosecution called its first witness.

It's hard to overstate the bravery displayed by Till's great-uncle. As journalist and historian Juan Williams has observed, "Mose Wright did not go down in the history books as a leader of the civil rights movement. But his individual act of courage, like the acts of so many unknown citizens, was just as important to the movement as the charismatic leadership of people like Martin Luther King Jr."

Just five feet three inches tall, Wright had been cowed by Milam and Bryant on the night of the kidnapping. Compared with the imposing Milam, the diminutive Wright looked like "a black pygmy standing up to a white ox," in the words of *New York Post* columnist Murray Kempton. Yet when the district attorney asked "Uncle Mose" to identify the men who had come to his home and taken Till away, Wright pointed a bony finger at Milam and said, "Thar he." Then he indicated Bryant.

The next day, the prosecution presented "surprise" witness Willie Reed, an eighteen-year-old sharecropper's son who lived near a plantation owned by Leslie Milam, another member of the Milam-Bryant brotherhood.

Roy Bryant and J. W. Milam sit with a defense attorney at the start of their trial. Because of the ninety-five-degree heat in the courtroom, the judge permitted men to take off their jackets.

This photograph taken outside the courtroom during the Till trial shows (from left to right) Walter Reed, Walter's grandson (and surprise witness) Willie Reed, Mamie Till Bradley, Detroit congressman Charles Diggs, Dr. T. R. M. Howard, and Reed neighbor Amanda Bradley.

Contradicting the story that the killers later told Huie, Reed testified that early on Sunday morning, August 28, he had been walking to the local general store when a pickup truck passed him on the road. "I saw four white men in the cab," Reed said, "and three colored men in the back." Shown a picture of Emmett Till, Reed identified the boy as one of the Negroes he had seen in the back of the truck.

Later, Reed continued, he heard cries of "Mama, Lord have mercy, Lord have mercy" coming from inside a shed on the plantation, outside of which the empty pickup truck was parked. At one point, he saw Milam emerge from the shed with a gun. Still later, he saw the truck being backed up to the shed so that a long object wrapped in a tarpaulin could be loaded onto its bed. Finally, Reed saw several black field hands washing out the bed of the truck in the afternoon. The water that was draining onto the ground, Reed testified solemnly, was blood red.

THE CASE FOR THE DEFENSE

The prosecution rested its case just before two o'clock on Thursday afternoon, at which point the defense began its presentation by calling Carolyn Bryant, whom the press had begun calling a "crossroad Marilyn Monroe." Recognizing that her testimony was primarily a play for sympathy, Judge Curtis M. Swango, who ran a fair trial, allowed her to testify but not in the presence of the jury. Neither defendant ever took the stand. Instead, the defense built its case on the contention that the body found in the Tallahatchie River was not that of Emmett Till. To support its claim, the defense called Sheriff Strider.

Although Mamie Till Bradley had already taken the stand to identify positively the body as her son's, Strider claimed that, in his professional opinion, the body had been in the river "about ten days, if not fifteen," in which case it could not possibly

Mose Wright points from the witness stand to identify J. W. Milam as one of the men who kidnapped Emmett Till. After a brief cross-examiniation, Wright walked out of the courthouse and, with the help of Medgar Evers and journalist James Hicks, left Mississippi entirely.

PETITION

TO THE PRESIDENT OF THE UNITED STATES:

We the undersigned, do hereby protest the brutal Lynch-murder of Emmett Till, in Sumner, Miss. on August 29th. This brutal killing of a 14 year old boy, reflects the type of terror used to deny Negro citizens their civil rights.

The Lynch-murder of Rev. C. W. Lee at Belzoni, Miss. on May 7th and of Lamar Smith at Brookhaven, Miss. on August 13th, are evidence that there is an organized movement to keep negro citizens from gaining their long denied right of full citizenship, which includes the right to vote and the right to equal and unsegregated educational facilities.

We the undersigned, therefore, demand that the federal Government take action, both legislative and administrative in order to stop this organized wave of terror against the Negro people.

We further demand, that the Attorney General's office be put into action investigating this conspiracy to deny American citizens their full constitutional Rights.

BRONX COUNTY, NAACP, 370 E. 162nd STREET

Members of the all-white, all-male jury listen to testimony before beginning their brief deliberations in the Emmett Till murder case.

have been Till's. Later, in his summation, defense attorney John C. Whitten suggested that "there are people in the United States who want to destroy the customs of southern people....They would not be above putting a rotting, stinking body into the river in the hope he would be identified as Emmett Till." Louis Till's ring, Whitten implied, was merely an NAACP plant.

Then Whitten segued to the emotional core of his argument. "Your ancestors will turn over in their graves [if Milam and Bryant are convicted]," he challenged the all-white, all-male jury, "and I'm sure that every last Anglo-Saxon one of you has the courage to free these men." The jurors deliberated for just sixty-seven minutes before returning a not-guilty verdict, and they would have taken even less time, said one juror, "if we hadn't stopped to drink pop."

Two months later, when a Leflore County grand jury refused to indict either Milam or Bryant on kidnapping charges, the two men were set free.

While it may have been true (as Hodding Carter's *Delta Democrat-Times* maintained) that the prosecution's case was weak and a guilty verdict would likely have been overturned on appeal, legal analyses tend to obscure the unique impact that the death of Emmett Till had on the modern

> "Before Emmett Till's murder, I had known the fear of hunger, hell, and the Devil. But now there was a new fear known to me—the fear of being killed just because I was black. This was the worst of my fears."
>
> ANNE MOODY IN HER MEMOIR *COMING OF AGE IN MISSISSIPPI*

civil rights movement. From a historical point of view, it didn't really matter what Bryant and Milam did, whether they intended to kill Till or not, whether he begged for mercy or not, whether he was castrated or not. What persisted after September 1955 was the emotional impact that Till's death had on a generation of young African Americans. It changed many of their lives.

This 1955 NAACP petition, addressed to President Eisenhower, protested the lynchings of Emmett Till, George W. Lee, and Lamar Smith.

John Lewis, for example, was just seventeen months older than Till. Five years after Till's death, as a college student in Nashville, Lewis became involved with the sit-in movement and emerged as a leader of the Student Nonviolent Coordinating Committee (SNCC). According to Lewis, Till's murder "galvanized the country. A lot of us young black students in the South later on, we weren't sitting in just for ourselves—we were sitting in for Emmett Till. We went on Freedom Rides for Emmett Till." They never forgot Emmett Till.

Although it temporarily assuaged southerners, the not-guilty verdict in the Till trial sparked large protest rallies in the North, such as this one held in New York City on October 11, 1955. The rally was organized by the NAACP and a local labor union.

Don't Ride the Bus

1955–1956

A **segregated bus** in Birmingham, Alabama, in 1933. Exceptions to the seating law were made only for Negro nurses caring for white children or infirm white adults.

In recounting the story of the modern civil rights movement, historians have to be careful not to create narratives that move too quickly from one confrontation to another without pausing to examine the specifics of each local situation. What the best civil rights scholars have learned from studying the events in Montgomery, Little Rock, Birmingham, Selma, and elsewhere is that each episode occurred not merely as the result of a national movement but primarily from an accumulation of local concerns.

In supporting local activism, national civil rights organizations certainly insinuated their own goals, such as the passage of public accommodations or voting rights legislation, but these objectives were usually supplementary and secondary to the goals already developed by the local community. Even in Montgomery, the Rev. Martin Luther King Jr. came rather late to the action.

During the mid-1950s, about 130,000 people lived in Montgomery, the state capital of Alabama. Some 40 percent of these residents were black, and like other biracial communities in the South, Montgomery was a city on edge. In a master's thesis submitted to the Atlanta University Department of Sociology in August 1958, the Rev. Ralph D. Abernathy described the social changes that had taken place during his seven-year tenure as pastor

of Montgomery's First Baptist Church. "World War II," Abernathy wrote, "served only to speed up the processes, heighten the tension, and sharpen the issues of Negro–white relations. As a result, there was an increase in racial tensions, fears, and aggressions which opened up the basic question of racial segregation and discrimination."

The *Brown* decision, Abernathy continued, "deepened the dissatisfaction of both white and Negro individuals over the state of affairs in their city. Generally, Negroes began to seek a way to implement the decision, and most whites, particularly the political leaders, started to look around for ways and means to circumvent, nullify, or resist the court decrees."

As elsewhere, the white opposition to *Brown* coalesced around the local Citizens' Council,

known in Alabama as the White Citizens' Council. On the other side was the Montgomery NAACP and, more importantly, the Women's Political Council (WPC). Founded in 1946 by a group of Alabama State College professors and black public school teachers, the WPC was the most militant civil rights group in town. Originally organized to press for voting rights, the WPC soon widened its mandate to include, in particular, the maltreatment of blacks on Montgomery's public buses.

In 1953, WPC president Jo Ann Robinson began meeting occasionally with the members of the Montgomery City Commission—Mayor W. A. Gayle, Commissioner of Public Works George L. Cleere, and Commissioner of Public Affairs Dave Birmingham—to lobby them for better treatment of Negro passengers. The mayor listened to the proposals, but the actions he took were marginal at best, never addressing the core grievances.

Chapter Six, Section Ten, of the Montgomery City Code required all bus lines operating in the city to "provide equal but separate accommodations for white people and Negroes." Alabama state law also required the physical separation of black and white passengers. In Montgomery, this was accomplished with a floating color line. The first ten seats in the front of each thirty-six-seat bus were reserved for white people. Informally, the last ten seats in the back of each bus (behind the rear door) were set aside for blacks. The middle sixteen seats were filled as passengers boarded the bus, with blacks seating themselves from the rear and whites from the front.

Small metal placards with arrows were used to indicate the row separating the white section from the black. As the bus filled with passengers, the two races would move closer to one another until separated by a single row. At this point, the bus driver adjusted the placards to define clearly the line between the two sections. If the racial balance of passengers shifted, so could the color line.

didn't stop at each corner as scheduled. They didn't like the way some drivers started the bus before a Negro passenger could get both feet on the ground. Most of all, they didn't like the way many bus drivers talked to them. 'Go on round the back door, Nigger.' 'Give up that seat, boy.' 'Get back, you ugly black apes.' "

THE COLVIN CASE

Jo Ann Robinson was initially patient with the mayor's lip service because, in 1953 and 1954, Montgomery city government seemed to be moving forward. Commissioner of Public Affairs Birmingham, who oversaw the police and fire departments, had been elected in 1953 with strong support from the black community, and a year later he repaid that support by pressuring the police chief into hiring Montgomery's first four black officers. In March 1955, however, he

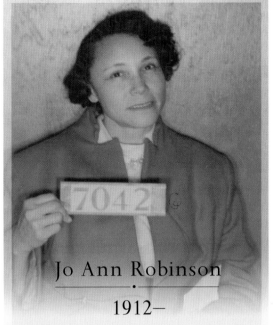

Jo Ann Robinson
1912–

Jo Ann Robinson was born on a farm in rural Georgia, the youngest of twelve children. Her family later moved to Macon, where she attended segregated public schools and became her high school's valedictorian. Later, she earned a bachelor's degree from Georgia State College at Fort Valley and a master's degree in English from Atlanta University. A failed marriage and several teaching positions later, she joined the English department at all-black Alabama State College in Montgomery in the fall of 1949.

That Christmas, her thoughts were elsewhere when she boarded a bus and absentmindedly sat in the fifth row. She was technically sitting in the unreserved middle section of the bus, but because there were still many seats available in the rear black section, the bus driver became angry.

"Suddenly," she recalled, "the driver left his seat and stood over me. His hand was drawn back as if he were going to strike me. 'Get up from there!' he yelled." Afraid that the driver was going to hit her, Robinson jumped out of the seat and ran off the bus in tears. "In all these years," she wrote in her memoirs, "I have never forgotten the shame, the hurt, of that experience."

> ## "Race relations in Montgomery have traditionally been 'good' in the sense that Negroes have seldom challenged their state of subordination."
>
> ALABAMA STATE HISTORY PROFESSOR L. D. REDDICK IN A SPRING 1956 *DISSENT* ARTICLE

At least that was how the system was supposed to work. In practice, few drivers bothered to get up from their seats to adjust the "race signs." Instead, they typically looked back, saw white passengers standing, and told blacks in the middle section to move back—sometimes courteously, sometimes not so courteously. On some buses at some times, whites did stand, but Negro seating was never secure.

In Montgomery, blacks made up about 75 percent of the riding public, and nearly all had stories about gratuitous humiliations to which they had been subjected. "They didn't like having to go to the front door of the bus to deposit their dimes, then going out again to the rear door to re-enter," Martin Luther King Jr. told the *Pittsburgh Courier* in March 1956. "They didn't like how the bus often took off while they were going to the back door, taking their dimes away with them. They didn't like the fact that in predominantly Negro areas buses just

A cap worn by a Montgomery City Lines bus driver during the boycott.

was defeated for reelection by Clyde C. Sellers, who ran the most racist campaign in Montgomery since the 1920s. Birmingham's ouster persuaded most of Montgomery's Negro leaders that working within the electoral system might not, after all, get their needs addressed.

Meanwhile, the bus issue escalated. On the afternoon of March 2, 1955, fifteen-year-old Claudette Colvin was arrested for refusing to give up her seat on a bus to a white person. Such arrests happened from time to time in Montgomery, resulting in small fines, but Colvin was the first Negro ever to plead not guilty.

Colvin had been sitting well back in a full bus next to an older woman named Mrs. Hamilton when driver Robert W. Cleere ordered them to stand because more white passengers were boarding. They both refused, and Cleere went for the police. Meanwhile, a black man got up and

left the bus, offering his seat to Mrs. Hamilton. She took it, leaving Colvin to face the arriving police by herself. Losing her nerve, she became hysterical and resisted arrest, kicking and scratching the policemen as they carried her off the bus and took her to jail.

Colvin was defended by local NAACP counsel Fred D. Gray, one of only two Negro lawyers practicing in Montgomery. Because of her age, she was brought to trial in juvenile court before

Rosa Parks (right) in August 1955 at the Highlander Folk School in Monteagle, Tennessee. Highlander was founded in 1932 by Myles Horton to promote his belief that ordinary people, if given training and guidance, could remake society. By the 1950s, Highlander had become a key training ground for civil rights activists.

Judge Wiley C. Hill Jr. The charges against her were violating the city's bus segregation law and resisting arrest. Gray offered two defenses. The first, that the segregation law was unconstitutional, Judge Hill quickly dismissed. But the second—that it was the bus driver, not Colvin, who had broken the segregation law— was much more nettlesome.

When Montgomery first adopted a segregated seating ordinance in 1900, the new law had produced a boycott of the trolley lines, which lasted the entire summer and ended only when the city agreed to revise the new ordinance so that passengers would never have to give up a seat unless another seat was available. Because this proviso was still part of the city code, Gray argued, Colvin had acted within her rights, and the bus driver had been the one at fault for requiring her to stand.

Circuit Solicitor William F. Thetford responded by amending the complaint to allege a violation of the state rather than city segregation law. In 1945, the state legislature had passed its own law requiring racially segregated seating. Unlike the Montgomery ordinance, the state statute gave bus drivers absolute power to seat passengers as they saw fit.

In general, state laws supersede local ones, but in Colvin's case the applicability of the state law was unclear because no one knew whether the Alabama Public Service Commission, charged with enforcing the bus law, had jurisdiction over municipal lines. (In fact, in federal litigation a year later, the state conceded it did not.) Nevertheless, Judge Hill overruled Gray's objection and found Colvin guilty of violating the state segregation law and committing assault and battery on the arresting officers. She was declared a juvenile delinquent and placed on probation.

Hoping that Colvin's case could serve as the basis for a constitutional challenge to the bus segregation law, Gray appealed her conviction to the Montgomery Circuit Court. However, Thetford outfoxed Gray by dismissing the segregation count and pressing only the assault and battery conviction, which was upheld.

With the Colvin case still in the headlines, Negro leaders met with city officials and the bus company to assert their complaints. They asked for first-come, first-served seating, with no reserved section for whites so that they wouldn't have to stand over empty white seats at rush hour. "First-come, first-served" already governed bus seating in most large southern cities and had been successfully adopted in Mobile, where the same state laws obtained and the bus franchise was held by the same Chicago company that operated the Montgomery City Lines.

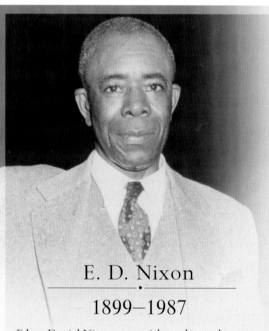

E. D. Nixon
1899–1987

Edgar Daniel Nixon was neither educated nor cultivated, but he was friendly, charismatic, and fearless. In 1924, after working for a year as a railroad baggage handler, he got a job as a Pullman porter. Three years later, he joined the relatively new Brotherhood of Sleeping Car Porters and became a lifelong disciple of BSCP president A. Philip Randolph.

"When I heard Randolph speak, it was like a light," Nixon remembered. "Before that time, I figure that a Negro would be kicked around and accept whatever the white man did. I never knew the Negro had a right to enjoy freedom like everyone else." Nixon later followed Randolph into political activity, organizing local voter registration drives and taking part in the 1941 March on Washington Movement.

According to Jo Ann Robinson, "Anytime a black citizen was arrested in the city and knew not whom to call for help in getting free, Mr. Nixon was called, often during the night, and he would go to city jail and get the prisoner out on bail." He was famous in Montgomery as the one Negro who knew every white policeman, judge, and city official. If a black person had a grievance, he would often ask Nixon for help. "Nixon seldom got anything close to justice," Taylor Branch writes, "but he usually got something."

Even so, many of Montgomery's more fashionable, college-educated blacks looked down on Nixon because of his proletarian manner and poor grammar. During the early 1950s, they gradually eased him out of his NAACP leadership role and otherwise marginalized his involvement.

Nevertheless, bus company lawyer Jack Crenshaw remained intransigent. Supported by City Attorney Walter Knabe, he insisted that city and state segregation laws required reserved seating for whites and dismissed out of hand Gray's legal analysis. Instead, he advised bus company manager James H. Bagley that the laws left no room for compromise. So there was none.

In late October, another young woman, Mary Louise Smith, was arrested for refusing to give up her seat on a bus. Once again, Montgomery's black leadership had to decide what to do, and once again, the most influential voice belonged to E. D. Nixon, a past president of both the local and state NAACP. Earlier, Nixon had vetoed plans to organize a highly public protest around Colvin when he learned that the high school student was pregnant. Now, he rejected Smith as similarly unsuitable because her father was an alcoholic and she lived in a see-through clapboard shack out in the countryside. In the end, Smith pled guilty and paid a five-dollar fine, while Nixon kept looking for the right defendant.

Rosa Parks
1913—

When Rosa McCauley was eleven years old, her parents sent her to live with an aunt in Montgomery. Until then, she had attended the one-room schoolhouse in Pine Level, Alabama, where her mother taught. Now, young Rosa needed more advanced instruction than she could get at home. There wasn't yet any public high school for blacks in Montgomery, but Alabama State College did operate a laboratory school that Rosa was able to attend. The tuition was more than her parents could realistically afford, but they worked hard and made sacrifices so that their daughter could get an education.

Still, economic opportunities for blacks in Montgomery were very limited—even for those few who had high school diplomas. Bitterly, Rosa (married in 1932 to Raymond Parks) learned that she could earn more money working with her hands as a seamstress than with her brain. This realization prompted her to join the NAACP in 1943, and she remained prominent in that organization even after Montgomery's professional class took it over during the early 1950s.

Unlike E. D. Nixon, Rosa Parks wrote and spoke impeccable English, and she always exhibited a quiet dignity. Her trade may have been working class, but her demeanor was entirely bourgeois. As a result, she was admired not only by Montgomery's teachers and ministers but also by its maids and laborers.

THE PARKS ARREST

Early on the evening of Thursday, December 1, 1955, Rosa Parks boarded a Cleveland Avenue bus at a stop not far from the Montgomery Fair department store, where she worked as a seamstress in the men's shop. She noticed a number of empty seats in the white section of the bus but only one seat in the back that she could take, located just behind the race sign. Several black passengers were already standing.

The bus next stopped at Court Square and then in front of the Empire Theatre. Once all those waiting had boarded, bus driver James F. Blake noticed that a white man was standing, so he told the first row of blacks to stand up and move farther back, even though there were no more seats available and the aisle was already crowded with standing passengers.

"At his first request," Parks recalled, "didn't any of us move. Then he spoke again and said, 'You'd better make it light on yourselves and let me have those seats.' At this point, of course, the passenger who would have taken the seat hadn't said anything. In fact, he never did speak to my knowledge. When the three people, the man who

The Cleveland Avenue bus on which Rosa Parks refused to give up her seat has been restored and put on display at the Henry Ford Museum.

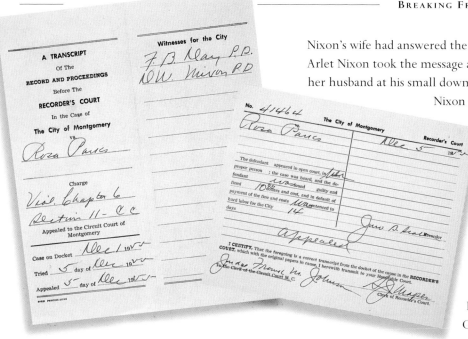

The front and back of Rosa Parks's December 1955 arrest record.

Nixon's wife had answered the telephone. Arlet Nixon took the message and relayed it to her husband at his small downtown office. Nixon telephoned the city jail to learn the charges on which Parks was being held, but the desk officer told him rudely that the charges were none of his business. Knowing that Fred Gray was out of town, Nixon then called Clifford Durr—a white lawyer and one of Montgomery's few racial liberals, who also happened to be a friend of Mrs. Parks's. Durr

Even before they reached the jail, Clifford Durr and E. D. Nixon were already discussing the practical aspects of using the arrest as a test case and rallying point for a communitywide boycott of the bus system. At Parks's home, they listened to her story while continuing to discuss the larger possibilities. Overall, Durr was encouraging, pointing out that the bus driver's actions had violated the city code (because there was no other seat for Parks to occupy) and also noting that there were no extraneous charges, such as the count of assault and battery that had made Colvin's case useless. Furthermore, Durr offered, Parks's dignified manner would make an excellent impression on white judges.

Upon hearing this, Nixon could no longer restrain his growing enthusiasm. *"This is the case,"* he said. "We can boycott the bus lines with this and at the same time go to the Supreme Court." Parks, however, was not yet persuaded that her simple act of disobedience could support such lofty endeavors. At the same time, her husband, Raymond, was scared. He told her that, if she pled guilty, the arrest might be forgiven as an isolated incident. But if she persisted, she would become a target, as Emmett Till had. "The white folks will kill you, Rosa," he begged. But Parks listened more receptively to Nixon and in the end told him, "If you think it is all right, I'll go along with you."

> ## "This movement was made up of just ordinary black people, some of whom made as little as five dollars a week, but they would give one dollar of that to help support the boycott."
>
> MONTGOMERY ADVERTISER CITY EDITOR JOE AZBELL

was in the seat with me and the two women [in the seat across the aisle], stood up and moved into the aisle, I remained where I was. When the driver saw that I was still sitting there, he asked if I was going to stand up. I told him, no, I wasn't. He said, 'Well, if you don't stand up, I'm going to have you arrested.' I told him to go on and have me arrested."

Unlike Claudette Colvin and Mary Louise Smith, the forty-two-year-old Parks was a mature woman and one of the more respected African Americans in Montgomery, having served as secretary of the local NAACP since 1943 and been active as a mentor to its Youth Council. In fact, Parks was such a impeccable choice for the focus of a public protest that some whites later accused her of planning her arrest. Parks, however, has always maintained that her decision to remain seated was spontaneous. She was simply tired, she has said, both physically from a long day on her feet and emotionally from years of humiliation on the buses.

After Parks was processed at the city jail, she was allowed to make a telephone call to her family, but word of her arrest had already spread. Another passenger on the bus had called a friend of Parks's to report what she had seen, and that friend had called the home of E. D. Nixon, where

had first met Parks through his wife, Virginia, who had asked Nixon to recommend a good seamstress to help with her daughters' clothes. Nixon recommended Parks, who became a regular presence in the Durr household.

Now Clifford Durr called the jail, got the information that was needed, and telephoned Nixon back. The two of them decided to drive to the jail so that Nixon could post the hundred-dollar bond. When Nixon pulled up in front of Durr's house, both Clifford and Virginia Durr got into his car. They all drove down to the jail, bailed Parks out, and took her home.

Clifford and Virginia Durr with three of their daughters in a family photograph.

THE BOYCOTT BEGINS

About this time, late on Thursday night, Fred Gray returned to Montgomery, learned of Parks's arrest, and quickly called Jo Ann Robinson, who had left him message. When Robinson got off the telephone with Gray, she called Nixon, who had just returned from Parks's house. They discussed the case and agreed that it was exactly what they needed. For several years, Robinson had been agitating for a boycott; now, she and Nixon made specific plans. Nixon would arrange for the Negro leadership to meet the next evening while Robinson produced handbills calling for a one-day boycott on Monday, December 5, the day of Parks's trial.

At five o'clock Friday morning, Nixon began making telephone calls. Knowing that even with the help of the WPC, the task of reaching the masses was more than his own circle of activists could handle, he started dialing ministers. Nixon began with twenty-nine-year-old Ralph Abernathy, who was secretary of the Baptist Ministers' Alliance and whose First Baptist Church was the most well attended in Montgomery. Abernathy said that he would support the effort and agreed to sponsor a meeting in the name of the Baptist Ministers' Alliance. He did, however, ask Nixon to call the Rev. H. H. Hubbard, president of the alliance, to obtain his blessing, which Nixon did.

Nixon's third call was to another young Baptist minister, twenty-six-year-old Martin Luther King Jr. of the Dexter Avenue Baptist Church. Nixon related the circumstances of Parks's arrest and asked King to support the boycott. King hesitated. Only two weeks earlier, his wife, Coretta, had given birth to their first child, and the responsibilities of running his church were also weighing heavily on him. He wasn't sure he could handle much more, so he put Nixon off. "Brother Nixon," he said, "let me think about it awhile, and call me back." But he did agree to make his downtown church available for the evening meeting, and soon his phone rang again. This time, it was Abernathy, who quickly pressured King into participating.

Meanwhile, Jo Ann Robinson didn't sleep that night. After getting off the phone with Nixon after midnight, she called her friend John Cannon, chairman of the Alabama State business

department, who had a key to the college's duplicating room. She also called two of her students for help. They met at the college in the middle of the night and by 4 A.M. had mimeographed, cut, and bundled some thirty-five thousand handbills. Each read:

Another Negro woman has been arrested and thrown into jail because she refused to get up out of her seat on the bus for a white person to sit down.

It is the second time since the Claudette Colbert [sic] case that a Negro woman has been arrested for the same thing. This has to be stopped.

Negroes have rights, too, for if Negroes did not ride the buses, they could not operate. Three-fourths of the riders are Negroes, yet we are arrested, or have to stand over empty seats. If we do not do something to stop these arrests, they will continue. The next time it may be you, or your daughter, or mother.

This woman's case will come up Monday. We are, therefore, asking every Negro to stay off the buses on Monday in protest of the arrest and trial. Don't ride the buses to work, to town, to school, or anywhere on Monday.

The Dexter Avenue Baptist Church at which King preached.

After teaching an 8 A.M. class, Robinson drove the bundles of handbills to various black public schools, where she passed them on to WPC members for door-to-door distribution. Even so, most blacks didn't learn about the boycott until it began receiving white media attention on Sunday. That morning, the *Montgomery Advertiser* ran a front-page story on the handbills, and in the evening Commissioner Sellers went on television to assure black riders that the Montgomery police would protect them from boycott-enforcing "Negro goon squads."

A copy of the printed handbill, based on Jo Ann Robinson's mimeographed flyer, that King and Abernathy produced for the new Montgomery Improvement Association.

Don't ride the bus to work, to town, to school, or any place Monday, December 5.

Another Negro Woman has been arrested and put in jail because she refused to give up her bus seat.

Don't ride the buses to work to town, to school, or any where on Monday. If you work, take a cab, or share a ride, or walk.

Come to a mass meeting, Monday at 7:00 P. M. at the Holt Street Baptist Church for further instruction.

By the time the Negro leadership gathered on Friday evening, the boycott was a fait accompli. All that remained to be worked out were the details. Even so, the meeting didn't go well. Nixon would have presided, but he had left that afternoon on his regular Pullman run to Chicago. Therefore, leadership fell by default to the Rev. L. Roy Bennett, president of the Interdenominational Ministerial Alliance, to which all the Negro ministers in Montgomery belonged. Unfortunately, Bennett's manner offended many. About seventy-five people showed up for the meeting, but half left early, many in disgust at Bennett's arbitrariness and dictatorial style.

The first edition of King's first book, published in 1958.

In the end, a few things were decided: The ministers would all preach in support of the boycott during their Sunday sermons. King and Abernathy would produce and distribute more handbills promoting not only the boycott but also a mass meeting to be held at the Holt Street Baptist Church on Monday evening. Finally, the group delegated the Rev. W. J. Powell to approach Montgomery's eighteen black taxi companies and ask them to lower their fares in support of the boycott, which they did. On Monday, more than two hundred cabs offered a ten-cent fare, the same fare that the bus company charged.

"My wife and I awoke earlier than usual on Monday morning," King wrote in *Stride Toward Freedom*, his 1958 account of the bus boycott. "We were up and fully dressed by five-thirty. The day for the protest had arrived, and we were determined to see the first act of this unfolding drama.…Fortunately, a bus stop was just five feet from our house. This meant that we could observe the opening stages from our front window." The first bus was scheduled to pass by about six o'clock.

"I was in the kitchen, drinking my coffee," King continued, "when I heard Coretta cry, 'Martin, Martin, come quickly!' I put down my cup and ran toward the living room. As I approached the front window Coretta pointed joyfully to a slowly moving bus: 'Darling, it's empty!' I could hardly believe what I saw. I knew that the South Jackson line, which ran past our house, carried more Negro passengers than any other line in Montgomery, and that this first bus was usually filled with domestic workers going to their jobs. Would all of the other buses follow the pattern that had been set by the first?"

Bus company receipts later showed that the Monday boycott was about 90 percent effective, with most of the black ridership limited to the elderly. The Negro community was overjoyed with its success, and hundreds of people gathered at bus stops to cheer as the empty buses passed. Hundreds more assembled at the courthouse to show their support for Parks, whose trial began at 9 A.M. before city court judge John B. Scott.

Like Colvin, Parks was initially charged with violating the *city* segregation law; however, because her bus had been full, the prosecution faced the same problem that it had in the Colvin case: The bus driver, not Parks, had violated the city law. So City Prosecutor D. Eugene Loe began the trial by dropping the original charge and substituting one based on the *state* segregation law. Again, Fred Gray argued that the state law didn't apply, but Judge Scott wasn't any more receptive than Judge Hill had been.

Parks smiles for a photographer at the Montgomery courthouse after her December 5 conviction. Standing beside her as a notice of appeal is filed on her behalf are E. D. Nixon (center) and attorney Fred Gray (right).

He quickly found Parks guilty and fined her ten dollars plus four dollars in court costs. Parks announced her intention to appeal.

MIA

Among the spectators at the courthouse were Nixon, Abernathy, and the Rev. Edgar N. French of the Hilliard Chapel AME Zion Church. After the trial, Nixon invited the two young men back to Fred Gray's office to talk about the next leadership meeting, scheduled for three o'clock that afternoon at Bennett's Mt. Zion AME Church. After some discussion, the three of them decided that a new permanent organization should be formed to extend the boycott and press for three concessions: first-come, first-served seating with no reserved section for whites; the disciplining of white bus drivers who failed to show proper courtesy; and the hiring of Negro bus drivers for predominantly Negro routes.

When Bennett convened the leadership meeting that afternoon, he continued to dominate its proceedings. "We are not going to have any talking," he told the gathering. "I am not going to let anybody talk. We came here to work and to outline our program." Abernathy tried to get the floor, but Bennett cut him off: "Well, Ab, although you're my good friend, I'm not going to even let you talk, so sit down."

Martin Luther King Jr.
1929–1968

Until 1934, the pastor of Atlanta's Ebenezer Baptist Church was known formally as the Rev. Michael Luther King Sr. That year, however, the Reverend King changed his first name (and that of his five-year-old son) to Martin. Even so, in later years at Morehouse College, Crozer Theological Seminary, and Boston University, the junior King was known to his closest friends as Mike.

It was during those university years that the younger King first became acquainted with the strategy of "passive resistance" that later guided the bus boycott. As an indifferent student at Morehouse between 1944 and 1948, King had followed the independence struggle in India, where Mohandas K. Gandhi used boycotts and other nonviolent means to oppose British rule. King also became familiar with Henry David Thoreau's seminal essay "On Civil Disobedience," which strongly influenced Gandhi as a young man and later informed his protest campaign.

However, it wasn't until King entered Crozer, a prominent biracial seminary in Pennsylvania, that he began to explore more deeply the intellectual roots of social activism. Among the theologians King studied at Crozer was Walter

The King family during the 1930s with young Martin Jr. seated at the right.

Martin Luther King Jr. at a March 10, 1960, press conference

Rauschenbusch, author of *Christianity and the Social Crisis* (1907), which had inspired the Social Gospel movement in American Protestantism. In his work, Rauschenbusch compared the Second Coming to Marx's postrevolutionary vision of a classless society and challenged ministers of the Gospel to make public morality—specifically, the reform of corrupt industrial society—their chief goal.

An even more important influence on King was Reinhold Niebuhr, an internationally known pacifist who began teaching at the Union Theological Seminary in New York City in 1928 after spending thirteen years in Detroit ministering to white and Negro autoworkers alike. Niebuhr's *Moral Man and Immoral Society* (1932) attacked the two fundamental premises of the Social Gospel: that the principal cause of injustice was ignorance, and that reason, coupled with goodwill, would eventually cure all social ills. Niebuhr countered that the real cause of injustice was "our predatory self-interest," which had never historically yielded to education.

According to Niebuhr, man was by nature sinful, which meant that cruelty and injustice could never be eliminated from the world. However, Niebuhr did draw a distinction between people acting individually and those acting as part of a social group. On an individual basis, he believed, people could be redeemed through love or reason; however, nations, corporations, and other large entities would always behave selfishly and always respond only to power. Niebuhr scorned, for instance, the idea that American blacks could one day obtain equality through moral suasion.

"However large the number of individual white men who…will identify themselves completely with the Negro cause," Niebuhr wrote, "the white race in America will not admit the Negro to equal rights if it is not forced to do so. Upon that point one may speak with a dogmatism which all history justifies."

King studied read Gandhi while a doctoral candidate at BU, but he was never the Gandhian that contemporary journalists made him out to be. Rather, his interest in nonviolence was that of the Christian pacifist, always rooted in the biblical directive to match hate with love. King never bothered to correct the media because, as Taylor Branch has pointed out, "he knew that within the American mass market there was a certain exotic comfort in the idea of a Gandhian Negro."

Then the current president of the local NAACP broke in to warn Bennett not to "go any further" because there were "stool pigeons" in the room, who were there to "get our strategy and take it back to the white man." Heeding this advice, the group chose an eighteen-member executive committee to meet in private. As the members of the committee adjourned to the pastor's study,

Ralph D. Abernathy
1926–1990

Ralph David Abernathy was born on a farm in rural Alabama about halfway between Selma and the Mississippi line. The grandson of a slave, he studied mathematics at Alabama State College, receiving a bachelor's degree in 1950. He went on to study sociology at Atlanta University, receiving his master's degree in 1951. That same year, he became pastor of Montgomery's First Baptist Church.

Initially, Abernathy eschewed nonviolence. After being threatened because of the role he was playing in the boycott, he went downtown to buy a pistol for self-defense, but he found that no white merchant would sell him (or any other Negro) a gun. "They stopped selling us even shells for shotguns to go hunting with," he recalled. "So it was dramatized to me…that counterviolence—that is, fighting back with weapons of physical destruction— was incompatible with Christian doctrine."

During the boycott, Abernathy became (and remained) King's closest confidant. After King returned to Atlanta, Abernathy followed him there in 1961, becoming pastor of the West Hunter Street Baptist Church.

Abernathy chastised Bennett for his stubbornness and again asked for the floor. "After much needling," Abernathy recalled., "he agreed reluctantly and promised that as soon as we got the meeting underway he might recognize me. Then I dropped back and started talking to Reverend King."

Abernathy told King about the proposal for a permanent organization he had worked out with Nixon and French earlier that day. "But who will be the president?" King asked. "Well, I feel that we owe it to Mr. Nixon," Abernathy replied. "Perhaps," King countered, "Mr. Lewis might make the better man."

Like Jo Ann Robinson, Rufus Lewis was another member of King's Dexter Avenue congregation active in political work. A successful businessman with interests in a mortuary and a supper club, among other ventures, he had once been the football coach at Alabama State and now

Rufus Lewis lights a cigarette on the steps of the Montgomery courthouse. His civic activities before becoming chairman of the MIA's Transportation Committee included the founding of a private nightclub that allowed only registered voters to become members.

headed a voting rights group called the Citizen's Steering Committee. Well acquainted with the sometimes schismatic nature of Montgomery Negro politics, he was concerned that factionalism would again take hold. Because he knew that his own nomination could revive old turf disputes, he decided to put forward instead the name of his pastor. As Lewis later explained,

he knew King could do better than Bennett, but "I certainly didn't know that [he] was the type of man of rare courage and rare abilities that he had—nobody knew that." By prearrangement, Lewis's motion was quickly seconded, and when no other candidates were put forward, King was unanimously elected president of the new Montgomery Improvement Association (MIA).

"The action had caught me unawares," King explained in *Stride Toward Freedom*. "It had happened so quickly that I did not even have time to think it through. It is probable that if I had, I would have declined the nomination."

The meeting then moved on to a discussion of the boycott, during which several ministers suggested that the protest be ended while it was still a success. How much longer could it go on, they argued. Certainly not past the end of the workweek, others said, and not even that long if it rained.

After listening to a few minutes of this, Nixon exploded. "What's the matter with you people?" he thundered. "Here you have been living off the sweat of these washerwomen all these years and you have never done anything for them. Now you have a chance to pay them back, and you're

The first issue of the MIA newsletter, published June 7, 1956.

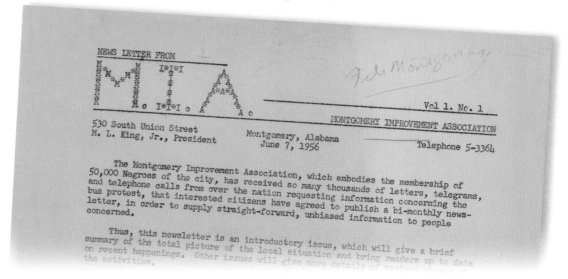

King leads a January 1956 meeting of the MIA board. Seated in the front row (left to right) are Ralph Abernathy, Rosa Parks, and Moses James.

too damn scared to stand on your feet and be counted! The time has come when you men is going to have to learn to be grown men or scared boys."

Within the African-American community, ministers had long been important civic leaders and spokesmen, but they also tended to be rather conservative. As a result, generations of black activists had excoriated them for their political recalcitrance, yet this criticism wasn't entirely fair. As Swedish economist Gunnar Myrdal pointed out in *An American Dilemma,* his landmark 1944 study of U.S. race relations, "If the preachers have been timid and pussyfooting, it is because Negroes in general have condoned such a policy and would have feared more radical leaders."

Since the end of World War II, however, attitudes within the black community had changed significantly. Appropriately chastened,

the ministers agreed to postpone any decision regarding the boycott until the public could be consulted at the mass meeting that night. The group then finalized the program for that meeting and created three committees. Abernathy, as chairman of the new Resolution Committee, would transform the three demands he had formulated with Nixon and French into a formal statement of resolutions upon which the mass meeting could vote. Nixon was placed in charge

"Here you have been living off the sweat of these washerwomen all these years and you have never done anything for them.... The time has come when you men is going to have to learn to be grown men or scared boys."

E. D. NIXON TO THE BLACK MINISTERS OF MONTGOMERY

of the Finance Committee, which would become the MIA's principal fund-raising arm and manage the contributions it took in. Lewis was chosen to head up the Transportation Committee, which would look into alternative ways for Montgomery's Negroes to get to work.

KING AT HOLT STREET

The Holt Street Baptist Church seated about fifteen hundred people. By 7 P.M. Monday, all of those seats were taken, and perhaps another five thousand people stood outside the church in front of a series of loudspeakers that had been hastily set up to accommodate the unexpectedly enormous crowd.

Joe Azbell covered the mass meeting for the *Montgomery Advertiser.* "I was two minutes late, and they were [already] preaching," Azbell remembered, "and that audience was so on fire that the preacher would get up and say, 'Do you want your freedom?' And they'd say, 'Yeah, I want my freedom!'"

The fourth item on the program—after an opening hymn, a prayer, and a scripture reading—was an address by the new MIA president, who may have been young but was already an accomplished public speaker. According to Taylor Branch, "King was controlled. He never shouted.

But he preached like someone who wanted to shout, and this gave him an electrifying hold over the congregation. Though still a boy to many of his older listeners, he had the commanding air of a burning sage."

King's performance that night was mesmerizing. "You know, my friends," he told those gathered at Holt Street, "there comes a time when people

bleakness of nagging despair. There comes a time when people get tired of being pushed out of the glittering sunlight of life's July and left standing amidst the piercing chill of an Alpine November. We are here this evening because we're tired now."

After Mrs. Parks was introduced, Abernathy presented his resolutions to the assembly, which voted by acclamation to accept them

welling-up of grievances in which the specific case of Rosa Parks was all but forgotten." (Thrasher was the white president of the Montgomery chapter of the biracial Alabama Council on Human Relations.) Meanwhile, Montgomery's whites were unable to accept the reality of the situation. According to Thrasher, "Those members of our community who believe that

"When the history books are written in the future, somebody will have to say, 'There lived a race of people…who had the moral courage to stand up for their rights.' And thereby they injected a new meaning into the reins of history."

MARTIN LUTHER KING JR. AT THE HOLT STREET BAPSTIST CHURCH

get tired of being trampled over by the iron feet of oppression. There comes a time, my friends, when people get tired of being flung across the abyss of humiliation, where they experience the

King preaches at the height of a 1956 mass meeting at the Holt Street Baptist Church. On the night of December 5, those unable to fit inside the church peered in through the windows.

and continue the boycott. Then, without the usual exhortation to do so, people began placing coins and bills on the collection table. The meeting closed, according to Azbell's front-page story, with "a wild whoop of delight" and more singing of hymns.

Afterward, blacks lingered inside the church, exchanging stories of their mistreatment on the buses. In fact, all over town, the Rev. Thomas R. Thrasher wrote in March 1956, "there was a general

the whole thing was staged by outside influences generally do not believe that the local press has given an accurate reporting of the facts."

On Thursday, December 8, at a meeting arranged by Thrasher, city and bus company officials met with the MIA leadership to discuss the situation. Bus company lawyer Jack Crenshaw insisted that his client had always responded to complaints of discourtesy and would continue to do so—even though, he gratuitously pointed out, the discourtesy

ORGANIZING

In 1953, blacks in Baton Rouge had successfully petitioned the city council to pass a first-come, first-served seating ordinance with no reserved section for whites. Baton Rouge bus drivers, however, continued to save seats for whites, and when black riders staged a one-day bus boycott, the state attorney general declared the new ordinance illegal.

Three months later, the Rev. T. J. Jemison led a second boycott that lasted nearly two weeks. It ended with city officials offering a face-saving compromise: first-come, first-served seating with a few token seats reserved for each race. Jemison, a college friend of King's who knew the minister well enough to call him Mike, happily accepted the deal.

Thus, when King needed advice about transportation, he immediately called Jemison, who passed along the details of the car-pool system he had organized. The key, according to Jemison, was to designate two sets of pickup points, one in the black neighborhoods for morning use and another downtown and in the white neighborhoods for people headed home from work.

Soon, unsigned and otherwise unidentified schedules began appearing on telephone poles and in other public places. They listed forty-three

Montgomery mayor W. A. Gayle sits in his office, smiling as he displays a stack of telegrams offering praise for his stance against the bus boycott.

was often provoked by Negro passengers. The other two MIA demands, Crenshaw rejected entirely. He never wavered from his earlier position that first-come, first-served seating was illegal, and he characterized the hiring of Negro bus drivers as "inappropriate."

Mayor Gayle mouthed some niceties, then created a biracial citizens' committee to resolve the dispute. During its first meeting, the committee reached an impasse and soon disbanded. This is how Abernathy later described the city commission's attitude: "Return to the buses, they said, and they would forget it, if we did."

Once the boycott entered its second week, the city commissioners decided to increase the pressure on the MIA. On December 14, they had the city comptroller send letters to all of the Negro cab companies, warning them that the forty-five-cent minimum fare set by city ordinance would be strictly enforced. This move surprised Rufus Lewis's Transportation Committee, which had persuaded the taxi companies to continue the ten-cent boycott fares on weekdays. Now, the MIA had no choice but to set up its own alternative transportation system for those who couldn't make private arrangements. Already, Lewis had been working on plans for a massive car pool.

The Mass Meetings

The mass meetings that took place every Monday and Thursday night during the bus boycott served a number of important functions. One was communication. Because there was no black-owned newspaper or radio station in town, the mass meetings got the latest news out. They also became powerful morale boosters.

"People come hours ahead of time to get a seat," Alabama State history professor L. D. Reddick wrote in March 1956. "A few read papers and books while waiting, but mostly the audiences sing. Hymns such as 'Onward Christian Soldiers,' 'Abide With Me,' and 'Higher Ground' are moving, but the really stirring songs are the lined, camp-meeting tunes, of low pitch and long meter. These seem to recapture the long history of the Negro's suffering and struggle."

Because working-class women tended to dominate the audiences, speakers often featured stories emphasizing the heroism of the walking women. At one meeting, a minister described his efforts to persuade an ancient woman known universally as Mother Pollard to drop out of the boycott because of her advanced age. Mother Pollard refused, explaining, "My feets is tired, but my soul is rested."

The audience at a February 1956 mass meeting held at the First Baptist Church gives an ovation to the MIA leadership.

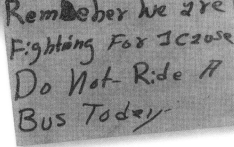

Remeber We are Fighting For JC2use Do Not Ride A Bus Today

This handwritten poster helped keep the boycott about 95 percent effective.

PREVIOUS PAGE: **Blacks in Mongomery** walk to work in February 1956. It helped that Montgomery was a relatively small city, encompassing only about twenty-five square miles.

ABOVE: **White passengers** ride a nearly empty bus in 1956. To offset its losses, the bus company raised its fare from ten to fifteen cents, but this only eroded white ridership.
BELOW: **A carpool driver** holds the door of a sedan open for riders while an empty bus passes behind him, headed in the opposite direction.

"dispatch stations"—most in front of black churches, which kept their doors open and heat on for the comfort of waiting passengers—and forty-two "pickup points" scattered conveniently throughout town.

Eventually, some three hundred people donated use of their cars, enough to carry several thousand people a day. But there had been seventeen thousand Negro bus riders before the boycott, so other arrangements also had to be made. Some boycotters organized share-a-ride systems. Some rode taxis. Many—at least several hundred and perhaps several thousand—were shuttled to and from work by white women unwilling to lose the services of their maids. And many, many walked.

The MIA car pool had to be free of charge; otherwise, it would fall under the city's taxi ordinances and be required to charge the forty-five-cent minimum fare. But the car pool wasn't free to operate. With the cost of gas, repairs, drivers, and other expenses, the MIA was spending more than five thousand dollars a week.

Riders were asked to contribute the money they would have spent on bus fares, but this amounted to only a few hundred dollars a week. For the most part, the MIA had to rely on donations from outside the black community. Some of these came from sources within

Montgomery, such as the Jewish community; the rest came from outside the city and, as word spread, outside the state. During the first month of the boycott, a Birmingham church group sent six hundred dollars, and an anonymous woman calling herself "The Club From Nowhere" began sending a hundred dollars a week.

To meet the growing demand for firsthand accounts of the boycott, the MIA set up a speaker's bureau, which sent MIA officers all over the country to meetings at which additional funds were solicited. For two months, the organization barely managed to get by. Then, a series of miscalculations on the part of the city fathers put an end to the MIA's financial worries.

THE WHITE RESPONSE

Even in late January 1956, as the boycott neared the end of its second month, the whites who ran Montgomery still couldn't accept what was happening. "There is," the Reverend Thrasher wrote, "the recurrent rumor of goon squads operating among the Negroes to force them to obey the boycott. Thus far only one arrest has

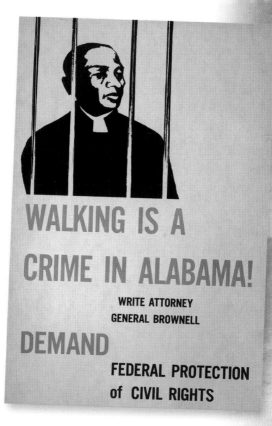

This handbill encouraged northerners to write to Attorney General Herbert Brownell in support of the bus boycott. Although the Eisenhower administration kept its distance, Brownell was personally sympathetic to the civil rights cause.

A black woman in Montgomery returns from a shopping excursion with a box of turnip greens on her head.

In the spring of 1956, the MIA purchased about twenty station wagons, which greatly increased the efficiency of its car pool.

been made on this count—a Negro youth picked up for preventing a Negro woman from boarding a bus. She testified in court that he was helping her across the street and the charge was dropped. If there has been widespread intimidation among Negroes, the police have been unable to get evidence of it."

If only the "radical" leadership of the MIA could be bypassed, it was thought, more "reasonable" ministers would surely accept a compromise. Pursuing this logic, the city commissioners invited three Negro ministers not connected with the MIA to a meeting ostensibly about group insurance. What happened at that

unenforceable promise that bus drivers would be nicer.

The announcement was a hoax, calculated to isolate the MIA "agitators" from the rank and file of Negroes. The hope was that working-class blacks would believe the story and return immediately to the buses. Once they did, it was believed, the spell would be broken, and the MIA would vanish.

Carl T. Rowan of the *Minneapolis Tribune* was working late that Saturday night when the settlement news moved over the Associated Press wire. Having only recently returned from covering the boycott in Montgomery, he was surprised to learn that the MIA had settled for so little, so he telephoned King for a comment.

Rowan's call was the first King had heard of any settlement, and while King made his own calls, Rowan telephoned one of Montgomery's city commissioners. This source confirmed the story but refused to reveal the names of the ministers involved, giving only their denomination. Rowan then passed this information on to King, who used it to deduce the identities of the ministers. None was an influential member of the Montgomery clergy.

Letting people know that the story was a hoax would be difficult late on a Saturday night, but

Sellers had walked dramatically into a meeting of the White Citizens' Council and paid his $3.50 membership fee, declaring, "I wouldn't trade my southern birthright for one hundred Negro votes." Now, Mayor Gayle and Public Works Commissioner Frank Parks (who had replaced George Cleere) also joined the White Citizens' Council, and the next day, January 25, they announced a new "get-tough" policy. Immediately, police officers began harassing MIA car-pool drivers, handing out tickets as fast as they could write them for minor and imaginary traffic violations. On Thursday, January 26, this campaign peaked when King was arrested for speeding.

When a large and irate crowd gathered in front of the city jail, King was released without bond. But four nights later, while he was preaching at the regular Monday night mass meeting, someone in a passing car threw a dynamite cap onto the porch of his house. King rushed home. The damage was minor, and his wife and infant daughter were unhurt, but they had been deeply shaken. The equally frightened and angry crowd outside King's house had grown to about five hundred people when the minister addressed it. The moment was, according to Abernathy,

> "Its main argument seems to be that if vigilance is relaxed in any measure there will be wholesale intermarriage across racial lines."

meeting on Saturday, January 21, has never been clarified, but afterward the commissioners announced to the press that unspecified "prominent Negro ministers" had agreed to a plan ending the boycott. (The ministers later claimed that they had been tricked.) The terms as reported were: courtesy to all, reserved sections at the front and back of each bus with unreserved seats in the middle, and special all-Negro buses during rush hours. In other words, *status quo ante bellum* with a few special buses and an

the leaders of the MIA believed that they had no choice. So they sent messengers or went themselves to every nightclub, bar, and roadhouse in the black community—places Baptist ministers weren't even supposed to know about—to keep people off the buses. The effort worked, and the next morning, the buses rolled empty as usual.

Angry at having lost so much face, the city commissioners began to increase the pressure on the MIA. Two weeks earlier, Commissioner

The city's get-tough policy included the issuance of tickets for dubious traffic violations, "loud talking," and "congregating in white neighborhoods."

"the most dramatic incident in [the history of] the Montgomery Improvement Association."

King implored his neighbors to remain nonviolent. "We believe in law and order," he said. "Don't get panicky. Don't do anything panicky at all. Don't get your weapons. He who lives by the sword will perish by the sword. Remember that is what God said. We are not advocating violence. We want to love our enemies....I did not start this boycott. I was asked by you to serve as your spokesman. I want it to be known the length and breadth of this land that if I am stopped this movement will not stop. For what we are doing is right. What we are doing is just. And God is with us." The words had their intended effect, and a race riot was averted.

King was right: The boycott had started without him and would have gone on without him, but his leadership was nonetheless irreplaceable. "King has captured the imagination and the devotion of the masses of the Negroes here and has united them and done a wonderful job—no doubt about it," Virginia Durr observed in a February 1957 letter. "They adore him and my wash lady tells me every week about how she hears the angel's wings when he speaks, and God speaks directly through him and how he speaks directly to God. There is a great deal of mysticism in him and the Negroes absolutely believe in his 'vision' and his 'sainthood.'"

The Men of Montgomery

During January 1956, the Men of Montgomery, a newly formed group of influential business owners, began to involve itself in the city's handling of the bus boycott. Because of reduced Negro travel downtown, these men had suffered a disappointing holiday season, and they wanted their customers back as soon as possible.

Most doubted that the city commissioners were competent enough to resolve the dispute on their own, and once the grand jury began its deliberations, the Men of Montgomery became particularly concerned that prosecuting the MIA leaders would generate a great deal of adverse national publicity.

King considered the businessmen honest brokers and was willing to negotiate with them, but Gayle and Sellers remained adamant. They offered only relief from prosecution—and that only if the MIA immediately accepted the city's original settlement terms. King and the others refused. The next day, the grand jury indictments were unsealed.

The view down Dexter Avenue, the second widest thoroughfare in the entire South. In the background, behind Montgomery's bustling downtown, the dome of the state capitol can be seen.

Ralph Abernathy (left) stands with his assistant, the Rev. W. J. Hudson, on the porch of his house, which was damaged by a January 10, 1957, bomb blast. INSET: **A handbill advertising** a 1957 speech by Abernathy in Lynchburg, Virginia.

Without this sort of appeal, the Montgomery bus boycott could not have become the truly *mass* movement it did. "There was no other leader there with the humility, with the education, with the know-how of dealing with people who were angry and poor and hungry," Jo Ann Robinson told David J. Garrow in 1984. Certainly the media, with its insatiable appetite for personalities, singled King out and highlighted his role, but the attention was justified, and King's importance was not lost on the Montgomery city commissioners.

THE MASS INDICTMENTS

Because the ministers who dominated the MIA had been hoping to preserve the city's preboycott social fabric, they stuck to their original three demands, all of which could be accomplished within the existing segregation laws. The demands were so modest, in fact, that the *Montgomery Advertiser* advised the city to accept them, and several national civil rights groups initially withheld their support because they felt that the MIA's goals fell too far short of integration. After the bombing of King's house, however, the pressure on the MIA to escalate became irresistible.

Since the start of the boycott, MIA attorney Fred Gray had been urging the ministers to file a federal lawsuit challenging the constitutionality

of bus segregation. Already, he had drawn up the necessary papers with the help of LDF attorney Robert Carter. As recently as January 23, however, the MIA board had voted again to delay action. Now, that decision was reversed, and on February 1, Gray filed *Browder v. Gayle* in federal district court in Montgomery. (Aurelia Browder and Claudette Colvin were two of the four plaintiffs who sued on the grounds that, at one time or another, they had been forced to comply with unconstitutional city and state segregation laws.) At the time, the local White Citizens' Council had six thousand members. Within a month, its membership doubled.

The whites escalated in other ways as well. On February 13, at the request of Circuit Solicitor Thetford, a grand jury met to consider indictments against the MIA leaders. The charges stemmed from a dubious state law passed in 1921 to control striking coal miners in Birmingham. Gray doubted that its prohibition against boycotts was constitutional, and its antipicketing provisions had already been struck down by the Supreme Court. Nevertheless, on February 21, eighty-nine indictments were unsealed. The story was, as the Men of Montgomery had feared, one of national interest. *Montgomery Advertiser* editor Grover C. Hall Jr. called the indictments "the dumbest act that has ever been done in Montgomery." The white opposition never recovered.

E. D. Nixon didn't wait for the law to come knocking on his door; instead, he turned himself in, which encouraged others to do so. Soon,

A crowd stands outside the Montgomery County courthouse on February 24, 1956, after the arraignment of eighty-nine Negroes charged with leading the bus boycott.

people began telephoning the police to find out whether their names were "on the list." This show of bravado transformed what had been a deeply dreaded experience (being sought by the police) into a humorous spectacle, and a joke went around town that several prominent Negroes were upset because their names had been left off the list.

The mass indictments recharged the boycotters' morale and severely weakened what Taylor Branch has called "the time-honored stigma of jail as a weapon of social control against Negroes."

Abernathy, King, and Bayard Rustin walk away from the Montgomery County courthouse on February 24 after King and Abernathy's arraignment on conspiracy charges.

The Fellowship of Reconciliation

On February 21, the day that the grand jury indictments were unsealed, Bayard Rustin arrived in Montgomery. Rustin was a close associate of both A. Philip Randolph and A. J. Muste, head of the Fellowship of Reconciliation (FOR), an interfaith organization founded in 1915 to promote "active nonviolence."

Rustin had traveled down from New York City to observe the boycott firsthand. Because he was both a former Communist and a homosexual who had served time on morals charges, he tried to keep a low profile, passing himself off to whites as a reporter from the Parisian *Le Figaro*. Meanwhile, he insinuated himself into the MIA and consulted with King.

Within a week, Rustin's cover was blown by national reporters brought to town by the indictments, but before he left, he called FOR executive director John Swomley to describe what he had seen and insist that the FOR send

down a staff person immediately. Rustin's visit thus put the relatively unsophisticated MIA leadership in touch with professional social activists, who could offer tactical advice and help expand the base of the movement beyond the black churches.

The FOR responded by dispatching Glenn Smiley. Two days later, after meeting with King, Smiley wrote this hurried report: "He had Gandhi in mind when this thing started, he says. Is aware of the dangers to him inwardly, wants to do it right, but is too young and some of his close help is violent. King accepts, as an example, a bodyguard, and asked for a permit for them to carry guns. This was denied by the police, but nevertheless, the place is an arsenal. King sees the inconsistency, but not enough. He believes and yet he doesn't believe.... At first, King was asked to merely be the spokesman of the movement, but as sometimes happens, he has really become the real leader and symbol of growing magnitude. If he can *really* be won over to a faith in non-violence there is no end to what he can do."

A. J. Muste (right) leads a 1939 Fellowship of Reconciliation antiwar protest on Fifth Avenue in New York City.

A black woman turns her head in November 1956 to watch two robed Klansmen walk past her in downtown Montgomery. Later that night, the Klan held a cross-burning rally on the outskirts of town.

The nationwide publicity also brought in a flood of donations, which ended the MIA's financial troubles. During the first ten weeks of the boycott, the MIA had collected a total of twenty-five thousand dollars. In early March, however, Nixon traveled to address a United Automobile Workers convention in Detroit, where he was given seven thousand dollars and told to expect another twenty-eight thousand in ninety days. In all, more than two hundred thousand dollars poured into the MIA's treasury after the indictments, creating a substantial surplus.

Back at the Montgomery courthouse, the city prosecutors

decided to hold eighty-eight of the indictments in abeyance and move ahead only against King. They wanted to make an example of him. The trial began on March 19 and lasted four days, at the end of which Judge Eugene Carter found King guilty and sentenced him to pay a five-hundred-dollar fine plus court costs or serve 386 days at hard labor. King appealed the decision and was released on bond.

After that, the lawyers did most of the work. On April 23, the Supreme Court dismissed an appeal of the Fourth Circuit decision in *Flemming v. South Carolina Electric and Gas Company*, which had used the logic of *Brown* to strike down bus segregation in South Carolina. (In South Carolina, utility companies typically owned bus lines as well.)

Even Jack Crenshaw realized what this meant, and he advised the bus company that it could no longer enforce segregated seating. Mayor Gayle, however, demanded that segregation continue, and Commissioner Sellers vowed to have the police arrest any driver who took part in "race mixing."

On June 5, the three-judge panel hearing *Browder v. Gayle* ruled two-to-one in favor of the plaintiffs. Two weeks later, the judges permanently enjoined the city from enforcing bus segregation but suspended this injunction pending a city appeal. On November 13, the Supreme Court voted unanimously (and without oral arguments) to reject the city's appeal and affirm the lower court's ruling. All that remained was the paperwork.

Because the Court allowed the city and state to file petitions for reconsideration (which were denied), and also because of the Thanksgiving

Noble Bradford, an employee in the Dallas Transit Company body shop, removes a separate-seating sign from the rear of a bus after the Texas company announced in April 1956 that it was voluntarily ending passenger segregation on all of its 530 buses.

holiday, the integration order took more than a month to reach the federal district court in Montgomery. The formal writs finally arrived on Thursday, December 20, when they were served on city officials just before noon. The next day, blacks boarded buses all over Montgomery, pointedly taking seats in the front.

Rosa Parks rides in the front of a Montgomery city bus shortly after the Supreme Court decision making bus segregation there illegal.

Showdown at Central High

1956–1958

With hindsight, one can see rather easily that the momentum of history favored the cause of racial equality. During the late 1950s, however, the people who were making that history couldn't see the big picture nearly so well. The *Brown* decision rattled the South, and the strong emotions it generated left many southerners vulnerable to the Citizens' Councils and their exhortations that *Brown* be defied.

Meanwhile, political and governmental leaders across the country faced important choices. Which side of history would they be on? Would they choose moral leadership or political opportunism? Today, their situation seems almost Shakespearean.

On the federal level, Pres. Dwight D. Eisenhower put off making his choice for as long as he could. During his first term in office, he offered little leadership on the civil rights issue and limited his commentary on *Brown* to the ambiguous statement that he would enforce all Supreme Court decisions whether he agreed with them or not.

One can understand why Eisenhower would have wanted to stay out of the politically sensitive desegregation mess. Even so, his unwillingness to act in support of *Brown* is generally considered to be the single greatest failure of his presidency.

Not until the president chose to seek reelection did his administration produce its first significant initiative on civil rights. The bill came about as the result of a meeting held in late 1955 between group of urban Republicans and Attorney General Herbert Brownell. Looking forward to the 1956 election, these men wanted Brownell to develop new legislation that could be used to attract the votes of northern blacks, who were registering in large numbers.

A bill was sent to Congress in April 1956. It consisted of four parts: Title I created a bipartisan U.S. Commission on Civil Rights to study racial discrimination in America and recommend further legislation to Congress. Title II created a new assistant attorney general for civil rights (and thus a new civil rights division) in the Justice Department. Title III empowered the attorney general to intervene in state civil rights cases and petition federal courts for injunctive relief. Title IV strengthened

An Arkansas National Guardsman stands watch at Central High School in Little Rock. His orders were to prevent Negro students from entering.

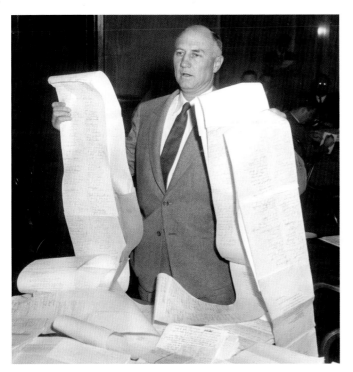

South Carolina senator **Strom Thurmond** holds up petitions supporting his record-setting filibuster of the Civil Rights Act of 1957.

the Justice Department's ability to seek injunctive relief in cases involving voting rights.

Of these provisions, Title III was the most important and the most controversial. It allowed the Justice Department to become involved in cases even when those whose rights had been abused were too frightened or intimidated to file suit themselves.

The House of Representatives passed a scaled-down version of Brownell's program in July 1956, but the bill never emerged from the Senate, where Sen. James O. Eastland of Mississippi killed it in the Judiciary Committee, which he chaired.

Following his landslide reelection in 1956, Eisenhower decided to resubmit the civil rights bill in 1957. Georgia senator Richard Russell, leader of the Senate segregationists, responded immediately by lambasting the bill as a "cunning device" to force the integration of black and white children in southern public schools.

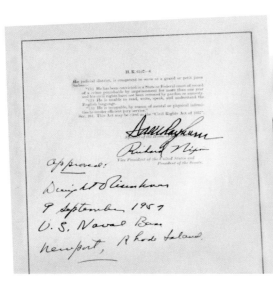

President Eisenhower signs the Civil Rights Act of 1957 into law. The act (inset) was the first piece of civil rights legislation passed by Congress in eighty-two years.

After the legislation passed the House intact on June 18, an undaunted Russell declared that he and his fellow southerners were "prepared to expend the greatest effort ever made in history to prevent passage of this bill in its present form." The shape that Russell's opposition took was an amendment regulating the criminal contempt proceedings that would take place should an injunction granted by a federal judge be violated. Specifically, the amendment granted anyone accused of contempt the right to a jury trial.

In the South, where jurors were culled from voter lists, the fact that few blacks were registered meant that nearly all jurors were white. More to the point, no one could imagine a southern jury in 1957 convicting a white man for violating the civil rights of a Negro. Therefore, Russell's amendment threatened to make the bill's other provisions unenforceable.

After several weeks of wrangling, congressional Republicans came up with a compromise that was only somewhat less offensive. Both sides agreed, and the bill moved swiftly toward passage. There was, however, some final grandstanding. On the evening of August 28, Strom Thurmond, now a senator from South Carolina, took the floor of the Senate and held it for twenty-four hours and twelve minutes, smashing the previous record by nearly two hours. Thurmond finally collapsed at 9:12 P.M. on August 29, at which point the Senate passed the final watered-down bill by a vote of 60–15.

During the initial Senate debate on the Civil Rights Act of 1957, Russell had complained that Title III gave the Justice Department the authority to use "the whole might of the federal government, including the Armed Forces if necessary, to force a co-mingling of white and Negro children" in southern public schools. At a presidential press conference held on July 17, a reporter followed up on Russell's statement by asking the president whether or not he already had the authority to use force to implement *Brown*.

Eisenhower replied that the president did have the necessary authority, but he couldn't "imagine any set of circumstances that would ever induce me to send federal troops…into any area to enforce the orders of a federal court, because I believe the common sense of Americans will never require it."

Two months later, Eisenhower no longer had to imagine those circumstances. He could see them for himself in Little Rock, the capital of Arkansas.

RACE RELATIONS IN ARKANSAS

Then as now, Arkansas was considered a racially moderate state of the Upper South. Like its southern neighbors, it had experienced a substantial population shift during the first half of the twentieth century, as blacks and whites left the countryside for industrial jobs in the state's briskly expanding cities. The rural whites who moved to cities such as Little Rock experienced a great deal of stress adapting to their new lives as urban

blue-collar workers. "For them," historian John A. Kirk has observed, "clinging to white supremacy provided a degree of order and stability in a rapidly changing environment and a safeguard from black competition for jobs."

Rural blacks had much less difficulty adapting to urban life because of the security provided by their new surroundings. In the countryside, where African Americans tended to live apart from one another, white vigilantes could terrorize families at will. The concentration of blacks in urban neighborhoods, however, meant that they could find safety in numbers. There was also much more opportunity for blacks to organize politically without fear of white retaliation.

For a time, desegregation proceeded uneventfully in Arkansas. The University of Arkansas Law School voluntarily enrolled its first Negro students, Wiley A. Branton and Silas Hunt, in February 1948. In Little Rock, the police force and the bus system were both integrated without incident, and there were even a few integrated residential neighborhoods.

Gov. Francis Cherry's statement in the wake of *Brown* that "Arkansas will obey the law" reflected a general acceptance of the decision across most of the state, especially in northern and western Arkansas, where few blacks lived. In Fayetteville, for example, the school board announced on May 21, 1954, that it would allow the district's nine black high school students to attend the local all-white school. At the time, the district's black students were being bused to segregated schools up to 150 miles away at an annual cost of five thousand dollars. "Segregation was a luxury we could no longer afford," the Fayetteville superintendent of schools told reporters.

An undated postcard of Central High. Built in 1927, Central was one of the top public high schools in the country according to National Merit Scholarship results.

In February 1948, Wiley A. Branton (left) and Silas Hunt (seated) became the first black students to enroll at the University of Arkansas Law School.

Such was not the case in the cotton lands of southeast Arkansas, where blacks made up a much larger percentage of the population. This was Delta country, and racial attitudes were similar to those in Mississippi. In Sheridan, the school board acted exactly as the Fayetteville board had, voting unanimously to integrate its twenty-one black students at a cost savings of four thousand dollars a year. The vote produced such a firestorm, however, that the school board was forced to meet again the next day to rescind the decision.

The rest of the state watched Little Rock to see what its board would do—whether it would choose the strategy of "maximum resistance" being encouraged by the Citizens' Councils or that of "minimum compliance," which relied on gradualism, tokenism, and delay to limit *Brown*.

THE BLOSSOM PLAN

While waiting for the *Brown II* implementation decision, Little Rock superintendent Virgil T. Blossom drew up an integration plan that could be used should the Supreme Court indeed force the district to desegregate. Privately, he assured influential whites that his plan would provide "the least amount of integration over the longest period."

Unveiled during the fall of 1954, the Blossom Plan began desegregation with the high schools. At the time, Little Rock had two senior high schools, all-white Central and all-black Dunbar. Two more were under construction: Horace Mann High on the predominantly black east side of town and Hall High in the affluent white western suburbs. Both were expected to open in September 1956, at which time Dunbar would become a junior high school.

Blossom's original plan was to divide the city into "attendance zones," one for each of the three high schools, and integrate all of them in September 1956. The junior high schools would follow in 1957, with the elementary schools being integrated sometime around 1960. L. C. Bates, editor of the *State Press* and husband of Arkansas NAACP president Daisy Bates, immediately criticized the Blossom Plan as "vague, indefinite, slow-moving and indicative of an intent to stall further," but most of the local NAACP leaders, worried about pushing the school board too hard too fast, considered the plan reasonable and wanted to give Blossom a chance to prove his good faith.

Like the Supreme Court, however, the school board gradually drew back from its initial commitment to integration, and by May 24, 1955, when the final details of the Blossom Plan

SENIOR HIGH SCHOOL, 14TH AND PARK AVENUE, LITTLE ROCK, ARK.

Daisy Bates

1914–1999

Daisy Bates and her husband, L. C., began publishing the *Arkansas State Press* in May 1941. From its first issue, the weekly newspaper offered in-depth coverage of problems, such as police brutality and racial injustice, that the white media ignored. "Our decision [to start the *State Press*]," Daisy Bates wrote in her 1962 autobiography, *The Long Shadow of Little Rock*, "was based on the conviction that a newspaper was needed to carry on the fight for Negro rights as nothing else can."

Like her husband, Bates was far more combative than most Arkansas blacks—to the extent that her militancy dismayed even the national NAACP, which quietly opposed her election as president of the Arkansas state NAACP in 1952.

During the school desegregation crisis, the Bateses' new home at 1207 West Twenty-eighth Street

A **January 1958 issue** of the Bateses' newspaper, the *Arkansas State Press*.

became a popular target for enraged segregationists. Passing cars fired gunshots into the house on several occasions, compelling the Bateses to replace their broken front windows with reinforced steel screens. At other times, crosses were burned on the lawn, and the house itself was set on fire twice.

Despite these incidents, the Bateses' appeals for police and federal protection went unanswered. Instead, armed friends and neighbors organized a nightly watch, which reduced the terrorism but had no effect on the economic reprisals (such as loss of ad revenue) that forced the Bateses to close the *State Press* in October 1959.

---

were published, "minimum compliance" had become much more minimal. The revised Blossom Plan pushed desegregation back an entire year (to September 1957) and limited it to the enrollment of a few token Negroes at Central. Junior high school integration, also on a token basis, would not take place until 1960, and no date was set for action on the elementary level. Furthermore, students would be allowed to transfer out of any school in which their race was a minority.

The revised Blossom Plan infuriated the leaders of the black community and prompted the Little Rock NAACP to begin to explore legal options. In December 1955, its executive board voted to file suit against the school board. Local LDF counsel Wiley Branton—working in consultation with Robert Carter of the LDF's national office and Ulysses Simpson Tate, the LDF's southwest regional attorney—filed the necessary papers in federal district court on February 8, 1956.

The changes in the Blossom Plan and the gerrymandering

Superintendent of schools Virgil T. Blossom during a January 1958 press conference. Blossom came to Little Rock in February 1953 from Fayetteville, where the high school integrated in September 1954.

of attendance zones made it obvious that the school board intended to establish Horace Mann and Hall as segregated schools and keep them that way. The NAACP suit, known as *Aaron v. Cooper*, demanded that Little Rock's high schools be integrated when they opened in 1956, as originally planned.

Branton built his case around the school board's delaying tactics. His plan was to ask the court to order implementation of the original Blossom Plan, and he marshaled his evidence accordingly, deposing students who would be adversely affected by the changes in the plan.

Tate flew into Little Rock the evening before the August 1956 trial. Because he was the senior LDF attorney present, he would be making the arguments. But he hadn't been paying attention to the work Branton was doing, and he declined to be briefed that night, saying he was too tired.

The next morning, rather than asking the school board to live up to its promises, Tate argued the same line that the LDF had taken in sixty-four other integration suits against school boards in the Upper South: that all of Little Rock's schools should be immediately and completely integrated. The school board's attorney, Leon Catlett, was ready for this and argued persuasively that the 1955 *Brown II* decision required no such precipitous action. (At the same time, Catlett less astutely referred to Tate's clients as "nigger leaders" and the state NAACP president as simply "Daisy.")

Agreeing with Catlett, Judge John E. Miller upheld the revised Blossom Plan as reasonable under the circumstances. Branton appealed, but the judges of the Eighth Circuit Court of Appeals reaffirmed the lower court's decision.

FAUBUS INTERVENES

For two years after the *Brown* decision, Arkansas governor Orval E. Faubus had been content, like President Eisenhower, to let others tackle the desegregation issue. During his first gubernatorial campaign in 1954, Faubus had managed to take both sides, telling whites in southeast Arkansas that he stood with them while hinting to the rest of the state that he approved of gradual integration. Seeking reelection in 1956, however, he was challenged in the Democratic primary (the only election that mattered) by Jim Johnson, leader of the Associated Citizens' Councils of Arkansas, whose single issue was opposition to integration in the schools. Faubus, who continued to vacillate and temporize, won because he was able to tar Johnson as a fanatical "purveyor of hate" while portraying himself as eminently calm and reasonable. Nevertheless, Faubus could tell that the political winds were shifting and that white public opinion was turning much more strongly against integration.

Faubus had two basic options: He could take a principled stand for integration and likely lose his bid for a third term in 1958, or he could join the segregationists and face the legal consequences while winning elections as far into the future as he could see. In August 1957, amid a flurry of lawsuits, he chose the latter course.

Orval E. Faubus

1910–1994

Growing up poor in the Ozark Mountains of northwest Arkansas, Orval Faubus had little contact with blacks during his formative years. His strongest political influence was his father, a true-believing socialist who was arrested for disloyalty during one of the World War I–era Red Scares. After attending leftist Commonwealth College briefly in 1935, Faubus decided to jettison his father's idealism and instead pursue a political career based not on ideals but on votes.

During his twenties, Faubus held occasional public office while working as a schoolteacher, postmaster, and the editor of a small weekly newspaper. He entered the army in 1942, serving as an intelligence officer with George S. Patton's Third Army. After the war, he joined the liberal administration of Arkansas governor Sidney McMath and became its director of highways.

On August 27, a newly formed group called the Mothers League of Central High filed suit in Pulaski County Chancery Court to stop the school's integration. Their case, based on a group of prosegregation laws enacted earlier that year by the Arkansas General Assembly, had little merit. But the league did have a star witness: Governor Faubus. On the stand, Faubus testified that there had been a recent surge in weapon sales and that revolvers had been confiscated from both white and black teenagers. For these reasons, he said, he believed that violence would likely occur at Central if the school board went ahead with its desegregation plan.

Based on the governor's unsubstantiated testimony, Chancellor Murray O. Reed, a Faubus appointee, found in favor of the Mothers League and issued a restraining order against the school board, blocking the desegregation of Central. Lawyers for the school board immediately petitioned federal district court judge Ronald N. Davies to countermand Reed's order, which Davies did on Friday, August 30, agreeing that the integration of Central should proceed the following Tuesday as planned.

Over the Labor Day weekend, Faubus decided to defy Davies's order. He called out the Arkansas National Guard, and at 10:15 P.M. on Monday, September 2, an hour after 250 guardsmen began cordoning off the school, he gave a televised speech explaining his action. He said he had called out the Arkansas guard "to maintain or restore order and to protect the lives and property of citizens." The troops, he said vaguely, would act neither "as segregationists or integrationists but as soldiers called to active duty to carry out their assigned tasks." He then made his point a little more clearly: "It will not be possible to restore or maintain order and protect the lives and property of the citizens if forcible integration is carried

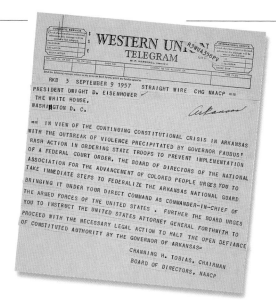

NAACP board chairman Channing H. Tobias sent this September 9 telegram to President Eisenhower protesting Governor Faubus's use of the Arkansas National Guard to prevent school integration. It urged the president to federalize the guard.

out tomorrow." Therefore, Faubus concluded, Little Rock's schools "must be operated on the same basis as they have been in the past."

After Faubus's speech, the school board issued a statement instructing black students "in view of the situation" not to attempt entry into Central "until this dilemma is legally resolved." The next day, the board asked Judge Davies to advise them on how to proceed. Davies replied that the board should take the governor at his word that the troops were there merely to prevent violence. Therefore, the integration of Central should proceed.

THE FIRST DAY OF SCHOOL

Concerned for the safety of the students, Daisy Bates spent that night making arrangements for the Little Rock Nine to gather the next morning at the corner of Park and Twelfth Streets, four blocks from the school at Sixteenth and Park. There, they would be met by a small interracial group of ministers and a city police escort. Once these plans were finalized about 2:30 A.M., Bates called all of the families involved except the Eckfords, who had no telephone. Exhausted, she decided to get some sleep and send a message to the Eckfords in the morning. Unfortunately, with everything else that was going on, she forgot.

On the morning of what she expected to be her first day at Central High School, fifteen-year-old Elizabeth Eckford put on a new black-and-white dress she had made for the occasion and took a public bus to school. As she walked from the bus stop, Eckford later told Daisy Bates, "the crowd began to follow me, calling me names.

The Little Rock Nine

Superintendent Blossom knew that white students assigned to Horace Mann would, of their own accord, transfer out. He also believed, correctly, that he could persuade the six black students living in the Hall High attendance zone not to enroll there because they would be unwelcome. That left only the black students who would be attending Central High. Blossom knew that he couldn't prevent the school's integration, but he did seek to limit its extent.

First, he required the black principals of Horace Mann and Dunbar to screen the seventy students who expressed an interest in attending Central, insisting that each have an IQ of at least 100 and a suitable personality. This narrowed the field to thirty-two. All were then interrogated by Blossom, who dissuaded most from continuing.

Finally, Blossom approved seventeen students, eight of whom later withdrew. Those who remained were Minnijean Brown, Elizabeth Eckford, Ernest Green, Thelma Mothershed, Melba Pattillo, Gloria Ray, Terrance Roberts, Jefferson Thomas, and Carlotta Walls.

I still wasn't afraid—just a little bit nervous. Then my knees started to shake all of a sudden and I wondered whether I could make it to the center entrance a block away."

When Eckford reached the line of guardsmen in front of the school, she walked up to one of them and waited for him to step aside so she could pass. But he didn't. Then she saw a soldier farther down allowing some white students pass. She walked up to him, but this soldier also blocked her way.

"When I tried to squeeze past him," Eckford continued, "he raised his bayonet, and then the other guards moved in and raised their bayonets. They glared at me with a mean look and I was very frightened and didn't know what to do. I turned around and the crowd came toward me. They moved closer and closer. Somebody started yelling, 'Lynch her! Lynch her!' I tried to see a friendly face somewhere in the mob—someone who maybe would help. I looked into the face of an old woman and it seemed a kind face, but when I looked at her again, she spat on me. They came closer, shouting, 'No nigger bitch is going to get in our school. Get out of here!' I turned back to the guards but their faces told me I wouldn't get any help from them. Then I looked down the block and saw a bench at the bus stop.

White students taunt Elizabeth Eckford as she walks away from the blocked entrance to Central High School on September 4. For a long time afterward, she occasionally woke up in the night, terrified, screaming about the mob.

I thought, 'If I can only get there I will be safe.' I don't know why the bench seemed a safe place to me, but I started walking toward it."

The mob trailed Eckford to the bench, where it again crowded around her and resumed screaming threats and insults. At this point, a white man sat down next to Eckford, patting her shoulder and telling her, "Don't let them see you cry." He was Benjamin Fine, an education reporter for the

New York Times. "Then," according to Eckford, "a white lady—she was very nice—she came over to me on the bench. She spoke to me but I don't remember what she said. She put me on the bus and sat next to me. She asked my name and tried

The scene outside Central High on September 5, as a huge crowd of students, parents, reporters, and thrill seekers congregates outside the school.

integration on the federal government. Eisenhower even instructed Brownell to give the governor "every opportunity to make an orderly retreat."

Meanwhile, Davies asked the FBI to do some fact-finding, and on Monday, September 9, he received a report stating that Faubus's claims about increased weapon sales and gun confiscation were fabrications. Concluding that Faubus had acted solely as a segregationist, Davies asked the Justice Department to enter the *Aaron v. Cooper* litigation and seek a preliminary injunction against Faubus. A hearing was set for Friday, September 20.

In a surprise move, Faubus failed to appear at the September 20 hearing. His attorneys told Davies that the governor didn't recognize the authority of the court, and then they left as well. The hearing continued, however, and ended with

to talk to me but I don't think I answered." This woman was Grace Lorch, whose husband, Lee, taught at all-black Philander Smith College and sat on the executive committee of the Little Rock NAACP.

Daisy and L. C. Bates were driving to the rendezvous when a report came over the car radio that a black student was being mobbed at Central. A shocked Daisy instantly realized that she had forgotten to contact the Eckfords, at which point L. C. jumped out of the car and ran to the school to find her. Daisy continued on to the rendezvous, where she, the ministers, and the students

> ## "The first day I was able to enter Central High School, what I felt inside was stark raving fear— terrible, wrenching, awful fear."
>
> MELBA PATTILLO BEALS

climbed into police cars for the short trip to Central. At the school, the other eight teenagers were turned away just as Eckford had been.

Later that day, Faubus confirmed that he had ordered the guardsmen to prevent the black students from entering the school. In doing so, he had intentionally disobeyed a federal court order. Nevertheless, President Eisenhower refused to condemn Faubus's stand publicly, still hoping that the courts could resolve the matter without the need for executive branch action. He also expected Faubus, now that a dramatic gesture had been made, to withdraw the Guard during the next few days and blame Central's

Grace Lorch (left) stands by Elizabeth Eckford as Eckford waits for a city bus at a stop near the school. When the bus finally did come, Lorch boarded it with Eckford and escorted her away.

Davies issuing an injunction prohibiting Faubus and anyone under his command from interfering with the school desegregation plan. Three hours later, Faubus went on television to announce that he was removing the National Guard troops from Central High in compliance with Davies's order. He went on to ask the black students to stay away from the high school until he could arrange for its peaceful desegregation. Then he unexpectedly left town to attend a meeting of the Conference of Southern Governors at Sea Island, Georgia. Later, Little Rock mayor Woodrow Wilson Mann confirmed that his police force would now assume responsibility for keeping order at Central.

THE SECOND DAY

By 8 A.M. on Monday, September 23, all nine students were in Daisy Bates's living room, awaiting instructions from the police. When the call finally came at 8:35 A.M., ten minutes before Central's first bell, Mrs. Bates was warned that a thousand whites had already gathered in front of the school. The plan was for the police to

Daisy and L. C. Bates in their Little Rock residence on September 26. Throughout the desegregation crisis, the Bates home functioned as a command center.

For the next several hours, the police struggled to keep order. Hysterical women began chanting for the white students to come out, and about eighty of them did. They also urged the men in the crowd to break down the barricades and "get the niggers out!" Eventually, sawhorses began to fall, and by 11:30 A.M., Assistant Chief of Police Gene Smith realized that his men couldn't control the crowd much longer.

"Even the adults, the school officials, were panicked," Melba Pattillo Beals remembered. "A couple of the black kids who were with me were crying. Someone made a suggestion that if they allowed the mob to hang one kid, then they could get the rest out while they were hanging the one kid. And a gentleman [Smith] said, 'How are you going to choose? You're going to let them draw straws?' He said, 'I'll get them out.'" And Smith did, leading them to a basement garage and placing them in cars with their heads down. Smith instructed the drivers to leave the building immediately and, once they started driving, not to stop under any circumstances.

EISENHOWER SENDS IN THE ARMY

Meanwhile, at City Hall, Mayor Mann called the Justice Department to ask the president to consider sending federal troops. In response, the president issued an emergency proclamation ordering all Americans "to cease and desist"

meet the students near Central and escort them into the school through the side entrance on Sixteenth Street.

The white reporters who had been camping out at the Bates home now left for Central, but four black reporters remained behind, drinking coffee around the Bateses' kitchen table. They had hoped to accompany the Little Rock Nine to the school and were disappointed to learn that they wouldn't be allowed to ride in the police cars. Instead, Daisy Bates told them of the side-entrance plan and gave them a head start.

"At Park Street, we came face to face with a mob of about 100 whites standing on the corner," wrote one of the reporters, James L. Hicks, in a special dispatch. "When they saw us, they rushed toward us yelling 'Here come the niggers.' We stopped and the mob rushed upon us.... A man threw a punch at [Alex] Wilson, another kicked [Moses] Newsom and a one-armed man slugged me beside me right ear. We turned to run."

Just at that moment, the Little Rock Nine arrived at Central. Temporarily distracted by the black reporters, the mob didn't realize what was happening until the students were already inside the building. Then someone began yelling, "They're in! The niggers are in!" and the mob regrouped at the school. As Hicks later told Bates, "We probably saved you and the children, but I know you saved us."

Journalist Alex Wilson is beaten by the mob outside Central High School on September 23.

blocking the court-ordered desegregation plan but withheld any further action, despite the mounting pressure.

In Little Rock, Daisy Bates announced that the students would remain at home until the president personally guaranteed their safety. The next morning, another mob gathered in front of Central, prompting Mann to send a second telegram to Eisenhower. This one formally requested federal troops.

In his nearly five years as president, Eisenhower had dealt successfully with crises by not acting quickly and instead conducting business as usual while passions cooled. Once he received Mayor Mann's second telegram, however, "Eisenhower realized immediately that his entire policy had broken down," Stephen Ambrose has written. "By allowing events to run their course, by attempting to negotiate with Faubus, by failing to ever speak out forcefully on integration, or to provide real leadership on the moral issue, he found himself in precisely the situation he had most wanted to avoid."

At 12:08 P.M., the president called Brownell to say that he was about to sign Executive Order 10730, federalizing the Arkansas National Guard, and send regular army troops to Little Rock. Seven minutes later, Eisenhower called army chief of staff Maxwell D. Taylor, who promptly dispatched one thousand troops of the 101st Airborne Division from Fort Campbell, Kentucky. Segregationists called the deployment "an invasion."

The next morning, September 25, soldiers of the 101st Airborne arrived at the Bateses' house to escort the Little Rock Nine to school. At Central, a crowd of segregationists had again gathered. Maj. James Meyers commanded them to disperse, and when they refused, he had them moved off at bayonet point. Local, national, and international media then watched the nine black students enter the high school, flanked by twenty-two armed federal troops. The rest of the school day passed uneventfully, and at its end, the soldiers returned the students to the Bateses' home. After a week of this escort duty, the soldiers

Minnijean Brown (center) arrives with the rest of the Little Rock Nine at Central High School on September 25 as members of the 101st Airborne Division stand guard on their first day of escort duty.

Daisy Bates (right) in her living room with the Little Rock Nine. Her picture window is taped because rocks such as this one (inset) were being thrown through her windows on a regular basis by people in passing cars.

of the 101st Airborne withdrew from Central High to Camp Robinson, leaving the federalized National Guard to maintain order at the school. The results were mixed.

On September 25, nearly one hundred of the most segregationist students had walked out of school in protest. Their absence, together with the shocking presence of soldiers in the hallways, made the Little Rock Nine's first week in school rather welcoming. Minnijean Brown was invited to join the glee club, and others were asked to eat lunch with white classmates. By October 1, however, the segregationists had returned, and the systematic harassment of the Little Rock Nine began.

The intention was to make life at Central so unbearable for the black students that they would all withdraw voluntarily. Tactics included verbal abuse, threatening notes, jostling in the halls, and even the occasional physical attack. Typically, the guardsmen on duty, many of them segregationists, failed to intervene, and their inaction invited more white students to join in the intimidation.

Maj. Gen. Edwin Walker, the commander of the federal forces in Little Rock, speaks with reporters outside Central High on September 25. (To his left is his subordinate Col. William Kuhn.) Walker said that he had a "mission" to accomplish and would take whatever steps necessary to carry out the integration decree.

"There is possibly going to be a concerted attempt to conduct a war of nerves to force the Negro kids to get out," NAACP director of branches Gloster B. Current told Daisy Bates during an October 7 telephone conversation. "We lose everything we have gained if they move out." Understanding this, the students somehow endured.

BACK TO COURT

Meanwhile, the legal maneuvering continued. During the spring of 1958, the Little Rock school board petitioned Davies's replacement, Judge Harry J. Lemley, for a two-and-a-half-year delay in its desegregation plan. On June 21, Lemley granted the request, using *Brown II*'s "local problems" exception to rule that the violence of the previous fall justified a cooling-off period. Working with local counsel Wiley Branton, LDF attorneys Thurgood Marshall, Jack Greenberg, and Constance Baker Motley filed an immediate appeal of Lemley's decision.

On August 18, the judges of the Eighth Circuit Court of Appeals voted, 6–1, to overturn Lemley's order. But they delayed implementation of their decision until the Supreme Court could hear the school board's appeal. Because the Court was out of session until the first Monday in October, this delay meant that Little Rock's schools would open on September 15, 1958, on a segregated basis.

Just as circumstances in Arkansas had finally forced the president to act, so the Supreme Court found itself in a similar situation. One week after the appeals court ruling, Chief Justice Earl Warren announced that the Supreme Court would meet on August 28 in special session to begin hearing the Little Rock case.

An unidentified member of the Little Rock Nine (probably Ernest Green) stands in front of a Central High class on September 25, his first full day in school, in this rare photograph.

A second hearing was scheduled for September 11, and on September 12, the justices ordered the Little Rock school board to proceed with its desegregation plan immediately.

Back in Arkansas, as the Supreme Court deliberated, Faubus called the General Assembly into a special session of its own to pass six new anti-integration laws. The most important of these was a statute empowering the governor to close any school forced to integrate by federal order. On the day that the Court ordered integration to proceed in Little Rock, Faubus used the new law to close all of the district's schools. For the next year, white students enrolled in out-of-district schools, attended segregated private academies, or took correspondence courses offered through the University of Arkansas in Fayetteville.

> "Evidence of the naked force of the federal government is here apparent in these unsheathed bayonets in the backs of schoolgirls."
>
> GOV. ORVAL FAUBUS, DISPLAYING THE PHOTOGRAPH BELOW

Troopers with fixed bayonets draw giggles from Central High coeds in this widely published wire-service photo taken on an otherwise tense September 25. The image caused a furor, according to Central vice principal for girls Elizabeth Huckaby, because segregationists used it to charge that whites were being mistreated.

The mass resignation of the school board, however, made it impossible for them to continue ignoring the adverse effects the ongoing crisis was having on northern investment in the city. Not a single new industry had chosen to locate in Little Rock since September 1957, and five anticipated plants had moved elsewhere. Therefore, when the school district held a special election in December 1958, the business community put up its own slate of candidates, three of whom won. The other three seats on the new school board went to single-issue segregationists.

An uneasy alliance prevailed until May 1959, when the segregationists on the board moved to fire all Little Rock school employees who supported integration. The board's business members walked out of the meeting in protest, but the segregationist president of the board

Four Central High students stand in front of a sign erected by the Little Rock school board to shift the blame for the closing of Central to the federal government. (Note the misspelling of *government*.)

Most black students attended schools outside the district, but some took a correspondence course taught by Horace Mann principal L. M. Christophe.

In November 1958, after Faubus won a third term as governor, a Gallup poll named him one of the ten most admired men in America. Citizens' Council leader Jim Johnson also won election that fall to the Arkansas Supreme Court, and Dale Alford, one of the more outspoken segregationists on the Little Rock school board, upset eight-term incumbent Brooks Hays to win Little Rock's seat in Congress. These victories

made it difficult to doubt the political power of segregationism. Meanwhile, the entire Little Rock school board resigned in exasperation. As one of its final acts, it bought out Virgil Blossom's contract so that the incoming board could begin anew.

THE REOPENING OF THE SCHOOLS

Until this point, Little Rock's business elite had remained largely disengaged. Their children didn't attend Central High, located in a working-class neighborhood, but rather Hall High in the city's wealthy western suburbs.

A Negro student, displaced by the closing of the Little Rock school system, watches instructional television in September 1958.

ruled that the meeting could continue, even though it now lacked a quorum. The three remaining school board members then voted not to renew the contracts of forty-four employees, including seven principals.

Three days later, a group of downtown business leaders met to form Stop This Outrageous Purge, an organization dedicated to recalling the three segregationist school board members. A week after that, the segregationists organized their own effort to recall the business members.

The showdown came on May 25, when voters narrowly retained the three businessmen and dismissed the three segregationists. The new board then moved to reopen the schools in August 1959, with token integration at both Central and Hall.

Six members of the Little Rock Nine pose outside the Supreme Court in 1958. They are (from left to right) Carlotta Walls, Melba Pattillo, Jefferson Thomas, Minnijean Brown, Gloria Ray, and Elizabeth Eckford.

Supporters of segregation gather at the state capitol in Little Rock in August 1959 to protest the resumption of integration at Central High.

The Hate That Hate Produced 1959–1965

From the death of Booker T. Washington in 1915 until the late 1950s, the central organizing force in the fight for African-American equality was the NAACP. Nearly all civil rights activists became NAACP members, and the association's basic strategy of using constitutional principles to shame white judges governed most of their political activity.

Yet the Little Rock desegregation crisis was something of a last hurrah for this pattern of activism. The emergence of the Montgomery Improvement Association in December 1955 offered a new paradigm, which appealed strongly to southern blacks because it was local and because it drew strength from the considerable institutional resources of the black church. With the NAACP suspended in Alabama as of June 1956 and under legal attack from white politicians elsewhere in the South, church-based organizing seemed the way of the future.

In May 1956, with the Montgomery boycott into its sixth month, the Fellowship of Reconciliation sponsored a one-day conference at the Rev. Martin

Luther King Jr.'s alma mater, Morehouse College in Atlanta. The purpose of the meeting was to bring King into contact with other southern civil rights leaders who might join him in forming a new, interracial movement based on the principles and tactics of nonviolence. The main topic of discussion was whether mass protests of the sort undertaken in Montgomery could be instigated elsewhere, or whether they had to develop on their own. In January 1957, the FOR staged another, much larger conference in Atlanta, out of which a new organization was expected to emerge. But Bayard Rustin had different plans.

Although Rustin shared the FOR's commitment to nonviolence, he disagreed that a new interracial

Elijah Muhammad (left) wanted the Nation of Islam to stay out of the civil rights movement, while Malcolm X (right) ached to get into it.

organization should be created in the South. The great strength of the Montgomery boycott, he felt, was that blacks had organized it themselves. Therefore, the same should be true of any future organization led by King, whose stardom had already become apparent.

Aiding Rustin in his counterplanning were two fellow veterans of the 1930s Left, Stanley Levison and Ella Baker, whose politics had also been shaped in the radical cauldron of Depression-era New York City. Levison, a Jewish lawyer-turned-mogul, had made enough money early in his business career (chiefly through real estate investments) to spend the rest of his life indulging his personal passion for politics. Among the many progressive organizations he backed was the NAACP, through whose offices he met Baker, then the national director of branches.

Martin Luther King Jr. at the founding meeting of the Southern Christian Leadership Conference on January 10, 1957. The Rev. Theodore Jemison (left) and the Rev. Fred L. Shuttlesworth (to King's immediate left) look on.

With the help of Levison and Baker, Rustin organized a rival conference in Atlanta to begin on the same day, January 10, as the FOR conference ended. The invitations—signed by King, the Rev. Fred L. Shuttlesworth of Birmingham, and the Rev. C. K. Steele of Tallahassee—weren't mailed until January 1. Nevertheless, sixty ministers responded and at the meeting agreed to establish a permanent organization, effectively sidelining the FOR effort. The new group was called, initially, the Southern Leadership Conference on Transportation and Nonviolent Integration; later, its name was changed to the more pleasing Southern Christian Leadership Conference (SCLC).

"Since [mentioning] the NAACP was like waving a red flag in front of some southern whites," the Rev. T. J. Jemison of Baton Rouge recalled, "we decided that we needed an organization that would do the same thing and yet be called a Christian organization."

Because it would have been politically inappropriate to compete with the NAACP for members, Rustin, Levison, and Baker designed the SCLC to be an umbrella organization—that is, a group of groups, rather than a group of individuals. Each SCLC affiliate would pay dues of twenty-five dollars a year, entitling it to seek advice and assistance from the SCLC staff.

In the South, at least, this church-based approach made sense because most of the prominent civil rights leaders were Christian ministers who felt comfortable with nonviolence because of its deep roots in the

Noble Drew Ali (standing, center, foreground) poses with his MSTA officers at the group's annual meeting in 1928.

Christian pacifist tradition. In the North, however, there lived many blacks who were neither Christian nor nonviolent, and they pursued a different path to the goal of equality.

THE FIRST BLACK MUSLIMS

About 1910, an East Indian missionary named Muhammad Sadiq arrived in the United States to spread the gospel of his teacher, the late Mirza Ghulam Ahmad. (In 1889, Ahmad had declared himself the Mahdi, or Messiah, prophesied in the Bible and the Quran.) Arriving at Ellis Island, Sadiq settled in New York City, where he opened a small mosque. Most of his converts were either Arabs or fellow East Indians (from the Islamic region now known as Pakistan), but Sadiq was able to bring into the Ahmadiyya movement a few American blacks.

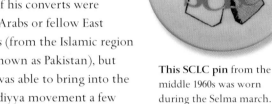

This SCLC pin from the middle 1960s was worn during the Selma march.

These people were not the first black Muslims in America. During the height of the transatlantic slave trade, tens of thousands of Africans were shipped to the New World from Islamic West Africa. During several generations of bondage, however, the Christian religion forced on them by their masters came to supplant their original Muslim beliefs.

Among those attracted to Sadiq's sect was a young Newark railroad worker named Timothy Drew, who began studying Islam under Sadiq in 1912.

A year later, though, Drew became disaffected and broke away from the Ahmadiyya community. He changed his name to Noble Drew Ali, declared himself a prophet of Allah, and formed his own sect, the Moorish Science Temple of America (MSTA). Ali's theology was a pastiche of Ahmadiyya beliefs, leavened with Christian spiritualism and some vaudevillian showmanship. He taught that all blacks were of Moorish (and thus Muslim) origin and preached a "return" to Islam as the only means of ending racial oppression.

Ali offered his followers an alternative to the Christian tradition—which many blacks, especially those who had participated in the Great Migration only to find unemployment and discrimination in the North, believed had failed them. The new, mythic "Moorish" identity that Ali gave temple members soothed their acute feelings of inferiority and relieved at least some of the burden of being an American Negro. By the mid-1920s, when Ali's movement reached its peak, the MSTA had acquired about thirty thousand members, most living in the northern urban centers of Harlem, Detroit, and Chicago (where Ali made his headquarters).

Not long before Ali's death in July 1929, a man of indeterminate race calling himself Wallace D. Ford arrived in Chicago and attached himself to the MSTA leader. Following Ali's death, Ford told others that he was the prophet's reincarnation. However, at least three other MSTA members also

Wallace D. Fard

1893–?

Although Wallace Dodd Fard told his followers that his birthplace was Mecca, he was actually born in New Zealand to Zared Fard, an East Indian immigrant, and Beatrice Dodd, a British New Zealander. In 1913, he entered the United States illegally through Canada and settled in Portland, Oregon, where he lived under the name Fred Dodd, the first of his many aliases.

By 1916, Fard had married, fathered a son, and abandoned his family, moving south to Los Angeles, where he found work as a cook. During Prohibition, he became a bootlegger and drug peddler. In January 1926, he was arrested for violating the Volstead Act (the federal prohibition law), and a month later, while awaiting trial, he was arrested again for drug trafficking. Fard paid a fine to satisfy the bootlegging conviction but had to serve three years in San Quentin on the drug charge. Following his release in May 1929, he headed east to Chicago.

During the 1950s, when FBI director J. Edgar Hoover became obsessed with discrediting the Black Muslim movement, the bureau began searching nationwide for Fard so that he could be exposed as a fraud. Agents learned that he had returned briefly to Los Angeles in 1934 but found no other trace of him.

made this claim, leading to a murderous succession battle. During the summer of 1930, when the situation in Chicago got too hot for him, Ford (now using the name *Fard*) fled for Detroit, where he began selling silks and satins door to door in the Negro ghetto. Even though his customers had little money, Fard found them eager to buy the garments he was offering once he described them as identical to the clothes worn by natives in their West African homelands.

Gradually, Fard's lectures on the secret history of the Negro superseded his peddling, and he soon announced that he was the Supreme Ruler of the Universe, though he was more commonly known as the Prophet. His new followers organized meetings in their homes, at which he explained that he had been sent by Allah to teach American Negroes the truth about their past. According to Fard, blacks were the "original" humans, and they ruled the world until their position was usurped during prehistory by a race of "blue-eyed devils"— i.e., the Caucasians. Nevertheless, Fard declared,

BELOW: **A view of the audience** at one of Elijah Muhammad's speeches. His followers dressed alike to show their unity.

RIGHT: **A ticket** to an August 1959 appearance by the Messenger, the Honorable Elijah Muhammad.

ADMIT TWO
1st Preference To RESERVED SECTION

ADMIT TWO
To See and Hear
MESSENGER ELIJAH MUHAMMAD
At ROCKLAND PALACE, 155th St. & 8th Ave.
SUNDAY, AUGUST 16, 1959 - 2:00 P.M.
Doors Open at 1:00 P.M.   This Ticket Admits FREE

the Day of Judgment was coming, when Allah would deliver blacks from oppression and condemn whites to eternal damnation.

According to Louis E. Lomax's 1963 study *When the Word Is Given*, Fard's preaching had "but one message: The white man is by nature evil, a snake who is incapable of doing right, a devil who is soon to be destroyed. Therefore, the black man, who is by nature divine and good, must separate from the white man as soon as possible, lest he share the white man's hour of total destruction."

to insulate himself from the violent excesses of some NOI factions by creating a new position, supreme minister, to which he appointed Elijah Poole. He also gave Elijah a new surname. *Poole*, Fard explained, was Elijah's "slave" name, given to his family by the white master of his slave forebear. *Muhammad* would be, in NOI's parlance, his new "original" name. With the addition of a suitable honorific, he became, for the remainder of his life, the Honorable Elijah Muhammad.

> ## "The Muslims demanded respect and they got respect, and I think that was the important thing in any prison population. But the administration was more scared of 'em than anybody."
>
> STANLEY JONES, AN INMATE WHO SERVED TIME WITH MALCOLM X AT THE NORFOLK PRISON COLONY

The lure of such a teaching to poor blacks living in fear of whites was strong, and before long Fard's informal meetings became so crowded that a hall had to be hired to accommodate the demand. Thus was founded the Nation of Islam (NOI) and its Temple Number One.

During the four years that Fard lived in Detroit before vanishing in June 1934, he gave his followers, who came to be known as Black Muslims, a strong dose of racial pride, which Fard called "knowledge of self." Christianity, he explained, had been forced on African Americans by masters who wanted to control the slave population. In Islam, however, especially in the Nation's rather unorthodox version of the faith, lay the path to salvation.

THE NATION OF ISLAM

Elijah Poole began attending Fard's meetings during the fall of 1931. The first one he attended, held in the basement of a follower's home, was so crowded that Poole had to stand outside a window and content himself with the occasional words that reached him. Unemployed, with few skills or prospects, he became entranced. Early NOI members recall him initially running errands for Fard, but he quickly moved up in the NOI hierarchy.

Despite his use of an alias, Fard's involvement in the MSTA succession fight eventually became known to the Detroit police, who began keeping him under closer surveillance. Not wanting to spend any more time in prison, Fard decided

Not long afterward, Fard dispatched Muhammad to Chicago to found Temple Number Two, which later became the NOI's national headquarters. In some ways, Muhammad was a worthy successor to Fard. He began by proclaiming himself the Messenger of the Prophet (the Prophet being Fard) and, having learned the basics of church administration from his clergyman father, founded and managed several more temples. But the movement gradually stagnated, and the number of believers remained in the low hundreds until Malcolm Little emerged from prison in August 1952.

"When Malcolm came out, he was full of fire," recalled his elder brother Philbert (now Abdul Aziz Omar). "He came to Detroit, and he was surprised to find that there were so few people in this powerful teaching. He got on the podium, and he told them, 'I'm ashamed, I'm surprised

A prison mug shot of Malcolm X from 1949. Elijah Muhammad had himself served time in federal prison for refusing induction into the army during World War II.

The Honorable Elijah Muhammad

1897–1975

Elijah Poole was one of thirteen children born to Georgia sharecroppers William and Mariah Poole. As a boy, he attended the local segregated elementary school but never finished the fourth grade (or the eighth grade, depending on which account one believes).

Becoming a laborer, he married Clara Evans in March 1919 and later moved with her and their two children to Detroit in April 1923.

An NOI button. In 1960, members tithed Elijah Muhammad eight dollars a week plus occasional special assessments.

"Of all the disenchanted Detroit Negroes," Louis Lomax has written, "Elijah Poole was probably the bitterest." Even before the Great Depression hit, Poole had difficulty finding work and was typically depressed himself.

One day in 1931, his father told him about an encounter he had recently had with a friend who once belonged to the MSTA. Now, this friend had associated himself with another quasi-Islamic prophet, W. D. Fard. The bits and pieces of conversation that William Poole could recall intrigued Elijah, who decided to learn more.

Malcolm X
1925–1965

Malcolm Little's father, Earl, was a dedicated Garveyite whose outspoken views often provoked Klan retaliation. Within Malcolm's first four years of life, the family moved at least three times—from Malcolm's birthplace in Omaha to Milwaukee to Lansing, Michigan, and finally to East Lansing. The last of these moves came after the Littles' house was set on fire in November 1929. According to Malcolm, "The firemen came and just sat there without making any effort to put one drop of water on the fire. The same fire that burned my father's home still burns in my soul."

Malcolm X at age fourteen.

In September 1931, when Malcolm was six years old, his father was run over by a streetcar under mysterious circumstances. Left alone and destitute with seven children to care for, Louise Little did her best but slowly began to deteriorate mentally. Finally, in January 1939, she was declared insane and committed to a state mental institution. Meanwhile, Malcolm and his siblings survived largely on their own. At night, for example, they roamed the streets, stealing whatever food they could find to ease their hunger.

After his mother's commitment, Malcolm entered foster care and was placed in a Mason, Michigan, junior high school, where he was the

Malcolm X wears a zoot suit in this photo taken with his half sister Ella Collins soon after Malcolm's arrival in Boston in 1941.

only black student. Initially, he adapted well, becoming class president, but the respite didn't last. "When I was in eighth grade," he recalled, "they asked me what I wanted to become. I told them I wanted to study law. But they told me that law was not a suitable profession for Negro. They suggested that I think of a trade such as carpentry."

Malcolm's performance nose-dived after that, causing the social service bureaucracy to move him from one foster home to another until, finally, in February 1941 he went to live with his half sister Ella Collins in the Roxbury section of Boston. There, he was drawn into Boston's swinging nightlife, and he quickly became a hustler, donning a zoot suit, conking his hair, and learning to smoke "reefer." Eventually, his criminal activity included numbers running, drug dealing, pimping, and burglary.

During December 1945, Malcolm and his partner, "Shorty" Jarvis, carried out a string of burglaries in Cambridge with the assistance of their white girlfriends. All four were arrested in January 1946, after Malcolm attempted to reclaim a stolen watch he'd left for repair at a

Malcolm's brothers (left to right) Philbert, Wesley, Wilfred, and Reginald in 1949.

jewelry store. Malcolm and Shorty received especially stiff sentences of eight to ten years each because of their association with the white women. According to Malcolm, the police even tried to bring a rape charge, but the women wouldn't cooperate.

In prison, Malcolm and Shorty Jarvis began to educate themselves, reading books from the prison library up to fifteen hours a day. Then, in 1948, Malcolm was converted to the Nation of Islam by several brothers who had recently adopted the faith. According to Malcolm's brother Wilfred, who joined the Nation of Islam in 1947, "We all got together and decided we better let Malcolm know about this.... We already had been indoctrinated with Marcus Garvey's philosophy, so [the Nation of Islam] was just a good place for us. They didn't have to convince us we were black and should be proud or anything like that."

that you are sitting here, and [there are] so many empty seats.' He said, 'Every time you come out here, this place should be full.' And that excited the Honorable Elijah Muhammad, it excited the believers who had any energy. And we brought in people, just hundreds of them."

At their first meeting a few weeks later in Chicago, Malcolm asked Elijah Muhammad what he could do to spread the Word. Muhammad told him, "Go after the young people," which Malcolm did. Shortly afterward, Muhammad gave Malcolm the new surname X, which represented the lost surname of his African ancestors.

Muhammad's strategy had been to wait, believing that Allah would provide the necessary converts. But the driven, energetic Malcolm had no such patience, and he took to the streets, recruiting the people whom he wanted. Malcolm's "fishing" expeditions quickly tripled the membership of Temple Number One and earned him the title of assistant minister in June 1953.

The experience prepared Malcolm well for his next two assignments: the establishment of Temple Number Eleven in Boston, followed by

Malcolm X and his wife, Betty, with their daughters Attallah (left) and Qubilah in their East Elmhurst, Queens, home about 1962.

"This is the day of warning, the hour during which prophecy is being fulfilled before your very eyes. The white man is doomed! Don't integrate with him, separate from him! Come ye out from among the white devils and be ye separate."

MALCOLM X

the founding of Temple Number Twelve in Philadelphia. Completing both of these tasks to Muhammad's satisfaction, Malcolm was then rewarded with the high-potential, high-profile prize that he most craved. In June 1954, he became chief minister of Temple Number Seven in Harlem—where, as Malcolm liked to point out, more blacks lived than anywhere else in America. He was by now clearly the second most powerful man in the church and Muhammad's heir apparent.

The Black Muslim movement was especially successful in reaching low-income blacks, Louis Lomax explained in *When the Word Is Given*, because "these people are in something of a prison, too; they see themselves as failures and need some accounting

for why they are what they are, why they are not what they are not. These needs are met when the wayward and the downtrodden sit at the feet of Malcolm X and hear him proclaim the divinity of the black man, hear him blame the white man for sin and lawlessness and then go on to herald the impending destruction of the 'blue-eyed white devil.'"

Like Marcus Garvey, the Black Muslims promoted separation from whites, either within the United States or in Africa, if that became necessary. They also advocated the use of violence in self-defense, blamed Christianity for the horror of slavery, and emphasized the importance of personal morality. NOI members were expected to abstain from drugs and alcohol, follow strict dietary laws, obey their ministers, and take care of their families. No excuses were accepted.

THE BEATING OF JOHNSON HINTON

As it had in Detroit, Boston, and Philadelphia, Malcolm's charismatic proselytizing won many converts to the faith, and Temple Number Seven began to thrive. Also as before, Malcolm worked rather quietly, remaining unknown outside the black community. On the evening of April 14, 1957, however, Malcolm X began to emerge as an influential public personality.

Shortly after dark that night, police officers at the Twenty-eighth Precinct received a call about a brawl on the corner of 125th Street and Seventh Avenue. Several radio cars were dispatched, and arriving police pushed their way through the crowd to get to the participants. In doing so, at least one officer got into a heated argument with Johnson Hinton, who as Johnson X belonged to Temple Number Seven. The confrontation ended with Hinton sprawled on the pavement, his head split open. The police then arrested him and took him to the precinct house a few blocks away.

Another Black Muslim in the crowd saw what had happened, and within an hour, hundreds of angry temple members (including the paramilitary Fruit of Islam) cordoned off the area around the police station. A race riot seemed

Malcolm leaves a Brooklyn mosque in 1963. He was a very disciplined man with the unusual habit (for a civil rights leader) of being always on time. He could function effectively on just one meal and four hours' sleep a day.

The NEW THERESA

"No man should have that much power over that many people. We can't control this town if one man can wield that kind of power."

Malcolm X uses an enlarged photo of a beaten Black Muslim to decry police at a Harlem rally in 1963.

A NEW YORK CITY POLICE CAPTAIN'S ASSESSMENT OF MALCOLM X

imminent. Then Minister Malcolm X arrived, demanding to see Hinton. The police resisted at first, but the presence of so many Black Muslims standing in intimidating rank formation persuaded the desk sergeant to produce a bloody, semiconscious Hinton.

When Malcolm insisted that Hinton be given immediate medical attention, an ambulance was called—which the Fruit of Islam, walking beside the car, escorted to the hospital fifteen blocks away. Only when Malcolm was satisfied that Hinton was receiving the proper care did he wave his hand, dispersing the crowd.

Later, *Amsterdam News* editor James Hicks reported that he had heard the precinct captain remark, "No man should have that much power over that many people.

The Fruit of Islam, shown here in 1965, were created by Wallace Fard as a paramilitary offshoot of the Nation of Islam. They were taught both judo and the use of firearms.

We can't control this town if one man can wield that kind of power."

Afterward, the streets of Harlem were abuzz with talk of how the Black Muslims had cowed the NYPD. Overnight, Malcolm became one of Harlem's most prominent leaders, and Hicks even gave him a regular newspaper column. The Twenty-eighth Precinct captain, who had never heard of Malcolm before that night, also began paying attention.

It wasn't until 1959, however, that the white world at large took notice of the Black Muslim movement. The precipitating event was a television documentary, "The Hate That Hate Produced," created by Mike Wallace and Louis E. Lomax. Wallace, a former game show host, was then anchoring a provocative current events show called *News Beat* on WNTA-TV Channel 13 in New York City. He had never heard of Malcolm X or the Nation of Islam when Lomax pitched him on the Black Muslim movement, but he knew a good story when he heard one. In fact, he was stunned by what Lomax told him was going on.

The report aired in five segments between July 13 and July 17. As with much of Wallace's later work on *60 Minutes*, the series enhanced the story's shock value by sensationalizing certain aspects of Black Muslim doctrine. Wallace even presented as factual Elijah Muhammad's claim that the Nation of Islam had 250,000 members. (The number was actually much closer to 25,000.)

A Black Muslim rally in Harlem during the summer of 1961. According to Elijah Muhammad, the resurrection of blacks would occur by 1970.

However, citing this exaggerated number gave the program a news hook and focused its overall message: that the Nation of Islam posed a hidden threat to white society.

"While city officials, state agencies, white liberals, and sober-minded Negroes stand idly by," Wallace's opening statement began, "a group of Negro dissenters are taking to street corner stepladders, church pulpits, sports arenas, and ballroom platforms across the nation to preach a gospel of hate that would set off a federal investigation if it were to be preached by southern whites."

Picked up by the wire services during a slow summer news period, the story caused such a sensation that Wallace quickly repackaged the program into an hour-long documentary that aired throughout the country on July 22.

A Black Muslim hawks copies of the NOI newspaper *Muhammad Speaks* on a Harlem street corner in 1962.

Afterward, Malcolm wrote in his posthumously published autobiography, "The telephone in our then small Temple Seven restaurant [next door to the temple] nearly jumped off the wall. I had a receiver against my ear five hours a day....Calls came, long-distance from San Francisco to Maine ...from even London, Stockholm, Paris....One funny thing—in all that hectic period, something quickly struck my notice: the Europeans never pressed the 'hate' question. Only the American white man was so plagued and obsessed with being 'hated.' He was so guilty, it was clear to me, of hating Negroes." As a result, Malcolm became a national figure, and membership in the Nation swelled.

White reporters then began hounding mainstream black leaders to declare where they stood on the issue of "black supremacy." Nearly all responded by condemning the Nation of Islam and its reportedly hate mongering. "We must not stoop to the low and primitive methods of some of our opponents," the Reverend King told the National Bar Association (the black counterpart of the American Bar Association) in August. Choosing another, rather foolish approach, NAACP executive secretary Roy Wilkins denied in an interview with Mike Wallace that he had ever heard of Elijah Muhammad.

Malcolm X lectures at an NOI temple in April 1962. Tall, handsome, and well spoken, he had a charismatic personality that attracted many converts.

MALCOLM'S APPEAL

Although most of these black leaders regretted having to disparage other blacks, the statements being made by Malcolm X in the name of Elijah Muhammad were simply too extreme (and too anti-Christian) to be acceptable. While Christian ministers such as King preached tolerance and acceptance, Malcolm had been using the most rousing language he could muster to deride the civil rights movement as pointless and even

An FBI transcript of "The Hate That Hate Produced."
In 1958, FBI director J. Edgar Hoover designated
Malcolm X a "key figure," which meant that, in the
event of a national security emergency, Malcolm
would be located and interned.

damaging to black aspirations because it suggested
that whites might one day willingly accept racial
equality. "There is nothing in our book, the Quran,
that teaches us to suffer peacefully," Malcolm X

told an audience in Detroit. "Our religion teaches
us to be intelligent. Be peaceful, be courteous,
obey the law, respect everyone; but if someone
puts his hand on you, send him to the cemetery."

In the Christian South, Malcolm made little
headway, but in the ghettos of the North, he
outperformed King in organizing urban blacks.
His issue was racism, and even some of King's
followers felt compelled to heed his words.
"We were willing to listen to Malcolm," SNCC
founder John Lewis explained, "because, on
one hand, Malcolm inspired us. Malcolm
said things in New York, in Chicago, around
the country, that maybe some people in the
South and in other parts of the country didn't
have the courage to say."

A large measure of Malcolm's appeal was
that he seemed so fearless. "My first impression
was how could a black man talk about the
government, white people, and act so bold, and
not be shot at?" recalled Cassius Clay, who was
given the name Muhammad Ali after joining the
Nation of Islam in 1964. "How could he say these
things? Only God must be protecting him."

Yet Malcolm's ideas about the civil rights
movement gradually began to change. As the
demonstrations in the South intensified—and
with them, the brutality of southern whites—
Malcolm and other Black Muslims became

ABOVE: **A flyer** promoting Malcolm X's appearance
at a Harlem rally on May 1961. The text of the flyer
highlights Malcolm's criticism of the NAACP.
BELOW: **Malcolm addresses** a crowd at a June 1963
rally in Upper Manhattan.

"Stop talking about the South. When you cross
the Canadian border, you're in the South."

MALCOLM X

This sign on the side of a Washington, D.C., bus advertised a 1961 appearance by Elijah Muhammad.

quietly but increasingly dissatisfied with Elijah Muhammad's insistence on noninvolvement. Muhammad taught that Allah would soon punish the whites, but Malcolm wasn't content to wait. According to his aide Benjamin Karim, "We weren't doing anything to help our people who were being brutalized by the whites and the police. We wanted to send some brothers down to Birmingham to train the black people to fight."

THE BREAK

This doctrinal rift widened in December 1962, when Malcolm first became aware of rumors that Muhammad had fathered six children in adulterous affairs with his secretaries. Because a large number of members was simultaneously leaving Temple Number Two, Malcolm decided to investigate. He talked with three of the secretaries involved and discovered that the rumors were true. He was devastated. "I felt almost out of my mind," he said.

Confronted by Malcolm, Muhammad admitted the affairs and asked Malcolm to help him make contingency plans in the event that the scandal became public. Malcolm did so and kept the damaging information tightly controlled, but his estimation of Muhammad changed fundamentally. He ceased being the obedient acolyte, and Muhammad, for his part, became much more concerned with Malcolm's still-growing prominence.

Publicly, Malcolm continued to honor Elijah Muhammad, but his sermons began to include subtle deviations from NOI orthodoxy. For example, according to his brother Philbert, "Malcolm began to talk less and less about how God was going to get rid of the Caucasians, and he began to talk about how we were going to be able to go into court and bring them to justice, that they are guilty according to the law of the

Muhammad Ali
1942–

Cassius Clay, the 1960 Olympic boxing champion, first learned of the Black Muslim faith in 1959, when he picked up a copy of *Muhammad Speaks*. "I can still feel the powerful way [it] impressed me," he later wrote. "It was speaking out boldly against the injustice and oppression of black people, saying things that I had thought and felt but had no one to talk to about."

Three years later in Detroit, Clay met Malcolm X, who immediately realized the public relations advantages of converting the charismatic young boxer. Clay, however, kept his interest secret. "For three years, up until I fought Sonny Liston, I'd sneak into Nation of Islam meetings through the back door," he remembered. "I didn't want people to know I was there. I was afraid if they knew, I wouldn't be allowed to fight for the title. Later on, I learned to stand up for my beliefs."

Cassius Clay (right) backs away from world heavyweight champion Sonny Liston during the sixth round of their February 1964 title fight. Liston failed to answer the bell for the seventh round.

At a press conference held the day after he beat Liston, Clay finally admitted that he had joined the Nation of Islam, disowned his "slave name," and become Cassius X. A month later, he reported that Elijah Muhammad had given him a new Islamic name, Muhammad Ali.

In March 1964, Cassius Clay signs autographs outside the Trans-Lux Theater on Broadway in New York City as Malcolm X (left) looks on.

land—which was not our argument at all. Our argument was that we were a divine people and that we would be protected and finally delivered, put in the seat of authority by Allah. That was our teaching at that time."

When Muhammad ordered Malcolm not to take part in the August 1963 March on Washington, Malcolm complied. But three months later, when Muhammad ordered all of his followers to avoid public comment on the assassination of Pres.

John F. Kennedy, Malcolm failed to restrain himself. Taking a question from the audience during a December 1 speech, he said of Kennedy's death, "It was, as I saw it, a case of 'the chickens coming home to roost.'" Three days later, Muhammad suspended Malcolm from his Harlem ministry and "silenced" him for three months.

On March 5, 1964, the day of his supposed reinstatement, Malcolm received word that his suspension was being extended for "an indefinite period of time." Anticipating expulsion, Malcolm resigned from the Nation of Islam three days later. He had no immediate plans, but his general intention was to ally himself in some way with the civil rights movement, broadening its scope and strengthening its militancy. At the same time, he began receiving death threats from his former brothers in the NOI.

ASSASSINATION

During March 1964, Malcolm began to involve himself in rent strikes, a school boycott, and other mass-based attempts to reduce the day-to-

In mid-April, Malcolm began a monthlong pilgrimage to Mecca and West Africa, during which he wrote a letter to his wife, Betty, that she made public. The letter suggested that Malcolm had moved beyond the NOI's black–white dualism to embrace a more humanistic, and therefore more properly Islamic, vision of the world. "There were tens of thousands of pilgrims from all over the world," Malcolm wrote of his stay in Mecca. "They were of all colors, from blue-

Malcolm X meets with Prince Faisal in Saudi Arabia during his April 1964 pilgrimage to Mecca.

> "I have no argument with Dr. Martin Luther King. He's doing the best he knows how. But what he's doing is out of style. It's out of date. And anybody who teaches Negroes today to turn the other cheek is actually committing a crime."
>
> MALCOLM X

day suffering of black people in New York City. He even traveled to Washington to monitor Senate debate on the 1964 civil rights bill. During this visit, he briefly crossed paths with Martin Luther King. It would be their only meeting.

eyed blonds to black-skinned Africans. But we were all participating in the same rituals, displaying the same spirit of unity and brotherhood that my experiences in America had led me to

believe never could exist between the white and the non-white. America needs to understand Islam, because this is the one religion that erases from its society the race problem.

"You may be shocked by these words coming from me," he continued. "But on this pilgrimage, what I have seen, and experienced, has forced me to rearrange much of my thought patterns previously held, and to toss aside some of my previous conclusions. This was not too difficult for me. Despite my firm convictions, I have always been a man who tries to face facts, and to accept the reality of life as new experiences and new knowledge unfolds it." He signed the letter with the new Islamic name he had taken: El-Hajj Malik El-Shabazz.

Soon after his return to the United States in late May, Malcolm announced that he would be forming the Organization for Afro-American Unity (OAAU). Its goal would be to enlist the help of Islamic nation-states in raising "the Negro struggle from the level of civil rights to the level of human rights." Malcolm's plan was to lobby African and Middle

Martin Luther King and Malcolm X wait for a press conference to begin following their chance meeting at the Capitol in Washington, D.C., on March 26, 1964.

The week before his assassination, Malcolm X steps from his car in front of his firebombed Queens home.

> "America needs to understand Islam, because this is the one religion that erases from its society the race problem."
>
> MALCOLM X

Eastern heads of state to charge the U.S. government with discrimination and genocide before the United Nations.

Many of Malcolm's admirers have speculated that, had he lived, his leadership might have changed the course of the decade. But none can say so definitively, because on the afternoon of February 21, 1965, as he began to address an OAAU gathering at the Audubon Ballroom in Harlem, Malcolm X was killed. Two men created a diversion, while three others standing near the

stage shot him repeatedly. All five assassins were eventually captured and later identified as members of the NOI's Temple Number Twenty-five in Newark.

Cleveland Sellers was among the many SNCC members who attended Malcolm's February 27 funeral. "We felt like we were bringing a message to Malcolm," Sellers has said. "And that message was, we heard you, we were listening. We have taken the best of what you offered, and we will continue to incorporate that movement in our struggle."

Elijah Muhammad sits surrounded by aides during a public appearance in Chicago just five days after the Malcolm X assassination. The bodyguards and microphones have been placed carefully around him to interfere with the sight lines of any potential assassin.

OVERLEAF: **Police escort** a dying Malcolm to Columbia Presbyterian Hospital, just across the street from the Audubon Ballroom, where he was shot.

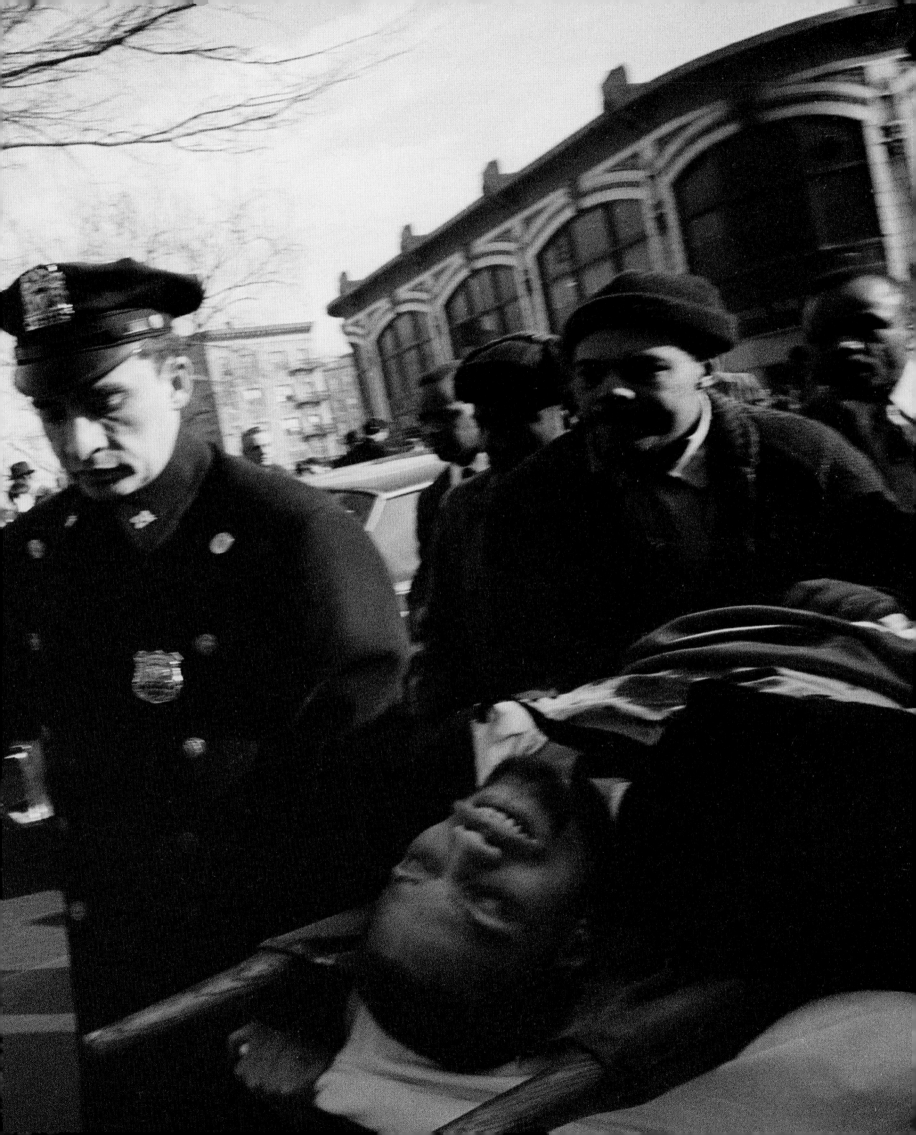

PART III
BECOMING FREE

As the 1960s began, young Negroes often found themselves at odds with members of their parents' generation about the direction the civil rights movement should take. Most student activists favored direct action, while older black leaders, many of them NAACP stalwarts, felt the battle should remain in the courts and not be taken into the streets. One reason for this difference was that, as in all eras, young people were generally less patient and more willing to take risks than older people, who had more to lose. What happened in the end was that the students went off on their own.

"Nonviolent tactics, particularly when accompanied by a rationale based on Christian principles," historian Clayborne Carson has written, "offered black students an appealing combination of rewards: a sense of moral superiority, an emotional release through militancy, and a possibility of achieving desegregation." These emotional aspects were particularly accentuated once student leaders began making the transition from part-time to full-time activism. The mental strains that resulted from full-time commitment in turn created emotional needs that were met, more often than not, by a moralistic passion that rejected all compromise.

Police arrest three sit-in demonstrators in Cambridge, Maryland, in July 1963, after they refused to leave a local lunch counter that wouldn't serve them.

Sitting In

1960

It took two decades of careful legal block-building to obtain the *Brown* decision. Those who carried out this work, all members of the NAACP, belonged to a black professional class that W. E. B. Du Bois would have instantly recognized as the Talented Tenth he had envisioned half a century earlier. After *Brown*, however, this elite continued to press the same strategy of block-building with the same methodical patience but not the same results.

Their children were much less patient. Contemporaries of Emmett Till, they had just entered adolescence when the Supreme Court overturned *Plessy v. Ferguson* in May 1954.

This comic book of the Montgomery boycott, created by the FOR for people who didn't like to read, was especially popular on college campuses.

Lacking historical perspective, they expected change to come much more quickly than it did. Five years after *Brown*, as many settled into college life, they found themselves staying up late at night discussing why more hadn't changed. The idea of racial segregation seemed almost silly to them. Furthermore, the isolated gains achieved by their parents in such places as Montgomery and Little Rock made the remaining inconsistencies of Jim Crow seem that much more irrational. What sense did it make for blacks and whites to go to school together and ride on buses together but not eat together in restaurants or drink from the same water fountains?

Even so, little was expected of black college students, who were generally thought to be apathetic. In his landmark 1957 study *Black Bourgeoisie*, sociologist E. Franklin Frazier had argued that the principal goal of upwardly mobile middle-class blacks and their college-aged progeny was not racial equality but social assimilation. In other words, according to Frazier, young blacks didn't want to overturn the values and institutions of white society; they merely wanted to join.

A student stages a lonely sit-in at a closed Nashville lunch counter in March 1960. The store manager has placed packages of linens on surrounding stools to discourage other protesters.

THE WOOLWORTH'S LUNCH COUNTER

Ezell Blair Jr., Franklin McCain, Joseph McNeil, and David Richmond entered North Carolina Agricultural and Technical College in Greensboro together in the fall of 1959. They became fast friends, eating together, studying together, and talking together about whatever happened to be on their minds. Often, their conversations turned to the subject of racial justice.

They assigned each other books to read. One was Robert E. Davis's 1954 work *The American Negro's Dilemma*, the foreword to which began: "It is the considered view of this writer that the problem of the Negro in the United States is basically the result of his own actions, or rather inactions. Whatever the original cause of the present dilemma, it is the Negro's apathy which is largely responsible for its continued existence.... Until the Negro realizes that he must do something on his own to alleviate his burdens, he will constantly be plagued by double standards of justice, cynicism, and other nefarious treatment."

One Sunday night, McNeil said to his friends, "It's time that we take some action now." They had recently watched a television program on Gandhi and had been deeply impressed by his use of nonviolence to achieve political ends. Additionally, at least one of them had read a comic book about the Montgomery bus boycott, published by the Fellowship of Reconciliation, that instructed readers in the tactics of passive resistance. The four freshmen were, therefore, aware of King's activities, although he wasn't their inspiration.

"The individual who had probably the most influence on us was Gandhi," McCain has said. "Yes, Martin Luther King's name was well known... [but] he was not the individual that we had upmost in mind." Later, Blair told a reporter that his motivation had come from the realization that older blacks were too fearful and that it was "time for someone to wake up and change the situation."

Their plan was to visit a downtown lunch counter, where, by custom, blacks weren't served. The counter they chose belonged to the F. W. Woolworth Co. store on North Elm Street. They chose Woolworth's because the chain explicitly advertised for Negro business.

The four North Carolina A&T freshmen who began the sit-in movement in Greensboro leave Woolworth's following their initial February 1 protest. They are (left to right) David Richmond, Franklin McCain, Ezell Blair Jr., and Joseph McNeil.

They entered the store about 4:30 P.M. on Monday, February 1, 1960. McNeil bought a tube of toothpaste. McCain bought some toiletries. Then all four sat down at the lunch counter and nervously ordered coffee. They were refused, McCain recalled, "and, of course, we said, 'We just beg to disagree with you. We've, in fact, already been served; you've served us already, and that's just not quite true.' The attendant or waitress was a little bit dumbfounded, just didn't know what to say under circumstances like that. And we said, 'We wonder why you'd invite us in to serve us at one counter and deny service at another.'"

They showed her their receipts and pointed out that Woolworth's wasn't a private club requiring membership for service. "That didn't go over too well," McCain continued, "simply because I don't really think she understood what we were talking about." So she called the store manager, a career Woolworth's employee named C. L. Harris, who explained that "corporate headquarters" set the lunch-counter policy, which he was not empowered to change.

About this time, a policeman entered the store and began pacing behind the students, slapping his billy club rhythmically into his palm. He was, McCain remembered, "just looking mean and red and a little bit upset and a little bit disgusted. And you had the feeling that he didn't know what the hell to do. You had the feeling that this is the first time that this big bad man with the gun and the club has been pushed in a corner, and he's got absolutely no defense, and the thing that's killing him more than anything else—he doesn't know

> "Some whites wrote off the episodes as the work of 'outside agitators.' But even they conceded that the seeds of dissent had fallen in fertile soil."
>
> *NEW YORK TIMES* REPORTER CLAUDE SITTON IN A 1960 ARTICLE

A **waitress at an S. H. Kress** lunch counter in Oklahoma City serves black patrons after a two-day protest in August 1958 reversed the segregated seating policy at a nearby soda fountain.

The First Sit-Ins

As early as 1942, the year that it was founded, the Congress of Racial Equality staged sit-ins at Chicago-area restaurants where blacks were being denied service. Some of these protests were successful, but the tactic didn't catch on regionally or nationally for several reasons. One was that CORE's membership was still very small; another was that its members were primarily white pacifists with no real connection to the black masses.

The first black students to carry out a sit-in were members of the NAACP Youth Council in Oklahoma City. Their campaign began on August 19, 1958, and ended two weeks later with four of the five targeted stores changing their seating policies. Learning of this success through NAACP channels, the Youth Council in Wichita began its own protest campaign on August 29. Integration in Wichita took only four days, with the sit-ins next spreading to Enid, Tulsa, and Stillwater in Oklahoma and to Kansas City, Kansas—but no farther.

what he can or what he cannot do." This was, the students realized, the power of nonviolence. Their action had been provocative—but not quite to the point at which the policeman felt justified in resorting to violence himself.

The reaction of white customers in the store was mixed. A pair of elderly white ladies told the young men kindly, "You should have done this ten years ago." Others cursed at them: "Nasty, dirty niggers, you know you don't belong here!" Nevertheless, the four remained on their stools until the five-and-dime closed at 5:30 P.M. Then, because a sizable

White youth described by reporters as "the duck-tailed, leather-jacket group" hold seats for whites at the Woolworth's lunch counter in downtown Greensboro. Many cursed and threatened the Negro protesters who sought service there.

crowd had gathered outside in front of the store, they left through the side exit.

"If it's possible to know what it means to have your soul cleansed," McCain has said, "I felt pretty clean at that time. I probably felt better on that day than I've ever felt in my life....I felt as though I had gained my manhood, so to speak."

THE SIT-INS SPREAD

Word spread quickly, and even before the freshmen returned to the A&T campus, students there were talking about what they had done. There had been sit-ins before, and some of those had even been successful, but as Fisk University student Diane Nash was later to recall, "We started feeling the power of an idea whose time had come."

Later that night, Blair, McCain, McNeil, and Richmond met with fifty other students to form the Student Executive Committee for Justice. The next morning, they led a group of twenty-seven A&T students back to the North Elm Street Woolworth's—where, observed by several members of the local press, they sat in for another two and a half hours before leaving around 12:30 P.M.

On Wednesday, the third day of the protest, students began arriving at the Woolworth's about 11 A.M. and at one point occupied all but three of the sixty-six lunch-counter seats. (These three were taken up by the idle waitresses, who had no one to serve.) On Thursday, when the protest was expanded to include

Civil rights sympathizers picket a New York City Woolworth's in April 1960, protesting lunch-counter segregation at the chain's southern stores. According to Woolworth's management, the company was simply "abiding by local custom."

the S. H. Kress & Co. store half a block away, the demonstrators were joined for the first time by white students from the Greensboro Women's College, a division of the University of North Carolina.

These three young women told reporters that they felt it was their "moral obligation" to support the Negro students. However, according to a report filed by one of the police detectives present, "The situation became immediately explosive upon their joining the colored group and remained that way until the store closed. Their presence among the colored students acted to inflame the feelings of all spectators and also the white students who were there in opposition to the colored demonstration."

On Saturday, a telephoned bomb threat forced Harris to close the store. As it turned out, there was no bomb, but city officials were thankful for the call because it defused what was becoming at Woolworth's an increasingly combustible situation. That night, at a mass meeting, the A&T students granted a mayoral request for a two-week truce while Woolworth's and Kress officials reconsidered their seating polices.

On February 21, the day that the truce was set to expire, the Student Executive Committee

Protesters receive no service at this Arlington, Virginia, lunch counter, where the staff walked out rather than serve them.

for Justice announced that it would continue to abstain from direct action while it pursued "peaceful channels of negotiation" and waited to see how the white community would ultimately respond. Soon, a committee appointed by Greensboro mayor George Roach recommended the adoption of integrated seating with a small section reserved for whites only. When downtown store and restaurant managers balked, however, the settlement effort failed, and on April 1, the sit-ins resumed.

According to one student, it was "like a fever. Everyone wanted to go." In the end, more than 90 percent of the A&T student body took part in the demonstrations, either sitting in at or picketing targeted stores, and participation percentages at the four other colleges in the area—white, black,

and integrated—were nearly as high. McCain later estimated that, at its height, the Greensboro movement could muster between ten and fifteen thousand students, allowing it to target any establishment that refused service to Negroes.

Meanwhile, the sit-ins spread. Over the first weekend, more than a hundred students met in Winston-Salem to organize demonstrations there, beginning on Monday, February 8. By Wednesday, February 10, protests were also under way in Durham, Charlotte, and Raleigh. By the end of the week, they had spread to High Point; Rock Hill in South Carolina; and Hampton, Concord, Norfolk, and Portsmouth in Virginia. By the end of the month, there were significant student protests taking place in more than thirty cities in seven southern states.

Although the initial sit-ins were polite and peaceful, the student participants gradually

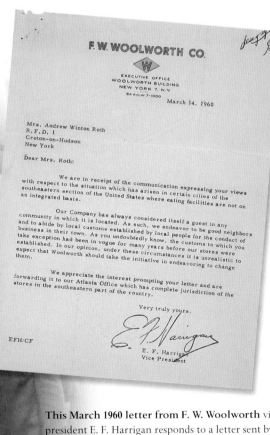

This March 1960 letter from F. W. Woolworth vice president E. F. Harrigan responds to a letter sent by a New Yorker objecting to lunch-counter segregation. Harrigan writes that expecting his company to take the lead in changing this "custom" is "unrealistic."

A street cleaner removes a sign that appeared in Montgomery, Alabama, after a March 1960 sit-in.

James Lawson

1928–

The son and grandson of Methodist ministers, James Lawson received his first preacher's license in 1947, the year of his graduation from high school. At college in Ohio, he became a pacifist and joined the Fellowship of Reconciliation. After refusing the Korean War draft in 1951, he was sentenced to three years in prison. Thirteen months later, he was released into the custody of missionaries who sent him to teach at Hislop College, a missionary school in Nagpur, India, where Lawson spent the next three years.

Nashville police officers escort James Lawson to a paddy wagon after arresting him on March 5, 1960.

While in Nagpur, he studied the recent Indian independence campaign and became an expert on Gandhism. Returning to the United States, he enrolled at the Oberlin School of Theology, where he met King at a dinner in February 1956. Because of his experiences in India, "Lawson was ahead of King as an activist," Taylor Branch has written, "but King had already realized Lawson's dream of starting a nonviolent mass movement."

A year later, Lawson decided to become a full-time activist and joined the FOR staff as its southern field secretary, opening a field office in Nashville and enrolling at Vanderbilt Divinity School to continue his studies. Meanwhile, Lawson traveled through the South, often in the company of Glenn Smiley, holding workshops to train black and white volunteers in the philosophy and tactics of nonviolence.

became more assertive in their requests for service, and the segregationists, especially those of high school age, began to respond with violence, underscoring the differences between the two groups. The contrast between the neatly dressed, strictly disciplined students on the one hand and the hooliganish white teenagers on the other was so stark, in fact, that even southern whites took notice.

In a widely read February 22 editorial, James J. Kilpatrick, editor of the strongly segregationist *Richmond News Leader*, commented on the juxtaposition: "Here were the colored students, in coats, white shirts, ties, and one of them was reading Goethe and one was taking notes from a biology text. And here, on the sidewalk outside, was a gang of white boys come to heckle, a ragtail rabble, slack-jawed, black-jacketed, grinning fit to kill, and some of them, God save the mark, were waving the proud and honored flag of the Southern States in the last war fought by gentlemen. Eheu! It gives one pause."

NASHVILLE

In some of the communities to which the movement spread, students claimed later that they had been planning sit-ins long before the Greensboro students acted in February 1960. In many instances, these

claims were born of jealousy, but not so in Nashville, where a group of black students had been schooling themselves in the philosophy and practice of Gandhian nonviolence.

The mentor of this group was Vanderbilt divinity student James Lawson, who initiated a series of Tuesday night workshops in nonviolence. Among Lawson's pupils was Chicagoan Diane Nash—whose school, Fisk, was one of twelve colleges and universities in the Nashville area. "I remember we used to role-play, and we would do things like pretend we were sitting at lunch counters in order to prepare ourselves to do that," she has said. "We would practice things such as how to protect your head from a beating, how to protect each other." At other times, they

The first organized sit-in in Nashville (shown here) took place February 13 at the downtown Woolworth's. Student protesters often worked in shifts so that every seat could remain occupied from opening to closing.

Young white men attack a sit-in demonstrator in Nashville on Big Saturday, February 27, the day the backlash began. Although eighty-one civil rights activists were arrested for "disturbing the peace," none of their attackers was detained.

would have to sit quietly while other members of the group, pretending to be segregationists, cursed, poked, and spit at them. Another member of the group, John Lewis, described the training as "the most important thing we were doing."

In December 1959, Lawson's group experimented with "test" sit-ins. They walked into several department-store restaurants and asked to be served. When they were refused, they asked to speak with the manager, whom they engaged in conversation about the store's segregation policy before withdrawing politely. Then, on Wednesday, February 3, 1960, Douglas Moore, a Methodist minister in Durham, called his friend Lawson to tell him about the protests overrunning North Carolina and asked whether the Nashville students wanted to join in.

Lawson's group held its first actual lunch-counter sit-ins on Saturday, February 13, after which the opposition mobilized as well. The first

violence came on February 27, when white teenagers began pulling student demonstrators off their stools, shoving them against the lunch counters, and pummeling them. "Curiously," according to Paul LaPrad, a white Fisk student who took part in the sit-in at McClellan's variety store, "there were police inside the store when the white teenagers and others [began] insulting us, blowing smoke in our faces, grinding out cigarette butts on our backs, and finally pulling us off our stool and beating us." Yet those policeman chose not to intervene and, when they did act, arrested only the demonstrators. The charge was disorderly conduct.

Nashville's black community responded by raising nearly fifty thousand dollars in bail money and persuading Z. A. Looby, a prominent black attorney, to represent the eighty-one defendants. In court, however, the trial judge turned his back on Looby and sat facing the wall as Looby presented his case. Eventually, Looby simply threw up his hands, cut short his presentation, and, staring directly at the judge's back, said, "What's the use!" before sitting down again. The judge then turned around,

pronounced the defendants guilty, and fined them each fifty dollars plus court costs.

The demonstrations continued, however, and by April, the Nashville business community was feeling the pressure. An estimated 98 percent of black customers were withholding their business from noncompliant stores, and even whites who preferred segregation were staying away, fearful of the disruptions caused by the protests. Something had to give.

Students serve time in a Nashville jail after being arrested in March 1960 for participating in lunch-counter sit-ins.

wanted to offer Negroes lunch-counter service weeks earlier, if only to bring back their business, but hadn't in fear of segregationist retaliation. Now, they simply avoided the responsibility by holding the mayor accountable.

"To me, the whole thing was like I had the feeling that we were involved in something like a crusade in a sense," John Lewis remembered. "It was a sense of duty. You had an obligation to do it—to redeem the city. Or, as Dr. King said so many times, to redeem the soul of America."

THE SHAW CONFERENCE

Once the sit-in movement demonstrated that young blacks could initiate effective protests without the guidance of older leaders, some

At 5:30 A.M. on April 19, dynamite hurled from a passing car destroyed Looby's home. Later that day, twenty-five hundred outraged students and community members marched on City Hall, where Diane Nash asked the mayor, who had been waiting for them on the building's front steps, if he personally believed that it was wrong for blacks to be served at the checkout counter and not the lunch. In response, Ben West nodded yes, he thought it was wrong.

"They asked me some pretty soul-searching questions, and one that was addressed to me as a man," Mayor West explained later. "And I found

that I had to answer it frankly and honestly— that I did not agree that it was morally right for someone to sell them merchandise and refuse them service. And I had to answer it just exactly like that.…It was a moral question—one that a *man* had to answer, not a politician."

The next day, store managers in Nashville began using the mayor's words as political cover for changing their seating policies. Most had

Nashville mayor Ben West (second from left) greets the Rev. C. T. Vivian (to West's immediate left) and Diane Nash on the steps of the Nashville City Hall.

John Lewis

1940–

John Lewis grew up on a farm in Pike County, Alabama, about fifty miles south of Montgomery. He was listening to the radio one Sunday morning in early 1955 when he heard Martin Luther King Jr. preach for the first time. "I didn't catch his name until the sermon was finished," Lewis wrote forty years later in his autobiography, "but the voice held me right from the start. But even more than his voice, it was his message that sat me bolt upright with amazement."

In the sermon that Lewis heard, King used St. Paul's letter to the Corinthians to explicate the problems that blacks were having at present in Montgomery. "This was the first time I had ever heard something I would soon

learn was called the Social Gospel," Lewis continued. "I was on fire with the words I was hearing. I felt that this man…was speaking directly to me."

The next morning, Lewis went to the local public library and found an old newspaper article about King, which mentioned that he had attended Morehouse College. "I decided right then and there that that was where I was going to go to school," Lewis wrote.

Sadly, his impoverished family couldn't afford the tuition, and his grades didn't merit a scholarship. But during his senior year in high school, Lewis learned of the American Baptist Theological Seminary in Nashville. This small school for black ministerial candidates charged no tuition and provided jobs for its students in exchange for their room and board. Lewis applied immediately and within a matter of weeks was accepted, becoming the first member of his family ever to attend college.

Ella Baker

1903–1986

Ella Baker grew up in North Carolina on the same land her maternal grandparents had once worked as slaves. After her graduation from Shaw University in 1927, she moved to Harlem, where she helped organize black consumer cooperatives during the Great Depression.

In 1941, Baker joined the NAACP's national staff, serving first as an assistant field secretary and later as director of branches. The work she did made her an expert on black activists and black activism in the South and prompted her to work within the top-down NAACP for more of a bottom-up approach. Failing to accomplish this, she resigned her staff job in 1946.

students began discussing the possibility of forming an organization to consolidate their newly won influence within the civil rights movement. The idea also occurred to Ella Baker, who was then preparing to leave her job as executive director of the Southern Christian Leadership Conference (because she had become increasingly skeptical of King's cautious leadership). Before Baker left, however, she invited the leaders of the various sit-in movements to an Easter weekend conference at Shaw University in Raleigh, her alma mater.

According to Julian Bond, who represented the Atlanta students at the conference, Baker "was very concerned about two things. One, she thought that SCLC hadn't been involved in the sit-in movement as much as it should have been, and by that I think she meant Dr. King. And, secondly, she felt that the student movement was really directionless, that it had narrow vision and thought the whole world was nothing but lunch counters." Baker's purpose in sponsoring the April 15–17, 1960, conference was to help the students come to terms with the leadership roles they had suddenly taken up.

Already, existing organizations from the Congress of Racial Equality (CORE) to the Communist party had begun to seek the affiliation of the student movement, tempting it with lawyers, money, and advice. But Baker appreciated the students' psychological need to remain independent of adult control and

encouraged them, against the wishes of her SCLC superiors, to go their own way—which was, of course, their intent.

The Shaw conference attracted more than two hundred delegates—most, but not all, of whom

were black. They represented fifty-two colleges and high schools in thirteen southern states. Also attending were representatives from eleven border and northern states, who participated but did not vote. "This move," according to sociologist Martin Oppenheimer, who wrote his 1963 dissertation on the student sit-in movement, "was apparently dictated not only by an acute sense of public relations (by attempting to offset opponents' charges of 'outside meddling in our affairs'), but also by a genuine feeling on the part of the Southerners that this was to remain their movement, indigenous, Southern, and predominantly Negro, not controlled by any organization, adult, Northern, or otherwise."

The large turnout was helped by the presence of Dr. King, who praised the students for "moving away from tactics which are suitable

This group portrait taken at the April 1960 SNCC founding conference at Shaw University shows (clockwise from the front) Martin Luther King, Wyatt T. Walker, Ralph Abernathy, Douglas Moore, James Lawson, and Fred Shuttlesworth.

James Lawson sits with fellow attendees on a Shaw University lawn during the April 1960 conference at which the Student Nonviolent Coordinating Committee was founded.

merely for gradual and long-term change"—a reference to the NAACP's legal strategy. The star of the conference, however, turned out to be Lawson, who had just been expelled from Vanderbilt for his involvement with the sit-ins. A few months older than King, Lawson delivered an electrifying keynote address that focused on moral and spiritual themes but also explicitly criticized the "too conservative" NAACP for its preoccupation with fund-raising and lawsuits at the expense of direct action.

At the end of the conference, after explicitly affirming their commitment to nonviolence, the delegates voted to form the independent Student Nonviolent Coordinating Committee (SNCC). Marion Barry, a Fisk University graduate student in chemistry (and later the controversial mayor of Washington, D.C.), was elected chair, and Baker's offer of office space at SCLC headquarters in Atlanta was accepted.

SNCC

Curiously, during this early formative period, SNCC (pronounced "snick") was parented by two young white women. To run the new office in Atlanta until a permanent administrator could be found, Baker recruited twenty-four-year-old Jane Stembridge, a Virginian then studying at the Union Theological Seminary in New York City. Equally important was Constance Curry, then director of southern programs for the National Student Association (NSA). At a time when SNCC had few resources, Curry made her equipment available to Stembridge and diverted funds to SNCC from a sixty-thousand-dollar grant that NSA had been awarded to support "human relations" workshops in the South.

"Whereas SNCC appeared to outsiders and even to many black student leaders to be merely a clearinghouse for the exchange of information about localized protest movements," Clayborne Carson has written, "to [Stembridge and Curry] it was potentially an organization for expanding the struggle beyond its campus base to include all classes of blacks."

This was a view that also came to be shared by Robert Moses, a twenty-six-year-old teacher of mathematics at Horace Mann, an elite private Jewish high school in New York City. "The sit-ins

New York," Bond admitted. "He wore glasses and picketed *for hours* by himself. His views and concerns were much broader than ours. We thought he was smarter than we were."

Stembridge particularly welcomed Moses's presence and talked to him at length about the SNCC strategy conference she was planning for that October. Among her problems was finding student activists in Alabama, Louisiana, and Mississippi, where the sit-in movement hadn't yet taken hold. According to Moses, he had already concluded that there wouldn't be much meaningful work for him in Atlanta that summer, "so when Jane suggested that I consider traveling and collecting names for SNCC's fall conference, I was open to the idea." Ella Baker made a list of her NAACP contacts in those states, and Moses was on his way.

Moses knew that, according to the Supreme Court's 1941 *Mitchell* decision, interstate bus companies couldn't segregate their passengers, but it still remained dangerous for Negroes in the South to challenge this custom. "Because I was now representing the student movement, I was

expected to ride in the front of the bus," Moses remembered. "I sat in the front until the bus neared the Alabama line. Then some kind of instinct made me move to the back. It was lucky I did because the highway patrol stopped the bus at the Alabama line; someone had alerted them that a black passenger was riding in the front. The patrolman, however, couldn't tell who; in the back mine was just another indistinguishable face among the black folk."

Moses's journey, which he undertook at his own expense, began the subsequent transformation of SNCC from a coordinator into an agent of change.

Robert Moses teaches mathematics at the Horace Mann School in a photograph from the 1960 Horace Mann yearbook.

woke me up," Moses recalled. "[They] hit me powerfully, in the soul as well as the brain." Thus inspired, he joined Bayard Rustin in opening an SCLC office in Harlem and that summer, carrying a letter of introduction from Rustin to Baker, he traveled by bus to Atlanta to volunteer at the organization's headquarters.

"Miss Baker was out of town when I arrived," Moses continued. "No one else directed me toward work that first day in the office, but I saw Jane stuffing envelopes and joined her, startling her a bit she told me later because I didn't even ask if it was all right for me to help."

Through Stembridge, Moses met Julian Bond and other leaders of the Atlanta student movement. Because Baker actually had little for Moses to do, he often joined Bond and the others on picket lines organized to protest employment discrimination at local A&P supermarkets. Initially suspicious of the northerner Moses, the southerners eventually came around. "We thought he was a Communist because he was from

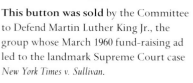

This button was sold by the Committee to Defend Martin Luther King Jr., the group whose March 1960 fund-raising ad led to the landmark Supreme Court case *New York Times v. Sullivan.*

ATLANTA

The first Atlanta sit-ins—which had begun on March 3, 1960—were limited but well organized. On March 15, for example, more than two hundred students had sat in at ten different public eating establishments in downtown Atlanta, including

Martin Luther King Jr. meets with a group of college students in the SCLC's Atlanta office in September 1960. The student sit-in organizers include Julian Bond (second from right).

cafeterias at the state capitol, county courthouse, City Hall, and railroad and bus stations. Under orders from Gov. Ernest Vandiver, police arrested seventy-seven demonstrators using a recently (and unanimously) passed state law making it illegal to refuse to leave a place of business after being ordered to do so by the management. After the arrests, the pressure on the students from school administrators and Atlanta's black elders became much more focused. They counseled delay and urged that downtown merchants who donated to the city's prestigious black colleges be spared. Two days later, a mass meeting of fourteen hundred students was held at which the sit-ins were temporarily suspended.

In fact, the Atlanta sit-ins weren't resumed for seven months, during which time the movement leadership continued to organize. They stocked up on two-way radios, protective parkas, and other gear while preparing laminated picket signs that wouldn't smear in the rain.

The student leaders also worked out a plan. Although many of their followers wanted to renew the protests immediately upon returning to school in September, the Atlanta movement co-chairs, Lonnie C. King and Herschelle Sullivan, held out for an October 19 start. This date was significant for two reasons: It came just three days after the close of the second SNCC conference and only three weeks before the November 1960 presidential election.

"Our strategy was to get Martin King arrested with us and do it in the middle of October, so as to influence the election," Lonnie King has explained. "The plan was we would send telegrams to Nixon and to Kennedy and ask them to take a position on the civil rights movement here. We thought that with Dr. King being involved in it, that would create enough of a national uproar in the black community and we would really see where these guys stand."

At first, Dr. King told Sullivan that he couldn't take part because he was currently serving a suspended sentence on a traffic violation and Wyatt T. Walker, Baker's SCLC replacement, was concerned that another arrest might jeopardize that suspension. King had been pulled over in May 1960 by a patrolman in suburban De Kalb County, just outside Atlanta, because the white passenger in his car had made his vehicle look suspicious. Unable to find anything else wrong, the police officer charged King with driving under an improper permit because he had not yet surrendered his Alabama driver's license even though he had moved back to Atlanta from Montgomery three months earlier. County judge Oscar Mitchell sentenced King to twelve months in jail, an unheard-of punishment for a first-offense misdemeanor that didn't involve dangerous driving, but then suspended the sentence in lieu of a twenty-five-dollar fine.

Others also asked King to participate, but he kept declining until he received a call from Lonnie King on October 18. A member of Dr. King's own congregation at Ebenezer Baptist, the student leader personally urged his pastor to reconsider: "I called him, and he gave me the long story, and I said, 'Well, Martin, you've got to go to jail.' I went through all the ramifications of it. I said, 'You are the spiritual leader of the

A white man sprays insect repellent along the lunch counter at Woolworth's main downtown Atlanta store on October 20. Nearly one hundred Negroes had been sitting in there for three hours. The store manager subsequently closed the counter, requiring the protesters to exit.

THE JAILING OF KING

At precisely eleven o'clock the next morning at eight different eating establishments around town, black students asked for and were denied service. The group waiting at the elegant Magnolia Room on the sixth floor of Rich's included Dr. King. The chairman of the department-store board interceded personally but, failing to persuade the protesters to leave, had them arrested for trespassing.

ordering them to continue holding King for violating the terms of his suspended sentence.

Early Tuesday morning, King emerged from the Fulton County jail in the custody of two detectives, who took him in a waiting squad car to De Kalb. That afternoon, Judge Mitchell revoked King's probation and ordered him to serve four months at hard labor on a road gang, beginning immediately. The decision was harsh, vindictive, and, in fact, illegal (because judges were required to grant bail on misdemeanor charges and Mitchell hadn't). Thus King faced the very real prospect of hard

> "I think the maxiumum sentence for Martin Luther King might do him good, might make a law-abiding citizen out of him, and teach him to respect the law of Georgia."
>
> A SPOKESMAN FOR GEORGIA GOVERNOR ERNEST VANDIVER

By prior arrangement, King and his thirty-five fellow defendants refused to post bail, and they were locked up pending trial. (It would be the first night King ever spent in jail.) The next day, two thousand more students picketed the restaurants, and twenty-five were arrested. None of these accepted bail, either. One of the reasons was the rousing "jail, no bail" speech delivered by Jim Lawson at the SNCC October conference, in which he had argued that accepting release on bond relieved the pressure on the system while refusing bail pressured "adults...to end the system which [puts] us in jail." The demonstrators' refusal to accept release prompted Atlanta's sympathetic mayor, William Hartsfield, to broker a weekend deal in which the county charges were dropped in exchange for a truce similar to that granted eight months earlier in Greensboro. A new obstacle developed on Monday morning, however, when jail officials received a bench warrant from Judge Mitchell in De Kalb County

time and told his crying wife, Coretta, who was six months' pregnant with their third child, that she would also have to be strong.

Meanwhile, Wyatt T. Walker and King's chief lawyer, Donald Hollowell, went into crisis mode.

Already under arrest, Martin Luther King Jr. walks beside Lonnie King as they pass through the picket line outside Rich's on October 19. The face of police captain R. E. Little can be seen over Lonnie King's right shoulder.

Picketers parade outside Rich's department store in downtown Atlanta on October 19, protesting the store's segregated eating facilities. At top can be seen the pedestrian bridge on which Martin Luther King met Lonnie King that morning.

movement, and you were born in Atlanta, Georgia, and I think it might add tremendous impetus if you would go.' He said, 'Well, where are you going to go tomorrow, L. C.?' He always called me L. C., because I grew up in the church down there. I said, 'I'm going to be on the bridge down at Rich's.' He said, 'Well, I'll meet you on the bridge tomorrow at ten o'clock.' So that's what happened."

In their view, according to Taylor Branch, "the state road gang meant cutthroat inmates and casually dismissed murders. King had to be freed or he would be dead. This was the emergency message that Walker and a band of colleagues sent to every person they could think of who might conceivably have influence."

Harris Wofford in a 1961 White House photograph. His duties there included helping Sargent Shriver form the Peace Corps.

Around eight o'clock on Wednesday morning, Hollowell called the De Kalb County jail to let the authorities know he would soon be arriving with a writ of habeas corpus demanding King's release. He was told not to bother because, during the night, King had been transferred to the maximum-security prison at Reidsville. When Coretta Scott King learned what had happened, she immediately called Harris Wofford. Along with black newspaper publisher and political operative Louis Martin, Wofford ran the civil rights office of John F. Kennedy's Democratic presidential campaign. Nearly hysterical, Mrs. King told Wofford, who had known her husband since the Montgomery bus boycott, of the secret middle-of-the-night transfer and stressed that no one knew what might happen next.

THE CALL TO CORETTA

With the exception of Wofford's direct superior, JFK brother-in-law Sargent Shriver, the candidate's top aides were paying little attention to the King situation. To the extent that they thought about it at all, they considered King's imprisonment the result of southern ignorance and believed that he would be released sooner or later. For this reason, they avoided returning Wofford's repeated telephone calls so that they wouldn't have to listen to his nagging.

Wofford finally got through to Shriver in Chicago, where Kennedy had just finished breakfasting with fifty important Illinois businessmen. Wofford reached Shriver in a

A police detective escorts a handcuffed Martin Luther King Jr. into the De Kalb County courthouse on the morning of Tuesday, October 25.

special holding suite at O'Hare Airport, where the candidate was consulting with a few top aides while his plane was being readied. Speaking as succinctly as he could, Wofford passed on the gist of what Mrs. King had told him and described her frantic tone.

He knew that campaign manager Robert Kennedy, after avoiding the issue of civil rights for months, would never allow his brother to make a controversial public statement just two weeks before the election. So Wofford told Shriver that he and Martin had another idea, one that was much less controversial: Senator Kennedy should simply call Mrs. King to express concern for her husband and sympathy for her own ordeal. "All he's got to do," Wofford said, "is show a little heart. He can even say he doesn't have all the facts in the case." Such a call, Wofford assured Shriver, "would reverberate all through the Negro community."

"All right, all right," Shriver replied, and asked for Mrs. King's home number in Atlanta.

Bobby and Jack Kennedy confer at a 1959 meeting of the Senate Rackets Committee. RFK served as the group's chief counsel before resigning to run JFK's campaign.

"I know this must be very hard for you," Kennedy told Mrs. King. "I understand you are expecting a baby, and I just wanted you to know that I was thinking about you and Dr. King. If there is anything I can do to help, please feel free to call on me." Mrs. King's reply was equally brief. "I certainly appreciate your concern," she said. "I would appreciate anything you could do to help." The entire call lasted little more than a minute.

When Robert Kennedy at the campaign's Washington headquarters learned about the call

As it turned out, Robert Kennedy's tirade was an overreaction. As Wofford and Martin had hoped, the white press played down the story, which the *New York Times* buried in a two-inch report on the bottom of page twenty-two. This would have given the civil rights office an opportunity to publicize the phone call quietly among black voters had it not been for Robert Kennedy's ban.

A bumper sticker from the 1960 Kennedy presidential campaign.

Then Shriver waited a few minutes until Kennedy had retired to a bedroom to rest before pitching him on the call. As Shriver had hoped, Kennedy was too tired to bring his staff back for another consultation and wearily agreed. After Shriver dialed the number, Kennedy took the phone.

later that day, he savaged Shriver with a curse-laden rebuke that permanently damaged their family relationship. "You bomb-throwers have lost the whole campaign," he stormed before hanging up the phone. Then he chewed out Wofford and Martin and ordered them not to involve the campaign in the King case ever again.

THE MARGIN OF VICTORY

On Thursday morning, October 27, Donald Hollowell finally persuaded Judge Mitchell to obey the law and grant King bail. Draining down the SCLC treasury, Wyatt T. Walker chartered a private plane and flew King the 230 miles back to Atlanta in time for a mass meeting at Ebenezer that night.

Negroes for Nixon

Although Franklin Roosevelt had gradually lured most northern blacks into the Democratic party, the South's Negro elders had generally stayed with the party of Lincoln, and in 1960 they backed the Nixon-Lodge ticket. President Eisenhower's decision to send troops into Little Rock also benefited the vice president, and a number of influential blacks campaigned on his behalf, including Jackie Robinson.

When the story of King's arrest broke, John Calhoun, the head of the Nixon campaign in Atlanta's black precincts, implored the vice president to issue a supportive statement. "Kennedy didn't know King, but Nixon did," Calhoun recalled, referring to their 1957 meeting at independence ceremonies in Ghana. Nixon decided not to comment, figuring that he might lose some black votes but gain more white ones. In fact, Nixon still failed to carry such states as South Carolina, Alabama, and Georgia while losing enough Negro votes to cost him Illinois and other northern states.

Republican nominee Richard Nixon greets young black supporters at W. C. Handy Park in Memphis.

Keeping a promise that he had made earlier that day to Wofford, the Rev. Martin Luther King Sr. told the crowd at Ebenezer that, although he had been a lifelong Republican, he was now shifting his support to the Democrat. "It took courage to call my daughter-in-law at a time like this," Daddy King said of Kennedy. "He has the moral courage to stand up for what he knows is right. I've got all my votes, and I've got a suitcase, and I'm going to take them up there and dump them in his lap."

"It's time for all of us to take off our Nixon buttons."

MARTIN LUTHER KING SR.

Armed with this statement, Wofford and Martin now reported to Shriver that the black community's acute sensitivity to the King case was causing a political "sea change" in the North as well as the South. They begged to exploit it with a pamphlet promoting the candidate's call to Mrs. King. It could be printed quickly and distributed quietly to black churches in battleground states on the final Sunday before the election, thus minimizing the danger of a white backlash. But there was still Bobby Kennedy's ban. So Wofford and Martin pressed Shriver to speak with the campaign manager and get him to change his mind.

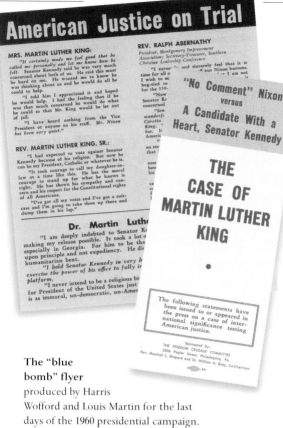

The "blue bomb" flyer produced by Harris Wofford and Louis Martin for the last days of the 1960 presidential campaign.

Shriver wasn't sure what to do. In the end, he decided to tell Bobby nothing and approved the plan himself. He told Wofford and Martin to print the pamphlets, for which he would find the money outside the campaign and take responsibility should Bobby find out. The following Sunday, about two million copies were distributed at black churches and schools, many in the Chicago area.

On Election Day, Kennedy won one of tightest presidential races ever. Afterward, analysts searched the results for issues and constituencies that might have made the difference. A postelection Gallup poll showed that Kennedy had won a surprising 70 percent of the Negro vote, or about 10 percent more than Adlai Stevenson had won in his 1956 race against Eisenhower. Closer inspection showed that in several key states, notably Illinois, this difference accounted for Kennedy's narrow margin of victory.

Because neither candidate had said much during the campaign about civil rights, and because Nixon's record on the issue was significantly stronger than Kennedy's, the only possible explanation for such a dramatic shift in

Coretta Scott King kisses her husband, Martin, after his release on a two-thousand-dollar bond from Reidsville state prison on Thursday, October 27. At the right are the Kings' two children, five-year-old Yolanda and three-year-old Martin Luther III.

African Independence

Many of the students who took part in the sit-ins considered their activism more than an isolated American phenomenon. Instead, they saw it as part a great international struggle then being waged for black liberation.

In March 1957, the Gold Coast, which had been a British colony for eighty-three years, became Ghana, the first sub-Saharan African nation to declare its independence

from a European empire. Other African colonies soon followed Ghana's example, and between June 30 and October 1, 1960, when the sit-ins were at their height, no fewer than ten colonies declared their independence.

These successes, many achieved by nationalist leaders trained at American colleges, helped prepare American blacks psychologically for the steps they were about to take. In the words of John Lewis, "Black Africans on their native continents were raising their own national flags for the first time in history, and we couldn't even get a hamburger and a Coke at a soda fountain."

Government officials carry Ghanian prime minister Kwame Nkrumah on their shoulders in April 1957 to celebrate their country's newly won independence from Great Britain.

the black vote was Kennedy's telephone call to Mrs. King. Little known at the time, the call nevertheless became, by Inauguration Day, the widely acknowledged tipping point of the election.

It also became more generally known at this time that Robert Kennedy had made a quiet call of his own on King's behalf. The morning after his tongue-lashing of Wofford and Martin, as King's fate hung in the balance, he had called Judge Mitchell to express the opinion that any decent judge would free King by sundown. The call violated not only his own ban on campaign involvement but also, and more importantly, basic legal ethics. The reason he made the call, he admitted later, was out of anger at how Mitchell's behavior was "screwing up my brother's campaign and making the country look ridiculous."

The white press had paid even less attention to the campaign manager's call than it had to the candidate's, but not so the black media, which had been reporting the interchange between King and the Kennedy campaign closely. Finally, the *Pittsburgh Courier* ran an editorial describing as "universal consensus" the opinion of one reader who said, "These white folks have now made Dr. Martin King Jr. the biggest Negro in the United States."

Negro voters line up to shake hands with President-elect Kennedy in January 1961. Some contemporary estimates suggested that Kennedy received as much as 80 percent of the black vote.

"These white folks have now made Dr. Martin King Jr. the biggest Negro in the United States"

A *PITTSBURGH COURIER* EDITORIAL

The Freedom Ride 1961

The day before John F. Kennedy's inauguration, Harris Wofford met with the president-elect to discuss the text of his inaugural address. The speech, to Wofford's dismay, was so focused on the Cold War that it contained not a single reference to civil rights. "You can't do this," Wofford pleaded. "There's an equal rights struggle here at home, too. You have to say something about it. You have to."

"Okay," Kennedy replied, and he inserted a few handwritten words near the beginning of the speech. Now the second sentence of the third paragraph read, "Let the word go forth from this time and place, to friend and foe alike, that the torch has been passed to a new generation of Americans—born in this century, tempered by war, disciplined by a hard and bitter peace, proud of our ancient heritage, and unwilling to witness or permit the slow undoing of those human rights to which this nation has always been committed today *at home* and around the world."

The reference, of course, proved hardly necessary. Kennedy's speech was so eloquent, so uplifting, so transformative that nearly all who

heard it felt as though the new president were speaking directly to their personal concerns—even though he was actually addressing the Soviets. The speech was so good, in fact, that it had important unintended consequences.

Students who had been active in the sit-in movement heard in Kennedy's words a recounting their recent life experience. When the president spoke of the need to "pay any price, bear any burden, meet any hardship…to assure the survival and the success of liberty," they thought of the risks they had taken, and would take, to end segregation in the South. When he spoke of the need to "ask not what your country can do for you, ask what you can do for your

country," they heard a call to action—even though, in truth, none was intended. As biographer Richard Reeves has observed, Kennedy "did not understand the reach and resonance of his own words."

Civil rights was simply not on Kennedy's early presidential agenda, and as he took office, he even backed away from the one promise he had made: to end discrimination in federally funded housing projects "with the stroke of a pen"—that is, by issuing an executive order to that effect. His excuse was that he didn't want to risk alienating southern Democrats, whose support he needed on the foreign policy issues that mattered most to him. For the same reason, the president also decided not to propose any new civil rights legislation.

Some Freedom Riders pose in Washington, D.C., on May 4, 1961, the day they began their bus trip. They are (from left to right) Edward Blankenheim, James Farmer, Genevieve Hughes, the Rev. B. Elton Cox, and Howard University sophomore Henry Thomas.

His policy to "litigate, not legislate" thus removed the issue from his desk to that of his brother, the new attorney general, who was in no particular rush himself. "My fundamental belief," Robert Kennedy said soon after taking office, "is that all people are created equal. Logically, it follows that integration should take place today everywhere....But other people have grown up with totally different backgrounds and mores, which we can't change overnight."

The Kennedys weren't bigots, and to the extent that they thought about prejudice, they considered it a waste of time and money. But neither were they passionate about the issue, and they remained willing to allow change to proceed slowly—a position disappointing to most movement leaders, who weren't satisfied with the knowledge that the Kennedys were friends at heart. In their view, the brothers owed blacks a large political debt, which civil rights leaders intended to collect.

TARGETING INTERSTATE BUSES

The seeds of the next crisis were sown on December 5, 1960, when the Supreme Court ruled in *Boynton v. Virginia*, a case argued by Thurgood Marshall, that interstate bus terminals could not operate as segregated facilities. The decision extended the Court's ruling in *Mitchell v. U.S.* (1941), which had outlawed segregated seating on interstate buses but not segregated restrooms and restaurants in interstate terminals. Even so, like the *Mitchell* decision before it, *Boynton* was widely ignored in the South, where WHITE and COLORED signs remained in place over terminal waiting rooms and coffee shops.

"When I became CORE's national director in 1961,"

A police sign indicates the whites-only waiting room at the Jackson bus terminal.

> "We felt we could count on the racists of the South to create a crisis so that the federal government would be compelled to enforce the law."
>
> JAMES FARMER

James Farmer
1920–1999

James Farmer grew up in Marshall, Texas, where his father, one of the few African-American Ph.D.s in the South, taught at Wiley College. Farmer himself entered Wiley at age fourteen and later attended Howard University's School of Religion. He received a degree in theology in 1941 and thereafter went to work for the FOR as its secretary for race relations.

Farmer soon proposed using Gandhian techniques to fight racial discrimination directly. The FOR leadership decided not to sponsor this project directly, but it did permit Farmer to organize the Congress of Racial Equality (CORE) while on the FOR payroll.

Farmer put together the first CORE chapter in Chicago in 1942. Its members were drawn primarily from his own circle of friends, most of them socialist and pacifist graduate students at the University of Chicago. By 1944, however, there were CORE chapters in New York City, Philadelphia, Pittsburgh, Detroit, and Los Angeles.

A CORE button

James Farmer recalled, "there were letters on my desk from blacks in the Deep South who complained that when they tried to sit on the front seats of buses or to use the bus terminal facilities, they were beaten, or jailed, or thrown out, or all three. This was in spite of the fact that the Supreme Court said they had every right to sit anywhere they wanted to on a bus or to use the bus terminal facilities without segregation. But those Supreme Court decisions had become merely scraps of paper gathering dust with cobwebs over them. They were not being enforced."

WAITING ROOM FOR WHITE ONLY

BY ORDER POLICE DEPT.

The Journey of Reconciliation

In April 1947, fourteen years before the Freedom Ride, the FOR and CORE jointly sponsored a similar undertaking called the Journey of Reconciliation. For two weeks, sixteen interracial volunteers rode through the Upper South to test the June 1946 Supreme Court decision in *Morgan v. Virginia*, which had extended the ban on segregated seating first enunciated in *U.S. v. Mitchell*. (The Deep South was still considered far too dangerous a place for such a provocative direct action.)

Notable participants in the Journey of Reconciliation included Bayard Rustin, who was arrested and sentenced to thirty days on a North Carolina road gang, and James Peck, a wealthy thirty-two-year-old pacifist from New York City, who would later become the only Journey of Reconciliation veteran to take part in the 1961 Freedom Ride.

Nine participants in the Journey of Reconciliation pose in front of Spotswood Robinson's law office in Richmond, Virginia. Those pictured are (from left to right) Worth Randle, Wallace Nelson, Ernest Bromley, James Peck, Igal Roodenko, Bayard Rustin, Joe Felmet, George Hauser, and Andrew Johnson.

To compel federal action, Farmer began organizing an operation that he called the Freedom Ride. His plan was to send a group of interracial volunteers on a bus trip through the South, during which they would exercise their rights under *Mitchell* and *Boynton*. To make the journey, Farmer chose seven Negroes and six whites—ten men and three women—ranging in age from twenty-one to sixty. Most were recruited from within the CORE membership, but two, John Lewis and Howard University's Henry Thomas, were SNCCers.

The Freedom Ride was scheduled to begin on May 4, 1961, in Washington, D.C., and end thirteen days later in New Orleans, where a large rally was planned to celebrate the seventh anniversary of the *Brown* decision. Beginning on May 1, Farmer trained the volunteers in Washington, where some of them ordered coffee at simulated lunch counters while others acted the parts of angry segregationists, pushing the protesters off their stools, clubbing them, and kicking them. "I think all of us were prepared for as much violence as could be thrown at us," Farmer recalled. "We were prepared for the possibility of death."

Following the Gandhian dictate to inform civil authorities in advance of any plan to protest, Farmer wrote letters to John Kennedy, Robert Kennedy, FBI director J. Edgar Hoover, the chairman of the Interstate Commerce Commission (ICC), and the presidents of the Greyhound and Trailways bus companies, informing them of the Freedom Riders' intentions. There was not a single response. As it turned out, both Kennedy letters had become lost in the vast federal bureaucracy. Yet Robert Kennedy did learn of the Freedom Ride just before its start, when Simeon Booker of *Jet* magazine stopped by to see him at the Justice Department.

Booker was one of three reporters, all Negroes, whom the CORE press office had persuaded to accompany the Freedom Riders on their trip. He was worried that violence would erupt en route and wanted to be sure that the attorney general was aware of his concerns. "Okay," a distracted Robert Kennedy told him, "call me if there is [any trouble]." Then Kennedy promptly forgot all about the Freedom Ride.

On Thursday, May 4, the Freedom Riders left Washington in two buses, one a Greyhound and the other a Trailways. The white members of the group sat in the back of each bus, and the blacks sat in the front. At each stop, the riders ignored the WHITE and COLORED signs in the terminals, and—in the Upper South, at least—the locals ignored them.

The first trouble came in South Carolina on May 9, when John Lewis and white Freedom Rider Albert Bigelow tried to enter the white waiting room at the Greyhound bus terminal in Rock Hill. "I noticed a large number of young white guys hanging around the pinball machines in the lobby," Lewis remembered. "Two of these guys were leaning by the doorjamb to the waiting room. They wore leather jackets, had those ducktail haircuts, and were each smoking a cigarette."

"When you go looking for trouble, you usually find it."

One stepped in Lewis's way and told him, "Other side, nigger," indicating the colored waiting room. Lewis replied calmly that, under *Boynton*, he had the legal right to use either waiting room. "Shit on that," said another of the toughs as he punched Lewis in the face. A second punch floored Lewis, who was then kicked as he lay unresisting on the ground. At this point, Bigelow, following his nonviolence training, placed himself between the attackers and Lewis. "They hesitated for an instant," Lewis recalled. "Then they attacked Bigelow, who did not raise a finger as these young men began punching him."

Finally, a watching police officer intervened, pulling one of the youths off Bigelow and telling them all, "All right, boys. Y'all've done about enough now. Get on home." Another officer asked Lewis and Bigelow if they wanted to press charges. Both declined because, from a Gandhian perspective, it was the segregationist system (and not those following it) that was at fault. The Rock Hill youths were simply another order of victim.

The next day, when the bus carrying the Trailways contingent stopped for lunch in Winnsboro, Jim Peck and Hank Thomas sat down at the white terminal lunch counter and ordered something to eat. Immediately, the owner called the police and had Thomas arrested for "trespassing." Peck was jailed for "interfering with an arrest," and both were held overnight in segregated cells until someone realized that, under *Boynton*, the charges wouldn't stick.

The Freedom Riders then proceeded uneventfully through Georgia to Atlanta, where on Saturday, May 13, they were greeted by a large group of welcoming students, a few of whom even volunteered to take part in the

Passengers look on as the Greyhound bus carrying Freedom Riders from Atlanta to Birmingham burns outside Anniston, Alabama, on Mother's Day 1961.

A fireman inspects the bus wreckage. Before leaving Washington, several Freedom Riders wrote letters to be delivered if they were killed.

final four legs of the trip. (At the same time, however, the Freedom Riders lost Farmer, who left for home after learning of the sudden death of his father.) That night, Martin Luther King Jr. visited the riders to express his support and admiration. The next morning, however, it was with some trepidation that they boarded Greyhound and Trailways buses for the Mother's Day ride to Birmingham.

MOTHER'S DAY VIOLENCE

The buses were scheduled to stop only once on the 150-mile trip—at Anniston, Alabama, a Klan stronghold about 20 miles west of the Georgia border and 60 miles from Birmingham. The Greyhound bus was the first to arrive, and as it pulled into the Anniston terminal, it was attacked by a mob of about two hundred angry whites. They broke some of its windows, dented its sides with iron bars, and slashed several tires. The driver managed to back the bus quickly out of the terminal, but the mob gave chase.

Six miles outside of town, the bus began to wobble as its slashed tires flattened. Pulling over, the driver scrambled out of his seat and ran. Again, an angry white mob surrounded the vehicle. After a few more of its windows were broken, someone tossed a homemade firebomb inside. A few passengers escaped through broken windows, but most crawled toward the front of the bus, where they found the door held shut by members of the mob outside.

According to Hank Thomas, he and eight other Freedom Riders remained trapped on the smoke-filled bus until someone in the crowd yelled that it was going to explode. At this point, the whites holding the door fell back, allowing the riders to escape just moments before the Greyhound's fuel tank indeed exploded and the bus was consumed by flames. Other accounts,

Gandhian Philosophy

In leading the campaign against British rule in India, Mohandas K. Gandhi developed a technique that he called "satyagraha," combining the Hindu words for "truth" and "persistence." The strategy was simple: First he publicly declared his opposition to an unjust law, then he broke it and accepted the consequences. The dignified suffering of those who resisted the injustice, Gandhi believed, would open the hearts of the powerful and weaken their will to oppress.

Yet Gandhi also saw that for satyagraha to work, the movement behind it had to be broadly based, because individual resisters could only suffer so much. "I do not believe in making appeals," Gandhi once wrote, "when there is no force behind them."

His most famous satyagraha targeted the Salt Laws, which prohibited the making of salt from seawater (because this evaded the salt tax). On April 6, 1930, he made salt himself on the beach at Dandi and called on others to do so. Sixty thousand people were later arrested in what became a turning point in the Indian independence campaign.

Gandhi and seventy-eight fellow satyagrahis set out on their Salt March to Dandi on March 12, 1930, meeting large crowds all along the way.

however, credit the opening of the door to E. L. Cowling, an undercover state investigator assigned to observe the Freedom Riders as they entered Alabama. By some accounts, Cowling made his way to the front of the bus, drew his pistol, and told the men holding the doors that he'd kill them if they didn't back away. After that, however, Cowling did little to prevent the mob from beating the Freedom Riders, and the police, when they finally arrived, made no arrests, either.

At the local hospital, where the injured Freedom Riders were taken, doctors would only treat Genevieve Hughes, the one white woman in the group. Soon, another angry crowd began to gather outside, at which point the Freedom Riders were asked to leave. They were likely saved another beating only by the fortuitous arrival of the Rev. Fred L. Shuttlesworth at the head of a fifteen-car caravan from Birmingham.

About an hour or so behind the Greyhound, the Trailways bus pulled into Anniston. When its passengers learned what had happened, most left the bus, but the Freedom Riders remained. Next, eight white men boarded and stood beside the driver as he announced that he would not leave Anniston unless the Negroes took seats in the back. When none of the blacks moved, according to Jim Peck, "the hoodlums cursed and started to move them bodily to the rear, kicking

> "I think it is particularly important at this time, when it has become national news, that we continue and show that nonviolence can prevail over violence."
>
> JAMES PECK TO REPORTERS

and hitting them at the same time." In the end, all seven Freedom Riders were forced to sit in the back, while the Alabamans occupied the bus's front seats and the middle seats remained empty. "For the entire two-hour ride to Birmingham,"

Peck recalled, "the hoodlums craned their necks to make sure we didn't move into any of the empty rows of front seats."

As the bus reached its destination, Peck could see more hate-filled men, most in their twenties, gathered outside the terminal. Beneath their coats were poorly concealed tire irons and wooden clubs. Strangely, there were no Birmingham police in evidence. As it turned out later, influential officials in the police department had promised the Birmingham Klan that it could have fifteen minutes alone with the riders. A Klansman on the FBI payroll had passed along this information to the bureau, but Director Hoover, who didn't support civil rights for Negroes, chose not to act on it. Asked later about the absence of police that Mother's Day, Birmingham commissioner of public safety Eugene "Bull" Connor told reporters that his men were all at home visiting their mothers.

Peck left the bus in the company of Charles Person, a Morehouse student, with whom he planned to test waiting-room segregation. As they entered the white waiting room, Klansmen grabbed them and carried them outside into an alleyway, where Peck was beaten unconscious. His scalp wounds required fifty-three stitches. The other Freedom Riders were also beaten, but none so severely as Peck.

Fred Shuttlesworth

1922–

Raised in the backwoods of Alabama, where he was arrested in 1941 for running a still, Fred Shuttlesworth worked as an itinerant truck driver and cement mixer before accepting his "call" to the ministry. As tough as they come, Shuttlesworth built a house for himself and his wife out of World War II scrap material while struggling financially through college and seminary. A year after his 1952 graduation from Alabama State College, he became pastor of the Bethel Baptist Church in Birmingham.

After an Alabama court banned the state NAACP in June 1956, Shuttlesworth declared that he had received a message from God. "Ye shall know the truth," God had said, "and the truth shall make you free." Shuttlesworth interpreted this to mean that he should welcome the casting out of the factious NAACP and found another organization in its place. The result, modeled on the Montgomery Improvement Association, was the Alabama Christian Movement for Human Rights (ACMHR).

Shuttlesworth's audacity, however, frightened several of his fellow ministers. After the ACMHR's founding meeting was set for June 5, one Birmingham minister reportedly told Shuttlesworth that God had also sent him a message, telling him to tell Shuttlesworth to cancel the meeting. "When did the Lord start sending my messages through you?" Shuttlesworth shot back.

The founding of the ACMHR went on as scheduled. According to Taylor Branch, "This deed first singled [Shuttlesworth] out as the preacher courageous enough or crazy enough to defy Bull Connor." On Christmas Day 1956, after some white men beat a fifteen-year-old black girl at a bus stop, Shuttlesworth announced that the next day he would lead a group of demonstrators onto Birmingham's buses. That night, as he sat in his parsonage, preparing for the protest with one of his deacons, someone dynamited the structure, collapsing it on top of them. The two men were later found in the basement beneath a pile of broken lumber. Somehow, both survived.

The police suggested that Shuttlesworth leave town, but the minister refused. Calling his escape miraculous, he told the officers, "God erased my name off that dynamite." The next day, he led two hundred Negroes onto city buses, where they sat down in the front seats. Connor had Shuttlesworth and twenty others arrested for violating the city's bus segregation law, but Shuttlesworth didn't care. His sense of divine mission had been renewed.

Fred Shuttlesworth discusses his efforts to end racial segregation in Birmingham on December 28, 1956, three days after the bombing of his house.

A mob of whites at the Birmingham bus station beats Freedom Rider James Peck. The clothing-store heir had shocked his Harvard classmates in 1933 when he arrived at a freshman dance with a Negro date. Later, he spent several years in prison for refusing army service during World War II.

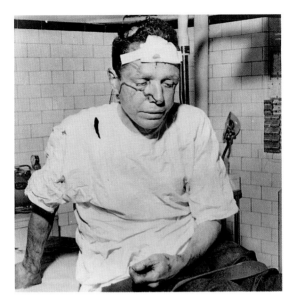

James Peck sits in a Birmingham hospital on May 14 after being taken there for treatment.

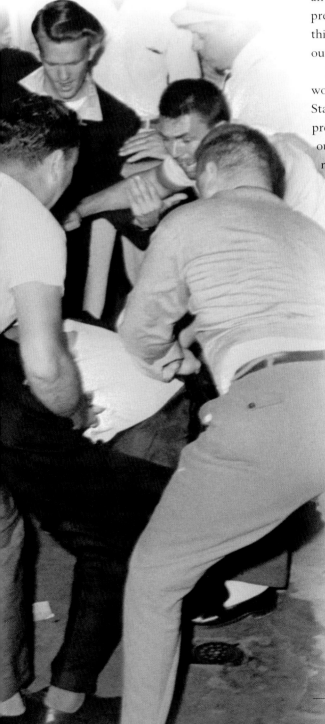

Pres. John Kennedy and Soviet premier Nikita Khrushchev conduct talks during their June 1961 summit meeting in Vienna.

THE FEDERAL RESPONSE

President Kennedy first learned of the Freedom Ride the next morning, when an Associated Press story about the beatings appeared on the front page of the *New York Times*. He was furious. Just four weeks earlier, his nascent administration had been rocked by the Bay of Pigs fiasco, and now, as he was preparing for an important June summit meeting with Soviet premier Nikita Khrushchev in Vienna, the last thing that he needed was a well-publicized outbreak of racial violence in the South.

Kennedy was concerned that the Communists would use the incident to embarrass the United States, but for the moment he had a more pressing problem: how to get the Freedom Riders out of Birmingham. They were determined to ride on to Montgomery, but no bus company would have them because there seemed to be too great a risk of violence. On Monday, May 15, they waited all afternoon in Birmingham's Greyhound terminal while Robert Kennedy carried on fruitless negotiations with the bus company. Finally, the menacing crowd unnerved them, and, deciding that further beatings would accomplish little, they headed for the airport. A direct flight to New Orleans, they reasoned, was the only way to ensure their presence at the May 17 rally.

At the airport, however, they fared no better. Each time a flight to New Orleans was announced, a bomb threat was telephoned in, and the flight was canceled. From a pay phone, Simeon Booker called the attorney general. "It's pretty bad down here, and we don't think we're going to get out," he told Robert Kennedy. "Bull Connor and his people are pretty tough." Later, Kennedy said that he had heard "terror" in Booker's voice.

A little while later, Kennedy walked into the office of John Seigenthaler, his thirty-one-year-old administrative assistant. A former reporter for the *Nashville Tennessean*,

Seigenthaler was the only southerner on the attorney general's personal staff. "Look," Kennedy explained to him, "they're at the airport, and they can't get off the ground. It's going to be about seven o'clock before we get them out of there. Do you think you can get down there and help them?"

Seigenthaler immediately flew down to Atlanta, where he caught a connecting flight to Birmingham, landing there about ten o'clock. In the airport, he found the Freedom Riders still trapped by the continuing bomb threats. He consulted with the police, the airlines, and the airport officials—all of whom wanted the Freedom Riders out of town as soon as possible. With their help, he was able to get the Freedom Riders on an unscheduled, unannounced flight to New Orleans shortly before midnight.

Seigenthaler escorted the group personally, and he had just gotten to sleep in a New Orleans hotel room when an urgent call roused him about four in the morning. "You know Diane Nash in Nashville," Assistant Attorney General for Civil Rights Burke Marshall asked him. "Yes, I know who she is," Seigenthaler replied, having become acquainted with Nash during the spring 1960 Nashville sit-ins. "Well, you come from that goddamned town," Marshall continued. "They started another group down to Birmingham to take over by bus where those others left off." Marshall then asked Seigenthaler to call Nash and talk her out of the plan, giving him a number in Nashville where she could be reached.

Diane Nash
1938–

During the years between the two world wars, Diane Nash's parents, like the Tills and so many other blacks, migrated from Mississippi to Chicago in search of economic prosperity and political freedom. Generally, the Nashes found both. Diane was raised as a Catholic in a middle-class home on Chicago's South Side. As a teenager, she considered becoming a nun but also entered beauty contests, a number of which she won (including several over white rivals). After high school, she enrolled at Howard University as an English major, but in the fall of 1959, she left Howard and transferred to Fisk University in Nashville.

Living in Tennessee gave Nash her first real taste of racial segregation. Feeling angry and degraded, she began attending Jim Lawson's workshops in nonviolent resistance, becoming part of a group of people who would provide leadership to the national civil rights movement for many years to come. In addition to Lawson, her comrades included John Lewis, Bernard Lafayette, and James Bevel (whom she later married, then divorced). Even among this illustrious company, Nash's personality was considered the most forceful, and she quickly became the group's leader.

THE NASHVILLE STUDENTS

On Mother's Day, the leaders of the Nashville student movement had gathered to enjoy a picnic lunch held in celebration of their recent success integrating local movie theaters (to which the sit-in movement had spread). They ate fried chicken and basked in the sunshine until the first reports of the Anniston bus burning began coming in over the radio. Nash quickly pressed James Bevel, the temporary chairman, to call an emergency meeting of the group's central committee. Bevel was reluctant to end the picnic, because he and others were having a good time, but Nash persisted and kept challenging Bevel until he relented.

John Lewis happened to be among those who adjourned to the First Baptist Church because he had temporarily left the Freedom Ride. After Rock Hill, he had flown to Philadelphia to be interviewed by the American Friends Service Committee, which had recently named him a finalist for a coveted scholarship. (The prize, which he won but subsequent events forced him to decline, would have allowed Lewis to spend two years living and working among Gandhians in India.) He was on his way back to the ride when he stopped off in Nashville to celebrate with his friends.

During the first few hours at the church—when it was feared that, at worst, the Freedom Riders might be arrested—the students discussed whether or not to travel down to Alabama and be jailed alongside them. Later, once the violence in Birmingham made it clear that the Freedom Riders' lives were in danger, the tenor of the discussion shifted. The principal issue became: If the Freedom Riders are killed, should the students risk becoming martyrs themselves?

This debate lasted all night Sunday and all day Monday until word reached the students that the Freedom Riders were giving up the bus ride and heading for the airport. Now, the discussion shifted again, this time from supporting the CORE effort to replacing it. "Farmer wanted to back down from that brutality," Lewis explained in his 1998 memoir *Walking with the Wind*. "We felt there was no choice but to face it."

Nash placed a call to Farmer, who was still in Washington, dealing with his father's death. She asked him whether CORE would object to a delegation of Nashville students picking up where its members had left off. After recovering his composure (because the boldness of Nash's question had startled him), Farmer warned her that such an effort would be extremely dangerous. He used words like *massacre* and *suicide* but in the end gave his consent.

When Seigenthaler tried calling Nash early the next morning at the church (for that was the number Marshall had given him), the line was busy and remained so. In between attempts, he called friends of Nash's whom he knew and described to them the perilous situation in Birmingham. His warnings and admonitions, however, had no effect. As Nash told Shuttlesworth later that day, "The students have decided that we can't let violence overcome. We are going to come into Birmingham to continue the Freedom Ride." After pausing for effect, Shuttlesworth asked her, "Young lady,

Members of the American Nazi party pose next to their "hate bus" in Montgomery on May 23. The Nazis were protesting the Freedom Ride by conducting their own trip to New Orleans. In Montgomery, they were forced to leave town by the National Guard.

Deputy Attorney General Byron White (left) with President Kennedy and First Lady Jacqueline Kennedy at the White House in January 1961.

do you know that the Freedom Riders were almost killed here?" "Yes," Nash replied, "that's exactly why the ride must not be stopped. If they stop us with violence, the movement is dead. We're coming. We just want to know if you can meet us." Shuttlesworth said that he would.

At dawn on Wednesday, May 17, ten Nashville students, led by Lewis, departed for Birmingham. At the city limits, Bull Connor's men stopped the bus and boarded it. Immediately, they arrested white student Jim Zwerg and black student Paul Brooks for violating state segregation laws by sitting next to each other. (Although local buses in Birmingham and Montgomery had been integrated since 1956, intercity buses in Alabama were still legally segregated.)

Next, the police escorted the bus to the terminal, where more officers boarded it. They covered the windows with newspaper, so that no one could see in or out, and inspected the tickets of the passengers. Anyone with a ticket originating in Nashville and calling for continuing travel on to New Orleans was detained. Initially, Connor's strategy was to intimidate the new Freedom Riders, but three hours' stalemate persuaded him that these students wouldn't be retreating quite yet to the airport, so he let them off the bus. Because the terminal was by now filled with a horde of angry whites, the police had to form a cordon through which the students passed into the white waiting room. They sat down there and began waiting for the five o'clock bus to Montgomery while the police struggled to control the crowd.

Just before five, Connor himself appeared at the terminal. When the students moved to board the Montgomery bus, he had them arrested to the cheers of the crowd. When Shuttlesworth objected, he was arrested, too. Later, as a sop to Birmingham's image-conscious city fathers, Connor told reporters that he had taken the Freedom Riders into "protective custody." To keep their morale up on their way to Birmingham jail, the students sang freedom songs.

THE PRESIDENT'S OPTIONS

At half past eight the next morning—Thursday, May 18—Robert Kennedy arrived at the White House for an emergency meeting with the president. The subject was contingency planning for a possible federal intervention in Alabama.

Accompanying the attorney general that morning were his two top deputies, Byron R. "Whizzer" White and Burke Marshall.

A former National Football League star, Deputy Attorney General White had been a close friend of the president's since World War II, when as a naval intelligence officer he had debriefed Jack Kennedy following the sinking of PT-109. Marshall, a Washington antitrust lawyer, had been given the top civil rights post at Justice so that Robert Kennedy wouldn't have to appoint Wofford, whom the brothers considered too emotionally involved with the movement to be effective. They chose Marshall because he seemed as detached as they were. (Wofford instead became the president's special assistant for civil rights.)

The meeting began in the president's bedroom. Because John Kennedy had returned late the previous night from a state visit to Canada, he was still in his pajamas. When the president's breakfast came, the four men moved into an adjacent sitting room. As the president ate, they discussed Alabama governor John Patterson's personality in detail. Patterson had been, by far, Kennedy's earliest and best political supporter in the South. The brothers hoped he would continue to help them now, but Patterson's own situation made that unlikely.

For Patterson, as for any southern governor, the Freedom Ride was a political trap: If he

Folksingers Guy and Candie Carawan compiled this book of southern freedom songs in 1963.

Freedom Songs

During the Montgomery bus boycott, the mass meetings always included a good deal of singing. Hymns were the mainstay, but old slave spirituals were also sung, often with lyrics updated for the twentieth century. These were the first "freedom songs," and as the movement grew, they became more and more closely identified with the civil rights cause. Popular examples included "This Little Light of Mine"; "We Shall Not Be Moved"; "I Ain't Scared of Your Jail"; "Keep Your Eyes on the Prize"; and, of course, the anthem of the civil rights movement, "We Shall Overcome."

When frightened protesters weren't sure what else to do, they usually sang. On May 24, 1961, for example, as the first group of Freedom Riders approached Jackson, Mississippi, one of them spontaneously broke into song:

I'm taking a ride on the Greyhound bus line
I'm riding the front seat to Jackson this time
Hallelujah, I'm traveling
Hallelujah, ain't that fine?
Hallelujah, I'm traveling
Down Freedom's main line.

protected the riders, the segregationists who held the political power in his state would disown him. If, on the other hand, he refused to guarantee the Freedom Riders' safety, he would invite federal intervention and suffer for that as well. So Patterson spent the Monday, Tuesday, and Wednesday after Mother's Day flip-flopping,

John Patterson
•
1921–

As Alabama's attorney general, John Patterson pursued the litigation that banned the NAACP from his state in 1956. Yet, as a racist, he wasn't really a true believer. Rather, he was an ambitious young politician who knew a popular issue when he saw one.

Building on the publicity from his NAACP fight, Patterson ran for governor in 1958 against Judge George C. Wallace, who had himself become well known for defying a U.S. Civil Rights Commission investigation into voting rights discrimination.

"I wished we didn't have a problem [with race]," Patterson told an interviewer during the mid-1970s, "but we did, and to be the governor and to do the things you wanted to do, you had to be right on that question as far as a majority of the people were concerned....George Wallace was considered soft on the issue in the '58 race, and that's one of the things that beat him."

Milking the segregation issue (and thereby gaining the Ku Klux Klan's public endorsement) got Patterson elected in 1958 and kept him popular during his term. But it also circumscribed his national ambitions because, as he admitted himself, "you couldn't be elected president of the United States if you were a segregationist."

The brothers Kennedy at the White House with FBI director J. Edgar Hoover in February 1961.

waffling, and dodging as best he could. In heated conversations with Robert Kennedy on Monday, he agreed reluctantly to safeguard the Freedom Riders, but when word of this agreement leaked to the press, Patterson denied it. "I refuse to guarantee their safe passage," he said later that day. "The citizens of the state are so enraged that I cannot guarantee protection for this bunch of rabble-rousers."

Meanwhile, President Kennedy was eager himself to avoid what he called the "Little Rock method." During the 1960 campaign, he had savaged Eisenhower for allowing the situation in Little Rock to reach the point of sending in troops, and he worried that, if he allowed the same thing to happen in Birmingham, voters would begin to question his basic competence, especially with the Bay of Pigs still fresh in their minds.

were middle-aged clerks, but at least they could all carry firearms while on duty.

After some discussion, the president consented and gave White the necessary authority. He hoped that White's preparations, when communicated to Patterson, would motivate the governor to take responsibility for the Freedom Riders. That way, the Kennedy administration wouldn't have to.

To accelerate the process, Kennedy had the White House operator place a call to Patterson at the Alabama statehouse. Soon, the operator came back on the line. The governor, she said, was

"The citizens of the state are so enraged that I cannot guarantee protection for this bunch of rabble-rousers."

JOHN PATTERSON

As the president picked through his breakfast, Marshall coolly laid out his legal options. At the extremes, he could do nothing or send in troops, either by federalizing the Alabama National Guard or using regular army soldiers. The only intermediate option that Marshall could suggest was using the FBI, but the president rejected this. He didn't trust Hoover, especially when it came to civil rights, and his brother agreed. "Hoover's on the other side," the attorney general commented.

"The brothers had already agreed on two things," Richard Reeves has written. "First, that this whole thing and the people behind it were a giant pain-in-the-ass—especially James Farmer of CORE—and second, that the federal government was on the side of the riders, that was the law and that was right." But the Kennedys wanted another enforcement option.

The next suggestion came from White, who proposed the creation of a special civilian force made up of U.S. Marshals, treasury agents, members of the U.S. Border Patrol, and federal prison guards. Most of these men

unavailable. Patterson's office was claiming that he was out of town, fishing somewhere in the Gulf of Mexico.

STUCK IN BIRMINGHAM

Meanwhile, inside the Birmingham jail, the Nashville students went on a hunger strike to protest their detention. Eventually, Connor decided he'd seen enough, and at eleven thirty Thursday night he walked into the black students' cell block and told them that he was taking them all back to Nashville—all except for Zwerg and Brooks, the only ones formally charged with a crime. The students refused to move, so Connor's men carried them out one by one. They were loaded into unmarked station wagons along with their luggage and driven out of town about one in the morning.

The caravan traveled north for about a hundred miles until it reached the Tennessee border. Here, still a hundred miles short of Nashville, the station wagons pulled over, and the luggage was unloaded. "This is where you'll be gettin' out," Connor said. "Y'all can catch a train home from here. Or maybe," he chuckled, "a bus."

The Alabama-Tennessee border, they all knew, was Klan country—dangerous for black strangers any time of the day and especially so in the predawn darkness. Fortunately, the seven students stumbled upon the home of an elderly Negro couple. When they knocked, the door opened a crack. "We're the Freedom Riders," Lewis said. "We're in trouble, and we need your help. Would you help us?" The man holding the door shook his head and said in a frightened voice, "I'm sorry. I can't." Lewis persisted. "Please, sir," he said. "We really need your help. If you could just let us make a telephone call." Then the door opened a little wider. Lewis could see the man's wife, and she could see him. "Honey, let them in," she said.

Using the couple's telephone, Lewis called Nash to let her know what had happened. As best he could, he described where they were and asked her to send a car to pick them up. She said someone would arrive by midmorning but wanted to know where they would be going, home to Nashville or back to Birmingham? "There was no question as far as I was concerned," Lewis remembered. "The others felt the same way. To a person, we believed there was no choice but to go back to Birmingham." Later, during the drive south, the students laughed when they heard a report on the car radio that the Freedom Riders were now back on their college campuses.

By early afternoon, after a stop at Fred Shuttlesworth's house to rendezvous with Jim Zwerg and Paul Brooks (who had just been released from jail) and twelve new volunteers, Lewis's group was back at the Birmingham Greyhound terminal, waiting to board the 3 P.M. bus for Montgomery. As before, the students were surrounded by a large, jeering crowd, now estimated at three thousand people. The police generally held the mob back, but occasionally they permitted people to walk by the Freedom Riders in order to step on their toes or "accidentally" spill drinks on them. To pass the time, the riders sang "We Shall Overcome," and Lewis led some of them in prayer.

A sharecropper's home in Lauderdale County, Alabama. This area just south of the Tennessee border was generally considered Klan county.

Just before three o'clock, they left the waiting room to board their bus. They found it idling in the loading area, but there was no driver in sight. Even so, they tried to board it but were told that the three o'clock had been canceled. So, amid cheers from the crowd, they returned to their seats and waited for the next Montgomery bus, scheduled to leave at five o'clock. It, too, was canceled, and the students were forced to spend the night on the terminal's uncomfortable wooden benches, with angry whites keeping watch from behind the police lines.

Meanwhile, late on Friday afternoon, Robert Kennedy finally got through to Patterson, whose refusal to take the president's calls had angered the attorney general and made him determined to see *Boynton* enforced. Their conversation was brief and unfriendly, but Patterson did agree to meet with a

Nashville students doze in the Birmingham bus station on the night of May 19–20 after being kept from boarding buses to Montgomery. They are (from left to right) Susan Hermann, Etta Simpson, and Frederick Leonard.

Alabama public safety director Floyd Mann was on hand at the Greyhound bus terminal in Montgomery when the Freedom Riders arrived. Watching one beating take place in front of him, he ordered the mob to stop. When his words went unheeded, he fired a warning shot, scattering the crowd. Then he called in the state police.

"personal representative" of the president. So Robert Kennedy called Seigenthaler, who was monitoring the situation in Birmingham, and told him to get down to Montgomery as quickly as he could. Renting a car, Seigenthaler drove the ninety miles to the state capital in little over an hour.

He arrived in Patterson's office to find the governor and his entire cabinet seated at a long table. Patterson rose to greet Seigenthaler. "I'm going to tell you something," Patterson said. "The people of this country are so goddamned tired of the namby-pamby that's in Washington, it's a disgrace. There's nobody in the whole country that's got the spine to stand up to the goddamned niggers except me. And I'll tell you, I've got more mail in the drawers of that desk over there congratulating me on the stand that I've taken against Martin Luther King and these rabble-rousers. I'll tell you, I believe I'm more popular in this country today than John Kennedy is. I want you to know if the schools in Alabama are integrated, blood's going to flow in the streets, and you take that message back to the president and you tell the attorney general."

"What I'm authorized to say," Seigenthaler replied, "is if you're not going to protect them,

A group of reporters listens to John Lewis (hidden) during his impromptu press conference at the Greyhound bus station in Montgomery. On the right is a young black woman whose expression reveals that she has just seen the approaching mob of several hundred violent white segregationists.

Greyhound bus driver Joe Caverno punches the tickets of Freedom Riders as the group leaves Birmingham for Montgomery on May 20.

the federal government will reluctantly but nonetheless positively move in whatever force is necessary to get these people through. They've got to be given protection, and so do other interstate passengers." Patterson paused for a moment and looked over at his cabinet. Then he responded, solemnly, that the state of Alabama was willing and able to protect all its visitors, including the Freedom Riders.

After that, state public safety director Floyd Mann took Seigenthaler aside and assured him that the state police would guard the Freedom Riders from the time they left Birmingham until they reached the city limits of Montgomery, where the Montgomery police would take over. Mann's briefing satisfied Seigenthaler, who used to governor's phone to call Robert Kennedy and convey Alabama's pledge of protection. Kennedy asked whether Seigenthaler believed Patterson, and Seigenthaler said yes.

The only problem left was finding a bus to carry the Freedom Riders, so early the next morning Robert Kennedy called the Greyhound superintendent in Birmingham,

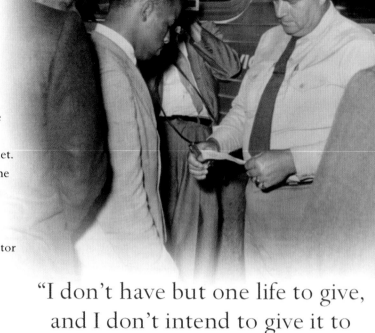

> "I don't have but one life to give, and I don't intend to give it to CORE or the NAACP."
>
> GREYHOUND BUS DRIVER JOE CAVERNO

George E. Cruit, and demanded to know why Cruit couldn't provide a bus. "Drivers refuse to drive," Cruit said. "Do you know how to drive a bus?" Kennedy asked. "No," replied Cruit. "Well," Kennedy continued, "surely somebody in the

damn bus company can drive a bus, can't they? …I think you should—had better be getting in touch with Mr. Greyhound or whoever Greyhound is and somebody better give us an answer to this question. I am—the Government is—going to be very much upset if this group does not get to continue their trip." Cruit got a bus ready.

THE MONTGOMERY MOB

At eight thirty Saturday morning, escorted by an army of state police, the twenty-one Freedom Riders finally departed for Montgomery. With so much force in evidence, the students eventually relaxed, and some who had been up all night even took short naps. At the Montgomery city limits, as expected, the state police cars turned around, but no Montgomery units replaced them. Nor were there any Montgomery police in evidence at the Greyhound terminal when the bus pulled in and discharged its passengers. In fact, the terminal seemed strangely deserted.

Lewis led the students off the bus and began speaking to the waiting television, magazine, and newspaper reporters. "It was really weird," he remembered, "an eerie feeling." He was in mid-sentence when his words trailed off. Over the shoulder of one of the reporters, he could see several hundred people approaching. All had remained carefully hidden until the Freedom Riders had disembarked. Now, the students and the reporters gave way, but the mob quickly surrounded them and beat all indiscriminately.

Seigenthaler arrived at the Greyhound terminal a few minutes later. He had been following the bus all the way from Birmingham but had dropped back near the city limits to get some coffee and gas. Hearing screams, he drove his car down an alley into the middle of a chase. Shouting whites were pursuing two young women. Seigenthaler pulled over, jumped out of his rental car, and grabbed one of the women while the other hustled into the backseat. The first woman resisted, telling Seigenthaler, "Mister, this isn't your fight. I'm nonviolent. Don't get hurt because of me." Seigenthaler later remarked that if she hadn't resisted, they likely would have gotten away.

"But that moment of hesitation," he recalled, "gave the mob a chance to collect its wits." One man grabbed him by the arm and turned him around, demanding to know "what the hell" he was doing. "Get back! I'm a federal man," Seigenthaler told him, and that was the last thing he remembered. A blow to the head knocked him out, and he learned later that the weapon had been a metal pipe. He lay unconscious

John Lewis and Jim Zwerg (right) confer after being beaten in Montgomery. Zwerg was a University of Wisconsin exchange student spending the year at Fisk.

on the pavement for the next half hour while the mob continued its rampage, hardly bothered by the Montgomery police, which finally arrived ten minutes into the riot. FBI agents on the scene took careful notes but did nothing to help either Seigenthaler or the riders.

After Little Rock, President Eisenhower had been reluctant to use force to safeguard the civil rights of blacks in the South. Now, movement leaders hoped that Kennedy would not back down so easily. The seven years since Brown had shown that, without executive branch enforcement, Supreme Court decisions were meaningless. What would the new president do?

Angered by the hospitalization of Seigenthaler and convinced that Patterson had broken his word, John Kennedy told his brother to send in Byron White's civilian army. That evening, White began assembling a force of six hundred marshals at Maxwell Air Force Base outside Montgomery.

John Seigenthaler (with cotton in his ear as a result of being beaten) talks with a wire-service reporter at the airport in Atlanta. On his way back to Washington after his release from the hospital, Seigenthaler was still "a bit woozy," he said.

Federal marshals sit across the street from the Greyhound bus terminal in Montgomery on Sunday, May 21, the day after the Freedom Riders were beaten there.

THE FIRST BAPTIST SIEGE

The next day—Sunday, May 21—Martin Luther King Jr. also arrived in Montgomery. He was just beginning to make a habit of flying into well-publicized trouble spots, and Robert Kennedy was worried that his presence might provoke more violence. Kennedy asked Patterson to protect King, and when the governor refused, Kennedy ordered White to assign King a fifty-marshal escort.

King drove to Ralph Abernathy's house, where he prepared for a mass meeting that night. Meanwhile, a dozen or so other

marshals nervously took up positions around Abernathy's First Baptist Church, where the meeting was to be held. As darkness fell over Montgomery, about fifteen hundred Negroes gathered inside the church, while a mob of three thousand whites assembled outside. The marshals remained on duty, but there were no city police.

Since the bus boycott, the racial mood in Montgomery had steadily deteriorated. Recently, for instance, the city had chosen to close all of its public parks rather than allow them to be integrated. Now, residual white anger over that decision rose to the surface and found expression in the verbal abuse (and occasional rock) being hurled at the blacks arriving at the church.

About eight o'clock, the passion of the crowd escalated when hooligans overturned a car and set it on fire. The resulting explosion was clearly audible and visible within the church, and it started the congregation talking. People began to whisper that such a large and angry crowd would never be satisfied with just one totaled car. At the same time—with instigators yelling, "Let's clean the niggers out of here!"—the mob began moving closer to the church.

The marshals radioed their situation back to White to Maxwell, and he relayed the information to Robert Kennedy on a continuously open phone line. "Get those marshals in cars and get down there," the attorney general ordered.

As reinforcements raced downtown in commandeered mail trucks, the marshals on the scene began using tear gas. In response, members of the crowd began throwing crude Molotov cocktails. (Fortunately, all of these fell short of their marks onto the church lawn.) Listening to the marshals' radio traffic, White told Kennedy, "It's going to be very close. Very touch and go."

Through the long night of May 21–22, Attorney General Robert Kennedy monitors the situation at the First Baptist Church in Montgomery by telephone from his office at the Justice Department in Washington.

The congregation, already singing hymns to dispel its fear, was exhorted by the Rev. S. S. Seay to sing even louder. "I want to hear everybody sing and mean every word of it!" he shouted from the pulpit. The crowd responded. "From the outside," according to historian Taylor Branch, "the church seemed to lift off the ground in song, but some of the men who had prepared for this moment were slipping out of the pews, reaching for knives, sticks, and pistols in their coat pockets." Downstairs in Abernathy's office, King called Robert Kennedy and told him that federal protection was urgently needed to save lives. Kennedy assured King that more marshals were on their way.

Minutes later, the reinforcements arrived and fired an enormous volley of tear gas that sent the

Ralph Abernathy and Martin Luther King wait patiently inside the First Baptist Church during the early stages of the May 21–22 siege.

mob stumbling backward. Soon, however, the cloud of tear gas drifted back over the church, allowing the enraged mob to reassemble. The boldest members reached the church's locked front doors and battered them until another volley of tear gas forced their retreat. Meanwhile, a brick shattered one of the church's large stained-glass windows and sent shards flying into the congregation. Other windows were broken, and the tear gas poured into the church.

With the help of a switchboard operator at the air force base, who was married to a state trooper on his personal detail, Patterson was able to monitor the telephone traffic into and out of Maxwell. When he learned about two o'clock in the morning that Robert Kennedy planned to ask the president to send in army troops, the governor finally acted to mobilize the Alabama National Guard and

declare martial law in Montgomery. He sent eight
hundred guardsmen to secure the First Baptist
Church, which they did quickly. Nevertheless,
Brig. Gen. Henry V. Graham, the officer in charge
of the operation, kept the stifled congregation
inside the church until dawn.

THE FINAL LEG TO JACKSON

On Tuesday, May 23, King and Abernathy
(representing the SCLC), Farmer (representing
CORE), and Nash and Lewis (representing the
Nashville students) held a press conference in
Montgomery to announce that the Freedom Ride
would continue. Robert Kennedy responded
by calling for a "cooling-off period." But as
Farmer told reporters, "We've been cooling
off for a hundred years. If we get any cooler,
we'll be in a deep freeze."

The next day, twenty-seven Freedom Riders—
including a charismatic young Howard student
named Stokely Carmichael, who had rushed
down the day before from Washington—boarded
two buses in Montgomery for the trip to Jackson,
Mississippi. In declining to join them, King cited
the terms of his De Kalb County probation. Many
of the students resented his reasoning. Some of
them were on probation, too, and were scared,
but were going anyway. They believed that if King
was going to share in the publicity, he should
share the danger as well.

The riders knew that the Alabama guard
would escort them all the way to the state line,
but what would happen in Mississippi? With only
rumors to go by, they struggled to contain their
imaginations, lest fear overwhelm them. "I don't
think any of us thought that we were going to
get to Jackson," Farmer recalled, and there was
good reason to be concerned. Mississippi
governor Ross Barnett was as cruel as he was
unpredictable, and even fellow Mississippians

considered him dangerous. For example, James P.
Coleman, Barnett's predecessor as governor,
telephoned Burke Marshall to warn him about
Barnett. If the Kennedy administration trusted
the governor, Coleman said, the Freedom Riders
would likely end up dead on their way to Jackson.

The first bus to leave was a Trailways, departing
just after 7 A.M. It had twelve Freedom Riders on
board, along with sixteen journalists, six Alabama
guardsmen, and no other passengers. More than
three dozen state police cars cleared traffic along
the way so that the bus could speed through
stoplights all the way to the border. One Freedom
Rider said later that he "felt like the president of
the United States touring Russia." At the border,
the bus stopped, and the Alabama guardsmen got
off. Then, to the relief of at least the journalists
on board, eight Mississippi guardsmen took their
places. Many more lined the route to Jackson.

Relieving their Alabama colleagues at the state line on May 24, Mississippi National Guardsmen take over protection duty for the Freedom Riders.

Some Freedom Riders were upset by this overwhelming show of military force, and while the transfer was being made, Jim Lawson (who had joined the ride in Montgomery) held

When the Trailways bus finally arrived in Jackson shortly after 2 P.M., there was no mob and no violence, but there were many police. The officers permitted the Freedom Riders to enter the white waiting room, but that was as far as they got. Once in the waiting room, all twelve Freedom Riders were arrested for breaching the peace.

the Freedom Riders not be made the subject of any more international headlines.

The day after their arrest, the riders were put on trial and quickly convicted. (As at Nashville a year earlier, the presiding judge, James L. Spencer, turned his back to the wall as the riders' lawyer presented their defense.) Each was given a two-

> "We've been cooling off for a hundred years.
> If we get any cooler, we'll be in a deep freeze."

JAMES FARMER

an impromptu press conference. "We would rather risk violence and be able to travel like ordinary passengers." he said, "We will accept the violence and the hate, absorb it without returning it." But the Mississippi authorities didn't care what he wanted, and the assembled reporters, according to historian David Halberstam, "looked at him as if he were crazy."

They learned later that Robert Kennedy had made a deal with Mississippi senator James Eastland. With less than a week to go before the president's trip to Vienna, the administration wanted no more violence, so the attorney general agreed not to interfere with Mississippi's enforcement of its unconstitutional segregation laws in exchange for Eastland's promise that

Jackson police watch as the Trailways bus carrying the first Freedom Riders arrives in the Mississippi capital on May 24. There was no violence in Jackson as the riders were immediatley arrested and jailed.

hundred-dollar fine and a sixty-day suspended sentence. When the riders refused to pay or even accept bail, they were transferred from the city lockup to Mississippi's notorious Parchman State Penitentiary.

But their imprisonment didn't stop the protest. More and more Freedom Riders kept arriving in Jackson until, by the end of the summer, a total of 328 had been jailed. Ross Barnett wasn't happy, nor was Robert Kennedy. Kennedy had come to respect the courage of the original Freedom Riders, but now, reflecting the cult of machismo to which he and his brother both subscribed, the attorney general disparaged the new recruits as having much less guts. Publicly, he accused them of merely creating "good propaganda for America's enemies."

Of course, Robert Kennedy had never been an inmate at Parchman—which, according to historian John Dittmer, "remains vivid in the memory of all movement veterans who did time there." The difficulty of this shared experience created a bond among the mostly young, mostly SNCC-affiliated men who endured Parchman. Before the summer of 1961, SNCC was primarily a clearinghouse for local student activists struggling to maintain the slowly dissipating momentum of the sit-in movement. Afterward, a new leadership emerged to give the organization a much more focused, militant identity.

Part-time campus-based activists such as Lewis and Carmichael now threw themselves fully into the struggle and became full-time organizers. Yet this wasn't the only important development to come out of the Freedom Ride. Farmer's campaign had also taught the movement that one didn't need thousands of students sitting in at lunch counters to attract publicity and compel action. Just a few dozen committed volunteers and an inflamed white citizenry would do. This was dangerous knowledge indeed.

Three of the nine Freedom Riders who successfully integrated the Montgomery Trailways station on May 28 sit in the whites-only waiting room. In the background, the manager of the closed lunch counter loiters on one of the roped-off stools.

Parchman

At Parchman, the Freedom Riders were initially isolated in wards in the death-row section of the prison. They were told that this was for their own protection, so that they wouldn't be exposed to dangerous criminals. But some of the activists suspected that the opposite was true: that prison officials were much more concerned about Freedom Riders infecting the regular prison population with their radical political ideology.

Because the Freedom Riders at Parchman considered themselves political prisoners, many protested their confinement by refusing to go along with prison routines. Some refused to leave their cells on the one day a week they were permitted to shower and exercise; others went on hunger strikes; most refused to "quiet down" when ordered to do so at night by their jailers.

The response to this behavior was sometimes brutal but also sometimes comical. In particular, the Freedom Riders' singing provoked regular confrontations with the guards. When the singers ignored repeated commands to shut up, the guards took away their toothbrushes, then their Bibles, and finally their mattresses, forcing them to sleep on the cold bare metal of the bunks. When Stokely Carmichael refused to give up his mattress, he was hauled out of his cell still clutching it. The singing continued, however, at which point the guards brought in fire hoses, directing powerful jets of water at the prisoners. The singing stopped temporarily, but once the hoses were turned off, it started up again.

Inmates at Parchman hoe cotton. When the first Freedom Riders arrived there on June 15, many felt that they had been sent back to another century.

Mississippi-ism 1961–1962

As one might expect, the Kennedy administration's reaction to the Freedom Ride set the pattern for its future behavior with regard to civil rights. The president—working through his brother, the attorney general—did everything he could to keep the issue from hijacking his Cold War foreign policy agenda. He cajoled the parties involved and threatened them, if necessary. He even made secret deals, when expedient, if he thought he could get away with them. Yet, when pressed, he usually enforced the law, albeit with great reluctance.

Ole Miss students wave a Confederate flag (inset) during campus demonstrations opposing the admission of Negro applicant James Meredith in September 1962.

In June 1961, however, the four-month-old administration didn't have much of a track record to demonstrate his goodwill, and the civil rights movement leaders, especially the students among them, didn't trust the Kennedys.

In the aftermath of the Freedom Ride, it became Robert Kennedy's job to prevent the next civil rights crisis from happening. The attorney general was already frustrated by the

way the Freedom Ride had ended—with the imprisonment of the riders at Parchman—and he knew that, if such divisive confrontations continued, the administration would be confronted itself with Hobson's choice: It would have to either back the demonstrators (and thus lose all electoral support in the South) or else abandon them to the southern white establishment (and thus ignore the law).

The answer, Kennedy thought, was voter registration. All the polling confirmed that integration was the toughest civil rights issue. Even northerners weren't sure that southerners should be forced to accept Negroes into their schools, neighborhoods, and public facilities. The first Gallup poll taken after the Freedom Ride showed that 63 percent of Americans questioned disapproved of the protest and considered it troublemaking. The principle that Negroes should be allowed to vote, however, was something on which nearly all Americans outside the South agreed. Furthermore, the work involved in registering voters was so tedious and mundane that few reporters would cover it. For these reasons, guaranteeing Negroes the right to vote seemed the easy way out for the Kennedys.

On June 16, 1961, Robert Kennedy met with representatives from SNCC, CORE, and the SCLC at the Justice Department. The purpose of the meeting, which Kennedy had convened, was to persuade these organizations to emphasize voter registration strategies. If they did, Kennedy promised, he would arrange funding through two Kennedy-connected philanthropies, the Taconic and Field Foundations and the Stern Fund. The attorney general also, it seems, guaranteed the safety of all registration workers sent out into the field. Although Justice Department officials later denied this, other participants insisted that he did, and all certainly left the meeting with the impression that Kennedy had promised Justice Department (and that included FBI) protection.

Kennedy's offer came at a time when a storm was already brewing within the SNCC leadership. Even before the Freedom Ride, tensions had existed between the SNCCers who identified with the group's Gandhian roots and those who had come to embrace the political activism that was quickly displacing SNCC's original religious inspiration. Now that a choice had to be made between nonviolent direct action and voter registration, the suppressed conflict became manifest.

Most of the leaders associated with direct action resisted the shift to voter registration, if only for the reason that the Kennedys were backing it. With some justification, they argued that the initiative was a diversion intended to sap their militancy without furthering the goal of desegregation in any way. On the other hand, those backing voter registration argued that the only way for blacks to gain real political power was through the vote.

At a crucial leadership meeting held at the Highlander Folk School beginning August 1, the direct action bloc nearly tore SNCC apart when it threatened to bolt should the registration advocates take control. That the organization survived was due largely to the presence of Ella Baker, who warned both sides that fights

such as this one kill movements and lead to "nobody accomplishing anything." After three days of acrimony, she was eventually able to arrange a simple compromise: SNCC would henceforth have two wings, one for direct action (headed by Diane Nash) and another for voter registration (led by Charles Jones of the Charlotte, North Carolina, student movement).

In the meantime, as his colleagues fought among themselves, Robert Moses set up shop in McComb, Mississippi, to begin the hard work of registering voters there.

MOSES RETURNS TO MISSISSIPPI

During the August 1960 trip that Moses took through the Deep South recruiting activists for the October 1960 SNCC conference, he made his first stop in Clarksdale, Mississippi, where he met with Aaron Henry, a pharmacist and president of the state NAACP. Since the murder of Emmett Till five years earlier, the national NAACP had assigned few resources to Mississippi, where most of the local branches were driven underground by severe Citizens' Council reprisals. Even its state field secretary, Medgar Evers, seemed to have little influence with the national organization.

The NAACP had dedicated itself half a century earlier to ending racial discrimination in the United States through the country's legal and political systems. But in Mississippi, where these systems were tightly held by a group of white supremacist oligarchs, that approach had floundered. Mississippi was so poor—the poorest state in the nation, in fact—that it had almost no black middle class, from which the NAACP traditionally drew its membership. A 1959 survey, for example, counted only five Negro lawyers, sixty Negro doctors, and one Negro dentist in the entire state.

Moses's next stop after Clarksdale was Cleveland, Mississippi, where he met Amzie Moore, president of the Cleveland NAACP and vice president of the state conference of branches. Like other Mississippi activists who had survived the wrath of the Citizens' Councils, the forty-nine-year-old Moore

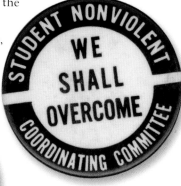

SNCC buttons from the early 1960s.

Members of SNCC, CORE, and the SCLC (including Diane Nash, second from left) wait outside Robert Kennedy's office before their June 16 meeting with the attorney general.

Robert Moses
•
1935–

According to historian Taylor Branch, the Robert Moses who showed up at the SCLC offices in July 1960 was "frail, bespectacled, and soft-spoken to the point of whispering," yet he "carried about him the strong presence of an Eastern mystic." Typically, the people who met Moses at this time sensed that there was something spiritual about him.

Moses grew up in a Harlem housing project but nevertheless attended Stuyvesant High, an elite Manhattan public school. Following his parents' wishes, he applied to several white colleges, receiving a scholarship to Hamilton in upstate New York, where he became one of three black students.

"One of the things I had taught myself to do [at Hamilton]," Moses recalled, "was to repress my feelings, or at least expression of my feelings, whenever I felt humiliated—to hide them. I think many African Americans becoming deeply involved with white society for the first time do this.... You put yourself in the role of the observer."

After his graduation from Hamilton in 1956, Moses entered a Ph.D. program in philosophy at Harvard, where he studied with Paul Tillich (the subject of Martin Luther King's own dissertation). In February 1958, however, Moses's mother died suddenly, and her unexpected death shocked his father into irrationality. He was treated in the psychiatric ward of Bellevue Hospital for several months before being released into his son's care. Thus unable to continue his studies at Harvard, Moses returned to New York City and took a job teaching mathematics at Horace Mann while his father continued to recover.

was economically independent, working part time at the local post office (a federal job) and the rest of the time at the Amoco gas station he owned on Highway 61, then the main road from Memphis to New Orleans.

Even more so than Henry and Evers, Moore had grown impatient with the NAACP's national leadership and privately questioned its commitment to Mississippi. The student sit-ins were only six months old, yet Moore was already thinking of possible local applications. He didn't think direct action would work in the Delta— local blacks were too poor to benefit from integrating facilities they couldn't afford to use— but the enthusiasm and volunteer labor could certainly be put to good use.

The key to solving Mississippi's race problem, Moore thought, was registering blacks to vote, because only political power could force open the doors of Mississippi's closed society. The congressional district in which Moore lived, for example, was two-thirds black, yet it elected racist white congressmen because so few blacks were registered to vote.

Moore agreed to attend the SNCC conference, but, more importantly, he persuaded Moses to return to Cleveland the following summer with enough help to launch an intensive grassroots registration campaign.

"He was the only adult I met on this trip who had clearly fixed the students in his sights," Moses later wrote. "It was as if he had been sitting there in Cleveland, watching the student movement unfold, waiting for it to come his way, knowing it had to eventually come, and planning ways to use it."

THE McCOMB PROJECT

Moses spent the next school year completing his teaching contract at Horace Mann. Then in June 1961, he returned to Cleveland only to discover that his mentor "just wasn't ready to start." Moore offered several logistical explanations— he hadn't been able to find appropriate meeting places, the equipment needed wasn't yet available, and so on—but the underlying reason

was that a lack of local commitment had made Moore reluctant to move ahead with such an ambitious campaign. Moses wasn't sure what to do next; then, a chance occurrence sent him downstate to McComb.

With Moses already in Mississippi, SNCC headquarters in Atlanta had sent out a press release announcing the start of a Delta voter registration drive. *Jet* magazine had picked up the story, which is how C. C. Bryant, president of the McComb NAACP, came to hear of it. Bryant then wrote to Amzie Moore, asking for some students to help register voters in McComb. As Moses was the only "student" worker then in Mississippi, Moore packed him up and put him on a bus for McComb. Moses arrived in mid-July and moved in with the Bryants.

An industrial city of thirteen thousand in Pike County, about seventy-five miles south of Jackson, McComb was founded during Reconstruction as a repair facility for the Illinois Central Railroad. Many of its black residents still worked for the railroad, which meant that they had a higher standard of living than most Negroes in the

Aaron Henry talks on the telephone in his Clarksdale, Mississippi, pharmacy in a 1964 photograph taken by a Freedom Summer volunteer.

state. Also, their jobs were unionized, and their paychecks came from Chicago, which meant that any who became involved in political activity had some real protection against white reprisals.

During Moses's first two weeks in town, he was taken around to all the black-owned businesses by Webb Owens, one of the most respected Negroes in McComb. Moses talked up the monthlong voter registration drive that he expected to begin on August 1, after which

This undated photograph from Amzie Moore's personal papers shows (left to right) Robert Moses, Julian Bond, Curtis Hayes, Willie Peacock, Hollis Watkins, Moore, and E. W. Steptoe.

"It was as if he had been sitting there in Cleveland, watching the student movement unfold, waiting for it to come his way, knowing it had to eventually come, and planning ways to use it."

ROBERT MOSES ON AMZIE MOORE

Owens hit up each proprietor for a five- or ten-dollar donation. In this way, the campaign was fully funded before it even began.

Had Moses pitched a sit-in or some other form of direct action, he probably would not have received any support from the adults in McComb, who tended to be rather conservative. But everyone he spoke with agreed that registering Negroes to vote was important, and they went along with his plan.

During the first week of August, Moses was joined in McComb by two more SNCC volunteers—Reginald Robinson, who arrived from Baltimore, and John Hardy, a Freedom Rider from Nashville who had just finished serving his time at Parchman. Soon, the trio began working the streets of McComb, going door to door and talking with black residents about the need for them to register to vote. In the past, the NAACP had focused its

registration efforts on the small Negro middle class in Mississippi, but Moses, Robinson, and Hardy included the entire community.

This was something new. Never before had poor blacks in Mississippi been asked systematically to involve themselves in political activity. It was mostly Moses's idea, based on Ella Baker's concept of "group leadership," and it informed all of the Mississippi organizing that followed. Local people, regardless of economic and social status, would be engaged and then relied upon—both for support and, when necessary, for protection.

At the time the SNCCers began their work in McComb, 250 blacks were registered to vote—not very many in a city of 4,000 Negroes. It did mean, however, that whites had permitted *some* Negroes to register, if not in large numbers.

All potential voters had to fill out a twenty-one-question form. They also had to read, copy, and interpret a section of the Mississippi constitution chosen by the county registrar. There were 285 sections from which the registrar could choose. Illiterate whites were usually given a simple, one-sentence section, such as "There shall be no imprisonment for debt." Black applicants got complicated, multiparagraph sections written in highly legalistic language.

To reduce the anxiety associated with the test, Moses offered voter registration classes on the second floor of McComb's Masonic Temple— a space provided by Bryant, who was also an

White customers expected Amzie Moore's gas station in Cleveland, Mississippi, to be segregated, but Moore refused to segregate any of his facilities, including the toilets.

Four members of an impoverished Delta family shell peas on the front porch of their home in Greenville in July 1967. In more rural areas, such as the red-clay country of Amite and Walthall Counties, many black homes lacked heat and indoor toilets. Water was typically provided by hand-dug wells.

After the 1955 murder of Emmett Till, the NAACP introduced a campaign in 1956 to "Stamp Out Mississippi-ism." Shown at the press conference holding up the campaign's poster are (from left to right) Henry L. Moon, Roy Wilkins, Herbert Hill, and Thurgood Marshall.

official of the lodge. All twenty-one questions were reviewed, and Moses explained the sections of the Mississippi constitution most likely to appear on the test. What he discovered, however, was that the educational climb wasn't nearly so daunting as the emotional chasm that had to be spanned. In Mississippi, where poor blacks had been taught for generations to feel they were inferior to whites, it required an extraordinary amount of courage merely to attempt to register to vote.

Few blacks wanted to risk what little self-esteem they had preserved on a test designed to humiliate them, so the SNCC canvassers kept

E. W. Steptoe signed this affidavit in January 1954 attesting to the fact that he was denied the opportunity to register to vote in Amite County.

their approach simple. They handed sample registration forms to whomever answered the door and asked, "Have you ever tried to fill out this form before? Would you like to sit down and try to fill it out now?" Just holding the form in one's hands was an important first step in breaking down the psychological barrier that had kept Mississippi blacks off the voter rolls for nearly ninety years.

On August 7, the first four Negroes recruited by Moses traveled to Magnolia, the Pike County seat, and took the test in the registrar's office there. Three passed. Two days later, three more applicants drove to Magnolia. Two of them were registered. Up to this point, the canvassing had been conducted rather quietly, but now word of the project began to spread.

AMITE AND WALTHALL

Reports in the *McComb Enterprise-Journal*, for instance, attracted the attention of NAACP leaders in neighboring Amite and Walthall Counties—who promptly asked the SNCCers

> ## "Just guns all over the house—under pillows, under chairs. It was just marvelous."
>
> ### ONE OF E. W. STEPTOE'S SNCC LODGERS

to help them as well. Amite and Walthall were typical Klan country—rural, poor, and violent. The Justice Department had already charged the Walthall County registrar with racial discrimination because in the entire county, despite its majority black population, there wasn't a single Negro registered to vote. In Amite, there was just one.

Moses, Robinson, and Hardy knew they'd find trouble there, but they didn't believe they could refuse. According to Moses, "The problem is that you can't be in the position of turning down the tough areas because the people in them, I think, would simply lose confidence in you." Leaving Robinson to run the McComb operation, Moses went to work in Amite, while Hardy took on the Walthall assignment. About this time, however, they were joined by more SNCC "field secretaries," or full-time activists, who had heard that the McComb project was *happening*.

Moses's local liaison was E. W. Steptoe, an Amite County native who owned a combination dairy and cotton farm on the Louisiana border. The small, wiry fifty-three-year-old had personally organized the local NAACP branch in 1954 and since that time had been subjected to ongoing death threats and police harassment. Not surprisingly, his house resembled an arsenal. According to one SNCCer who lodged with him for a time, "As you went to bed, he would open up the night table, and there would be a large .45 automatic sitting next to you. Just guns all over the house—under pillows, under chairs. It was just marvelous." (Because Moses was committed to nonviolence, he was uncomfortable around all of Steptoe's weaponry but said nothing to his host.)

Moses began holding registration workshops in a little church owned by the Steptoe family.

Meanwhile, Steptoe recruited a neighbor, farmer Herbert Lee, to drive Moses around the county so that he could be introduced to its people. Although a father of nine, Lee was, unlike Steptoe, prosperous enough to own a car.

At first, the local whites were caught off guard, but they soon began paying increasingly hostile attention. On August 15, Moses accompanied three black applicants to the courthouse in Liberty, the Amite County seat. The registrar kept them waiting for six hours before finally letting them fill out the required form.

It was already dusk as Moses headed back to Pike County. A highway patrolman who had been following him the entire way pulled him over just beyond the Amite County line. "You the nigger that came down from New York to stir up a lot of trouble?" he asked. "I'm the Negro who came down from New York to instruct people in voter registration," Moses replied and began taking down the officer's badge number. "Get in the car, nigger!" the irate policeman ordered, meaning his patrol car. Moses obeyed and was taken to the county jail in Magnolia, where he was charged with interfering with a police officer in the discharge of his duties.

From the jail, Moses made a collect call to Deputy Assistant Attorney General John Doar, Burke Marshall's number two in the civil rights division. To the shock and consternation of Moses's jailers, Doar answered the phone and accepted the charges. Moses had already been in touch with Doar, who was supervising the Justice Department's voting rights litigation, being conducted under the Civil Rights Act of 1957.

John Doar, a graduate of Princeton and the Boalt Hall School of Law, practiced family law in Wisconsin before joining the Eisenhower Justice Department in July 1960.

Moses had written to Doar a month earlier to let him know of SNCC's voter registration plans in Mississippi, and Doar had responded with his private number so that Moses could contact him quickly in the event of trouble.

Using as loud a voice as he could muster, Moses demanded an immediate federal investigation. He didn't get one, but his performance did cow the local sheriff and probably saved him from a beating. Instead, the county judge gave him a ninety-day suspended sentence plus a five-dollar fine to cover court costs. Because he refused to pay the fine, which would have been an admission of guilt, Moses spent the next two days in jail until an NAACP lawyer arrived from Jackson to post his bond, at which point Moses reluctantly accepted his release.

Two weeks after that, on August 29, Moses was back in Liberty escorting two more potential voters to the registrar's office. Outside the courthouse, he was approached by Billy Jack Caston, a cousin to the Amite County sheriff and son-in-law to Mississippi state representative E. H. Hurst. Without uttering a word, Caston began beating Moses

John Doar wrote this letter to Robert Moses in August 1961, politely rejecting Moses's request for Justice Department protection for registration workers in Mississippi.

Members of the Ku Klux Klan burn a forty-foot-tall cross at the climax of a 1965 rally held in a cow pasture in Brandon, Mississippi. About one thousand Klansmen attended, hearing speeches by Grand Dragon E. L. McDaniel and Imperial Wizard Robert Shelton.

with the butt of a knife, opening up three deep gashes in his scalp and leaving him covered in blood and semiconscious.

Moses knew that, for whites in Mississippi, violence was the ultimate weapon used to keep blacks obedient. Therefore, if he hoped to succeed in his work, he couldn't give in to fear himself. So he pressed charges against Caston to show that this sort of intimidation would no longer go

Quickly, he filed a suit on Hardy's behalf, eventually succeeding in having the charges dropped. For the moment, the Justice Department seemed to be honoring its commitment to protect the registration workers. Yet the attacks on Moses and Hardy had already set back the registration effort, and gradually the Kennedy administration pulled back from Doar's forward position.

> "It's okay to put our own lives in jeopardy, but when you cause somebody else to get killed, that's a different question."
>
> CHARLES McDEW

unchallenged. Along with several other Negroes who were present, Moses testified at Caston's August 31 trial, but he never heard the all-white jury's verdict. Before the trial ended, Caston's cousin, the sheriff, advised Moses and his companions to leave town, warning them pointedly that he couldn't guarantee their safety once the trial was over. Moses read about the acquittal in the next day's newspaper.

Over in Walthall County, John Hardy accompanied two people to the Tylertown courthouse on September 7. When the registrar refused to let them fill out the voter registration form, Hardy asked why. The question led to an argument, during which the registrar removed a pistol from his drawer and ordered Hardy out of the office at gunpoint. As Hardy left, the registrar struck him on the side of the head and shouted, "Stay out of here, you dumb son of a bitch." When the dazed SNCC worker finally staggered outside, the local sheriff arrested him for disorderly conduct.

About two weeks after Hardy's arrest, Doar traveled down to McComb to investigate the situation.

On September 24, just before Doar headed back to Washington, he met with Moses and Steptoe to talk about the dangers facing any Amite County Negro who became involved with the voter registration effort. Steptoe specifically singled out Caston's father-in-law, E. H. Hurst, as a threat and Hurst's neighbor Herbert Lee as a potential victim. The very next morning, about nine o'clock, Hurst put a bullet through Lee's head as Lee got out of his truck at a cotton gin near Liberty. The day after the murder, Hurst was cleared by a coroner's jury after he and other whites testified that Lee had attacked him with a tire iron and his gun had gone off accidentally.

Lee's death brought the SNCC effort in southwest Mississippi to a standstill. In its wake, the dozen or so field secretaries now working in the McComb area gathered together to take stock. "It's okay to put our own lives in

Mug shots of Bernard Lafayette (top) and James Bevel taken as a result of their Freedom Ride arrests in Jackson.

Ross Barnett cheers along with the rest of the crowd at the October 6 Mississippi-Houston college football game. Barnett's popularity, which had been sagging, rebounded sharply after the Meredith crisis as the issue galvanized the state's many segregationists.

General Walker subsequently resigned from the army in protest, declaring that he had been "on the wrong side" in Little Rock. Several days before, he had turned up in Mississippi, calling for ten thousand "patriotic Americans" to join him in the defense of Ross Barnett.

On the open pay telephone line, Robert Kennedy kept telling Katzenbach that the troops were just "twenty minutes away," yet four hours passed before the first 117 MPs arrived at 2:04 A.M. local time. "Where's the army? Where are they? Why aren't they moving?" the president demanded of Vance, but the army secretary himself couldn't explain the delay. Several times, he told the president that the troops were airborne only to report later that they were, in fact, still on the ground in Memphis. "They always give you their bullshit about their instant reaction and their split-second timing," the president complained to his staff gathered in the Cabinet Room, "but it never works out. No wonder it's so hard to win a war."

By dawn, however, there were sixteen thousand U.S. soldiers in Oxford (normally a city of ten thousand), and by eight that morning, the situation was sufficiently calm for Meredith to register at the Lyceum and attend his first class, a course on American colonial history. Just before going to bed at five thirty in

the morning Washington time, the president asked his brother to call Solicitor General Archibald Cox and find out what authority he needed to arrest Barnett. (He never followed up.)

In all, about 160 marshals and 40 soldiers were injured in the rioting. Two hundred people, including Walker, were arrested. Two others died: Agence France-Presse reporter Paul Guihard, who was shot in the head at close range, and jukebox repairman Ray Gunter, who was hit by a stray bullet. Afterward, nearly every state official blamed the Kennedys for the rioting, and Mississippi congressman John Bell Williams compared the president and the U.S. marshals to "Adolf Hitler and his infamous Gestapo."

In Mississippi's black community, however, there was quiet amazement. For the first time since Reconstruction, one of their number had won a substantial civil rights victory. Perhaps there was reason for hope.

ABOVE: **The Ole Miss riot** became front-page news around the world.
BELOW: **Accompanied by John Doar** (right), James Meredith walks to his first class on October 1.

Confrontation 1961–1963

Charles Sherrod, one of SNCC's first full-time field secretaries, grew up in the devoutly Baptist home of his grandmother in Petersburg, Virginia, before attending Virginia Union University in nearby Richmond. Several weeks after his 1961 graduation, the twenty-four-year-old Sherrod traveled down to Mississippi to help Robert Moses scout McComb. Then, at the end of July, he returned north to attend the August 1 SNCC leadership meeting at Highlander. Taking a rather circuitous route, he passed briefly through Albany, Georgia, where he did some more scouting.

Albany was a regional center of fifty-six thousand people, 40 percent of whom were black. Surrounded by peanut, pecan, and corn farms, the city boasted a prosperous Negro middle class, but in 1961 it remained thoroughly segregated and few blacks were registered to vote. In addition, the Albany City Commission tended to allocate municipal services disproportionately to white neighborhoods at the expense of black ones. For instance, there were no sewer systems in the black sections of town, and the streets there were generally unpaved. Furthermore, despite the seven years

that had passed since *Brown*, the Albany public school system was still separate and unequal.

Sherrod reported on these conditions at the Highlander meeting and then returned to McComb, where he helped Marion Barry organize the Pike County Nonviolent Movement. When that effort fell apart, Sherrod returned to SNCC headquarters, regrouped, and bought a bus ticket for Albany. He and eighteen-year-old SNCCer Cordell Reagon arrived there in early October.

As in McComb, many black adults in Albany, especially those belonging to the local NAACP, distrusted direct action and all those associated

Firemen use high-pressure hoses to move a group of young Negro demonstrators off the sidewalk on the first day of the Children's Crusade in Birmingham.

with it. Dentist E. D. Hamilton, for example, who had presided over the Albany NAACP since the late 1930s, gave the SNCCers a rather chilly reception and made it clear that he wasn't used to having his authority questioned. So, rather than take on the black power structure along with the white, Sherrod and Reagon focused their organizing efforts on younger members of the community, high school and college students, with whom they built a strong rapport.

The post–Freedom Ride Interstate Commerce Commission ruling prohibiting segregated facilities in interstate terminals was scheduled to take effect on November 1. To gauge its impact, Sherrod and Reagon decided to test the ruling at the Albany Trailways bus terminal. They recruited several high school students who were members of the NAACP Youth Council

This segregationist sign in an Albany, Georgia, restaurant window was photographed in August 1962, after Martin Luther King had left town.

but would not be acting in that organization's name; then they left town to attend Robert Moses's trial in McComb.

On November 1, Sherrod and Reagon returned to Albany on the 6:30 A.M. bus, expecting to find the Youth Council members waiting for them at the station. Instead, they found a dozen of Albany police chief Laurie Pritchett's most intimidating officers. The SNCCers decided to bypass the white waiting room and quickly left the terminal to find out what had happened.

It turned out that word of the test had reached Pritchett through his sources within the black community. The chief had then informed Mayor Asa D. Kelley Jr., who had convened a special closed session of the city commission on October 30. The commissioners had listened to Pritchett and then endorsed his plan to arrest the demonstrators using the public order statutes (that is, laws against disturbing the peace) rather than the segregation codes, which they all knew were vulnerable to legal attack.

Rumors in the Negro sections of town that the police intended to beat (and perhaps even massacre) the young demonstrators led to widespread paranoia and kept the students away. It took Sherrod and Reagon all morning and most of the afternoon to calm them down again. Finally, around three o'clock, with the SNCCers waiting outside, nine Youth Council members entered the bus terminal's white waiting room. Pritchett's men immediately ordered them to leave, which they did because their purpose was to test the ICC ruling, not to get arrested.

The Albany business district in 1962. According to Chief Pritchett, the city's racial problems were being caused by "outside agitators with criminal records."

Even though no one went to jail, this simple act of courage galvanized Albany's Negro community. Attendance at the nightly SNCC workshops swelled as students brought along their parents and relatives and locals began talking excitedly of the need for an arrest so that a legal challenge to the terminals' segregation could be brought.

THE ALBANY MOVEMENT

On Friday night, November 17, about twenty people representing various local civil rights organizations gathered at the home of insurance agent Slater King to discuss how to proceed. Although none could ignore the obvious tension that existed between Hamilton and the young SNCCers, there was much talk of shared goals, and in the end the Albany Movement was formed to coordinate their efforts. Osteopath William G. Anderson was chosen as president of the new umbrella organization, with Slater King as vice president and retired postal worker Marion Page as secretary. Hamilton, however, withheld his group's participation because, he said, he couldn't endorse the Albany Movement without first consulting NAACP regional director Ruby Hurley and state field secretary Vernon Jordan, both of whom were based in Atlanta.

Already aware that Sherrod and Reagon were draining the NAACP Youth Council in Albany, Hurley and Jordan strongly advised Hamilton to regain the initiative there as quickly as possible. Together, they made plans for three Youth Council members to sit in at the Trailways bus terminal until they were arrested. Then, in the

Charles Sherrod (left) speaks with Carl Braden, an influential field organizer with the interracial Southern Conference Educational Fund (SCEF).

traditional NAACP way, Legal Defense Fund lawyers would pursue enforcement of the ICC ruling in the federal courts.

On Wednesday, November 22, the day before Thanksgiving, the three volunteers entered the terminal's white waiting room and refused to leave. They were arrested (for "failing to obey the orders of a law enforcement officer"), processed, and bailed out within an hour. The NAACP and Pritchett were both satisfied, but neither had considered that soon hundreds of Albany State students would be descending upon the same terminal to catch buses home for the holiday. As word of the arrests spread, students began discussing the possibility of taking an uninvited part in the protest themselves.

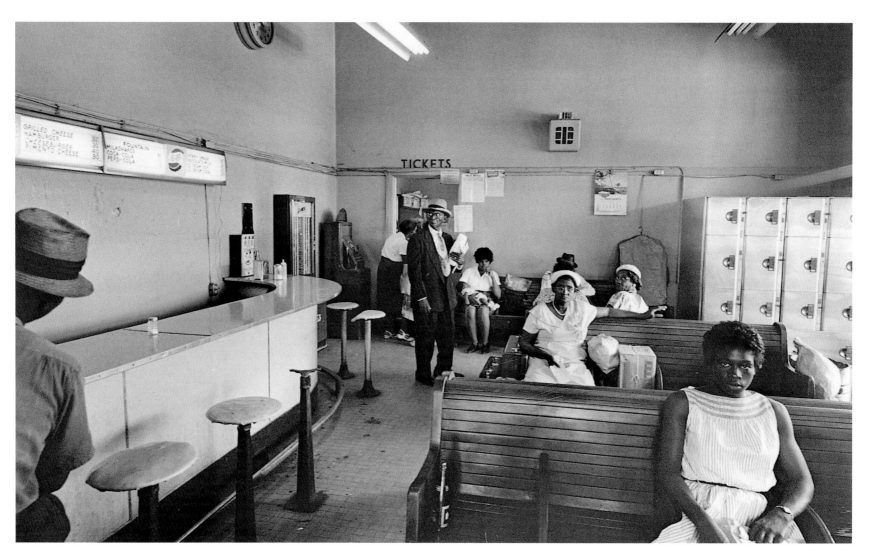

Passengers sit in the black waiting room of the Trailways bus terminal in Albany. On the left is the closed lunch counter.

Representing the conservative college administration, Dean Charles Minor went down to the bus station himself to ensure that his charges obeyed the segregation laws. Nearly all did, but two, Bertha Gober and Blanton Hall, slipped past him into the white waiting room, where they were both arrested and taken to jail. With the NAACP unwilling to bail them out as well, they spent Thanksgiving behind bars. Later, Hurley and Jordan explained to William Anderson that the NAACP would support only those protests approved and organized by its local branch. They did, however, suggest quietly to Anderson that he might consider replacing Hamilton as local branch president.

William Anderson could lead the Albany Movement because he had a black clientele.

The five protesters were tried together on Monday, November 27. Slater King's brother, attorney C. B. King, represented Hall and Gober, while Hurley and Jordan brought in Atlanta lawyer Donald Hollowell, who had fought Martin Luther King's October 1960 sit-in arrest, to defend the Youth Council members. The proceeding was brief, and at its end Judge Abner Israel found all five defendants guilty, sentencing each to fifteen days' probation and a one-hundred-dollar fine.

Sherrod and Reagon—who, by this time, had been joined by Charles Jones—were stymied. On the one hand, they could organize another direct action, but that would likely antagonize their new allies in the Albany Movement. On the other hand, they could do nothing, but then the momentum for change in Albany would surely dissipate. Finally, they hit upon a third way: recruiting demonstrators

from outside Albany whose arrest and imprisonment wouldn't ruffle local feathers.

In consultation with SNCC's new executive secretary, James Forman, they arranged for nine interracial Freedom Riders to travel from Atlanta by train to Albany on Sunday, December 10. The group included Forman himself, Robert Zellner, Tom Hayden of the National Student Association (and later Students for a Democratic Society), and SCLC youth director Bernard Lee. Reporters were notified in advance, and SCLC's Wyatt T. Walker paid for the train tickets. A large crowd of several hundred local Negroes greeted them at the station.

In keeping with his strategy to avoid a legal challenge to the segregation laws, Pritchett arrested eight of the Atlantans plus Charles Jones, Bertha Gober, and an Albany State student mistaken for a Freedom Rider. The charges against them were blocking the sidewalk, obstructing traffic, and refusing to obey a police officer. Following SNCC's "jail, no bail" policy, all refused release on bond.

The arrests greatly enhanced SNCC's prestige in Albany and generated national publicity.

At a crowded mass meeting on Monday night, December 11, the Albany Movement expressed its support for the Freedom Riders and voted to stage a protest march the following morning to coincide with the start of the Freedom Riders' trial. Led by Sherrod, about four hundred high school and college students braved a steady rain to march on City Hall. Trailed by squad cars, they circled the building twice, singing. As they began a third lap, however, Pritchett herded 267 of them into a blind alley behind the jail, where his officers stood guard over them for two hours until all were processed. About a third subsequently posted bond, but the remaining 150 or so filled up not only the city jail but also the county jail and work farm.

At another emotional mass meeting that night, the community voted to continue the marching on Wednesday, when hundreds more led by Slater King were arrested for parading without a permit. This brought the total number in jail to 471, including nearly all of the SNCC leadership in Albany. C. B. King thought the Albany Movement was now in over its head, and when Anderson suggested that it bring in Martin Luther King, there was enthusiastic agreement. The next morning, Anderson sent an urgent telegram to SCLC headquarters in Atlanta, and the day after that, Dr. King came to Albany.

Demonstrators in Albany are placed under arrest on December 12 by Laurie Pritchett (right) after marching around City Hall twice to protest the prosecution of eleven Freedom Riders.

KING COMES TO ALBANY

The crowd at Shiloh Baptist, where King addressed the Friday night mass meeting, was so large that a sound system had to be set up outside for those who couldn't fit inside. The understanding was that King would make this one appearance and then return to Atlanta. However, an obviously transported Anderson took the pulpit soon after King's speech and invited his guest to remain in Albany to lead the next day's protest march. A brief huddle followed, during which Anderson pointed out that King's mere presence might well induce Mayor Kelley to negotiate. Reluctantly, the SCLC leader agreed to stay.

James Forman
1928–2005

James Forman was ten years older than most of the SNCC staff, older even than Martin Luther King, but he wasn't bound like King to established institutions and old ways of doing things.

Born in Chicago, he spent the first six years of his life in rural Mississippi, living with his grandmother, before his divorced mother brought him back north. After high school, Forman spent several years in the air force before entering college in 1952. Following his 1957 graduation from Roosevelt University in Chicago, he covered the Little Rock desegregation crisis for the *Chicago Defender*.

Forman was working as a substitute elementary school teacher in early 1961, when he began taking part himself in civil rights protests. He traveled to Fayette County, Tennessee, where he counseled sharecroppers who had been evicted for trying to register to vote. Later, in Monroe, North Carolina,

he was arrested for taking part in a Freedom Ride–related direct action. When the judge in Monroe suspended his jail sentence, Forman headed down to Atlanta, where he began working for SNCC in September. A week later, he became the group's new executive secretary.

Forman replaced the Rev. Ed King, who was returning to college. The change was symbolic— the secular replacing the religious—but also important for practical reasons because SNCC was facing two major challenges. First, the organization's direct action and voter registration wings had to be reconciled; second, numerous accumulating bills had to be paid. SNCC was on very shaky ground, and had it not been for Forman's strong leadership, it might have foundered. Instead, Forman began raising funds, reorganized the Atlanta office, and stabilized SNCC's haphazard structure. "Without a leader like Forman," historian Clayborne Carson has written, "it is unlikely that SNCC could have become a durable organization."

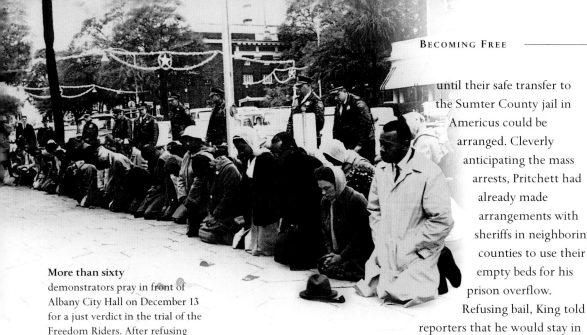

More than sixty
demonstrators pray in front of
Albany City Hall on December 13
for a just verdict in the trial of the
Freedom Riders. After refusing
Mayor Asa Kelley's order to
disperse, several were arrested.

until their safe transfer to the Sumter County jail in Americus could be arranged. Cleverly anticipating the mass arrests, Pritchett had already made arrangements with sheriffs in neighboring counties to use their empty beds for his prison overflow.

Refusing bail, King told reporters that he would stay in jail until the city agreed to desegregate. The media attention he was given, however, irritated many locals, who felt that the SCLC was taking over their movement. The SNCCers also took umbrage at what they considered grandstanding and began referring to King derisively as De Lawd. As a result, the rivalry between the two groups, which had been on the wane, took firmer hold.

To get King out of town, the city commissioners made a deal with Marion Page. (Much later, Page was revealed to have been Pritchett's chief informant.) In exchange for an end to the marches, the city agreed to release the jailed demonstrators, desegregate the bus and train terminals, and create a biracial committee to hear the Albany Movement's other grievances. Under this arrangement, King was freed on Monday, December 18, and he left Albany that evening, explaining to reporters that he had broken his promise to stay in jail because "I would not want to stand in the way of meaningful negotiations."

This was, however, as Albany's Negroes soon found out, not the city commission's understanding. Speaking for the three commissioners once King had left town, Chief Pritchett declared that the Negroes had won nothing. According to Pritchett, the city had always been in compliance with the ICC ruling, and as for the released prisoners, all of them still faced pending charges. Furthermore, there were no immediate plans to establish any biracial committee.

The Albany Movement persevered, staging occasional protests and instituting a boycott of the segregated municipal bus system. Yet absent King and the national attention he brought, Albany's white politicians could afford to ignore the movement, and they did.

On Saturday afternoon, December 16, Anderson, King, and Ralph Abernathy led 250 demonstrators to City Hall. Realizing that any harm done to King would bring even more unwelcome attention to Albany, Chief Pritchett assigned several of his officers to protect the minister from possible vigilante violence. Later, after the marchers were taken into custody, he kept King, Abernathy, and Anderson in his private office

The Velvet Fist

Police chief Laurie Pritchett became a favorite of the national media covering the Albany Movement because, although he looked like a stereotypical southern lawman, he was studious and reflective and had the subtlety, if not the grammar, of a college professor.

"I did research," Pritchett recalled of his experience with Martin Luther King. "I found his method was nonviolence—to fill the jails, same as Gandhi in India. And once they filled the jails, we'd have no capacity to arrest and then we'd have to give in to his demands. I sat down and took a map. How many jails was in a fifteen-mile radius? How many was in a thirty-mile radius? And I contacted those authorities. They assured us that we could use their [jails]."

After reading King's *Stride Toward Freedom*, Pritchett decided that the best way for a police department to counter nonviolence was to be nonbrutal. Having also reviewed the work of the Birmingham and Montgomery departments during the Freedom Ride, he saw that their chief mistake had been to employ violence, which had led to the federal intervention. Those police would have been better off, Pritchett realized, had they simply relied on polite law enforcement.

King called Pritchett's misuse of the public order statutes to perpetuate unconstitutional segregation laws "subtle and conniving." The national press called it "the velvet fist."

Chief Prichett informs December 16 march leaders Martin Luther King (left) and William Anderson that they are under arrest because they could not produce a valid parade permit.

On February 27, 1962, King and Abernathy returned briefly to Albany for a one-day trial on charges relating to their December 16 arrest. After listening for two hours to arguments about just what constituted a "parade" under the applicable statutes, Judge A. N. Durden Sr. recessed the proceedings and told the defendants that he would issue a verdict within sixty days.

Martin Luther King Jr. leads a line of marchers through downtown Albany on December 16.

In fact, the verdict wasn't issued until Tuesday, July 10, when Durden found King and Abernathy guilty and sentenced them each to a fine of $178 or forty-five days in jail. Both men said they would rather go to jail than cooperate with injustice by paying the fine.

King's jailing made segregation in Albany once more a national issue. White House beat reporters began hounding presidential press secretary Pierre Salinger for official comment, and most wanted to know specifically whether President Kennedy would again be calling Mrs. King. Later on July 10, President Kennedy announced that he had asked his brother, the attorney general, to look into the situation. Meanwhile, he called Burke Marshall at Marshall's vacation home in the Poconos and asked him to begin talking to both Coretta King and Mayor Kelley.

The next day, while presumably looking into King's situation, Robert Kennedy met secretly in Washington with B. C. Gardner, one of Asa Kelley's law partners. Several weeks earlier, the Albany Movement had sent its own delegation to Washington to meet with John Doar. Doar had listened

About two hundred marchers, arrested on December 16 for disorderly conduct, await processing in an alleyway behind the Albany jail. In the doorway at the far left, a protester conducts an impromptu prayer service.

politely to the Albany Movement representatives and then told them rather disingenuously that the federal government had no authority to act on their complaints. Gardner, however, received better treatment, and he returned home that night with a plan: The Albany establishment could get King out of jail simply by paying his fine surreptitiously.

At dawn the next morning—Thursday, July 12—while the jailhouse was still lifeless, Gardner appeared to pay both King and Abernathy's fines. Pritchett soon called the two ministers into his office and told them they would have to leave. When they demanded an explanation, the police chief said that "a well-dressed Negro male" who didn't wish to be identified had paid their fines. Pritchett later repeated the same story to the media.

Martin Luther King Jr. talks to reporters after his release from jail. Standing behind him are Ralph D. Abernathy (left) and William Anderson (right).

JUDGE ELLIOTT'S ORDER

It took a week for the movement to recover its momentum. Then, on Friday, July 20, Anderson and King made plans for another march to be held the following afternoon. They were finalizing the details at Anderson's house when a deputy U.S. marshal knocked on the door. The marshal was there to serve them with a temporary restraining order, issued by federal district court judge J. Robert Elliott, barring further marches until a hearing

could be held on the City of Albany's request for a permanent injunction.

Elliott was a committed segregationist who had only recently been appointed by President Kennedy to the federal bench. (Acceding to the judicial recommendations of Dixiecrat senators was an important way in which the Kennedy administration sought to curry favor with them.) In granting the unusual temporary restraining order, Elliott

"This is one time I'm out of jail that I'm not happy to be out."

MARTIN LUTHER KING JR. ON HIS JULY 12 RELEASE

had accepted the rather dubious argument that the Albany protests violated the Fourteenth Amendment because they drew police resources away from white neighborhoods and thus, literally, denied those whites equal protection of the laws.

King's legal advisers, notably William Kunstler, insisted that Elliott's order was unconstitutional, and they immediately petitioned the Fifth Circuit Court of Appeals to have it vacated. In the meantime, however, King had a decision to make: Was he going to obey the federal court order? Discussions went on all afternoon and well into the night. The SNCCers argued strongly for ignoring the order—pointing out that, if they obeyed it, the whites would gain control over the all-important matter of timing. Whenever a direct action campaign in the future reached a critical point, all the whites would have to do was find a sympathetic federal judge and obtain a similar injunction. By the time the order was lifted, perhaps weeks later, the movement's momentum would have been lost.

King also spent nearly two hours that afternoon on the telephone with Robert Kennedy, their conversation often escalating into near-shouting argument. How could King even consider violating a federal court order, Kennedy demanded to know. If King did violate the order, Kennedy insisted, he would be giving school officials all over the South exactly the excuse they needed to disobey federal court orders desegregating their districts.

Later that evening, after shutting himself away for a time, King emerged with a decision: He would obey Elliott's order. The march was off. Instead, he spent all day Saturday meeting with the SNCCers and listening to their recriminations. His leadership was too cautious, too media-driven, and too "bourgeois," they said. The movement, they continued, would surely suffer from his capitulation.

RETREAT

On Tuesday, Elbert P. Tuttle, chief judge of the Fifth Circuit, vacated Elliott's order, allowing the Albany Movement to march again. But its leaders paused, hoping that their legal victory might finally persuade the city commissioners to

Chief Pritchett (with bullhorn) asks 130 demonstrators praying outside City Hall on July 21 whether they have the proper permit before arresting them for violating an Albany city ordinance regulating parades. This "pray-in" also violated federal district court judge J. Robert Elliott's order banning marches and other demonstrations.

Busily at work in July 1962 in the home of William Anderson are SCLC and Albany Movement leaders (from left to right) Jean Young (wife of Andrew), Wyatt T. Walker, lawyer Carsie Hall, Andrew Young, and German-born ACLU leader Henry Schwarzchild.

negotiate in good faith. They sent Mayor Kelley a telegram inviting him to talk. "We…beg you once more, in the name of democracy, human decency and the welfare of Albany, to give us an opportunity to present our grievances to the City Commission immediately." Kelley replied that he and the other commissioners were willing to discuss the problems of local Negroes but only after King left town.

Movement morale, which had been low, now sank even lower. At a mass meeting that Friday afternoon, a call for jail volunteers was made, but few people responded. Not knowing what else to do, King marched that day with Abernathy, Anderson, Slater King, and seven female volunteers to City Hall, where they knelt in prayer. Pritchett arrested them for disorderly conduct and then gloated to reporters that the small number of protesters meant that King had lost his popular support.

This time, King remained in jail for two weeks, coming to trial on Friday, August 10. Anderson, who had bailed out of jail to appear on NBC's *Meet the Press* in King's stead, and Wyatt Walker worked as best they could to mobilize a renewal of the campaign for that day, either to celebrate King's release or to protest his conviction.

The trial was brief. Judge Durden found the defendants guilty and sentenced them each to a two-hundred-dollar fine plus sixty days in jail. Then, unexpectedly, he suspended the sentences on the condition that the defendants violate no laws in the future. King, Abernathy, Anderson, and Slater King were free to go. The SCLC leader spoke at three mass meetings that night and then left Albany for Atlanta.

The following Wednesday, the city commission finally granted an audience to a delegation of local Negroes, who presented the movement's list of grievances. The commissioners listened politely and then told the assembled crowd that because racial matters were currently the subject of litigation before Judge Elliott, they had no comment to offer. After that disappointment, Anderson and King concluded that further arrests would be pointless. Instead, the Albany Movement focused its remaining energy on voter registration, while King turned to rebutting press reports that his leadership in Albany had been a failure and the worst setback of his seven-year civil rights career.

However, just as Robert Moses benefited from his troubled experiences in McComb, so did Martin Luther King learn from his difficult time in Albany.

First, King learned that media attention was not, in and of itself, sufficient to reform a resistant yet nonviolent white power structure. Second, he learned that, in the absence of truly violent repression, the federal government would not intervene to protect Negro civil rights, nor would the American public pay much attention to their denial. King especially regretted that he had once again allowed himself to be drawn into an ongoing crisis not of his own creation. After Albany he told his staff, "I don't want to be a fireman anymore."

Nevertheless, King was caught between the stalling tactics of the Kennedy administration and the determination of SNCC to move ahead more aggressively. While first the Ole Miss rioting and then the October 1962 Cuban Missile Crisis captivated the nation's attention, King consulted with his closest advisers and decided, after a lengthy internal debate, that he would have to force the Kennedys' hand. This time, the SCLC

A view of downtown Birmingham, photographed on one of the few quiet days in May 1963.

would create its own crisis and design it so that the federal government would be compelled to act. For the setting, he quietly chose Birmingham.

BIRMINGHAM

Nicknamed Bombingham because of the eighteen "unsolved" bombings that rocked black neighborhoods between 1956 and 1963, the city was a bastion of southern segregation. Thanks to Public Safety Commissioner Eugene "Bull" Connor, nowhere was the repression of blacks meaner and more pervasive. In 1956, crooner Nat King Cole was beaten on stage while performing at the

Birmingham Municipal Auditorium, and a year later, a carload of drunken whites kidnapped a Negro off the streets at random, took him to a rural shack, and castrated him with a razor blade. Also in 1957, Fred Shuttlesworth, Connor's chief antagonist, tried to enroll his children in a white public school only to be chain-whipped on the street outside as several Birmingham police officers stood by but did nothing.

Similar incidents, culminating in the Mother's Day 1961 beating of the original CORE Freedom Riders, gave Birmingham such an unpleasant national reputation that its economy began to lag. This development deeply concerned the city's business elite, more than a few of whom blamed Connor. Finally, in 1962, a group of reformers fronted by chamber of commerce president Sidney Smyer moved to undermine Connor's authority by eliminating his job. Specifically, they put on the November ballot a proposal to replace the city commission with a mayor and nine-member city council. The initiative passed, and a special election was set for March 5.

The leading mayoral candidates were Connor and reformer Albert Boutwell,

Bethel Baptist in December 1962 after its third bombing. By then, Shuttlesworth had left the church to take a job in Cincinnati yet stayed on as ACMHR president.

The Rev. Fred L. Shuttlesworth in 1957 after his attempt to enroll his children in an all-white Birmingham school.

who had just finished serving four years as John Patterson's lieutenant governor. Although King later criticized Boutwell as "just a dignified Bull Connor," Boutwell's views on segregation were, in fact, relatively moderate for a native of Birmingham, and, more to the point, King's remark was disingenuous because he knew that Connor had no equals. King had chosen Birmingham for the new SCLC campaign specifically because of Connor's unparalleled ruthlessness and because King knew that, if provoked, Connor would do something so outrageous that otherwise ambivalent Americans would feel new sympathy for the southern Negro and force the Kennedys into the game. In comparison with Pritchett's "velvet fist," Connor was simply the fist.

Another reason that King chose Birmingham was its open playing field. The NAACP was still outlawed in Alabama, and with SNCC busy in Mississippi, there wasn't any other national civil rights organization in Birmingham to rival King's SCLC. Instead, there was only Fred Shuttlesworth's Alabama Christian Movement for Human Rights (ACMHR), with which King was closely allied. As long as King and Shuttlesworth continued to get along, the possibility of an Albany-style schism ruining the movement was negligible.

PROJECT C

Believing that the defeat in Albany had resulted from a lack of strategic planning, King secretly assigned Wyatt Walker to develop a comprehensive battle plan for Birmingham. Accompanied by

Andrew Young, the detail-oriented Walker scouted the city in December 1962 and took voluminous notes—making a list of Negro churches, for instance, and then recording the time it took to march from each to the downtown shopping district.

When the plan was ready for review, King arranged for a secret retreat to be held at the SCLC's Dorchester, Georgia, training center. Eleven people were present, nine of them SCLC staffers: King, Abernathy, Walker, Young, Stanley Levison, James Lawson, lawyer Clarence Jones, Citizenship Education Program head Dorothy Cotton, and Jack O'Dell, who ran the SCLC's direct-mail fund-raising operation in New York City under Levison's supervision. The other two participants were Shuttlesworth and his Alabama colleague Joseph Lowery.

Walker's plan was designed to force all of Birmingham's hidden racial problems to the surface. Called Project C (for "confrontation"), it had four stages. The first was lunch-counter sit-ins that would emphasize the importance of Negro consumers to downtown prosperity and also call attention to the campaign's primary goal, which was desegregation. Next would come a general boycott of the downtown shopping district, along with slightly larger demonstrations. The third stage would feature mass marches to fill the jails. Finally, if necessary, King would invite sympathizers from all over the country to gather in Birmingham for a biracial shutdown of the city under the overlapping pressures of negative publicity, economic boycott, and overflowing jails.

King and the others quickly accepted Walker's proposals without modification, then moved on to a lengthy discussion of the plan's implications. Their chief concern was whether or not Project C could withstand the sort of brutal, systematic oppression of which even a distracted Connor was capable. Should this campaign suffer the same fate as the Albany Movement, the consequences would be much more severe, not only for the SCLC but also for Birmingham's

exasperated Negro population, which might well riot if its hopes were raised and then dashed. Walker also pointed out certain demographic realities. With 350,000 people, Birmingham was Alabama's largest city. The marches there would have to be significantly larger than those in Albany or else seem paltry by comparison. Specifically, Walker explained that Stage Three would have to produce at least one thousand arrests, with the average jailgoer spending at least five nights in jail before bailing out. (He arrived at these figures by calculating the onetime bail costs to the SCLC against the money the city would be spending each day housing and feeding the jailed demonstrators.)

Andrew Young then brought up the subject of the Birmingham ministers, reporting that his talks with them hadn't gone well. With Shuttlesworth currently out of town, pastoring a church in Cincinnati, the conservatives who dominated the city's Baptist Ministers Conference had begun a whisper campaign against King, suggesting that he would bring only trouble to town. Young was worried that some of these men might even oppose Project C publicly, and he began listing their names until Shuttlesworth interrupted him.

"Don't worry, Martin," Shuttlesworth said. "I can handle the preachers."

Walker had timed the campaign to coincide with the Easter shopping season in order to maximize the effect of the downtown shopping boycott. It did seem prudent, however, to delay the start of Project C until after March 5, in case Boutwell won the special mayoral election and the disposition of City Hall changed. What Walker hadn't expected was a no-decision, but that's what he got. Because neither Boutwell nor Connor received a majority of the vote in the initial multicandidate election, a runoff was set for April 2.

King's choices now were to proceed as planned, to delay the start of the protest until April 3 (less than two weeks before Easter), or to wait nine months until the Christmas shopping season began. Having already pushed the starting date

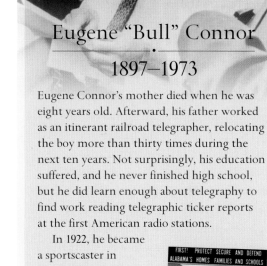

Wyatt T. Walker at a meeting of the SCLC staff held at an Atlanta restaurant in 1964.

Eugene "Bull" Connor
1897–1973

Eugene Connor's mother died when he was eight years old. Afterward, his father worked as an itinerant railroad telegrapher, relocating the boy more than thirty times during the next ten years. Not surprisingly, his education suffered, and he never finished high school, but he did learn enough about telegraphy to find work reading telegraphic ticker reports at the first American radio stations.

In 1922, he became a sportscaster in Birmingham, calling the Birmingham Barons baseball games. Because live, remote broadcasts weren't yet technologically feasible, Connor had to work from the WKBC studio. A ticker providing the basic game details, but Connor had to make up the rest—hence his new nickname, *Bull*.

Making use of this visibility, Connor entered politics in

A brochure from Bull Connor's 1962 mayoral campaign.

1934, winning a seat in the state legislature. Three years later, he became Birmingham's public safety commissioner and served four consecutive four-year teams before taking a break after one of his detectives caught him in a hotel room with his secretary in December 1951. In 1957, however, Connor reclaimed his job and won reelection again in 1961.

Although he had entered public life as a New Deal reformer, by 1963 Connor was the most established member of the Birmingham establishment. The police and fire departments were his private fiefdom, and he even exerted a loose supervision over the Klan.

back from March 6 to March 14, Birmingham's conservative ministers counseled further delay. In fact, the Rev. J. L. Ware, president of the Baptist Ministers Conference and Shuttlesworth's chief rival, nearly broke his pledge of public silence concerning King's plans by offering up a resolution that warned the SCLC to stay out of town. (Because it didn't pass, knowledge of King's plans remained within the group.)

Even Shuttlesworth, still in Cincinnati, was reluctant to offer support for an immediate start. Instead, this viewpoint fell to James Lawson, who argued strongly that the logistical issues being raised were merely a mask for the fear that all of them were feeling. For the past several weeks, Lawson had been making regular trips to Birmingham from his church in Memphis to train local people in nonviolence. These recruits, he said, were ready *now*; delay would only demoralize them. There were always good reasons to postpone, he went on, but then nothing would ever get done. King listened and decided to wait—but only until April 3.

On Tuesday, April 2, as Boutwell narrowly defeated Connor in the mayoral runoff, King slipped unnoticed into Birmingham. Although he would be sleeping at the home of insurance executive John Drew, he nevertheless registered at the Gaston Motel, where he had taken Room 30, the motel's only suite, for use as

Fred Shuttlesworth (right) leads thirty demonstrators in prayer outside Birmingham's city hall on Saturday, April 6. The group was arrested five minutes later for parading without a permit.

the Project C headquarters. The Gaston Motel was strategically located on the edge of downtown, just across Sixteenth Street from Kelly Ingram Park and across Sixth Avenue from the Sixteenth Street Baptist Church, which would serve as the campaign's principal staging area. Meanwhile, Walker and his staff began calling the 350 names on Lawson's "jail list."

On the morning of April 3, sixty-five of those people gathered at Sixteenth Street Baptist, where they were given instructions and exhortations and assigned to sit in at one of five downtown lunch counters. All were ready for arrest, but the store owners were ready as well. At four of the five targeted locations, well-rehearsed waitresses politely asked their white customers to leave and simply closed down the lunch counters. Only at the Britling Cafeteria, where twenty-one demonstrators were arrested, did management call the police.

Bull Connor was disappointed that the other store owners hadn't called. Because his popular support emanated from his standing as a bulwark against racial chaos, he needed high racial drama to keep seeming indispensable. Already, he and his colleagues on the defunct city commission had announced that they would remain in office, in defiance of the charter reform, until the terms to which they had originally been elected were up. Boutwell filed suit immediately, but it still took nearly two months for the Alabama Supreme Court to decide the matter in the reformers' favor. In the meantime, Birmingham had two governments, and no one was quite sure which to obey.

THE CAMPAIGN FALTERS

The defensive tactics of the store owners slowed the campaign considerably. On April 5, the *New York Times* ran its first story on Project C, headlined "4 Negroes Jailed in Birmingham as the Integration Drive Slows— Sit-Ins and a Demonstration Plan Fail to Materialize." Quickly, the leadership abandoned the sit-ins and switched to mass marches. The first of these took place

Nineteen-year-old college student Dorothy Bell waits at a downtown Birmingham lunch counter on April 4 for service that never comes.

on Saturday, April 6, as Shuttlesworth led about forty people from Sixteenth Street Baptist to City Hall and on to jail, charged with parading without a permit.

The next day, Palm Sunday, twenty more demonstrators were arrested during a similarly peaceful march. But several of the onlookers in Kelly Ingram Park, lacking Lawson's training, couldn't resist baiting Connor's men. One young man named Leroy Allen reportedly slashed at a police dog with a clay pipe, causing the German shepherd to lunge at him, tearing the sleeve of his coat and pinning him to the ground. Rioting followed, and for the next fifteen minutes, police used their K-9 units and nightsticks aggressively to clear the park and the streets around the church.

Now it was King's turn to be disappointed, not only at the violence but also in the rather low energy being generated by the campaign. After five days of demonstrations, there were only 102 people in jail, less than half the number imprisoned on just the *first* day of the Albany

marches. Even worse, jailgoing volunteers were becoming scarce and the media wasn't paying much attention. King decided again to change strategies. Walker's plan had called for him to go to jail on the third day, which would have been April 5, but King chose to remain at large indefinitely so that he could work on rebuilding local enthusiasm for Project C.

Realizing that Shuttlesworth had not, in fact, handled the local conservatives, the SCLC leader invited himself to a gathering of the Baptist Ministers Conference on Monday, April 8. At the meeting, King appealed to the ministers for their active support. Although most of those assembled (notably J. L. Ware) agreed with Birmingham's white liberals that Boutwell should be given a chance to prove himself, they were nevertheless impressed by King's eloquence, not to mention his fame, and found it more difficult to turn him down than it had been to refuse Shuttlesworth. By the end of the meeting, King had persuaded most of them either to join the crusade or, at the very least, not to oppose it publicly.

Meanwhile, the white authorities also held strategy meetings. Connor and his political ally, Alabama governor George C. Wallace, wanted to bring heavily armed state troopers into Birmingham to intimidate the local Negroes and, if necessary, crush their demonstrations. But Birmingham's reformers—including the Boutwell administration, the county sheriff, the newspapers, and the business elite—objected to this plan, fearing more violence and more bad publicity. They advocated Pritchett-style resistance and even consulted with the Albany police chief to get his advice.

In the end, a compromise was reached: For the time being, there would be no state troopers, but the city would seek an injunction barring further protests. Responding to Connor's request, state circuit court judge William A. Jenkins Jr.

Martin Luther King Jr. (second from right, foreground) talks with Ralph Abernathy (third from right) at the Gaston Motel on April 16, just before the start of another march.

George C. Wallace
1919–1998

When George Wallace first ran for governor of Alabama in 1958, he was considered—compared with his rival, John Patterson—rather soft on civil rights. Part of the reason was that Wallace's mentor in Alabama politics, outgoing governor Big Jim Folsom, had been the rare southern moderate on segregation. But what had worked for Folsom blew up in Wallace's face as Patterson ran hard to the racial right. The NAACP endorsed Wallace, but the Klan backed Patterson, and he won in a landslide. "John Patterson outniggered me," Wallace said afterward, "and I'm never going to be outniggered again."

When Wallace ran again in 1962, he took the hardest line possible on segregation and won the largest vote yet of any Alabama gubernatorial candidate. In his January 1963 inaugural address, Wallace told his constituents:

Today, I have stood where once Jefferson Davis stood and took an oath to my people. It is very appropriate then that from this cradle of the Confederacy, this very heart of the great Anglo-Saxon Southland, that today we sound the drum for freedom as have our generations of forebears before us done, time and time again through history. Let us rise to the call of freedom-loving blood that is in us and send our answer to the tyranny that clanks its chains upon the South. In the name of the greatest people that have ever trod this earth, I draw the line in the dust and toss the gauntlet before the feet of tyranny, and I say, Segregation today! Segregation tomorrow! Segregation forever!

George C. Wallace pledges "segregation today, segregation tomorrow, segregation forever" in his 1963 inaugural address.

issued a temporary restraining order about nine o'clock on the night of Wednesday, April 10. Four hours later, the papers were served on King at the Gaston Motel.

King's earlier decision not to defy Judge Elliott's order had significantly damaged Albany Movement morale. Now, he faced a similar choice. Eight days into Project C, there were still just 150 demonstrators in jail. "The black business community and some of the clergy [were] pressing us to call off the demonstrations and just get out of town," Andrew Young recalled. "We didn't know what to do." After the mass meeting that night, the Project C leadership sat in Room 30 of the Gaston Motel and talked.

The campaign was clearly in a downward spiral. As King later recalled, "Our most dedicated and devoted leaders were overwhelmed by a feeling of hopelessness." Earlier that day, Connor had informed James Esdale, the movement's bail bondsman, that he had reached the limit of his credit with the city. Esdale had already posted twenty thousand dollars' worth of appeal and appearance bonds to free seventy-one demonstrators, but there would be no more. Anyone who went to jail from this point on might be in there for a spell.

For two hours, King listened to various arguments about whether or not to obey the injunction, most of which he had heard before in Albany. Then, without a word, he stood up and went into the suite's bedroom to think by himself. When he emerged a little while later, he was wearing a work shirt, blue jeans rolled up at the cuffs, and clodhoppers—each item conspicuously new and all the more startling because most of those present had never seen him before in anything but a dark business suit. From his clothing, they could tell that he had decided to go to jail. "I don't know what will happen," King said. "I don't know where the money will come from. But I have to make a faith act." According to Andrew Young, "That was, I think, the beginning of his true leadership."

A Birmingham police officer writes down the names of demonstrators picketing outside a downtown store on April 11. By this time, the SCLC and the ACMHR had instituted nightly mass meetings, which continued until the end of the campaign, and a boycott of downtown stores that cut deeply into the Easter trade.

BEVEL'S INSPIRATION

The next day, Good Friday, King, Abernathy, and about forty others were arrested by Connor as they marched toward City Hall. King and Abernathy were then separated from the others and placed in solitary confinement—"for your safety," they were told. "Those were the longest, most frustrating and bewildering hours I have lived," King later wrote. Yet his arrest made instant national news.

After this initial spark, however, the doldrums returned, and as King's incarceration dragged on, Project C languished. Finally, on Saturday, April 20, King and Abernathy accepted release on bond, telling reporters that they had to confer with their lawyers. Their contempt trial began two days later, and at the end of it, Judge Jenkins found them guilty. He did, however, stay their five-day sentences and fifty-dollar fines pending appeal.

Although King and Abernathy remained free, Project C seemed on the verge of collapse. Now that the movement's bail fund had been exhausted, volunteers for jail were even harder to come by. The boycott was falling apart, too, and King was concerned that the media's interest was flagging. It seemed clear that a decisive move would have to be made. So, on the same day that Judge Jenkins issued his guilty verdict in the contempt trial, Shuttlesworth applied to the city for a permit to parade on Thursday, May 2. Both governments turned him down.

The model for this march was quite consciously the April 19, 1960, march staged by the Nashville students at the climax of their sit-ins. The problem was, Who would march? With no bail funds available, few adults were willing to risk jail. They feared losing their jobs and becoming unable to support their families. But Nashville veteran James Bevel, who had recently joined the SCLC as its Mississippi field secretary, had another idea. He wanted to enlist the children of Birmingham because their incarceration wouldn't imperil any family's economic well-being. "A boy from high school has the same effect in terms of being in jail,

in terms of putting pressure on the city, as his father," Bevel told King, "and yet there's no economic threat to the family, because he is still on the job."

Bevel also pointed out that, as a result of the daily youth workshops he had been leading, many of those children were already well acquainted with nonviolent practice and, unlike their parents, were enthusiastic about marching. "This was not the first time that young veterans of the Freedom

"Injustice anywhere is a threat to justice everywhere."

MARTIN LUTHER KING JR. IN "LETTER FROM BIRMINGHAM JAIL"

Rides had pressed King to jump off the cliff," historian Taylor Branch has observed, "but none of them had been quite like Bevel," who "possessed the unique charm of a spellbinding eccentric."

The leading Negro businessmen of Birmingham—including King's host, John Drew, and millionaire A. G. Gaston (owner of the

On Good Friday, Fred Shuttlesworth, Ralph Abernathy, and Martin Luther King lead the march that resulted in the arrest and jailing of King and Abernathy.

Gaston Motel, among other concerns)—thought that the idea of using children younger than college age both unwise and immoral—an altogether terrible idea. Nearly every Birmingham minister consulted by King agreed. What would be the effect on their school and criminal records? How would their young lives be scarred by exposure to the violence of Connor's police and the indecency of his jail? Would they be beaten? Would they be raped?

Letter from Birmingham Jail

While in jail following his Good Friday arrest, King was given a copy of the *Birmingham News* to read. On page two, beneath photographs of himself and Abernathy, was a story headlined "White Clergymen Urge Local Negroes to Withdraw from Demonstrations." In an open letter to the community, eight liberal white ministers, who had earlier criticized Governor Wallace's "segregation forever" speech, now condemned the "unwise and untimely" Project C protests, praising the police for the "calm manner in which these demonstrations have been handled." King and the other Negro leaders, they declared, were inciting violence in Birmingham, and it had to stop.

Although King rarely responded to public attacks, he couldn't get this one out of his head, so he began composing a rebuttal in the margins of the newspaper, which was the only writing paper he had. When Clarence Jones came to visit him the next day, King surprised the lawyer by unbuttoning his prison

shirt, removing the marked-up newspaper, and discreetly slipping it into Jones's briefcase. "I need more paper," King said.

Over the next week, Jones brought more paper, along with typewritten copies of the sections already smuggled out. Thus, the writing and editing continued.

Because of its excellence and subsequent notoriety, King's "Letter from Birmingham Jail" is sometimes credited as the turning point of the Project C campaign. But such credit is misleading because, at the time, few people knew about King's letter. It wasn't mentioned in any media reports until the middle of May and remained unpublished

This first edition of "Letter from Birmingham Jail" was printed as a pamphlet by the American Friends Service Committee in May 1963.

until May 28, when the American Friends Service Committee issued it as a pamphlet.

"I have yet to engage in a direct action campaign that was well-timed in the view of those who have not suffered unduly from the disease of segregation," King wrote. "For years now, I have heard the word *Wait*. It rings in the ears of every Negro with piercing familiarity. This *Wait* has almost always meant *Never*. We must come to see with one of our distinguished jurists that 'justice too long delayed is justice denied.'"

One of Bull Connor's men places Martin Luther King Jr. into a paddy wagon on Good Friday.

A police dog lunges at a seventeen-year-old
Negro bystander during the demonstrations in
downtown Birmingham on May 3. The next day at
the White House, President Kennedy discussed the
photo publicly, expressing the horror and sadness
he felt after seeing the image for the first time on
the front page of that day's *New York Times*.

King understood and sympathized with these
concerns, but he also felt a terrible pressure to do
something, anything, to save the campaign.
Having no better ideas, he gave Bevel permission
to address the mass meeting on Tuesday, April 30.

Bevel began by announcing that, although
Shuttlesworth's request for a permit had been
turned down, they would march regardless.
Then he revealed that the marchers would be
high school students. During the next twenty-
four hours, however, the minimum age required
of jail volunteers fell steadily as younger and
younger children begged to be included. To
accommodate them, Bevel devised a simple
rationale: If a child was old enough to be a church
member, he was old enough to march. King
approved this policy even though he knew as
well as Bevel that most Baptist congregations
allowed children as young as six years old to
become church members.

THE CHILDREN'S CRUSADE

The Children's Crusade began early on Thursday
afternoon, when fifty youngsters marched out of
Sixteenth Street Baptist and began heading
downtown. They walked as schoolchildren—
orderly, two abreast—laughing, clapping, and
singing high-spirited freedom songs. Some
carried picket signs. At first, Connor wasn't sure
what to do with them, but soon enough he
decided they would have to be arrested. Stopped
by police before they reached the downtown
shopping district, they obeyed instructions and
were calmly loaded into paddy wagons.

Then another group of children emerged from
the church, and another, and another. For nearly
three hours, hooky-playing children poured out
of Sixteenth Street Baptist until Connor ran out
of paddy wagons and had to bring in school buses
to transport the hundreds of new prisoners. Nor
was there room for all of them at the city jail.
As many as seventy-five children were crammed
into cells built for eight, and they still didn't fit,
so a barracks was set up at the local fairgrounds.
Citing Wyatt Walker's meticulous jail registry,
King announced that 958 children had
volunteered for jail that day, about 600 of
whom were currently in custody.

On Friday, May 3, a thousand more children
gathered at Sixteenth Street Baptist for a repeat
performance. Connor's men showed up as
well, this time with new orders. Under no
circumstances were they to make any
more arrests. Instead, the police
and firemen were to block
access to downtown and keep
the demonstrators confined
in the Negro section.

Police captain Glenn V. Evans
confronted the first group of
children at the corner of Fifth
Avenue and Seventeenth Street.

James Bevel (with megaphone)
attempts to disperse a large crowd
of demonstrators on May 4. He told
the crowd that a disturbance "like
this could easily cause a riot."

Pointing to the fire hoses behind him, he told
them to "disperse or you're going to get wet."
The teenagers kept marching, however, at which
point Evans signaled the firemen to spray them
with fogging nozzles. Most retreated, as did
the adult bystanders in Kelly Ingram Park, but
ten or so held their ground. Evans then ordered
through his bullhorn an evacuation of the area.
There was general compliance until people
began to notice the holdout children, singing
the word *freedom* over and over again as though
it were *amen*.

As the emboldened crowd surged back into
the park, the firemen increased the pressure in
their hoses and concentrated the outflow on the
defiant students, who sat down on the sidewalk
to stabilize themselves. The firemen then hooked
their hoses up to pieces of equipment called
monitor guns. Fed by two hoses simultaneously,
the monitor guns produced jets of water so
powerful that they stripped the bark off trees.
The force of these jets lifted the
children up off the ground
and sent them rolling
down the sidewalk.

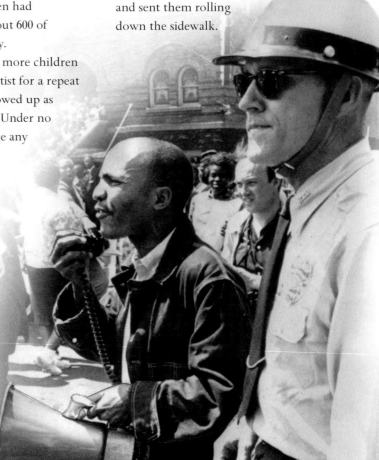

Young Negroes taking part in the Children's Crusade sit down on the sidewalk with their hands behind their heads to protect themselves from the firemen's high-pressure hoses.

Some were slammed into the curb; others were tossed over parked cars.

A. G. Gaston had been talking on the telephone with attorney David Vann, a leader of the white reformers, when the demonstration began. Through the window of his office in the Gaston Building, catercorner to Kelly Ingram Park, he could easily see the scene as it unfolded. Gaston and Vann had been complaining to one another about King's tactics, which they both deplored.

Birmingham firemen use a monitor gun to clear Kelly Ingram Park on May 4.

Even if the marches succeeded, moderate whites would be alienated, and if they failed, the segregationists would be strengthened. Either way, King was undermining the delicate, discreet efforts Gaston and Vann were making to turn Birmingham around.

Suddenly, Gaston paused in his conversation. Then he came back on the line. "But, Lawyer Vann," Gaston exclaimed. "they've turned the fire hoses on a little black girl. And they're rolling that girl right down the middle of the street!"

Like Gaston, bystanders watched in horror as children were flushed down the sidewalk like bits of debris. Enraged, they began to pick up rocks and bricks that had been dislodged by the jets and throw them at the firemen. In response, the police K-9 units went into action, charging the crowd and tearing at clothes and flesh until the park was cleared. Despite Connor's orders, several hundred more people were arrested before the riot ended near 3 P.M. In the meantime, the movement received exactly what its leaders had sought.

That night, the national television networks showed graphic footage of Negro children being savaged by Connor's fire hoses and German shepherds. Not merely Birmingham's Negro community but white and black Americans all over the nation instantly unified behind King. According to Arthur Schlesinger, the footage even persuaded President Kennedy that he finally had to take on southern intransigence with regard to civil rights.

Until the May 3 violence, John Kennedy had paid even less attention to Project C than he had to the Albany Movement. The water and the dogs changed all that. The next day, he sent Burke Marshall and John Doar down to Birmingham to mediate.

OVERLEAF: **A young girl is soaked** by firemen on May 8. Meanwhile, as Burke Marshall and John Doar began their negotiations, Treasury Secretary Douglas Dillon brought additional pressure to bear by calling the heads of the big department-store chains with branches in Birmingham.

Police escort a group of Negro children to jail on May 4. More than two hundred of those arrested were still waiting in the jailyard to be processed when night fell.

SHUTTLE DIPLOMACY

With the marches and the violence both continuing, Marshall and Doar conducted a form of shuttle diplomacy, moving back and forth between the whites and the blacks, hoping to start a dialogue. Meanwhile, on Monday, May 6, another thousand demonstrators were jailed, and the mass meeting that night, set for St. James Baptist, filled three other churches as well. Project C treasurer William Shortridge and his assistants collected forty thousand dollars, and Bevel told King that he would have six thousand jail volunteers ready for Tuesday.

This was the situation as chamber of commerce president Sidney Smyer convened on Tuesday morning a meeting of the Senior Citizens Committee, Birmingham's informal yet exceedingly powerful business club. Its members, who employed

about 80 percent of the city's workforce, were decidedly unhappy. They despised Project C and couldn't bear the idea of negotiating under the pressure of ongoing demonstrations. But those demonstrations had now emptied the downtown stores of nervous white (as well as black) shoppers, so something had to be done. This point was made even more forcefully at noontime, when the "big mules," as they were called, emerged for lunch to find young Negroes seemingly running wild in the streets.

King and Walker had concluded that one of the key mistakes made in Albany was the movement's focus on politicians who didn't need Negro votes to stay in office. In Birmingham, therefore, they targeted white businessmen who needed Negro trade to stay in business. To increase the pressure on the members of the

A young boy peers through the jailyard fence on May 7 during his second day of imprisonment. Horror stories abounded about maltreatment of the children.

Senior Citizens Committee that Tuesday, the SCLC leadership arranged for small groups of the best-trained young volunteers— six hundred in all— to make their way inconspicuously downtown. Meanwhile, adult volunteers filled up the trunks of their cars with picket signs and then parked their vehicles at a dozen downtown rendezvous points. At noon precisely, the youngsters dashed for the cars, retrieved the picket signs, and began

With Burke Marshall facilitating, the Senior Citizens subcommittee met that evening with a Negro delegation led by A. G. Gaston. Not until midnight, however, did they all abandon the fiction that they could somehow craft a settlement without King. Reaching that point, they secretly adjourned their meeting to the Drew house, where the negotiations continued with King included. By 4 A.M., the basic parameters of an agreement had emerged, but they all felt they could do little more without first getting some sleep.

The settlement framework called for an end to the demonstrations in exchange for the gradual desegregation of public facilities in the downtown shopping district. The sticking point, however, turned out to be the two thousand demonstrators still in jail. The white negotiators repeatedly pointed out that they

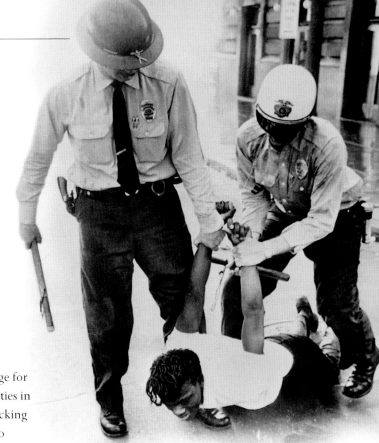

Police make another arrest on May 7. By this time, according to Wyatt Walker's count, there were 148 reporters in Birmingham, some from as far away as Japan and the Soviet Union.

"I waited a week to see Shuttlesworth get hit with a hose. I'm sorry I missed it.... I wish they'd carried him away in a hearse."

BULL CONNOR ON THE MAY 7 HOSING OF FRED SHUTTLESWORTH

picketing the downtown shopping district.

From his observation post in an office building near the Sixteenth Street Baptist Church, Walker could see the police transferring more and more units downtown. Finally, when he judged that their lines had sufficiently thinned, he used his walkie-talkie to order a general charge. The doors of the church burst open, and thousands of children dashed out. Ignoring crosswalks and traffic signals, they sprinted around the undermanned police and headed for downtown.

The big mules returned from their lunch break with no doubt left that their world was in crisis. Either they would have to begin negotiating with the Negroes soon, or else bloodshed was likely. Then the troops would come—whether state or federal, it didn't matter—after which their businesses would suffer, perhaps for years to come. Facing this eventuality, they formed a subcommittee that afternoon to open settlement talks immediately.

were only businessmen and that, even if they could manipulate the city's judicial system, they certainly couldn't admit to it in a public settlement document. They offered instead a

After his 1943 Yale graduation, Burke Marshall worked for army intelligence as a Japanese linguist and cryptanalyst. After the war, he attended Yale Law School and then went to work for Covington and Burling in Washington.

private promise to do their best, but that wasn't good enough for King, who wanted them at least to raise the $250,000 necessary for bail. When the big mules refused, the parties deadlocked.

At this point, Robert Kennedy entered the negotiations, pressuring King to relent. Instead, King pushed Kennedy to come up with the bail money himself. After all, King pointed out, the attorney general had raised $53 million from private sources to ransom back the Bay of Pigs prisoners. Surely he could find $250,000 now?

Some counterpunching followed, as Kennedy warned King that the possibility for settlement would disappear once Governor Wallace sent in the National Guard and King warned Kennedy that he was thinking about asking New York governor Nelson Rockefeller for the money. (A man of great personal wealth, Rockefeller was also the current front-runner for the 1964 Republican presidential nomination.) Finally, the attorney general told King that if the SCLC could raise $90,000 of the total, he would arrange for the rest.

King announced the settlement at a press conference held in the courtyard of the Gaston Motel on Friday, May 10. Shuttlesworth read the final terms: The downtown fitting rooms would be desegregated by Monday; a biracial committee would be created within fifteen days; downtown restrooms and water fountains would be integrated within thirty days of the anticipated court order establishing the Boutwell administration. In addition, within sixty days of that court order, the downtown stores would end lunch-counter segregation and begin hiring Negro clerks. Finally, all jailed demonstrators were either out of jail or on their way out.

Newsmen jam the courtyard of the Gaston Motel for a May 9 press conference held by King and Abernathy (seated at the table). All King had to say, however, was that negotiations were still under way.

BOMBINGHAM REDUX

The violence, however, wasn't over. On Saturday night, the Klan held a large rally in Bessemer on the outskirts of Birmingham, after which two attempts were made to assassinate Martin Luther King. (The perpetrators didn't know that King had already left town for Atlanta.) At 10:45 P.M. a stick of dynamite exploded at the home of his younger brother, Birmingham minister A. D. King. There was extensive structural damage, but no one was hurt. About an hour later, another bomb missed its target (Room 30 of the Gaston Motel) but nevertheless destroyed the motel's office.

A sign on an automobile announces the May 11 Ku Klux Klan rally in Bessemer, where Grand Dragon Robert Shelton spoke to a crowd of about one thousand Klansmen. Later that Saturday night, two bombs exploded in nearby Birmingham.

The wrecked home of the Rev. A. D. King, located in a pleasant Birmingham neighborhood called Ensley.

As the Saturday night bar crowd gathered to survey the damage, shock swiftly turned to rage.

Having calmed his family and neighbors, A. D. King rushed downtown to Kelly Ingram Park, where he grabbed a bullhorn and began preaching to the angry mob. "Our *home* was just bombed," he said. "Now, if we who were in jeopardy of being killed, if we have gone away *not* angry, *not* throwing bricks, if we could do that and we were in danger, why must *you* rise up to hurt our cause?"

It was now about two o'clock in the morning, and everyone was tired. With the police showing commendable restraint, the crowd slowly began to disperse. From atop a parked Cadillac, A. D. King was singing "We Shall Overcome" to several hundred stragglers when an irregular regiment of 250 state troopers, fish and game wardens, and tax agents arrived on the scene. Led by state public safety director

State public safety director Al Lingo (left) confers with his colleague Bull Connor on May 10, the day before the rioting began in Birmingham.

Al Lingo, these men carried carbines along with their billy clubs. The senior police officer in charge asked Lingo politely to leave, assuring him that the situation was under control, but Lingo ignored the request and led his men in a charge down the street. The violence that ensued was, according to some journalists, worse than anything they had seen at Ole Miss. "Negroes fled in terror as they were clubbed with gun butts and nightsticks," the *New York Times* reported. "The 'thonk' of clubs striking heads could be heard across the street."

By the next morning, a nine-block area looked as through it had been struck by a hurricane.

It soon became clear that Lingo's charge was part of a Wallace-Connor strategy to sabotage the settlement by provoking Negro violence. Indeed, feeling betrayed, many blacks spent the next day arming themselves for a battle Sunday night. Immediately, King returned to Birmingham and overspread the city, urging his followers to remain nonviolent and assuring them that the federal government would

protect them. Meanwhile, the president, thinking of Oxford, backed up King's words by announcing on national television that he was sending federal troops to Fort McClellan, just thirty miles outside the city. "The Birmingham agreement was and is a fair and just accord," Kennedy said, "The federal government will not permit it to be sabotaged by a few extremists on either side who think they can defy both the law and the wishes of responsible citizens by inciting or inviting violence." The efforts worked, Sunday night passed without violence, and the settlement held.

At the same corner where firemen turned their hoses on protesters three years earlier, Mayor Albert Boutwell (center) walks with A. G. Gaston (left) and John Drew, all of whom continued the work of improving race relations.

Marching on Washington

1963–1964

Before the Project C demonstrations in Birmingham, the Kennedy administration had been a rather reluctant partner in the Negro struggle for civil rights. Although the president and his brother, the attorney general, sympathized with the goals of the movement, they considered the demands of its leaders unreasonable and politically naive. The 1960 Democratic party platform had, it was true, called for the introduction of new civil rights legislation, but the political climate in Washington, the Kennedys believed, didn't yet permit meaningful change. Sixty-seven votes were needed to overcome the promised Senate filibuster of any new civil rights initiative, and the votes simply weren't there. So the Kennedys kept postponing the introduction of a bill because they didn't want to waste any of their precious political capital on a sure loser.

Civil rights activists on their way to the Lincoln Memorial during the August 1963 March on Washington for Jobs and Freedom.

The violence in Birmingham, however, changed their minds, just as it changed the minds of whites all over America. On May 24, two weeks after the announcement of the Birmingham settlement, Robert Kennedy met in New York City with a group of influential black celebrities and intellectuals. Those present included the writer James Baldwin, singer Harry Belafonte, psychologist Kenneth Clark, and SCLC lawyer Clarence Jones. During the generally angry conversation, the attorney general was told bluntly that the federal government was not living up to its moral responsibility to defend the rights of its Negro citizens.

Robert Kennedy's immediate reaction was indignation at the lack of gratitude for all the Kennedy administration had done for civil rights. Once the attorney general calmed down, however, he realized that the criticism was largely correct. "The more lasting impact of the encounter," historian David J. Garrow has written, "was to sensitize [Kennedy] more deeply than ever to the fact that what the federal government had done

still fell short of what was morally necessary." A week later, he assembled the administration's top political strategists and told them that, however poor the chances of passing a civil rights bill might be, the time had come to try.

The president generally supported his brother's initiative but did impose one important restriction. In his view, equal access to public accommodations and voting rights were too much to take on simultaneously. So voting rights would have to wait.

Alabama governor George Wallace (second from left) stands, as promised, "in the schoolhouse door" to block integration at the University of Alabama. Standing opposite him is Deputy Attorney General Nicholas Katzenbach.

STANDING IN THE SCHOOLHOUSE DOOR

Meanwhile, Alabama governor George Wallace, having lost the battle in Birmingham, opened up a new front in Tuscaloosa, home of the all-white University of Alabama. The school was being

> "We have a responsibility, Governor, to insure that the integrity of the courts is maintained… and all of the force behind the federal government will be used to that end. "
>
> ROBERT F. KENNEDY TO GEORGE WALLACE

compelled by a federal court to admit two Negro students, James Hood and Vivian Malone. Fearing a repeat of the Ole Miss violence, the university president had decided to acquiesce in their admission. Now Wallace overrode this decision and, emulating Mississippi governor Ross Barnett, appointed himself temporary university registrar so that he could personally refuse Hood and Malone admission.

During the 1962 campaign, Wallace had promised his segregationist constituency that he would "stand in the schoolhouse door," if necessary, to block school desegregation. On June 11, 1963, he did just that outside Foster Auditorium, the main administration building on the Tuscaloosa campus. Surrounding him were one hundred state troopers commanded by Col. Al Lingo, the state public safety director whose inflammatory charge had set off the May 12 rioting in Birmingham. Surrounding the state troopers was an even larger army of reporters, photographers, and television cameramen.

The curtain went up as scheduled at 11 A.M., when Hood and Malone arrived on campus accompanied by Deputy Attorney General

Nicholas Katzenbach. The temperature in Tuscaloosa was about one hundred degrees that day. "Stop!" Wallace ordered Katzenbach, who replied, "I have a proclamation from the president of the United States ordering you to cease and desist from unlawful obstructions. I'm asking you for an unequivocal assurance that you will not bar entry of these students and you will step aside peacefully and do your constitutional duty. Do I have your assurance?"

Rather than answer Katzenbach directly, Wallace read his own prepared statement: "I, George C. Wallace, as governor, do hereby denounce and forbid this illegal and unwanted action by the central government." The use of the word *central*, rather than *federal*, was significant. Wallace liked its connotation of Communist totalitarianism.

Taking this statement to mean "No," Katzenbach walked back to his car and drove Hood and Malone to their respective dormitories. (The Justice Department had obtained the keys the day before, having explained to the housing office that the rooms had to be checked for bombs.) Simultaneously, as planned, the president

federalized the Alabama National Guard. Four hours later, Brig. Gen. Henry Graham, the same officer who had commanded the May 1961 Freedom Ride operation, arrived on campus with a force of one hundred soldiers. Sixteen hundred more remained on alert back at the local armory, and at Fort Benning, Georgia, four hundred regular army troops sat in their helicopters, ready for immediate deployment should the situation turn violent. The Kennedys had learned at least this much from Oxford.

Graham walked up to Wallace, who was again blocking the Foster Auditorium doorway; saluted him; and said, "Governor Wallace, it is my sad duty to inform you that the National Guard has been federalized. Please stand aside so that the order of the court may be accomplished." Wallace returned Graham's salute, stepped aside, and left the campus quickly in a lights-flashing motorcade. Moments later, Hood and Malone were registered.

Vivian Malone passes by a line of University of Alabama registrars on June 11 as she registers for classes at the Tuscaloosa campus.

KENNEDY TAKES A STAND

In Washington, John Kennedy had watched the Wallace-Katzenbach encounter on television. After federalizing the Alabama National Guard, he had informed the three national networks that he wanted to go on television himself that night. The president planned to discuss civil rights, and his surprise decision threw the White House staff into a frenzy of activity.

Robert Kennedy addresses civil rights demonstrators outside the Justice Department on June 14.

The president's chief speechwriter, Theodore Sorensen, had already been assigned the task of developing text to accompany a new civil rights bill, but he didn't yet have a first draft ready, and now his deadline was suddenly hours—not weeks—away.

Sorensen worked all day toward the eight o'clock deadline but didn't make it. Instead, Kennedy went on the air and spoke live for eighteen minutes, working from an incomplete text. He filled in the holes with improvisations based on a recent memo written by Louis Martin that had stuck in his mind.

"The heart of the question," the president told the nation,

is whether all Americans are to be afforded equal rights and equal opportunities, whether we are going to treat our fellow Americans as we want to be treated. If an American, because his skin is dark, cannot eat lunch in a restaurant open to the public; if he cannot send his children to the best public school available; if he cannot vote for the public officials who represent him; if, in short, he cannot enjoy the full and free life which all of us want, then who among us would be content to have the color of his skin changed and stand in his place? Who among us would then be content with the counsels of patience and delay?

One hundred years of delay have passed since President Lincoln freed the slaves, yet their heirs, their grandsons, are not fully free. They are not yet freed from the bonds of injustice. They are not yet freed from social and economic oppression. And this nation, for all its hopes and all its boasts, will not be fully free until all its citizens are free.

We preach freedom around the world, and we mean it, and we cherish our freedom here at home, but are we to say to the world and, much more importantly, to each other that this is a land of the free except for the Negroes; that we have no second-class citizens except Negroes; that we have no class or caste system, no ghettos, no master race except with respect to Negroes?

Now the time has come for this nation to fulfill its promise. The events in Birmingham and elsewhere have so increased the cries for equality that no city or state or legislative body can prudently choose to ignore them. The fires of frustration and discord are burning in every

city, North and South, where legal remedies are not at hand. Redress is sought in the streets, in demonstrations, parades, and protests which create tensions and threaten violence and threaten lives. We face, therefore, a moral crisis as a country and as a people.

Although Kennedy kept his remarks somewhat vague with regard to specific remedies, his lack of detail didn't bother Martin Luther King, who was thrilled by the unexpected show of support.

> "It is time to act in the Congress, in your state and local legislative bodies, and, above all, in all of our daily lives."
>
> JOHN F. KENNEDY IN HIS JUNE 11 SPEECH

Handwritten notes made by President Kennedy in preparation for his June 11 speech.

At last, King thought, the president of the United States had taken a side. In a congratulatory telegram to the White House, he called the speech "one of the most eloquent, profound and unequivocal pleas for justice and the freedom of all men ever made by any president."

Of course, the southern Democrats in Congress also got Kennedy's message, and the next morning they killed funding for the Area Development Administration, a public works program created by the president to help the nation's most economically depressed regions, especially Appalachia. About the same time, House majority leader Carl Albert of Oklahoma told the president that southern defections were threatening the administration's farm and mass transit bills. "Civil rights," Albert said, "it's overwhelming the whole program."

THE KENNEDY CIVIL RIGHTS BILL

The new civil rights bill was delivered to Capitol Hill on June 19, the same day that recently assassinated NAACP field secretary Medgar Evers was laid to rest in Arlington National Cemetery. Containing seven carefully limited titles, the bill was, in the end, more cautious than bold.

Title I made completion of the sixth grade sufficient proof of literacy, so Negroes with sixth-grade educations could no longer be excluded from voting by literacy tests. Title II banned racial discrimination in public accommodations. Title III empowered the attorney general to file his own school desegregation lawsuits.

A thousand angry blacks marched spontaneously down Capitol Street after Evers's funeral, throwing rocks and bottles. Before the police could let loose their dogs, however, a white man (left) intervened. "My name is John Doar," he said. "I'm from the Justice Department, and anyone around here knows I stand for what is right."

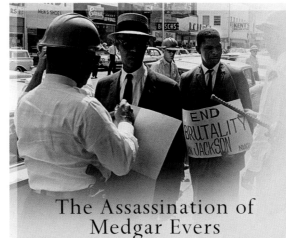

Deputy Police Chief J. L. Ray (right) arrests Roy Wilkins (left) and Medgar Evers for picketing outside a Woolworth's in Jackson on June 1, 1963.

The Assassination of Medgar Evers

From the day in December 1954 that Medgar Evers signed on as the NAACP's first full-time field secretary in Mississippi, he became an obvious target for assassination. In his house, the window blinds were always drawn. He owned several guns and kept one in his Oldsmobile, which had a V-8 engine powerful enough to outrun most threatening situations. He coached his children on what to do if they heard gunfire. Telephoned death threats to the Evers home were common, and by June 1963, they had become a daily event.

At the time, Evers was deeply involved in the Jackson Movement. This direct action campaign had begun inauspiciously in December 1962, when the North Jackson NAACP Youth Council (advised by white Tougaloo College professor John Salter) organized a boycott of downtown stores. Evers supported the effort, but the NAACP's national office remained aloof, ignoring his requests for bail money. After Birmingham, however, NAACP executive secretary Roy Wilkins realized that he had some catching up to do if he wanted to keep up with the SCLC, so he reversed himself and began flooding Jackson with aid and attention.

With all of this new support, the Jackson Movement escalated, and after a disappointing May 27 meeting with Mayor Allen Thompson, it took to the streets on May 28. At first, Evers expressed reservations, pointing out that direct action campaigns often have long-term negative consequences. But he couldn't argue with the campaign's success. According to his wife, Myrlie, "For the first time, the entire Negro community was

behind him; for the first time, volunteers were everywhere." The enthusiasm was contagious, and even Evers was caught up in it.

His excitement lasted about three days. Then, on May 31, Roy Wilkins and the NAACP's national staff came to town. They took over the movement and, backed by local conservatives, slowed things down considerably. For the foreseeable future, it was announced, there would be no more demonstrations. Morale plummeted, and Evers found himself caught between his old allies in the NAACP and his new constituency among the young. Unable to choose between them, he simply withdrew.

On the night of June 11, he attended a disappointing rally at the New Jerusalem Baptist Church, where there was more talk about selling NAACP T-shirts than about freedom. He arrived home at 12:20 A.M., emerging from his Oldsmobile with a bundle of the JIM CROW MUST GO T-shirts in his arms. Meanwhile, from the shelter of a honeysuckle thicket 150 feet away, a gunman took aim and shot him in the back with a deer rifle. Evers's neighbors rushed him to the local hospital. but he died later that night from internal injuries and acute loss of blood.

The murder weapon, which the killer had left behind in the honeysuckle, belonged to Byron de la Beckwith, a Citizens' Council member from Greenwood, a small city in the Delta about eighty miles north of Jackson. Beckwith's fingerprints were found on the gun's sight, and several taxi drivers remembered him asking them for directions to Evers's house. Despite this compelling evidence, two different trials ended with hung juries. After the second one, the charges against Beckwith were dropped. His case was reopened in 1989, however, and in 1994, he was convicted of Evers's murder and sentenced to life in prison, where he died in 2001.

Myrlie Evers comforts her son Darryl during the funeral of his father.

Title IV established a Community Relations Service to help resolve race-based disputes. Title V extended the life of the Civil Rights Commission. Title VI withheld federal funds from any state or local programs that engaged in racial discrimination. Title VII created the Equal Employment Opportunity Commission to police discrimination in the federal civil service.

Lyndon Johnson, who had spent six years as majority leader in the Senate before becoming vice president in 1961, didn't think the bill would pass in any form unless the president got energetically behind it. At a June 1 strategy session on the legislative politics of the bill, Johnson insisted that it would be "just another gesture" unless the president toured the South to urge its passage.

Two days later, he told Ted Sorensen that when he was Senate majority leader, "I slept on this couch I'm looking at for thirty-seven nights…and produced quorums at two o'clock and four o'clock and that's what you've got to be prepared to do.…We've got a little pop gun, and I want to pull out the cannon. The president is the cannon. You let him be on all the TV networks, just speaking his conscience, not at a rally in Harlem but at a place in Mississippi or Texas or Louisiana and just have the honor guard have a few Negroes in it. Then let him reach over and point and say, 'I have to order these boys into battle.…I don't ask them what their name is… or what color they got, what religion. If I can order them into battle, I've got to make it possible for them to eat and sleep in this country.'"

Johnson also felt strongly that the president needed to make an early moral appeal to Republicans from the North, Midwest, and West, whose support would be crucial in offsetting southern Democratic defections.

Unfortunately—but not surprisingly, given the bitter nature of the personal relationships among Johnson and the Kennedys—the advice was mostly ignored. The president never toured the South. Instead, at his

brother's suggestion, he invited groups of clergymen, chain-store owners, labor leaders, educators, newspaper publishers, and other businessmen to the White House for a series of meetings designed to build support for the civil rights bill. These guests, nearly every one of them white, gathered weekly in the East Room, hundreds at a time, to listen to the president and the vice president and the attorney general urge voluntary action on racial discrimination. Otherwise, they were told, Birmingham-style demonstrations would eventually force the federal government to intervene on the Negroes' behalf.

By the time the last of these meetings took place on June 21, the omission of black civil rights leaders from the list of invited constituencies had become obvious enough that it had to be

Bayard Rustin, deputy director of the March on Washington for Jobs and Freedom, addresses a press conference on August 7, 1963.

FBI Wiretapping

•

Early in 1962, the FBI began receiving reports from informants in the American Communist party that CPUSA members were bragging about Stanley Levison, crowing that one of their own had become Martin Luther King's chief adviser. From this information, J. Edgar Hoover concluded that Levison must be working secretly for the Soviets to exert influence over the civil rights movement. Although he had no evidence of any direct connection between Levison and the CPUSA (which Levison left in 1955), the FBI director nevertheless reported his surmise to Attorney General Robert Kennedy.

Kennedy refused Hoover's request to tap King's phone but did approve the wiretapping of Levison. The surveillance was ostensibly put in place to detect secret communication between Levison and his Soviet handler (if one existed). More practically, the taps recorded King's regular late-night telephone calls to Levison, during which he discussed candidly and in detail all that he was thinking and doing.

An FBI transcript of a wiretapped telephone conversation between Stanley Levison and Martin Luther King on May 21, 1963.

redressed. Another meeting was scheduled for Saturday morning, June 22, and both King and NAACP executive secretary Roy Wilkins were told that they would be granted private audiences with the president beforehand.

Kennedy expected to offer the movement leaders the usual counsels of patience and gradualism until he learned several days before that King and A. Philip Randolph were jointly planning a massive protest march on Washington for later that summer. This development changed the nature of the meeting entirely. The president, under no circumstances, wanted tens of thousands of Negroes marching in Washington, and he moved cancellation of the march to the top of his agenda.

THE MARCH FOR JOBS AND FREEDOM

Randolph, of course, had been the driving force behind the planned 1941 March on Washington, called off at the last moment when Pres. Franklin Roosevelt agreed to ban racial discrimination in government and defense industry employment. Bayard Rustin had worked closely with Randolph on the 1941 march, and in December 1962 they began discussing the feasibility of staging a similar March for Jobs and Freedom sometime during 1963.

By April, they had come far enough along that Randolph began inviting other civil rights organizations to participate. First he approached Wilkins and National Urban League executive director Whitney M. Young Jr., both of whom reacted coolly. Then he tried contacting the SCLC, but with Project C in full deployment, no one even returned his call.

In the aftermath of Birmingham, however, King independently came up with the idea of staging a large protest in the nation's capital. On June 1, he mentioned the idea to his close adviser Stanley Levison in a telephone conversation recorded by the FBI. (J. Edgar Hoover had used Levison's past association with the Communist party to obtain permission for this wiretap, which allowed him to monitor King's activities because King treated Levison as a something of a father confessor.)

King told Levison that he had been thinking about organizing a huge "march on Washington" because "the threat itself may so frighten the president that he would have to do something," meaning new civil rights legislation. (This conversation, of course, took place before Kennedy's June 11 speech.) Levison replied that Randolph was already planning such a march and that he should be contacted, either by Clarence Jones or Levison himself. King agreed, and a few days later, Jones called Randolph, who enthusiastically accepted King's involvement. The seventy-four-year-old Randolph was the elder statesman of the civil rights movement, but King, after Birmingham, was undeniably its most popular and visible leader.

Randolph had wanted the march to emphasize jobs and job training. At the time, black unemployment was 11 percent, or more than double the white rate of 5 percent. Similarly, the average black family earned $3,500 a year, compared with the $6,500 earned by the average white family. With King's involvement, however, the focus of the march shifted away from economic issues to the Kennedy administration's civil rights bill.

In another FBI-recorded telephone call, a transcript of which was passed on to the Kennedys, King told Levison that the Washington protest would have to be aimed at Congress, not the president. Nevertheless, President Kennedy wanted the march called off entirely. He was worried that it would degenerate into violence, and he believed sincerely that the best way for Negroes to encourage passage of the bill was to stay off the streets. The worst thing they could do, he planned to tell the movement leaders on June 22, was to present themselves as threatening.

THE JUNE 22 MEETING

The president began by warning them that rioting would set the movement back a decade; and even if there was no violence, Kennedy went on, some congressmen would resent the implicit

threat and oppose the civil rights bill rather than vote for it "at the point of a gun." Wilkins took this opportunity to point out that the NAACP was not yet a march sponsor and that "quiet, patient lobbying tactics" were the best means he knew of to support the civil rights bill.

Ironically, SNCC was also opposed to the march. At the June 22 meeting, the group was represented by John Lewis, its new national chairman, elected just seven days earlier following the resignation of an exhausted Chuck McDew. "From the first mention of this march," Lewis has written, "a good number of SNCC people wanted nothing to do with it," believing that its outcome would be "lame" and that it would likely be controlled by the federal government.

Such a response was typical of SNCC's insubordinate attitude, and the group would likely have been kept out of the White House meeting had it not been for the fact that its members were disproportionately among those activists being jailed and beaten in the South.

Robert Kennedy talks with Negro leaders on the White House lawn after their June 22 meeting with the president. Standing beside Kennedy are (from left to right) Martin Luther King, Roy Wilkins, and A. Philip Randolph.

Even President Kennedy, who considered the group a "very radical" organization with a leadership that promoted violence, didn't contemplate excluding SNCC.

Lewis, however, was one of the few SNCCers who thought the march was a good idea. He believed that it could dramatize for whites the burden of oppression carried by so many blacks, and thus he withheld SNCC's organizational disdain. Meanwhile, Randolph seized the floor and, ignoring Wilkins's comment, made it clear to Kennedy that the march was going to happen. "Mr. President," he said, "the Negroes are already in the streets. It's very likely impossible to get them off....Isn't it better that they be led by organizations dedicated to civil rights and disciplined by struggle, rather than leave them to other leaders who care nothing about civil rights nor about nonviolence?"

When King and James Farmer backed up Randolph's statement with strong defenses of their own, Kennedy had little choice but to nod his head and change the subject to the legislative situation. "Okay," the president said, "we're in this up to our necks. The worst trouble of all would be to lose the fight in Congress. We'll have enough troubles if we win; but, if we win, we can deal with those. A good many programs I care about may go down the drain as a result of this. I may lose the next election because of this. We may all go down the drain as a result of this—so we are putting a lot on the line. What is important is that we preserve confidence in the good faith of each other."

Kennedy was referring to good faith between himself and the civil rights leaders gathered in the Cabinet Room, but there was also reason to be concerned about good faith within the movement itself. Between Wilkins and King, for example, there had been recent trouble over a new SCLC bail fund named to honor the later Medgar Evers. "To Roy Wilkins," historian Taylor Branch has written, "King might as well have stolen Evers's body." Financial exploitation of the slain Mississippi field secretary's memory belonged exclusively to the NAACP, Wilkins believed, and he was furious at King's poaching. After Wilkins persuaded Evers's widow to sign an agreement stipulating that all funds raised in her husband's memory be controlled by the NAACP, the SCLC backed down, but resentment lingered.

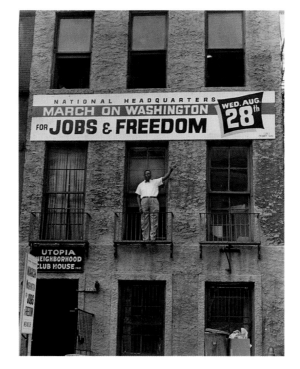

March on Washington administrative chairman Cleveland Robinson stands on the balcony of the event's West 130th Street headquarters.

At an August 3 planning meeting, A. Philip Randolph (left), Roy Wilkins, and Anna Arnold Hedgeman look over a map of the march route.

Fund-raising competition was nothing new. As early as February 1956, King had complained to Wilkins that the NAACP was raising money for itself "in the name of our [Montgomery] movement." After Project C, however, the stakes became much, much higher. With King now elevated to leadership of the movement in the public's mind, Wilkins feared deeply that King's SCLC, rather his own venerable organization, would enjoy the primary financial benefits of expanded public interest in civil rights work.

THE PLANNING OF THE MARCH

On July 2, the Big Six—Randolph, King, Wilkins, Farmer, Lewis, and Whitney Young—met in New York City to work out the organizational hierarchy of the march. By this point, Wilkins had realized that the NAACP would have to participate, and he moved to establish his own group's primacy by blocking the appointment of Rustin as march director. Wilkins's opposition, as one might expect, emphasized Rustin's

homosexuality and Communist past. King and Farmer joined Randolph in defending Rustin, pointing out that neither of these issues had ever caused serious problems before. But Wilkins insisted that increasingly desperate segregationists would now fight more fiercely (and more sordidly) than ever before. To resolve this impasse, Whitney Young suggested that Randolph be named director, and even Wilkins couldn't object to this suggestion. Randolph consented and, as his first act, made Rustin his deputy. Thereafter, Rustin handled all march logistics.

Wilkins then made it clear that he would not consent to any direct action protests, which both Lewis and King had been considering as possible supplements to the march itself. According to Lewis, Wilkins "seemed to assume that because he was the head of the largest organization among us he was the master and we were nothing but a bunch of upstarts. He clearly assumed that we were naive—all of us, including Dr. King. He didn't trust us young people in SNCC, and that was not surprising. But he didn't trust King either. He seemed to feel that King was basically a careless, unsophisticated country preacher and to envy the power and position Dr. King had attained. He didn't think King deserved it."

Lewis was ever more impressed by what he saw outside the meeting on this, his first visit to New York City. "The one thing I will never forget about that trip," he wrote later, "was the great sense of anger and hopelessness I felt in Harlem. It was very different from the South, where we were moving and marching and acting with a sense of community and purpose. In Harlem I saw boarded-up buildings, metal grates on store windows, a different kind of poverty. I felt a great sense of despair. I passed a crowd of people on a corner, listening to a speaker chant and rave about what they were going to do with 'Whitey,' and it seemed very sad, very hopeless."

The goal set for the march was one hundred thousand participants, and it would be Rustin's job to get them smoothly into and out of Washington. "This required all kinds of things that you had to think through," Rustin later recalled. "You had to think how many toilets you needed, where they should be. Where is your line of march. We had to consult doctors on exactly what people should bring to eat so that they

> "The march can serve to restore the dignity and validity of the Negro cause and refocus the Nation's attention and conscience on the big issue: that the Negro wants the breaks that other Americans have."
>
> AN AUGUST 25 *WASHINGTON POST* EDITORIAL

wouldn't get sick." These and innumerable other details were managed from the march's Harlem headquarters in an old church building on West 130th Street.

Meanwhile, in Washington, once the Kennedys realized that they couldn't stop the march, they decided to join it in order to maximize their

Thirteen members of Brooklyn's CORE chapter begin a 240-mile "freedom walk" to Washington on August 15. They indeed arrived on August 28.

influence. At a news conference on July 17, the president endorsed the march; at the same time, his brother began quietly channeling hundreds of thousands of Justice Department dollars into the event. Meanwhile, John Doar led the successful government effort to persuade Randolph and Rustin to hold the march on a Wednesday— specifically, August 28—so that most of the marchers (who couldn't afford to take *two* days off work) would have to come late and leave early. The Justice Department also arranged for the massive rally to be held at the Lincoln Memorial, which was conveniently surrounded on three sides by water (thus easing crowd control in the event of violence). The government even paid for a state-of-the-art sound system, the fear being that if people at the edges of the crowd couldn't hear, they might wander off and get into trouble.

Such extensive government involvement made more than a few blacks suspicious of the event, which Malcolm X soon began calling "the Farce

Volunteer marshals prepare for crowd-control duties on the morning of the march. Among them were a large number of off-duty black policemen from New York City.

on Washington." At the time, Malcolm was finding more and more converts among the restless, resentful youth of the North to whom King's message of nonviolent love held little appeal. "They told those Negroes what time to hit town, how to come, where to stop, what signs to carry, what songs to sing, what speeches they could make, and then they told them to get out of town by sundown," Malcolm sneered.

Members of the Broadway Congregational Church in New York City prepare to board buses to Washington after attending a special midnight prayer service.

But few whites heard Malcolm. Instead, President Kennedy controlled their perception of the march, and in his endorsement remarks, he was careful to emphasize the protest's "peaceful" nature. This characterization irritated some militant SNCCers, who saw it as a ploy "to take the steam out of the movement," but it appealed to the white liberals being courted by Randolph and Rustin, and many soon signed on.

In early August, Randolph announced the addition of four white co-chairs to the March on Washington Committee: United Automobile Workers president Walter Reuther, whose union had the largest Negro membership; Dr. Eugene Carson Blake, vice chair of the Commission on Race Relations of the National Council of Churches; Rabbi Joachim Prinz, president of the American Jewish Congress; and Mathew Ahmann, executive director of the National Catholic Conference for Interracial Justice. With white participation thus assured, Rustin now felt confident that he would reach his goal of one hundred thousand marchers.

THE MARCH ON WASHINGTON

As it turned out, no fewer than 250,000 people took part, and even this figure is probably low. (John Lewis has called it "one of the great undercounts of all time," possibly by half.) To give one a sense of the magnitude of the gathering, consider that at one thirty in the morning on August 28 there was a huge traffic jam outside the Lincoln Tunnel in New York City. The cause was the confluence of chartered buses, all leaving for Washington shortly after midnight to get their passengers to the march on time.

The marchers assembled at the Washington Monument, where a stage had been set up so that speakers could inspire and performers entertain the waiting crowd. Folksinger Joan Baez opened the morning program about ten o'clock with a

RETURN STUB
NEW YORK BRANCH
N. A. A. C. P.

Nº 64

"March On Washington"
WEDNESDAY, AUGUST 28th, 1963

BUSES

Departs 5:00 A. M. from
NEW YORK BRANCH, N. A. A. C. P.,
239 West 125th Street

ROUND TRIP - - - - - - - $6.00

A ticket for one of the buses chartered by the NAACP to carry marchers to Washington.

Marching along the Mall to the Lincoln Memorial are (from left to right) Floyd McKissick, Martin Luther King, and Eugene Carson Blake.

rendition of the movement anthem "We Shall Overcome." Later, Peter, Paul & Mary sang their version of Bob Dylan's "Blowin' in the Wind," which had recently peaked at Number Two on the *Billboard* singles chart. Dylan himself sang a new composition about Medgar Evers and then invited the SNCC Freedom Singers to join him on stage. Jackie Robinson also addressed the gathering crowd, and Roy Wilkins announced that W. E. B. Du Bois, who was then living in Ghana, had died in his sleep at the age of ninety-five.

The mile-long march down Independence and Constitution Avenues was scheduled to start at eleven thirty, with the Big Six in the lead (except for Farmer, who had recently been jailed while organizing Negroes in Louisiana). At about eleven twenty, however, some marchers set off spontaneously behind a local drum-and-bugle corps called the Kenilworth Knights. Already growing restless in the August heat and humidity, the rest of the crowd soon followed.

Randolph, Wilkins, King, Lewis, and Young were at the Capitol, paying their respects to the congressional leadership, when they learned that the march had begun without them. They rushed out of the building and climbed into their cars only to discover that the avenues were impassable. "So we just climbed out of the cars, joined hands, and began walking," Lewis remembered. Meanwhile, aides engineered a break in the line so that photographers could shoot King and the others apparently "leading" the marchers.

JOHN LEWIS'S SPEECH

There was a problem, however, with Lewis's speech. When the texts of the major addresses had been distributed to the press the evening before, Kennedy administration officials had

obtained copies and read them carefully, becoming alarmed at the tone and content of the SNCC leader's rhetoric. For instance, Lewis began his speech by announcing that SNCC could *not* support the administration's civil rights bill because it was "too little and too late." Then he went on to warn the country, using Marxist phraseology, that "the revolution is at hand, and we must free ourselves from the chains of political and economic slavery." Finally, he concluded:

> *The time will come when we will not confine our marching to Washington. We will march through the South, through the heart of Dixie, the way Sherman did. We shall pursue our own "scorched-earth" policy and burn Jim Crow to the ground—nonviolently. We shall fragment the South into a thousand pieces and put them back together in the image of democracy. We will make the action of the past few months look petty. And I say to you, wake up America!*

A Justice Department official made sure that a copy of Lewis's speech was immediately messengered to the Very Rev. Patrick O'Boyle, the Roman Catholic archbishop of Washington, who had consented to deliver the march's invocation. O'Boyle was no racist; in fact, he had integrated the city's parochial schools in 1948, six years before *Brown*. But his reaction was nevertheless predictable: He let it be known that if the Sherman line wasn't changed, he would not take part, placing the march's interracial coalition in jeopardy.

Joan Baez and Bob Dylan perform at the Washington Monument. They sang Dylan's "Blowin' in the Wind," which had been a hit that summer for Peter, Paul & Mary.

vacation in the resort town of Warm Springs, Georgia, he said, and it bothered him that restaurants there refused to serve his driver, who was black. When Kennedy look surprised, Halleck said, "Once in a while, a guy does something because it's right."

In the end, the Judiciary Committee voted against Celler's bill and for the bipartisan compromise. H.R. 7152 then traveled to the Rules Committee for transmission to the House floor. The Rules Committee, however, was chaired by Democrat Howard Smith of Virginia, who strongly opposed integration and referred to the legislation as the "civil wrongs" bill. The bill arrived on his desk on October 29, and there it sat on November 22, when President Kennedy was killed in Dallas.

THE EARLY DAYS OF THE JOHNSON ADMINISTRATION

When Lyndon Johnson became president in November 1963, the Democratic national convention was just nine months away. Johnson badly wanted to remain in the White House, and he knew that to accomplish this, he would have to establish leadership of the party soon. Otherwise, contenders, sensing a political opportunity, would begin entering the race.

At the time of John Kennedy's death, there were two major administration bills pending before Congress: the civil rights legislation and a tax cut. Unable to focus on both, Johnson chose the former because, although riskier, it offered greater benefits, both for himself and for the country. If Johnson could get the bill passed, he would win the allegiance of the party's powerful northern liberal wing, which regarded him with suspicion and was already considering a draft of Bobby Kennedy for president. The civil rights bill immediately became the centerpiece of his new administration.

On November 24, two days after the Kennedy assassination, while the late president's body still lay in state in the Capitol Rotunda, the new president telephoned Whitney Young, with whom he had served on a White House committee looking into employment discrimination. Johnson liked to work on the telephone, using it both to stay in close touch with his allies and to intimidate his adversaries.

The president called Young to let him know that he was making the civil rights bill his top priority and to ask whom else (in addition to Roy Wilkins) he should call. Young suggested James Farmer and gave the president Farmer's number. "He called me at home," Farmer recalled.

New York City newspaper headlines on November 23, 1963, report the assassination of Pres. John F. Kennedy the previous day in Dallas.

The new president, Lyndon B. Johnson, meets with Martin Luther King, Whitney Young, and James Farmer (face cropped) in January 1964. (Roy Wilkins was also present but is not shown in this photo.)

House Judiciary Committee chairman Emanuel Celler sits at his desk on October 23, 1963, beside a stack of testimony given at the hearings his committee held on the Kennedy civil rights bill. This photograph was taken the day after the committee rejected Celler's stronger bill and voted instead for a bipartisan compromise.

"And I was astonished. I'd never been called by a president before. It was impressive." Even during the best of times, President Kennedy had kept the Negro leaders at arm's length; now President Johnson was wooing them, and they were charmed, as Johnson knew they would be.

Next, Johnson invested the bill with the mantle of the martyred president. On November 27, before a special joint session of Congress, he declared, "No memorial oration or eulogy could more eloquently honor President Kennedy's memory than the earliest possible passage of the civil rights bill for which he fought so long. We have talked long enough in this country about equal rights. We have talked for one hundred years or more. Yes, it is time now to write the next chapter—and to write it in books of law."

Lyndon Johnson could never match John Kennedy's oratorical skill, nor his ability to inspire people, but as a legislator he was without peer in twentieth-century American history. The process of lawmaking is, by its nature, rather prosaic and dull. Yet, if done properly, its effects—though lacking the drama of nonviolent direct action—are much more pervasive and long-lasting.

THE CIVIL RIGHTS ACT OF 1964

As Johnson began his work, it still seemed extremely unlikely that a substantial bill would emerge. At the time, House chairmen exerted near-dictatorial control over their committees, and Howard Smith occupied a particularly powerful position in the chain from bill to law: He could kill almost any legislation simply by refusing to send it to the floor. This was his plan for the civil rights bill. Smith knew that Johnson's time was short and that if he could keep the bill in committee until Congress recessed in July, nothing more would happen until after the 1964 election, when there might well be a new president in the White House—one less interested in the cause of civil rights.

To force the bill out of Chairman Smith's Rules Committee, Johnson had to persuade the full House to approve a parliamentary maneuver called a discharge petition. His argument emphasized Smith's refusal even to hold hearings on the bill. "They'll be saying they don't want to violate procedure," the president told one sympathetic labor leader. "Our answer, it'll have to be, 'Well, a man won't give you a hearing at all—that's the way they treated Oswald in Dallas. They just shoot him without a hearing. And...a man's entitled to a hearing.'" Johnson also made it clear than he would tar any congressman who failed to sign the petition as an opponent of civil rights.

The pressure mounted rapidly, especially on Smith, and in mid-December the Rules Committee chairman made the surprise announcement that he would begin holding hearings on the civil rights bill in early January. This tactical retreat undermined the petition drive and bought Smith another six weeks of delay, but it eventually backfired. The nine days of hearings that Smith was forced to hold in January brought so much attention to the process that the politics of the bill became impossible to control. On January 30, the Rules Committee voted out the bill, 11–4, and eleven days later, H. R. 7152 passed the House, 290–130. Next stop: the Senate, Johnson's old stamping ground.

The key to the bill's success there would be Minority Leader Everett Dirksen of Illinois, who generally supported civil rights reform but was troubled by the strong enforcement provisions in the House bill (because he sincerely believed them to be unwarranted extensions of federal power). "The bill can't pass unless you get Ev Dirksen," Johnson told Majority Whip Hubert Humphrey of Minnesota, floor manager of the bill. "You and I are going to get Ev. It's going to take time. We're going to get him....You get in there to see Dirksen. You drink with Dirksen! You talk with Dirksen! You listen to Dirksen!"

NAACP lobbyist Clarence Mitchell (right) eats breakfast with Oregon senator Wayne Morse in the Senate dining room after the first all-night session of round-the-clock debate on the Civil Rights Act of 1960.

Humphrey often resented the tone that Johnson took with him, treating him as though he were a political naif. On the other hand, Humphrey wanted the Democratic vice presidential nomination in 1964 and knew that Johnson would likely control the choice, so he tolerated the abuse.

The opposition was led, ironically, by Johnson's closest friend in the Senate, Richard Russell of Georgia. Both men understood, however, that politics and friendship existed in different spheres and that each man would do his utmost to prevail over the other.

Johnson's plan was to intercept the civil rights bill before it could be sent to the Senate Judiciary Committee, chaired by James Eastland of Mississippi, from whose clutches it might never emerge. Therefore, as soon as the bill passed the House, the president immediately went into action. In the House anteroom where the lobbyists congregated, a pay telephone rang.

The man on the other end of the line asked to speak to NAACP lobbyist Clarence Mitchell.

"To our amazement," Mitchell remembered, "it was the president calling. I don't know how he ever managed to get us on the phone, but he was calling to say, 'All right, you fellows, get over there to the Senate and get busy because we've got it through the House and now we've got the big job of getting it through the Senate.' Well, that was the really fascinating thing to me, that the chief executive of a country could have followed this legislation so closely that immediately on the passage of it by the House, he knew how to get the fellows who were working over there on a pay telephone."

BEATING THE FILIBUSTER

Russell's filibuster, which began on March 9, gradually developed into a major news story, and by early May, the media focus on the civil rights bill had again become intense. As in 1957, Senate segregationists proposed a jury-trial amendment that would have undermined the bill's enforcement mechanisms by granting jurisdiction to all-white southern juries. Dirksen, however, supplanted this amendment with language of his own addressing the trial-by-jury issue in a manner acceptable to the Johnson administration. This compromise paved the way for the resolution

"You drink with Dirksen! You talk with Dirksen! You listen to Dirksen!"

LYNDON JOHNSON TO HUBERT HUMPHREY

At a congressional leadership meeting on the 1964 civil rights bill, Robert Kennedy talks to Everett Dirksen (left) as Hubert Humphrey looks on.

of several other issues, including Dirksen's concerns about federal intervention in state affairs, and on May 13, Dirksen, Humphrey, Senate majority leader Mike Mansfield of Montana, and Robert Kennedy agreed on the final form the bill would take. Celler, McCulloch, and Halleck later went along.

The cloture vote still lay ahead, however, and by late May, the Russell-led filibuster had become the longest in Senate history. Finally, on Tuesday, June 9, Humphrey told the president that he and Dirksen had the necessary votes to end it. In a largely symbolic gesture reminiscent of Strom Thurmond's 1957 performance, Robert Byrd of West Virginia took the Senate floor that night and held it for the next fourteen hours, reading into the record the text of the Magna Carta and speaking at length about states' rights. Less than an hour after he finished, forty-four Democrats and twenty-seven Republicans voted to bring debate to a close. Nine days later, the

CLOSED IN DESPAIR CIVIL RIGHTS BILL UNCONSTITUTIONAL

credit for passing the bill, and because they were about to leave town for their party's convention, the ceremony went ahead as scheduled.

Because of all the attention the bill had received, its signing was televised, ensuring a large turnout of dignitaries. Packed into the East Room of the White House were Johnson, the congressional leadership, cabinet officers, Justice Department officials (including Nicholas Katzenbach and Burke

Sid Kelly, owner of the Subway Club in the basement of the Robert E. Lee Hotel in Jackson, Mississippi, closes his establishment on July 6, 1964, rather than admit Negroes.

Marshall), and numerous movement leaders, including Whitney Young, Randolph, Wilkins, King, Clarence Mitchell, and even Rosa Parks. The president signed seventy-two copies of the law and distributed most of them as souvenirs to his guests, along with the pens he had used to sign them. Then Lyndon Johnson shook hands all around and basked in his accomplishment. A month later, in Atlantic City, he was nominated overwhelmingly as the Democratic candidate for president.

Lyndon Johnson shakes hands with Martin Luther King as he gives King the pen he has just used to sign the Civil Rights Act of 1964. Later, Johnson's relationship with King soured, in part because he failed to oppose the vendetta being waged against King by FBI director J. Edgar Hoover.

"The white power structure has bred a New Negro, and he is angry and impatient. It's not just the Black Muslims. It's the man on the street."

NEW YORK CITY CORE MEMBER OMAR AHMED TO A REPORTER

bill passed, 73–27, with twenty-one Democrats and six Republicans voting against it. On July 2, the House passed the Senate version of the Civil Rights Act of 1964 without amendment, 289–126.

Anticipating its passage, Johnson had arranged a White House signing ceremony for that afternoon. Robert Kennedy wanted to delay the signing until after July 4, fearing that civil rights activists would take advantage of the Independence Day holiday to stage large celebrations—which, in turn, might provoke a violent white response. But Johnson had promised the congressional Republicans that they would share in the

President Johnson addresses the nation on television from the East Room before signing the Civil Rights Act of 1964.

PART IV
FREE ELECTIONS

or many years in the Deep South, members of the Citizens' Councils and other segregationist groups routinely visited county registrars around their states, instructing them in the best ways to keep Negroes off the voting rolls while simultaneously allowing all manner of whites to register. One of the most effective methods they devised was unequal application of the literacy test, which typically required applicants to read and interpret sections of their state constitutions. Blacks were given lengthy, arcane sections and assessed harshly, while white applicants were either given simple sections or not required to take the test at all.

Justice Department efforts to promote fairness through voting rights litigation had little effect. In 1958, for example, federal judge Frank M. Johnson Jr., who presided over Alabama's Middle District, ordered Barbour County to turn over its voter registration records to the U.S. Civil Rights Commission. The county judge who held these records refused and complied only after Johnson threatened him with contempt. As it happened, Johnson knew the man well. It was his law-school classmate George Wallace, who was still considered a racial moderate. That would not be the case when the two men clashed again in 1965.

A team of COFO volunteers, canvassing door to door, talks to a woman in Jackson, Mississippi, about registering to vote.

Freedom Summer

1964

Freedom Summer
volunteer Dick Landerman
(right) discusses voting
rights with Hattiesburg,
Mississippi, resident Horace
Laurence on Laurence's
front porch in July 1964.

Martin Luther King Jr. and Robert Moses were, in the words of historian Taylor Branch, "opposing symbols for the holy wars within the civil rights movement." King was the epitome of the charismatic leader. His SCLC organization extended little beyond his personal retinue, yet its reach and influence were greatly magnified by King's shrewd manipulation of his own fame. In contrast stood Moses, who embraced instead Ella Baker's vision of "group leadership." Characteristically, Moses kept himself in the background while encouraging others to become empowered. As King roamed the South, holding press conferences and leading marches, Moses remained in Mississippi, methodically building an organization of the downtrodden on a county-by-county basis.

In early 1962, Moses had become program director of the Council of Federated Organizations (COFO), Mississippi's unique civil rights umbrella group. COFO was founded in the aftermath of SNCC's failed McComb project, when Moses realized that internal dissension could be as disabling to the movement as external repression. The NAACP brought to the coalition its state president Aaron Henry, who became COFO's president as well; SNCC and CORE, however, provided the bulk of COFO's staffing and funding.

Together, Moses, Henry, and CORE state field secretary Dave Dennis agreed that COFO should forgo direct action and concentrate instead on voter registration work.

Moses had already learned from his experiences in McComb that direct action didn't work well in Mississippi.

The COFO logo
from a 1964 summer
project brochure.

The white establishment was too strong and too lawless, and the older NAACP Negroes were either too intimidated or too prudent, depending on one's point of view, to support such an inflammatory strategy. The downside of registration work, however, was that it generated little national attention. "A heavy curtain seemed to have dropped down on the state, making us invisible to the nation," Moses recalled.

Without national attention, there was little reason for the Kennedy administration to reverse its policy of accommodating Mississippi's white establishment. Without federal pressure, there was little reason for that establishment to restrain its oppression of blacks. As a result, COFO's registration work went poorly.

In December 1962, in a report to the Voter Education Project (VEP), Moses admitted, "We are powerless to register people in significant numbers anywhere in the state." He went on to list three conditions that would have to be met

"We killed two-month-old Indian babies to take this country, and now they want us to give it away to the niggers."

A WHITE MISSISSIPPIAN TO A REPORTER IN APRIL 1963

for the work to succeed: The Citizens' Councils' hold on Mississippi state politics would have to be broken, the Justice Department would have to begin enforcing the right of Negroes to register, and Negroes themselves would have to begin demanding the right to vote.

After the success of Project C in Birmingham, Moses became particularly aware that, for a breakthrough to take place in Mississippi, he would have to attract national attention to the state as never before. In July 1963, he was searching for ways to accomplish this when thirty-four-year-old Allard Lowenstein gave him a call.

THE FREEDOM VOTE

Lowenstein, a northern liberal lawyer who had once been president of the National Student Association (NSA), had traveled down to Jackson on July 4, most likely at the request of Aaron Henry, an old friend from his NSA days. Although Lowenstein himself never explained the exact circumstances, he did say that he went to Mississippi to provide legal assistance, which was then badly needed. At the time, there were only three black lawyers in the state, and the one white attorney in Jackson willing to handle civil rights work had been recently run out of town.

Lowenstein initially intended to stay just a few days, but he was so appalled at the conditions he found that he lingered. The abuse of governmental authority was so profound that he couldn't see how one more movement lawyer defending arrested demonstrators would make any difference. "What was needed instead," historian William H. Chafe has written, "was the kind of bold action that would highlight, glaringly and dramatically, the systemic ways in which Mississippi was 'different in principle' from the rest of America."

This photograph from the early 1960s was found in the NAACP archives in the Library of Congress.

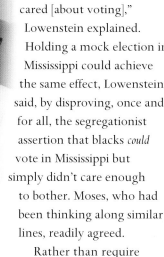

Allard Lowenstein in an undated photograph, probably from the mid-1960s.

According to Lowenstein, he soon contacted Moses in his role as COFO program director and pitched him on the idea of holding a mock election. While touring South Africa on a fact-finding mission in 1959, Lowenstein had witnessed a "day of mourning" staged by African blacks, who were also being denied the right to vote. "The day of mourning touched the conscience of the people who [had] never understood that Africans cared [about voting]," Lowenstein explained. Holding a mock election in Mississippi could achieve the same effect, Lowenstein said, by disproving, once and for all, the segregationist assertion that blacks *could* vote in Mississippi but simply didn't care enough to bother. Moses, who had been thinking along similar lines, readily agreed.

Rather than require blacks to vote at regular polling places, where they would be subject to white intimidation, Lowenstein and Moses planned to hold their Freedom Vote at polling places within the black community itself, at Negro-owned businesses and especially at black churches. Furthermore, on the ballot alongside the Democratic and Republican candidates would be a slate of candidates nominated by COFO so that Freedom Voters could support candidates who also supported civil rights.

COFO kicked off the Freedom Vote campaign at its monthly statewide meeting in Jackson on Sunday, October 6. Those in attendance, acting as though they were delegates to a party convention, adopted a platform calling for racial justice, school desegregation, and the right to vote. They also nominated Aaron Henry for governor, and a week later, Moses filled out the ticket with the Rev. Edwin King, who became COFO's candidate for lieutenant governor. King was the white chaplain at Tougaloo College, a black school in Jackson with many white faculty members and also, to the consternation of local segregationists, more than a few white students from outside Mississippi.

With a goal of two hundred thousand ballots, the Freedom Vote became COFO's first statewide project. It also marked the first time that any Mississippi civil rights organization used a large number of northern white volunteers. According to Moses, "We realized that a statewide election campaign required more manpower than we had in Mississippi." Given Lowenstein's strong connections among white student activists, it made sense to invite these people to participate.

Lowenstein concentrated his recruiting efforts at Yale, where he had attended law school, and Stanford, where he had been an assistant dean of students. "There was a belief [at the time]," recalled one of the students Lowenstein recruited, "that if people

ABOVE: **A handbill** for the Freedom Vote.
RIGHT: **A campaign button** for Aaron Henry.

"Lowenstein was convinced that if the 'best and the brightest' students from the American 'establishment' would make a commitment to show that the 'system' of American democracy worked, they could provide the energy, the publicity, and the talent to end inequality and rally the forces of social justice."

Guided by the COFO staffers, the Yale and Stanford students went door to door in the black community, spreading word of the Freedom Vote. From the start, they were harassed by whites. On October 22, the day after the first Yale students arrived in Mississippi, fourteen canvassers were arrested in Indianola for distributing leaflets

beat up Payne. The next day, in Natchez, the same group of whites began tailing the two civil rights workers.

Greene, who had a reputation for flashy driving, led the thugs on a wild 105-mile-per-hour chase before being forced off the road. One of the whites got out of his car and, holding a gun, ordered Greene and Payne to get out of theirs. Thinking quickly, Greene shifted his "votemobile" into gear and peeled out onto the highway. The stunned gunman got off four shots before hustling back into his car and resuming the chase. Greene had to run three red lights and cross the double line, driving into oncoming traffic, before he could lose them.

Reports of more than two hundred such incidents were collected by COFO headquarters in Jackson and passed on to the press. Lowenstein's own phone calls to the editor of the *Stanford Daily* produced a string of front-page articles that spurred Stanford students to raise five thousand dollars in support of their classmates' efforts. Meanwhile, reacting to similar stories in the *Yale Daily News*, Yale students wrote letters to their hometown newspapers, their parents (many of whom were politically influential), and their congressmen, expressing outrage at what was happening in Mississippi and insisting that something be done.

The Freedom Vote took place between Friday, November 2, and Sunday, November 4. In particularly dangerous areas, ballots were distributed and returned by mail. Elsewhere, boxes were set up at convenient locations

"What we have discovered is that the people who run Mississippi today can only do so by force. They cannot allow free elections in Mississippi, because if they did, they wouldn't run Mississippi."

ALLARD LOWENSTEIN

did the right thing, then that would really have an impact. That was great stuff to hear. It was straightforward and one of the most powerful things you can imagine."

In the end, Lowenstein's message that the actions of just one moral person could change the world persuaded about a hundred Yale and Stanford students to spend the last two weeks of the campaign in Mississippi, working on the Freedom Vote. COFO's three dozen black staffers had some misgivings about opening up their movement to rich, naive young whites from out of state, but they understood the need and felt that they could make do for such a short period of time, after which the white students would leave.

To Lowenstein, however, the inclusion of northern whites was the most important aspect of the Freedom Vote. According to Chafe,

without a license. Two days later, Lowenstein and two more Yale students were arrested in Clarksdale for violating the local curfew law.

As the election grew nearer, the intimidation intensified. Twenty-one-year-old Yale graduate student Bruce Payne spent the week leading up to the Freedom Vote canvassing in southwestern Mississippi with twenty-year-old SNCC field secretary George Greene. On Thursday, November 1, four white men surrounded Greene's car at a gas station in Port Gibson and

An October 28 article from the *Yale Daily News* about students leaving to help with the 1963 Freedom Vote.

around town—beauty parlors, diners, groceries, pool halls—so that participation could be as easy as possible. Not surprisingly, the greatest number of votes was cast at church services on Sunday morning.

More than eighty-three thousand blacks (and even a few whites) took part, nearly all of them marking their ballots for Henry and King. Although this total fell well short of the original two-hundred-thousand-ballot goal, COFO declared the Freedom Vote a victory— and reasonably so, given the campaign's short duration and the ardent white harassment.

There was one lingering irritation, however. Nearly all of the news stories that came out of the Freedom Vote played up the role of the northern white volunteers, marginalizing the work of the veteran black organizers. "The bitterness of the SNCC workers was very understandable and intense," Lowenstein observed in a 1965 interview.

THE GREENVILLE WORKSHOP

After the Freedom Vote, the returns were examined closely. Because Aaron Henry's base was in the upper Delta, no one was surprised that the neighboring counties of Coahoma, Quitman, and Panola produced more than thirty thousand votes, or 40 percent of the total. It was somewhat disappointing, however, that twenty-five of Mississippi's eighty-two counties yielded fewer than one hundred votes each.

Negroes attempt to register in Greenwood, Mississippi, in March 1963.

Even more disappointing was the low turnout in Leflore County, whose county seat (Greenwood) had been the center of SNCC's flagship project in Mississippi for more than a year. COFO ran a slate of fourteen local candidates headed by veteran organizer Willie Peacock, but only two thousand Freedom Votes were cast. In adjacent Sunflower County, where Fannie Lou Hamer lived and organized, just three hundred votes were cast. These were areas of extreme white hostility, of course, but great efforts were being made and little seemed to be changing.

The movement in Mississippi, it seemed, had reached a cusp: Either it could return to the type of community organizing that had characterized COFO's activities before the Freedom Vote, or it could build on that campaign by recruiting more outside volunteers. Neither choice was very appealing. The former would almost certainly result in continued slow progress on narrow fronts with little hope of dramatic federal intervention. The latter risked losing control of the movement entirely.

On November 14, the COFO staff gathered in Greenville for a three-day workshop sponsored by the Highlander Folk School. Typically, most of the seven whites and thirty-five blacks present were SNCCers. The workshop agenda included

A SNCC button
from 1964.

several important items, such as COFO's relationship to the NAACP and the merits of forming an independent political party. But only one issue mattered: whether or not to invite whites back to Mississippi for the summer of 1964.

Most black staff members argued that bringing in inexperienced white volunteers was too dangerous, both for the volunteers and for local Negroes. Whites working in black neighborhoods, they said, generated the wrong kind of visibility, and the interracial friendships-*cum*-romances that would inevitably develop, especially between white women and black men, would surely provoke a violent white reaction. Furthermore, SNCC veterans such as Charles Cobb, Curtis Hayes, and Hollis Watkins pointed out that the proposed heavy reliance on untrained volunteers would undermine SNCC's primary mission to empower local blacks.

There was also an emotional component to these objections. Most of the SNCCers harbored proprietary feelings about the movement they had created and were far from eager to share it with rich white newcomers. During the Freedom Vote, the SNCCers had gotten a taste of what it

felt like to be snubbed, and they didn't much like it. Now some field staff, notably Ivanhoe Donaldson, complained that whites had "taken over" the Jackson COFO office. Donaldson had been a student at Michigan State in December 1962 before dropping out to work for SNCC in Greenwood. "I came into SNCC and saw Negroes running the movement and I felt good," Donaldson said, "and then the whites take over leadership. We're losing the one thing where the Negro can stand first."

On the other side were the obvious benefits that white volunteers would bring: free labor, financial support, and national attention. No one denied these, and some even pointed out another important reason for inviting the whites back. "If we're trying to break down this barrier of segregation," Fannie Lou Hamer said, "we can't segregate ourselves."

Although Bob Moses didn't arrive in Greenville until the second day of the workshop, he was quickly brought up to speed and realized that a consensus was developing either to keep the whites out entirely or else to restrict them to nonleadership roles. Aware of the issue's importance, Moses uncharacteristically took a strong position in the ongoing debate. "Whiteness is no argument," he said. "That's an irrational, racist statement. That's what we're fighting. [If] no white person can be head of any project, [then] I don't want to be part of an operation like that."

Moses's statement came as something of a surprise because for more than two years he had been restricting his own recruiting efforts to local blacks—a practice that he justified by citing the SNCC shibboleth that organizing work was too dangerous for whites. With hindsight, however, one can see that Moses's growing frustration with the slow pace of change was causing his attitude to evolve. The success of the Freedom Vote, in particular, had offered him a tantalizing new vision: By bringing in enough white volunteers

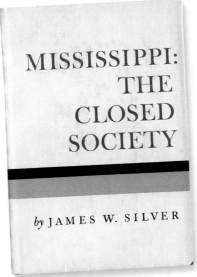

Ole Miss historian James W. Silver supported the cause of James Meredith, and his book-length critique of attitudes in the state became a 1964 best seller.

the following summer, he could possibly bypass several methodical movement stages with a single bold thrust. At the same time, he also found Mrs. Hamer's point of view quite compelling.

"In part," Moses wrote later, "what she and others were seeing very clearly was that the summer project would help open up Mississippi some more. And that couldn't do anything but help them, they felt. That was their experience. Exposure was an important part of what defined the movement—had been from the very beginning—exposure to ideas, to people, to places that had been closed to them."

The debate continued on into the winter. Meanwhile, a week after the Greenville workshop, President Kennedy was shot in Dallas. In classrooms across Mississippi, white children cheered the news, reflecting the prejudiced views of their parents.

> "If we're trying to break down this barrier of segregation, we can't segregate ourselves."
>
> FANNIE LOU HAMER

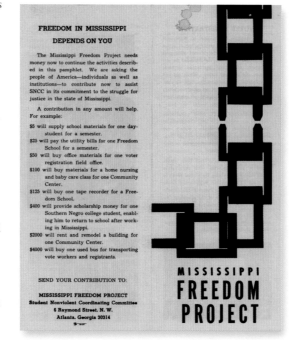

This SNCC brochure contained information for potential volunteers about the various aspects of the group's 1964 summer project.

THE DEATH OF LOUIS ALLEN

During December and January, Moses became increasingly certain that recruiting white students was the only way to go. He even persuaded himself that the use of whites might well limit Klan violence (because so many reporters would be present); and even if violence did occur, Moses told himself, it would serve the end of provoking the federal–state confrontation that Moses believed was necessary for the movement to succeed.

Given what later happened, it has been suggested that Moses cynically brought whites into Mississippi, knowing that a few would likely be killed. This interpretation is much too harsh. Certainly, Moses engaged in a good deal of rationalizing, but that is not sufficient to conclude that he risked lives consciously. A more likely explanation is that the pressure he was under directed his thinking. In mid-November, for example, Wiley Branton reluctantly cut off VEP funding to voter registration work in Mississippi because the fifty thousand dollars already spent had yielded just 3,228 new voters.

Additionally, Moses knew that his staff of just thirty full-time SNCC organizers was both physically and emotionally exhausted. "They were butting up against a stone wall," he later recalled, "no breakthroughs for them." Yet Moses didn't make the final decision to push through the use of white volunteers until he learned of the death of Louis Allen.

Moses still thought often about the death of Herbert Lee, whom E. W. Steptoe had recruited to drive Moses around Amite County in August 1961. Lee had been shot through the head by state legislator E. H. Hurst as he got out of his truck at a local cotton gin in September 1961. A coroner's jury had cleared Hurst, accepting the story that Lee had attacked Hurst first with a tire iron. Allen had witnessed the murder and knew that Hurst was lying. He told Moses as much but refused to testify in court without federal protection. Moses asked the Justice Department for help but was turned down. According to Moses, "They told us that there was no way possible to provide protection for a witness at such a hearing and that probably, in any case, it didn't matter what he testified and that Hurst would be found innocent."

Allen did, however, speak with an FBI agent, who tipped off local law enforcement. At that point, Louis Allen became a marked man in Amite County. He suffered economic reprisals, was jailed on false charges, and had his jaw broken by a deputy sheriff. Although he thought often of leaving Mississippi, he had debts to pay and an elderly mother to look after. Finally, when his mother died during the winter of 1963–1964, Allen made plans to join his brother in Milwaukee. His departure date was February 1, but on the night of January 31, he was gunned down outside his home. The sheriff's department and the FBI both conducted perfunctory investigations; no suspects were ever charged.

"For me, it was as if everything had come full circle," Moses later wrote. "Louis Allen's death after two years of harassment was the latest in a string of murders—lynchings. There had to be a response, a larger response than we had been able to provide two years before, or would be able to provide with the people we had working now. I spoke up for the summer project, threw all my weight behind it. In my mind, the need for a major gesture outweighed legitimate worries of how the influx of white students would affect black leadership. Until then, the staff had been deadlocked, at loggerheads with each other; this decided it."

THE RECRUITMENT AND TRAINING OF VOLUNTEERS

The goals of the 1964 summer project, as Moses subsequently explained them, were: 1) to expand black voter registration within the state; 2) to challenge actively the legitimacy of the all-white Mississippi Democratic party; 3) to open multiple community centers at which black Mississippians could obtain legal and medical services; and 4) to establish "freedom schools," where volunteers would teach the basics of African-American history and contemporary race relations along with reading, writing, and arithmetic.

Friends of SNCC groups in northern cities worked hard to meet the target of one thousand summer volunteers. So did Allard Lowenstein, but Lowenstein's habit of keeping his own counsel further irritated the Mississippi SNCCers. Particularly troubling was his rather arrogant assumption that he had the authority not only to recruit volunteers on his own but also to accept them into the program.

In late February 1964, Dorothy Zellner, a leader of the Boston Friends of SNCC (and the wife of

The Freedom Schools

During the winter of 1963–1964, while the COFO leadership moved to implement the community center program that Dave Dennis of CORE had been pushing for several months, SNCCer Charlie Cobb came up with the concept of the Freedom School. Because there was no mandatory school attendance law in Mississippi, poor black children tended to spend more time working in the cotton fields than learning in the classroom.

Cobb knew from his organizing work in the Delta that, a decade after *Brown*, the state of Mississippi still maintained a dual school system that spent four times as much money on white children as on black ones. Local funding was even more discriminatory. The Holly Bluff school system, for example, spent $191.17 annually on each white student and only $1.26 annually on each black student. The purpose of the Freedom Schools, as Cobb envisioned them, was to begin rectifying this imbalance; what the Freedom Schools achieved, however, was a revolution in educational methodology.

In March 1964, the National Council of Churches sponsored a Freedom Schools curriculum conference in New York City. Among the fifty-three participants were Ella Baker; Highlander Folk School director Myles Horton; and Staughton Lynd, a white professor at black Spelman College in Atlanta, who subsequently became the director of the Freedom School program. The curriculum developed at this conference paired traditional academic subject matter with lessons in black

A sign announcing registration hours at a Freedom School.

history, contemporary race relations, and the development of political leadership—all of which were banned subjects in Mississippi's black public schools. As taught at the Freedom Schools, however, these topics complemented and supported the summer project's political work, especially its formation of an alternative political party.

The premise of the new curriculum was that students brought with them valuable experiential knowledge—especially with regard to the culture of black Mississippians—that deserved to be explored and preserved. Therefore, student participation was emphasized, as was group learning.

In pedagogical terms, this was something of a revolution and marked a dramatic shift away from traditional methods of rote memorization, which tended to discourage student inquiry. Its effect on American education as a whole lasted well beyond Freedom Summer.

In all, the summer project operated forty-one Freedom Schools with a total enrollment of about twenty-five hundred students. Although their average age was fifteen, some students were preschool children; others, senior citizens. Teaching them were approximately 250 summer volunteers, mostly young white women from the North. The schools were SNCC's first attempt to replace dysfunctional white-run public institutions with more effective black-oriented institutions of SNCC's own creation.

Bruce Soslomon, a twenty-four-year-old volunteer from Brooklyn, works with students at a Freedom School in Jackson.

McComb project veteran Bob Zellner), wrote to a fellow SNCCer in Mississippi complaining that Lowenstein had set up his own recruitment operation in Boston (headed by Harvard graduate student Barney Frank). Lowenstein "was up here and left several times without having contacted a single person I knew or me," she reported.

reject the guild's offer, and when Moses refused, Lowenstein walked away.

The actual source of Lowenstein's alienation, however, was much larger than the guild; it involved his master plan for the political development of southern blacks. As deeply

> "This is it. They are not bluffing, and we are not bluffing. We are going to be ready for them....They won't have a chance."
>
> JACKSON MAYOR ALLEN THOMPSON

The Mississippi leadership soon made it clear to Lowenstein that all decisions on volunteers would be made in Jackson by the COFO staff.

For a time, Moses defended Lowenstein because he respected Lowenstein's passion and believed that Lowenstein's connections among student activists were indispensable to the recruiting effort. It was Lowenstein, however, who ultimately chose to disengage from Moses. The proximate cause was COFO's acceptance of free legal counsel from the National Lawyers' Guild, a left-wing organization that had been attacked during the McCarthy years as a Communist front. Lowenstein (along with the NAACP Legal Defense Fund) insisted that COFO

committed as Lowenstein was to the cause of social justice, he also had a parallel political agenda: He wanted to register Mississippi Negroes so that they could take their place within the liberal Democratic coalition that he so fervently supported. It was for this reason that Lowenstein found so much common ground with the NAACP. SNCCers, however, took a different view. Their prolonged interaction with poverty, violence, oppression, and the indifference of the federal government had radicalized them. "Symbolized by the overalls that SNCC workers wore as a movement uniform," historian Chafe has written, "the organization's identification

with the black proletariat—and with a poor people's critique of power and wealth—proved problematic for the NAACP and for Lowenstein."

Meanwhile, Mississippi's white establishment prepared for war—or at least, as the *Jackson Daily News* wrote, "an invasion." Jackson mayor Allen Thompson expanded his city's police force from two hundred officers to more than three hundred and also purchased a thirteen-thousand-pound armored personnel carrier that the press called

The Revival of the Mississippi Klan

The admission of James Meredith to Ole Miss was a turning point for whites in Mississippi. Many of them, perceiving their "way of life" to be under assault, turned violent.

White violence against blacks in Mississippi was nothing new, of course, but for thirty years it hadn't been well organized. The Mississippi Klan had largely disbanded after the 1920s, and the elite Citizens' Councils that dominated segregationist politics after the *Brown* decision disavowed violence because of the bad publicity it brought. Yet the failure of the business and professional classes to stop Meredith and destroy COFO persuaded many less affluent rural whites that the old methods were the best.

The Mississippi Klan revival began in Adams County, where still-active Louisiana Klansmen had recently begun recruiting white factory

workers in Natchez. In December 1963, these new recruits broke away from the Louisiana klavern and formed their own organization, the White Knights of the Ku Klux Klan, which soon became the most active and violent Klan faction in Mississippi. The White Knights' leader, twenty-nine-year-old E. L. McDaniel, was a Natchez native with just a tenth-grade education but a much more sophisticated understanding of how to terrorize black people. The local police, as expected, looked the other way.

On February 15, 1964, two hundred Klansmen from different parts of Mississippi came together in Brookhaven to establish the White Knights as a statewide organization under Imperial Wizard Sam Bowers. (Bowers, a thirty-nine-year-old resident of Laurel, ran the Sambo Amusement Company, a jukebox and vending machine operation.) The Brookhaven convention also adopted a forty-page constitution and a four-stage program for ensuring white supremacy. Each stage, or "project," called for a new and more extreme level of violence. Project 4 was "extermination."

This poster was nailed to a tree outside the home of Hattiesburg activist Vernon Dahmer in 1965. Less than a year later, Dahmer was killed by the Klan.

LEFT: **A Jackson policeman** poses inside the riot car dubbed Thompson's Tank for a national magazine story about the city's plans to cope with the coming summer "invasion" of civil rights workers.
BELOW: **Two police officers** in riot gear stand outside the same riot car after quelling a demonstration.

Thompson's Tank. In Ruleville, where Fannie Lou Hamer lived, Mayor Charles Durrough visited the homes of black families to warn them against hosting summer project volunteers— who, he said, would surely beat and kill them. When those people Durrough visited refused to heed his friendly advice, the mayor made sure that nearly all of them lost their jobs.

Before summer volunteers were accepted into the project, they were screened by psychologists and experienced civil rights workers so that any who might be "dangerous to the movement" or themselves could be weeded out. According to a COFO memo, screeners were to reject anyone "wrapped up in himself." Also on the exclusion list were the "well-meaning idealist who wants to secure equality and brother love for all and is solidly anti-politics" and the "bright young college student" with "all the answers" who knows "what's being done wrong [and] how to do it right."

The approximately five hundred volunteers who passed these interviews were told to report in June to the Western College for Women in Oxford, Ohio, for weeklong orientation sessions. The training for voter registration workers (about half the total number) began on Sunday, June 14, with the Freedom School teachers scheduled to arrive a week later.

Because each volunteer was required to bring five hundred dollars in bail money, plus enough cash to cover transportation and medical expenses, fewer than 10 percent of the students who gathered at Oxford were black. (Typically, black

students had to earn money over the summer to pay for tuition in the fall.) Conversely, those students who did make their way to Oxford were at least 90 percent white and generally well off— the sons and daughters of professional people from the Northeast, especially New York State.

From the start, their race and middle-class backgrounds set them apart from the mostly black, working-class organizers who had come north to train them. Writing home to his parents on June 16, white volunteer Bill Hodes observed that the Mississippians were "very much an in-group, because of what they have gone through together. They tend to be suspicious of us, because we are white, northern, urban, rich, inexperienced. We are somewhat in awe of them and conscious of our own inferiority."

That evening, the volunteers were shown the CBS television documentary "Mississippi and the Fifteenth Amendment." According to Hodes, the film featured an "idiotic registrar" explaining in a southern drawl why Negroes didn't want to vote. The obese, rednecked registrar in question, Theron Lynd of Hattiesburg, seemed a comic figure to the students, and they began to laugh at him.

The black Mississippians were appalled. They knew Lynd to be a bulwark of white repression in Forrest County and considered him anything but a joke. Six trainers were so offended that they walked out of the auditorium. Afterward, an older staff member informed the students through tears, "Maybe you won't laugh when you meet these guys and hear them talk and know that they are doing it every day."

Back in the dormitories, Hodes recalled, some of the volunteers began discussing among themselves what had happened. A few complained that the Mississippians were too

"distant"; others defended the COFO staff, pointing out that they "have a lot on their minds." Eventually, some of the trainers joined these discussions, and one, describing violence he had witnessed in Mississippi, told the students that if they weren't scared, they should "get the hell out of here because we don't need any favors from people who don't know what they are doing here in the first place." Another trainer said, "We cried over you in the staff meeting because we love you and are afraid for you."

Such exchanges improved the relationship between the volunteers and the trainers, but the underlying tension remained unresolved. The staff continued to resent the wealth, superior numbers, and academic skills of the white volunteers, while the whites continued, for the most part unconsciously, to expect from the staff both praise for their righteousness and appreciation of the sacrifices they were making.

At the summer project training in Oxford, SNCC field secretaries Bruce Gordon (left) and Cordell Reagon (right) demonstrate how volunteers should protect themselves from assault. They were to fall to the ground, roll themselves into a ball, and use their hands and arms to shield their head and vital organs.

NOW

STUDENT NONVIOLENT COORDINATING COMMITTEE
8½ RAYMOND STREET, N.W. ATLANTA 14, GEORGIA

A SNCC poster from the summer of 1964. Other SNCC slogans that year included "One Man, One Vote" and "Come Let Us Build a New World Together."

According to volunteer Sally Belfrage: "*I want to be your friend, you black idiot,* was the contradiction evident everywhere."

On Saturday, June 20, the first caravan of volunteers left Ohio for Mississippi. Inside one of these cars, a blue 1964 Ford station wagon, was the group headed for Meridian. The drivers were twenty-four-year-old Michael Schwerner (a Brooklyn Jew) and twenty-one-year-old James Chaney (a native black Mississippian), both of whom worked full time for CORE. Accompanying them were four summer volunteers, among them Andrew Goodman and Louise Hermey.

GOODMAN, SCHWERNER, AND CHANEY

Mickey Schwerner was a Cornell graduate who had started work on a master's degree in sociology at Columbia before dropping out of school to become a social worker in a New York City housing project. During the summer of 1963, after watching the violence in Birmingham on television, he had applied for a job with CORE and asked to be posted to the South. In January 1964, he and his wife, Rita, drove down to Mississippi, where he became CORE's first full-time white organizer in the state. Schwerner's initial task was to establish in Meridian Mississippi's first black community center; Moses and Dennis were so impressed with the result that they named Schwerner head of the summer project in the eastern half of the state's Fourth Congressional District.

Chaney had started volunteering in the Meridian CORE office soon after it opened in October 1963. Quickly he became indispensable to its first director, Matt Suarez, and later to Suarez's replacement, Schwerner, who asked that Chaney be put on the CORE payroll. In Schwerner's letter to the national office, he wrote, "James has never asked us to buy him a cup of coffee, though he has no means of support."

The six counties for which Schwerner was responsible included Neshoba, whose county seat was Philadelphia. On Memorial Day, Schwerner and Chaney had driven out to Longdale, a black community outside Philadelphia, to meet with members of the Mount Zion Methodist Church. COFO wanted to use the church as a Freedom School, and the congregation's leaders proved

"I may be killed. You may be killed. The whole staff may go."

JAMES FORMAN AT THE OXFORD TRAINING

willing. On the night of June 16, however, while Chaney and Schwerner were training summer volunteers in Ohio, a group of Klansmen burned the church to the ground. When news of the fire reached Schwerner and Chaney in Oxford, both knew that their first duty upon returning to Meridian would be to visit Longdale again to rally and reassure the movement's supporters there.

The drive from Oxford to Meridian took sixteen hours, with the blue Ford station wagon pulling up outside the CORE office on Fifth Avenue about five o'clock on Sunday morning. After a few hours' sleep, Chaney and Schwerner set off for Longdale around ten, taking with them Goodman, the twenty-year-old Queens College student assigned to Neshoba County.

SECURITY HANDBOOK

1. Communications personnel will act as security officers.

2. Travel

    a. When persons leave their project, they must call their project person to person for themselves on arrival at destination point. Should they be missing, project personnel will notify the Jackson office. WATS line operators will call each project every day at dinnertime or thereabouts, and should be notified of changes in personnel, transfers, etc. (If trips are planned in advance, this information can go to Jackson by mail. Phone should be used only where there is no time. Care should be taken at all times to avoid, if possible, full names of persons travelling.) Checklists should be used in local projects for personnel to check in and out.

    b. Doors of cars should be locked at all times. At night, windows should be rolled up as much as possible. Gas tanks must have locks and be kept locked. Hoods should also be locked.

    c. No one should go anywhere alone, but certainly not in an automobile, and certainly not at night.

    d. Travel at night should be avoided unless absolutely necessary.

    e. Remove all unnecessary objects from your car which could be construed as weapons. (Hammers, files, iron rules, etc.) Absolutely no liquor bottles, beer cans, etc. should be inside your car. Do not travel with names and addresses of local contacts.

    f. Know all roads in and out of town. Study the county map.

    g. Know locations of sanctuaries and safe homes in the county.

    h. When getting out of a car at night, make sure the car's inside light is out.

    i. Be conscious of cars which circle offices or Freedom Houses. Take license numbers of all suspicious cars. Note make, model and year. Cars without license plates should immediately be reported to the project office.

Living at Home or in Freedom Houses

    a. If it can be avoided, try not to sleep near open windows. Try to sleep at the back of the house, i.e., the part farthest from a road or street.

    b. Do not stand in doorways at night with the light at your back.

    c. At night, people should not sit in their rooms without drawn shades.

    d. Do not congregate in front of the house at night.

Summer project staff produced this security handbook for student volunteers unfamiliar with Mississippi's unspoken rules of racial conduct. Topics included "Travel," "Living at Home or in Freedom Houses," and "Personal Actions."

During Andy Goodman's orientation, COFO's trainers had repeatedly emphasized the dangers of civil rights work in Mississippi. Volunteers were instructed to shave their beards (which might attract unwanted attention), to avoid speeding, never to travel alone, and never to travel at night. Before leaving for Longdale, Schwerner showed Louise Hermey the office communications setup and reminded her that every hour on the half hour she needed to check in with Jackson to let COFO headquarters know that all was well. He also told her, "There's an immutable rule here: No one is to remain in Neshoba County after four P.M. If for any reason we aren't back by four P.M., you should alert Jackson and begin checking every city jail, county jail, sheriff's office, police station, and hospital between Meridian and Neshoba." A list of the necessary phone numbers was kept conveniently beside the telephones.

Schwerner, Chaney, and Goodman reached Longdale without incident. After inspecting the remains of Mount Zion, they visited with several church members to learn more about the arson. About three o'clock, they began heading back to Meridian along Highway 16. Just outside the Philadelphia city limits, they were pulled over by Neshoba County deputy sheriff Cecil Price, who recognized Schwerner's car. Earlier in the spring, the governor's State Sovereignty Commission had circulated a description to local sheriffs of Schwerner, his car, and license-plate number. "Schwerner was not wanted for any crime," historian John Dittmer has written, "but the implied message was clear: Civil rights workers were the enemy, and the highest state officials supported their local police." Price, who was also a Klansman, arrested the three young men for suspicion of involvement in the church burning and took them to the county jail in Philadelphia.

Price next contacted Edgar Ray Killen, the kleagle (or chief organizer) of the Neshoba County klavern. Killen told Price to keep the civil rights workers locked up without use of the telephone while he organized a death squad. All was ready by 10 P.M., when Price returned to the jail and released his prisoners. Then, according to the Neshoba County authorities, Goodman, Schwerner, and Chaney simply disappeared.

Andrew Goodman sits in an audience of Freedom Summer volunteers during one of the training sessions at the Western College for Women in Oxford, Ohio.

About fifteen minutes later, Goodman, Schwerner, and Chaney were driving east on Highway 19 near the Lauderdale County line when Price and two carloads of Klansmen pulled up behind them. Chaney, who was driving, accelerated. He swerved at high speed onto Highway 492 but then, for some unknown reason, braked and stopped the car. At this point, the three young men surrendered.

Price put them in his car and, followed by the other Klansmen, drove down an unmarked dirt track called Rock Cut Road. The end of the line was a construction site on the 253-acre Old Jolly Farm, where an earthen dam was being built. After the civil rights workers were shot, their bodies were placed in a hollow, which was covered over with tons of dirt moved by a Caterpillar D-4.

Back in Meridian, as the afternoon came and went, Louise Hermey got nervous. At 4 P.M., she telephoned COFO headquarters in Jackson as

LEFT: **Mickey Schwerner** in a photograph from 1964. RIGHT: **James Chaney** in an undated photo. Neshoba County sheriff Lawrence Rainey dismissed their disappearance, saying, "If they're missing, they're just hid somewhere, trying to get a lot of publicity."

instructed to report Goodman, Schwerner, and Chaney missing. She was told to stay calm, that it might take hours for the three men to reach a telephone if their car had broken down, and that she shouldn't begin making her emergency phone calls until five o'clock. When another hour passed without any contact, Hermey began methodically calling the jails, police stations, and hospitals on her list. About 5:20 P.M., she called the Neshoba

County jail, where the receptionist told her untruthfully that there were no such people in custody.

At 10 P.M., law student Sherwin Kaplan made the first contact between COFO headquarters and the FBI when he called Special Agent H. F. Helgesen in Jackson. Because the FBI in Mississippi had a close relationship with local law enforcement (and thus, indirectly, the Klan), its agents tended to ignore SNCC and CORE requests for investigations of disappearances, murders, and other segregationist violence. Helgesen was no different, and he quickly brushed off Kaplan's call.

At 1 A.M., SNCC headquarters in Atlanta began calling John Doar in Washington. Five hours later, during their third conversation of the night, Doar said that he had just "invested the FBI with the power to look into this matter." It wasn't until late

Deputy Sheriff Cecil Price

Monday, however, that the first FBI agents appeared in Philadelphia. By then, the disappearances had become national news.

The resulting media attention placed so much pressure on FBI director J. Edgar Hoover that on July 10 he flew down to Jackson to open personally a new FBI office there. The Jackson field office soon become the FBI's largest with 153 agents assigned to it.

"It's tragic," Rita Schwerner told reporters after flying into Mississippi herself from Ohio,

Meanwhile, President Johnson and Director Hoover both made it clear that the men they had sent to Mississippi were on hand to investigate a suspected crime, *not* to prevent future ones. During his July 10 press conference in Jackson, Hoover said, "We most certainly do not and will not give protection to civil rights workers." Privately, however, he warned Mississippi's new governor, Paul Johnson, that the Klan violence would have to stop and the state would have to comply with the new civil rights law, signed by the president eight days earlier.

Hoover's own racial prejudices ran deep, but now that his reputation was on the line in Mississippi, he intended to deliver results. Governor Johnson was also under pressure, fearful that more Klan violence could lead to a military occupation of his state. Therefore, the two men together began to crack down. Hoover gave Johnson a list of state highway patrolmen known to the FBI as members of the Klan, and the governor promptly fired them.

Even so, the summer of 1964 still saw the most violence in Mississippi since Reconstruction with thirty-five shootings, sixty-five burnings and bombings, and at least six murders.

At the same time, as the search for Goodman, Schwerner, and Chaney continued into August,

"The arrogance they showed in wanting to reform the whole state…created resentment."

CITIZENS' COUNCIL SPOKESMAN WILLIAM SIMMONS

"that white northerners have to be caught up into the machinery of injustice and indifference in the South before the American people register concern. I personally suspect that if Mr. Chaney, who is a native Mississippian, had been alone at the time of the disappearance, that this case, like so many others,… would have gone completely unnoticed."

After meeting with the parents of Schwerner and Goodman at the White House, President Johnson sent two hundred sailors to Neshoba County to help drag the swamps and rivers. These sailors found no trace of the missing men but did discover the bodies of several murdered Negroes whose disappearances the FBI had declined to investigate. Even so, according to Dave Dennis, "as soon as it was determined that they were not the three workers, then those deaths are forgotten."

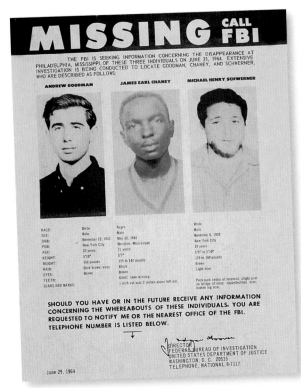

The Goodman, Schwerner, and Chaney "Missing" poster that was produced and widely circulated by the FBI.

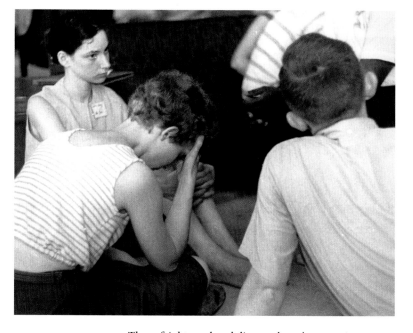

Three frightened and distraught volunteers sit on the floor of the Western College auditorium in Oxford after learning that three of their number have disappeared in Mississippi.

On June 23, federal agents tow the blue Ford station wagon driven by Goodman, Schwerner, and Chaney out of its hiding place off Highway 21 about fifteen miles northeast of Philadelphia. It was then taken to a Philadelphia garage for further inspection by the FBI and officers of the Mississippi Highway Patrol.

> "We most certainly do not and will not give protection to civil rights workers."
>
> J. Edgar Hoover

the work of the summer project proceeded all over the state, albeit in an atmosphere of seldom-relieved fear and tension. Three hundred ministers from the National Council of Churches joined the student volunteers in Mississippi, as did 150 lawyers and law students and 100 doctors, nurses, and psychologists from the Medical Committee for Human Rights. Although these adult volunteers usually stayed only a week or two, their presence provided invaluable expertise and helped local blacks secure some of the basic rights and services they had long been denied. With their participation, in fact, COFO reached and exceeded its one-thousand-volunteer goal.

To the public at large, however, by far the most compelling achievement of Freedom Summer was the creation of the Mississippi Freedom Democratic party (MFDP). The purpose of the MFDP was to challenge the state's "regular"—that is, white—

Searchers lower grappling hooks into the Pearl River near Philadelphia on June 27 as the hunt continues for the bodies of Goodman, Schwerner, and Chaney.

U.S. v. Price et al.

Early on—according to Joseph Sullivan, the FBI agent in charge—it became obvious that the Goodman, Schwerner, and Chaney case, code-named MIBURN (for Mississippi Burning), "would ultimately be solved by conducting an investigation rather than a search." Thus the bureau concentrated its efforts on developing informants and offered a thirty-thousand-dollar reward for any tips that would lead it to the recovery of the bodies. For weeks, the Neshoba County Klan hung tough, but finally one tip was passed along that led Sullivan on August 4 to the Old Jolly Farm.

Autopsies of the three bodies found there showed that Schwerner and Goodman had been shot once each; Chaney, however, had been shot three times, twice in the head and once in the chest. Whether the three men were also beaten remained a matter of dispute. The FBI's Klan informants insisted that they had not been, but forensic evidence suggested to New York pathologist David Spain, who conducted an independent autopsy, that Chaney at least had been excessively punished. "In my extensive experience," Spain told reporters, "I have never witnessed bones so severely shattered, except in tremendous high-speed accidents such as airplane crashes." The FBI concluded, however, that the bone damage was caused by the Caterpillar as it buried Chaney's body.

Using additional paid informants—notably James Jordan, who admitted to participating in the murders—the Justice Department brought a case against Cecil Price and twenty others in

December 1964. The federal charge, arising from a Reconstruction-era law, was conspiracy to deprive Goodman, Schwerner, and Chaney of their civil rights. (Only the State of Mississippi could bring murder charges, and it declined to do so.)

After nearly three years of legal wrangling, Price and seventeen others—including Sam Bowers, Edgar Ray Killen, and Neshoba County sheriff Lawrence Rainey—were eventually brought to trial in October 1967. John Doar prosecuted the case personally for the Justice Department, but he was up against federal district court judge Harold Cox, a notorious segregationist. Cox was the worst of several unfortunate judicial appointments made by President Kennedy at the urging of Mississippi senator James Eastland, who happened to have been Cox's college roommate. The judge's racism was well known—he had publicly referred to Negroes as "chimpanzees" and had only recently survived a congressional effort to impeach him—so Doar's expectations were low.

In the end, the all-white jury—which included at least one former Klan member, whom Cox refused to disqualify—delivered a compromise verdict. Seven defendants, including Price and Bowers, were found guilty. Eight others, including Rainey, were acquitted. In three cases, including Killen's, the jury deadlocked. Even so, the *New York Times* described the verdicts as "a measure of the quiet revolution that is taking place in southern attitudes."

Sheriff's deputies remove the corpses of the slain civil rights workers from an ambulance outside the University Medical Center in Jackson, where the remains were positively identified as those of Goodman, Schwerner, and Chaney.

Democratic party, which systematically excluded blacks. The goal of the MFDP goal was to supplant the "regular" Democrats at their party's 1964 national convention in Atlantic City, New Jersey.

THE MISSISSIPPI FREEDOM DEMOCRATIC PARTY

Bob Moses remembered being deeply influenced by John Lewis's March on Washington speech, particularly the passage in which Lewis declared, "The party of Kennedy is also the party of Eastland. The party of [liberal Republican senator Jacob] Javits is also the party of [conservative Republican senator Barry] Goldwater. Where is *our* party?" As Moses wrote later, "These questions were going to lead us step-by-step to formation of the Mississippi Freedom Democratic party." Although Moses's plans for the MFDP were initially announced at the monthly COFO meeting on February 9, 1964, the party itself wasn't formed until the April 26 COFO conclave.

For the MFDP challenge to be successful, the insurgents would have to prove that Mississippi's Negroes had indeed been excluded from the process of delegate selection. That process began with precinct caucuses, at which delegates to county conventions were chosen. The county conventions then sent representatives to district-level gatherings, at which delegates to the state convention were chosen. The state convention finally selected Mississippi's allotment of thirty-four delegates and thirty-four alternates to the national convention.

On June 16, the Mississippi Democratic party held 1,884 precinct caucuses around the state. Here and there in larger cities, a few blacks were allowed to vote; elsewhere, they were stymied. Some black registered voters arrived to find that the caucus site had been changed without notice; others were told upon arrival that the caucus had been canceled; most were simply turned away at the door. At several county conventions a week later, Negroes claiming to represent precincts in which no caucus had been held were similarly denied entry. From that point on, no black was allowed to participate in party deliberations.

Anticipating this, the MFDP set up its own parallel structure, enrolling over eighty thousand voters; holding precinct, county, district, and statewide meetings; and nominating its own slate of thirty-four delegates and thirty-four alternates to the Atlantic City convention. While this was going on, SNCC opened an office in Washington, out of which Ella Baker worked to build national support for the MFDP. Her most valuable ally in this task was Joseph Rauh, an influential Washington lawyer with powerful connections inside the Democratic party. In addition to being a founder of the liberal lobbying group Americans for Democratic Action (ADA), Rauh was general counsel to Walter Reuther's United Automobile Workers, and now he became the MFDP's general counsel as well. "If the Mississippi delegation is challenged, it will be unseated," Rauh promised Moses.

The seating of delegations, Rauh explained, was controlled by the Credentials Committee, a 108-member body dominated by supporters of President Johnson (who opposed the MFDP challenge because, like his predecessor, he didn't want trouble with the South). However, Rauh pointed out, if just 10 percent—in this case, eleven members—of the committee voted for a minority report supporting the MFDP, its challenge would proceed directly to the floor of the convention. At that point, the Johnson-controlled chair could order a voice vote and declare that, in his judgment, the Mississippi regulars had prevailed; on the other hand, with the backing of just eight

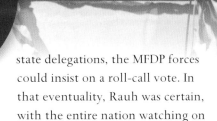

MFDP sticker

state delegations, the MFDP forces could insist on a roll-call vote. In that eventuality, Rauh was certain, with the entire nation watching on television, most convention delegates would abandon the segregationists and vote instead with the MFDP. Thus the MFDP's mantra became "eleven and eight."

Moses appreciated Rauh's enthusiasm but doubted his promise that the MFDP would be seated. Moses's own experience with the Democratic party had led him to believe that it would never take on its powerful southern wing. In June, however, the ADA approved a resolution of support for the MFDP, and soon the Michigan and New York delegations followed suit. At the same time, the Mississippi regulars made it even more difficult for northerners to support them. At their state convention in late June, they adopted a platform that

A summer volunteer urges two Negroes to register. Although the disappearances of Goodman, Schwerner, and Chaney cast a pall over Freedom Summer, only a handful of student volunteers quit.

Robert Moses speaks from the podium at the state convention of the Mississippi Freedom Democratic Party, held in Jackson on August 6. A crowd of 2,500 watched the election of 64 black and 4 white delegates.

denounced the civil rights bill, demanded a purge of the Supreme Court, and specifically rejected the platform of the national party. Their behavior raised the issue of party loyalty—especially after the *New York Times* reported that "virtually every delegate" to the Mississippi state convention supported Republican presidential candidate Barry Goldwater—and more backing shifted to the MFDP. Perhaps, it now seemed, there was cause to be optimistic.

ATLANTIC CITY

Once the Republicans chose ultraconservative Barry Goldwater as their presidential nominee in mid-July, Lyndon Johnson knew that he would win the election. What he wanted, however, was the largest mandate of all time so that he could ram his ambitious social agenda down Congress's throat. The Atlantic City convention was to be an important step along that path, and he didn't want any (in his view) ragtag Negroes from Mississippi spoiling it.

Because Goldwater had voted against the Civil Rights Act of 1964, Johnson felt certain that his base among black voters was secure.

What he feared was a backlash among white southerners should the Mississippi regulars be unseated. Johnson knew that Mississippi was already lost to him; his concern was that the rest of the Deep South not follow.

The MFDP delegates arrived in Atlantic City by bus on Friday, August 21, three days before the official start of the convention but just one day before the crucial Credentials Committee hearing at which their fate would be decided. The delegates stayed in the Gem Hotel, a small, ramshackle affair about a mile from the convention hall.

With events in Mississippi so prominent in the national news—especially after the August 4

Members of the Ku Klux Klan demonstrate on July 12 at the Republican national convention in San Francisco in support of eventual nominee Barry Goldwater. The black man in front is attempting to push the signs back.

Rauh's star witness that day was Fannie Lou Hamer, vice chair of the MFDP delegation, who poignantly described three years of involvement with the civil rights movement: how she had been chased off the Marlow plantation for attempting to register to vote; how she had been shot at; how she was beaten in June 1963 at the Winona, Mississippi, jail. Graphically, she described "the sounds of licks and screams" as other women in her voter registration group were beaten in the Winona jail and then the terror she herself felt as she was led away by state highway patrolmen to be savaged with a blackjack. Her story, expressed in broken yet highly evocative English, proved so deeply compelling—so emotionally powerful—that Lyndon Johnson became worried about the effect it was having on the American public.

"If the Freedom Democratic party is not seated now, I question America," Hamer concluded. "Is the America, the land of the free and the home of the brave, where we have to sleep with our telephones off the hook because our lives be threatened daily, because we want to live as decent human beings in America?" Unfortunately, only those present with Hamer in the convention hall heard these final heartrending words because the president, now fixated on the MFDP, had hurriedly called a press conference for no other reason than to get the MFDP off the air.

The networks, eager for news about Johnson's vice presidential choice, interrupted their hearing coverage to pick up the president live at the White House.

When Johnson merely voiced a few platitudes and left, however, the network executives knew they had been duped. They got even later that night by filling their evening newscasts with lengthy excerpts from Hamer's testimony. These, in turn, produced a deluge of telegrams and telephone calls to members of the Credentials Committee, demanding that they seat the MFDP.

Fannie Lou Hamer testifies on television before the Credentials Committee at the Democratic national convention in Atlantic City on August 22.

This COFO poster proved effective in channeling the emotional energy produced by the murders of Goodman, Schwerner, and Chaney into positive, constructive action.

discovery of the bodies of Goodman, Schwerner and Chaney—the MFDP delegates attracted a great deal of media attention, which somewhat dazzled them at first. Nevertheless, they recovered quickly and began circulating through the convention hotels, cornering other delegates, describing the terrible conditions in Mississippi, and pressing them for their votes. Meanwhile, SNCC and CORE supporters conducted a vigil outside the convention hall, holding up large portraits of the three slain civil rights workers.

Because the only suspense at Atlantic City involved Johnson's choice of a running mate, the news media gratefully played up the story of the MFDP challenge. As a result, several million Americans tuned in to watch the nationally televised Credentials Committee hearing on Saturday afternoon. Going into the hearing, Rauh was confident that he had his "eleven and eight" with support to spare.

As the committee reconvened on Sunday afternoon, Rauh had seventeen votes pledged to his minority report and ten state delegations ready to back a roll-call vote on the floor. Aware of the situation, Credentials Committee chair David Lawrence reluctantly postponed the final vote and instead formed a subcommittee headed by Minnesota attorney general Walter F. Mondale to recommend a compromise.

The choice of Mondale, a protégé of Hubert Humphrey, was far from accidental. Humphrey was on the spot. He wanted the vice presidential nomination badly, and because he had delivered the civil rights act for Johnson, he was the leading candidate. Yet before the president would give Humphrey his blessing, he wanted one more favor. Johnson knew that Humphrey had credibility with the civil rights movement. After all, it was Humphrey's insistence on a strong civil rights plank at the 1948 Democratic convention that had provoked the Dixiecrat walkout. Now Johnson wanted the Minnesota senator to use that credibility make the MFDP mess go away.

On another front, Johnson had already quietly arranged with Hoover for the FBI to gather political intelligence at the convention. According to the final report of the Church Committee, which investigated such abuses in the aftermath of Watergate, thirty special agents "were able to keep the White House fully apprised of all major developments during the convention's course... by infiltration of key groups through use of undercover agents." Specifically, the FBI agents

Committee (to prove to Lawrence that it had sufficient support for the challenge to reach the floor), Courtland Cox urged Moses to go along. What happened next, according to Cox, "was something unbelievable. Every person on that list, every member of that credentials committee who was going to vote for the

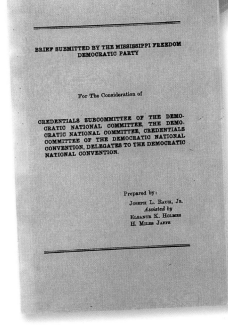

BRIEF SUBMITTED BY THE MISSISSIPPI FREEDOM DEMOCRATIC PARTY

For The Consideration of

CREDENTIALS SUBCOMMITTEE OF THE DEMO-
CRATIC NATIONAL COMMITTEE, THE DEMO-
CRATIC NATIONAL COMMITTEE, CREDENTIALS
COMMITTEE OF THE DEMOCRATIC NATIONAL
CONVENTION, DELEGATES TO THE DEMOCRATIC
NATIONAL CONVENTION.

Prepared by:
JOSEPH L. RAUH, JR.
Assisted by
ELEANOR K. HOLMES
H. MILES JAFFE

Joseph Rauh's Credentials Committee brief

At an August 21 press conference, Joseph Rauh (left) and Aaron Henry hold up a copy of the brief prepared by Rauh, which argued the case for the MFDP to be seated.

General Motors to fly into Atlantic City at 3 A.M. so that he could take part in an all-night strategy session with Humphrey, Mondale, Lawrence, and other insiders. The result was the compromise that Mondale presented to the Credentials Committee: Only those Mississippi regulars who agreed to sign party loyalty oaths would be seated; two of the MFDP representatives, delegation chairman Aaron Henry and national committeeman Edwin King, would be given "at large" seats; the remaining members of the MFDP delegation would be welcomed as "honored guests" but seated in the hall as spectators. Finally, the national party pledged to adopt new rules designed to prevent the seating of discriminatory delegations at future conventions.

After Mondale's presentation to the committee, Rauh pleaded for an adjournment so that he could consult with Henry, but the Johnson supporters on the committee pushed for an immediate vote. They were

"They beat me and they beat me with the long, flat blackjack. I screamed to God in pain. My dress worked itself up. I tried to pull it down. They beat my arms 'til I had no feeling in them."

FANNIE LOU HAMER BEFORE THE CREDENTIALS COMMITTEE

wiretapped Martin Luther King's hotel room, planted a microphone in the storefront that SNCC and CORE were using as their Atlantic City headquarters, and posed as television reporters to conduct "off-the-record" interviews.

Although the MFDP certainly didn't trust Johnson, none of its leaders imagined that the president would employ such low tactics in order to defeat them. Therefore, when a black congressman asked Moses on Sunday night for the list of MFDP supporters on the Credentials

minority, got a call. They said, 'Your husband is up for a judgeship, and if you don't shape up, he won't get it.' 'You're up for a loan. If you don't shape up, you won't get it.' And you began to see how things worked in the real world." By the time the Mondale subcommittee presented its recommendation on Tuesday afternoon, the White House had brought MFDP support on the Credentials Committee down to just eight votes.

The night before, at Johnson's insistence, Walter Reuther had abandoned critical negotiations with

concerned that a strong negative reaction from the MFDP might persuade wavering members to buck the White House pressure and vote their conscience instead.

While all this was taking place, Aaron Henry, Ed King, and Bob Moses were meeting with Humphrey, Reuther, Bayard Rustin, and

OVERLEAF: **Demonstrators on the boardwalk** outside the Atlantic City convention hall hold up posters of Goodman, Chaney, and Schwerner as they listen to Martin Luther King on August 24.

"I will have nothing to do with the political system any longer."

ROBERT MOSES

The interior of the meeting hall at the height of the Democratic national convention. Huge images of Lyndon Johnson bracket the speaker's platform.

Martin Luther King in the senator's suite at the Pageant Hotel. According to Ed King, "It was soon clear to us from MFDP that everyone else at this session was already 'in the know' about the details of the compromise" and was committed to support it. Unlike Moses, King and Henry

were willing to discuss the offer, but they joined Moses in stating that no question could be decided until it was first presented to the entire delegation.

Rustin was complaining that time was too short for such a presentation when a Humphrey aide interrupted to report that some important news was coming over the television set. The senator and his guests immediately removed themselves to an adjoining room, where they

watched a network correspondent explain that the Credentials Committee had just voted to accept the two-seat compromise. "You tricked us!" the normally placid Moses shouted before storming out on the next vice president of the United States.

Moses took a cab back to the Union Temple Baptist Church, where the MFDP had been caucusing. A little while later, Rauh arrived with the seven other committee members who had voted against the compromise. He quickly outlined its details and advised the delegates to accept. An emotional debate followed. Martin Luther King also appeared and asked to address the delegation, but, because he was associated with the perpetrators of the

The seats at the Democratic national convention reserved for the Mississippi delegation stand empty on August 24, after the Credentials Committee gave up for the day trying to decide who should rightfully occupy them.

MFDP delegates were given floor passes by other delegates friendly to their cause. Those sitting in the vacant Mississippi seats on Tuesday night included (from left to right) Annie Devine, Fannie Lou Hamer, and Edwin King.

Lyndon Johnson used his record mandate to launch the greatest social welfare program in American history, and it paid for, among other things, health clinics, legal aid, and educational programs in rural Mississippi. Nevertheless, after Atlantic City, young blacks in the civil rights movement began to question the motivations of white liberals whom they had once accepted uncritically as allies. Could whites be trusted to go all the way on civil rights, or would they always compromise, as so many had in Atlantic City?

Viewed through this prism, the 1964 summer project came to be seen as a failure by many of the SNCC and CORE activists who spent the fall of 1964 closely analyzing their past political assumptions. "Never again were we lulled into believing that our task was exposing injustices so that the 'good' people of America could eliminate them," Cleveland Sellers has written. "We left Atlantic City with the knowledge that the movement had turned into something else. After Atlantic City, our struggle was not for civil rights, but for liberation."

compromise, he was denied the opportunity to speak. The Mississippians felt that King—along with Rustin, Rauh, and other white liberals—had sold them out. The chaotic session ended with a defiant vote to reject the compromise.

That night, however, leaders of the civil rights establishment persuaded Henry, who was already inclined to support the compromise, to

opposition clear, and Jim Forman delivered a stinging, emotional attack.

When the speakers had all finished, they left the room so that only the delegates remained. Support for the compromise had grown stronger among the urban, middle-class members of the MFDP delegation—who acknowledged that, for championing the civil rights acts, President Johnson was due some deference—but the deal remained highly unpopular among the rural poor in their midst. "We didn't come all the way

"For many people, Atlantic City was the end of innocence."

SNCC ORGANIZER JOYCE LADNER

hold another meeting the following morning. In preparation for that meeting, visits were then made to other members of the MFDP delegation, especially those associated with the NAACP, in the hope that the political situation might still be smoothed out.

"NO TWO SEATS"

On Wednesday morning, the MFDP delegates reassembled at the Union Temple Baptist Church to listen to a host of civil rights luminaries urge them to accept the compromise. Martin Luther King told the delegates that this was the most important decision they would ever make in their lives. Bayard Rustin lectured them on the difference between protest and politics. "The former," he said, "is based on morality, and the latter is based on reality and compromise." Other speakers urged the MFDP delegates to accept the compromise on the grounds that doing so would reinforce the movement's alliance with white liberals. Moses, however, made his

up here to compromise for no more than we've gotten here," Fannie Lou Hamer said. "We didn't come all this way for no two seats." So the compromise was again rejected, and the proffered seats went unfilled.

"Atlantic City was a watershed in the movement," Moses later recalled, "because up until then the idea had been that you were working more or less within the Democratic party. We were working with them on voting, other things like that. With Atlantic City, a lot of movement people became disillusioned.... You turned around and your support was puddle-deep."

Many Freedom Summer projects continued on long after the white students left, if in somewhat altered forms.

This 1974 photograph, taken on the tenth anniversary of Freedom Summer, shows the building in Philadelphia, Mississippi, that once held the town's COFO office.

The Right to Vote

1964–1965

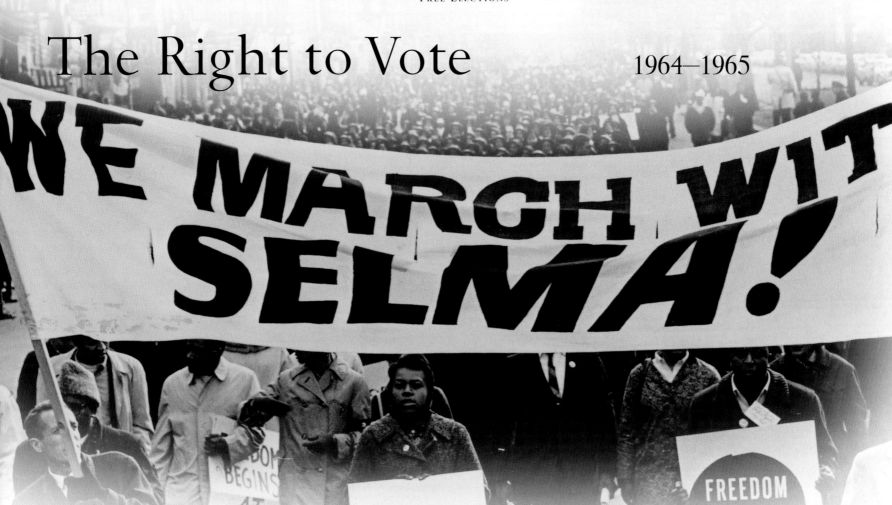

WE MARCH WIT SELMA!

John Lewis and Jim Forman flew to New York City to take part in this March 15, 1965, demonstration in support of the voting rights campaign in Selma, Alabama.

After the Atlantic City convention, the top SNCC leaders felt as though they wanted to leave the country—and, coincidentally, most of them did. Through Harry Belafonte, SNCC had received an offer from the government of Guinea to send a delegation to Africa, and eleven people took part, including Robert Moses, John Lewis, Jim Forman, Julian Bond, and Fannie Lou Hamer.

A former French colony, Guinea had decided after receiving its independence in 1958 to become a nonaligned nation, favoring neither the capitalist West nor the Communist East. Visiting such a place dominated by blacks gave the SNCCers a new perspective on their struggle at home. "I saw black men flying the airplanes, driving buses, sitting behind big desks in the bank, and just doing everything that I was used to seeing white people do," Hamer recalled.

While SNCC's chairman, executive secretary, and Mississippi project director were away, Courtland Cox acted in their stead. A former Howard University student, Cox was part of the organization's northern wing led by Stokely Carmichael, another former Howard student. The northerners tended to be more political and

more outspoken than their southern counterparts, especially on the subject of race. Many had grown up in white communities with white friends but were now disowning their pasts and embracing their "black consciousness." This largely internal pressure to identify more closely with the culture of southern Negroes was often expressed as bitterness toward whites. According to John Lewis, the racial radicalism of northerners was "almost inversely proportional to the degree to which they had, for one reason or another, kept down their 'blackness' when they were younger."

Lewis has written that when he left for Africa in September 1964, he knew that he was leaving behind a frustrated, angry staff. Already people were beginning to question SNCC's goals and

direction. "But," Lewis continued, "I had no idea they would move so far and so fast."

At the end of Freedom Summer, at least eighty white volunteers had asked to stay on in Mississippi and become full-time members of the SNCC staff. This development nearly doubled the organization's size and significantly altered its racial and class composition. It also brought into doubt whether SNCC remained committed to the development of indigenous leadership, because the expanding presence of paternalistic northern whites seemed to indicate otherwise. During the 1963 Freedom Vote, the white volunteers had been asked to stay for two weeks; during Freedom Summer, they had been invited for two months; now, they wanted to remain indefinitely.

With all this roiling the staff, Cox called a meeting for October 10 at the Gammon Theological Seminary in Atlanta. Forman and Moses were both there, having returned from Africa six days earlier; Lewis was not, having extended his tour from three to ten weeks.

Black and white volunteers at a meeting of the Mississippi Summer Project. Some of the whites who returned to school in the fall became active in other causes, such as free speech and opposition to the Vietnam War.

Forman began the meeting by introducing for discussion a program he and Moses had devised, the Black Belt Project, which sought to apply to the rest of the Deep South the lessons and methods of the Mississippi Summer Project. It would take place during the summer of 1965—only this time the summer volunteers would be black students rather than whites.

Moses had become convinced during the summer of 1964 that local blacks would never gain the confidence necessary to become leaders if they had to do so in the presence of large numbers of self-assured whites. But this subject never really came up. Instead, according to Forman, the meeting took "a disastrous turn" when staff members began complaining that they hadn't been adequately consulted. "A few people were raising the cry, 'Who made that decision?' as if somebody had tried to sneak something over on them," Forman wrote later. Who had set the agenda? Who was in charge. *Why* were they in charge? These were the questions people wanted answered, so the Black Belt Project was shelved.

Since 1960, SNCC had operated under a loose, even anarchic, decision-making structure. With fewer than one hundred people involved, it was possible for all of them to know one another and to reach consensus easily. But the sudden, explosive growth of SNCC's staff necessitated a reappraisal, which many of the organization's veterans resented. Forman, whose job made him particularly aware of the growing logistical problems, pushed for more structure and formality; others opposed him, charging that he was simply making a power grab. All were feeling the emotional aftereffects of a long and difficult summer—a sort of battle fatigue. As a result, it didn't take long for the meeting to degenerate into shouting and finger pointing.

Voting rights activists picket the front of the Leflore County courthouse in Greenwood, Mississippi, in March 1964.

The only person present who could have held the group together was Bob Moses, and he refused to say anything. Of late, Moses had become increasingly concerned that he was exercising "undue influence" over SNCC, and this made him very uncomfortable. Because of his extreme selflessness, he had become more and more revered within the organization, especially among the white staff. Now the hero worship had reached the point at which, he feared, too many people were willing to follow him blindly. Unwilling to bear this responsibility, he chose to remain silent rather than determine the outcome of the debate.

Voting Rights

Although Title IV of the Civil Rights Act of 1957 had somewhat strengthened the Justice Department's ability to protect Negro voting rights, the Eisenhower administration did little to explore its new powers. Assistant Attorney General for Civil Rights Wilson White decided that he would act only on receipt of formal written complaints from people who had personally been victimized by discrimination. Of course, there were but a handful of these complaints because few affected Negroes had the awareness or the legal knowledge necessary to file them. As a result, between 1957 and 1960, not a single Negro voter was registered as a result of Justice Department action.

Not all of this problem was White's fault. Even an aggressive prosecutor would have had trouble with the law's limited enforcement provisions, which relied almost entirely on the cooperation of recalcitrant southern courts. A second civil rights bill, passed in May 1960, sought to remedy some of these deficiencies, but its final watered-down language offered little improvement. The new law, for instance, failed to reduce the enormous amount of tedious, time-consuming work needed to

bring a single case, and it also neglected to broaden the application of successful verdicts to neighboring jurisdictions. As long as the Justice Department was forced to file its suits one by one, county by county, there was little hope that it could register more than a tiny percentage of the South's disfranchised Negroes.

Once the Kennedy administration took office in 1961, the pace and vigor of voting rights litigation accelerated rapidly. Both the president and the attorney general wanted badly to solve this problem through the courts so that they could avoid a politically costly confrontation with southern Democrats in Congress over yet another civil rights bill. Unfortunately, the administration defeated its own strategy by appointing inappropriate federal judges—in a foolish attempt to appease southern senators—who were zealous segregationists.

Even so, given the problematic state of the law, it's unlikely that the Justice Department would have succeeded in any case. As Robert Moses observed during the summer of 1963, "It is impossible to register Negroes in Mississippi," and the statistics backed him up. Despite all of COFO's work, the number of blacks registered to vote in that state increased from 5.3 percent of those eligible in 1962 to just 6.7 percent of those eligible in 1964. Clearly, more voting rights legislation was needed.

Selma's White Leadership

Unlike Montgomery and Birmingham, where King had faced off against united white municipalities, Selma was factionalized. Judge James Hare and Sheriff Jim Clark represented Selma's hard-line segregationists, while Mayor Joseph Smitherman and Public Safety Director Wilson Baker spoke for a much more moderate, though still segregationist, constituency.

The youthful Smitherman, once an appliance salesman, had served four years on the Selma city council before winning his first run for mayor in 1964. His chief campaign promise had been to bring new industry to Selma's sagging cotton economy. Though hardly a champion of racial understanding—he once called Martin Luther King "Martin Luther Coon"—Smitherman recognized

Selma mayor Joseph Smitherman speaks to reporters in March 1965. Standing to his right is Public Safety Director Wilson Baker.

that, unless he was careful, Selma could easily suffer the same economic fate as Little Rock after its school desegregation crisis.

Smitherman chose Wilson Baker for the newly created position of public safety director because Baker was a disciplined professional. A former police captain in Selma, he sometimes taught criminology at the University of Alabama and always could be counted on to keep his head.

THE NEXT STEP

Martin Luther King's SCLC certainly had a loose organizational structure as well, which made it highly adaptable to changing circumstances. But there was a crucial difference between the SCLC and SNCC: The SCLC had a strong leader, King, who was quite willing to give orders, and a staff that followed those orders without question.

Between November 10 and November 12, a month after the SNCC meltdown, King presided over an SCLC retreat at the Gaston Motel in Birmingham. Its purpose, he wrote, was "to chart our course in the nonviolent movement over the next six months." To no one's surprise, the key issue that emerged was voting rights.

Presidents Kennedy and Johnson had kept voting rights out of the Civil Rights Act of 1964 because they both feared that its inclusion would kill the legislation entirely. Freedom Summer and the saga of the MFDP, however, had recently made plain the acute need for a voting rights bill.

Johnson certainly knew that new legislation was needed, but it wasn't yet a top priority for him. During a mid-December meeting with King, he told the SCLC leader, "Martin, you're right.…I'm going to do it eventually, but I can't get a voting rights bill through in this session of Congress." The new attorney general, Nicholas Katzenbach, was already working on the legislation,

Johnson assured King, but the Justice Department would have to move slowly because the country was tired of civil rights and needed time to adjust. (Like his predecessor, Johnson was also thinking about the southern votes he would need to pass his ambitious new antipoverty program.) The president wasn't sure when the right time would come—perhaps late in 1965, he said, but more likely 1966. King replied politely but firmly that the Negroes weren't going to wait that long.

King had already made up his mind to force the issue in Selma, Alabama, the seat of Dallas County, where blacks made up half of the voting-aged population, yet only 1 percent were registered to vote (compared with 65 percent of whites). The decision to target Selma had been made on the second day of the Birmingham retreat, after Amelia Platts Boynton of the Dallas County Voters League (DCVL) had presented a report on Selma and asked King for help.

Some of the groundwork was already under way. For the past several months, SCLC organizer James Bevel had been working on the SCLC's Alabama Project with the goal of holding a statewide alternative election that could, in the manner of the MFDP, challenge the legitimacy of the Alabama state legislature. (In this work he was joined by Diane Nash, who had married Bevel in late 1961.) A direct action campaign

in Selma, the SCLC staff believed, would make a fine centerpiece to that campaign because it could bring intense national attention to the state.

SNCC IN SELMA

SNCC's presence in Selma, a city of twenty-seven thousand, dated back to February 1963, when newlyweds Bernard and Colia Lafayette moved there to organize Dallas County. (Bernard had been a leader of the 1960 Nashville sit-ins and a Freedom Rider who had done time at Parchman; Colia was a student at Tougaloo College.) "It was sort of our honeymoon," Bernard Lafayette recalled in a 1968 interview. "The first SNCC worker there came back and said that we might as well scratch Selma off the list because the people there just weren't ready for a movement. We didn't get any different impression when we were there. We had trouble finding a place to live; most people were afraid to put us up. But we worked on this assumption: No matter how bad a place is, some people got courage."

Fearful of white retaliation, the city's Negro ministers initially refused to allow voter registration meetings in their churches, but Amelia Boynton befriended the Lafayettes and allowed them use of her office. Out of this space, they organized monthly classes and taught eligible blacks how to fill out Alabama's complicated registration forms. The work went slowly, however, because of Selma's climate of fear. The root of that fear was Dallas County sheriff James G. Clark Jr.

The Lafayettes' classes eventually attracted Clark's attention, and he began harassing them, arresting them on dubious charges, and ignoring the beatings they and other activists occasionally received from local whites. Clark also sent officers to the monthly classes so that the names of those attending could be taken down and distributed to employers. At the same time, he issued a call for all white men over twenty-one years of age to come down to the courthouse for deputization as "possemen." In this way, he created his own small segregationist army.

Clark's thuggish behavior was, in fact, an important contributing factor in the SCLC decision to enter Selma. Like Bull Connor, Sheriff Clark looked the part of the southern segregationist lawman: redxnecked, overbearing, quick to lose his temper. He could be counted on to resort to violence, and that violence, once reported in the nation's newspapers and shown on national television, would expose the pattern of physical intimidation that kept whites in power in Alabama despite black-majority populations in many, many counties.

Clark had already gained something of a national reputation in July 1964, when he ordered his deputies to use cattle prods on protesters at the Dallas County courthouse, where both he and the Board of Registrars had their offices. Following that demonstration, circuit court judge James Hare, Clark's political mentor, had issued an order banning all civil-rights-related gatherings of more than three people. For the next six months, no mass meetings were held in Selma.

When Bernard and Colia Lafayette both went back to school in September 1964, SNCC sent Worth Long and John Love to continue what John Lewis has called "the dirty work" of the movement—the unseen, untold, and often unappreciated organizing that SNCC carried out long before other organizations and the media arrived. Even so, by the time that

Amelia Boynton traveled to Birmingham in November 1964, SNCC's effort to organize Selma had come nearly to a halt. The chief reason was a stark lack of results: In the two years since the arrival of the Lafayettes, only one hundred or so voters had been registered.

With the issue of voting rights foremost in his mind, with Jim Clark's methods likely to attract media attention, and with the DCVL's invitation in hand, King announced on December 28 that he would be kicking off the SCLC's new campaign in Selma with a speech there on Saturday, January 2. It would be the first mass meeting held in Selma since the issuance of Judge Hare's injunction.

Whatever concerns King and his staff might have had about stepping on SNCC toes in Selma were erased by Mrs. Boynton's invitation—but that invitation didn't make the SNCCers in Selma or at the Atlanta headquarters feel any better about the situation. According to John Lewis, "It was the same old story all over again.

Dallas County sheriff Jim Clark (left) uses a nightstick to prod one of several Negroes attempting to register at the Selma courthouse in February 1965. Clark was a large man weighing about 230 pounds, and very imposing.

"They picked Selma just like a movie producer would pick a set. You had the right ingredients."

JOSEPH SMITHERMAN

Martin Luther King Jr. addresses a wildly cheering crowd at Brown Chapel in Selma on January 2, 1965.

Fred Shuttlesworth (left), accompanied by Ralph Abernathy (center) and Martin Luther King, leads the January 18 voter registration march in Selma.

We dug in early, did the groundwork, laid the foundation, then the SCLC came in with their headline-grabbing hit-and-run tactics, doing nothing to nurture leaders among the local community but instead bringing in their own leaders, then leaving after they'd gotten what they needed out of it."

CONTROLLING CLARK

The last thing that Selma mayor Joseph Smitherman wanted was Jim Clark running amok all over Dr. King. Images of racial violence in the national press wouldn't help Selma's industrialization campaign any more than similar images had helped Little Rock's. So Smitherman and his public safety director, Wilson Baker, made plans for a moderate, Laurie Pritchett–style response to King, which they hoped would keep Jim Clark out of the picture. To begin with, Baker announced that he would not be enforcing Judge Hare's order at the January 2 mass meeting.

Seven hundred people attended that meeting, held at the Brown Chapel AME Church, where King told the overflow audience, "We will seek to arouse the federal government by marching by the thousands to the places of registration. When we get the right to vote, we will send to the statehouse not men who will stand in the doorways of universities to keep Negroes out but men who will uphold the cause of justice."

Later that night, members of King's staff met with the DCVL leadership and SNCCers Long and Love to present their plans and solicit support. Andrew Young, who had replaced Wyatt T. Walker

as SCLC executive director a year earlier, explained that he wanted to focus the Selma campaign on the two days a month—the first and third Mondays—when state law required the Dallas County Board of Registrars to accept applications.

Typically, the registrars arrived late, took long lunches, and left early, the point being to limit the number of Negroes who even got in the door. Those few brave enough to enter Sheriff Clark's domain were given a long and complicated literacy test so difficult that few applicants passed, unless those applicants happened to be white.

In advance of the next registration day—Monday, January 18—Young wanted to recruit hundreds of people to form long lines outside the county courthouse. He didn't expect any of them to be registered, but their mere presence, he said, would "establish in the mind of the nation that a lot of people who want to register are being prevented from doing so."

Sheriff Jim Clark shoves Amelia Boynton violently down the street after arresting her during the January 19 voting rights demonstration at the Selma courthouse.

The next day, King and Young returned to Atlanta, leaving behind Hosea Williams to supervise the work. A World War II veteran, Williams had become one of SCLC's most capable and trusted advance men, and by the time King returned to Selma on January 14 for another mass meeting, Williams had put Young's plan into action. He did so with the particular help of Long and Love, who set aside their wariness of the SCLC to help with the door-to-door canvassing.

Meanwhile, Smitherman had Baker meet with Clark to remind the sheriff that, except for the county courthouse, the city of Selma was Baker's jurisdiction. Clark got the message but didn't heed it, even though he knew that Smitherman and Baker spoke for the Selma business community, which didn't want a repeat of Birmingham. Beyond his self-centered racism, Clark was motivated by a personal grudge against Baker, who had opposed him for sheriff in 1958.

Knowing what King intended, Smitherman and Baker impressed upon Clark the need for the sheriff to remain calm and avoid unnecessary confrontations. For a time, this worked. When four hundred Negroes led by King and John Lewis arrived at the county courthouse on January 18, a restrained Clark informed them that they would have to clear the sidewalk and wait in an adjacent alleyway until they were called, one at a time, by the registrars. The demonstrators did as they were told and waited for several hours without any interference from Clark; none, however, were called by the registrars.

That night, a disappointed SCLC staff caucused with King. As everyone in the room understood, no violence meant no headlines, and no headlines meant that the campaign was a waste of King's precious time. If Baker and Smitherman could indeed keep Clark in check, then the SCLC would have another Albany on its hands, and no one wanted that. The possibility of rapidly shifting the direct action campaign to a nearby town such as Marion or Camden was discussed, but in the end it was decided to try one more demonstration and see what happened.

The next morning, King and Lewis led another group from Brown Chapel to the courthouse, but this time when

Clark told them to wait in the alleyway, they refused. The sheriff became agitated, yelling orders to his deputies, who began to push people off the sidewalk. "Clark had a big club in his hand," Amelia Boynton recalled, "and he yelled to me, 'Where are you going?…You all got to get in this line.' Before I could gather my wits, he had left the [courthouse] steps and jumped behind me, grabbed me by my coat, propelled me around, and started shoving me down the street. I was stunned. I saw cameramen and newspaper reporters around and…I said, 'I hope the newspapers see you acting this role.' He said, 'Dammit, I hope they do.'"

Sixty-seven demonstrators, including Boynton, were arrested and jailed. More important, the next day, photographs of Clark manhandling Boynton ran on the front pages of most major national newspapers. "You could hear the news photographers' cameras clicking," John Lewis has written, "and I knew that now it was starting, that cycle of violence and publicity and more violence and more publicity that would eventually, we hoped, push things to the point where something—ideally, the law— would have to be changed."

On Wednesday, January 20, while King traveled to Pennsylvania for two speaking engagements, another march on the courthouse produced 226 more arrests. Baker and Smitherman's strategy was clearly breaking down.

King returned to Selma on Friday, January 22, for a special demonstration that Andrew Young called, albeit with some exaggeration, "the most significant thing that has happened in the racial movement since Birmingham." More than one hundred teachers led by DCVL president Frederick Reese, a high school science teacher himself, marched through Selma that day, convening at the courthouse to protest Boynton's arrest.

The teachers' presence at the courthouse made the important propaganda point that few of them had been judged literate by the registrars. Much more significant, however, was the fact that a traditionally reluctant constituency had now joined the Selma campaign in earnest. As a group, black teachers were generally conservative, cautious, and averse to doing anything that might offend the whites who controlled their jobs; they were also among the

best-paid black professionals in any town and very influential. Having them on board was meaningful because where they led, others followed. As Reese himself explained, "The undertakers got a group, and they marched. The beauticians got a group, and they marched. Everybody marched after the teachers marched."

Martin Luther King kneels with other marchers in prayer before being led away to jail on February 1.

A SELMA JAIL

Like those made for Birmingham, the SCLC plans for Selma included, at some point, the arrest and jailing of King. After the teachers marched, it was decided that the best time for King to go to jail was the next registration day— Monday, February 1. Previously, the marchers

Selma public safety director Wilson Baker (right) tells Martin Luther King on February 1 that he and "all those folks behind you" are being arrested for violating a Selma ordinance requiring a permit for a parade.

assembling at Brown Chapel had been careful to walk to the courthouse in small groups so as not to violate the city's parade ordinance. This day, however, the 260 demonstrators walked in an unbroken line. Within a few blocks, Wilson Baker's police brought the column to a halt, and Baker informed King that he and the others were breaking the law. When the marchers refused to comply with Baker's order to realign themselves, they were arrested.

Refusing bail, King and his familiar jail companion, Ralph Abernathy, settled in for a stay of several days. SCLC's hope was that King's presence in the Selma jail would re-create the magic of Birmingham. The author of "Letter from Birmingham Jail" had even composed, before entering prison, a Selma "letter" to be published as part of a fund-raising advertisement in the *New York Times* later in the week.

Also that Monday, in another echo of Birmingham, five hundred schoolchildren mobilized by Bevel marched to the Dallas County courthouse. Some carried protest signs written in crayon; all were arrested. Meanwhile, thirty miles away in Marion, six hundred Perry County residents marched and were arrested

in one of the first protests held in an outlying community. On Tuesday and Wednesday of that week, hundreds more Selma schoolchildren were arrested, overflowing the jails and forcing the housing of some prisoners in embarrassing camps where buckets served as toilets and the inmates slept on the floor.

Malcolm X speaks to a group of mostly young Negroes at Brown Chapel in Selma on February 4. Press reports emphasized what reporters described as Malcolm's call for more militancy in the demonstrations.

Hundreds of schoolchildren sing freedom songs as they are marched under police guard to a detention compound on February 3.

On Thursday, February 4, Malcolm X came to town. While traveling in Kenya the previous fall, he had met John Lewis, who had invited him to visit the movement in the South.

Jim Forman had subsequently made arrangements for Malcolm to speak at the Tuskegee Institute, and, being so close to Selma, Malcolm had added a day trip there.

Initially, King's aides feared that the fiery Nation of Islam exile would incite violence, but Malcolm assured Coretta Scott King that he had come merely to help. Later in the day, he honored his word, telling a SNCC-organized gathering at Brown Chapel that the whites of Selma "should thank Dr. King for holding people in check, for there are other [black leaders] who do not believe in these [nonviolent] measures."

Just as Malcolm was leaving town, word came that Daniel Thomas, the federal district court judge with jurisdiction over Selma, had issued an order instructing the Dallas County Board of Registrars to halt administration of the literacy test and to process at least one hundred applications a day (if that many were submitted). Coming in response to a Justice Department lawsuit, Thomas's order, reportedly drawn up with the support of Dallas County officials, represented a significant attempt to accommodate disfranchised blacks—at least to

accommodate them enough to stop all the demonstrating.

Presented with these major concessions, Andrew Young called a temporary halt to the demonstrations. But King, acting from jail, soon reversed that decision. "Please don't be too soft," King urged Young. "We have the offensive. It was a mistake not to march today. In a crisis, we must have a sense of drama. Don't let Baker control our movement. We may accept the restraining order as a partial victory, but we can't stop." The next day, King's last in jail, Clark arrested five hundred more people outside the courthouse.

On Tuesday, February 9, King flew to Washington to meet again with President Johnson about voting rights legislation. The men agreed that any administration bill should ban literacy tests and provide for the appointment of federal registrars in counties where racial discrimination was pervasive; even so, Johnson still had the issue on the slow track. According to historian David J. Garrow, "King returned to Alabama pleased at how the discussion had gone but knowing that additional public pressure would be necessary to move the administration forward."

Martin Luther King meets on February 9 with Vice Pres. Hubert Humphrey (center) and Attorney General Nicholas Katzenbach (right) to discuss the legislative steps that need to be taken to protect Negro voting rights. In the background are Andrew Young (left) and James Forman.

C. T. Vivian leads demonstrators outside the Selma courthouse in prayer before being arrested by Sheriff Jim Clark (center) on February 5.

Exactly one week later, the Rev. C. T. Vivian—an early member of the Nashville sit-in group, a Freedom Rider, and now a top SCLC staffer—led twenty-five demonstrators to the Dallas County courthouse, where Clark and several armed deputies blocked his way. The highly articulate Vivian responded by lecturing the sheriff on his inadequacies. "You're racists in the same way Hitler was a racist," Vivian said.

In Clark's retelling, Vivian "started shouting at me that I was Hitler, I was a brute, that I was a Nazi....I lost my temper then." First, the sheriff ordered the television cameras turned off; then he punched Vivian so hard in the mouth that he fractured a finger. "You can arrest us, Sheriff Clark; you don't have to beat us. You beat people bloody in order that they will not have the privilege to vote," Vivian, bleeding from the mouth, shot back as Clark arrested him.

Or at least that was the story widely reported in the next day's newspapers. Years later, Vivian admitted that he was actually punched by one of Clark's deputies. Neither he nor Clark saw fit to correct the story because it suited both of them—Clark's ego and Vivian's aims.

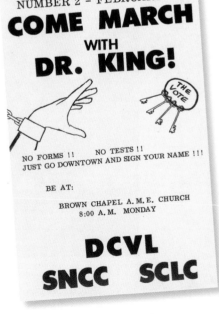

A mimeographed handbill advertising a February 22 march in Selma.

THE DEATH OF JIMMIE LEE JACKSON

Two days after his confrontation with Clark, Vivian was asked to address a mass meeting at Zion's Chapel Methodist Church in Marion, where nearly as many protests and arrests had taken place since February 1 as in Selma itself. Unusually, this meeting ended with a nighttime march from the church to the city jail. Nighttime marches were unusual in the movement because they were considered dangerous—too much could be hidden, too many things could go wrong. In this case, however, the jail was just a few hundred yards away, and with 450 people marching, it seemed safe enough. Not so.

Outside the church, the marchers were confronted by a mob of state troopers, local police, and angry white civilians. "This is an unlawful assembly. You are hereby ordered to disperse. Go home or go back to the church," Marion's police chief announced over a public address system. Then, all of a sudden, the streetlights went out.

In the ensuing gloom, troopers and policemen began clubbing marchers while well-prepared civilians spray-painted the lenses of television

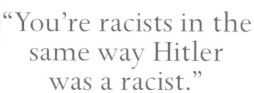
cameras and attacked news photographers. (NBC's Richard Valeriani was beaten so badly with an ax handle that he had to be hospitalized for several days with a large gash in his head.) Meanwhile, panicked demonstrators sought shelter wherever they could find it.

When twenty-six-year-old army veteran Jimmie Lee Jackson found his eighty-two-year-old grandfather, Cager Lee, beaten and bleeding on the street, he rushed him into Mack's Cafe. Unfortunately, several state troopers followed them into the restaurant and began assaulting the several dozen people inside. When one of these troopers hit Jimmie Lee Jackson's mother, Viola, and sent her screaming to the floor, the son leaped to his mother's defense. The state trooper then hit Jimmie Lee Jackson in the face before slamming him against a cigarette machine; meanwhile, a colleague drew his gun and shot Jackson point blank in the stomach.

Jackson held on for a week but finally succumbed to a massive infection on Friday, February 26. Two days later, a memorial service was held at Zion's Chapel in Marion. More than four hundred mourners packed the pews while another six hundred stood outside in the rain. Bevel delivered the sermon, preaching from two texts. The first was Acts 12, verses 2 and 3: "Herod killed James, the brother of John, with a sword; and when he saw that it pleased the Jews, he proceeded to arrest Peter also."

"I'm not worried about James anymore," Bevel shouted. "I'm concerned about Peter, who is still with us. James has found release from the indignities of being a Negro in Alabama, and no longer can he be cowed and coerced and deprived of his rights as a man. James knows the peace this world cannot give and lives eternally the life we all hope someday to share. I'm not worried about James. I'm concerned with Peter, who must continue to be cowed and coerced and beaten and even murdered."

What could be done to save Peter? Bevel asked the congregation. Then he turned to the second text, Esther 4, verse 4: "Also Mordecai gave Hetach the copy of the writing of the decree that was given at Shushan to destroy the Jews, to show it unto Esther, and to declare it unto her, and to charge her that she should go unto the king, to make supplications unto him, and to make requests before him for her people."

It was Bevel's idea that they all, like Esther, "go see the king"—in this case, Gov. George Wallace in Montgomery. Bevel wanted to take Jimmie Lee Jackson's body, carry it to Montgomery, and place it on the steps of the capitol—thereby confronting the governor, the state, and the nation.

Bevel's inspiration immediately took hold, though the idea of transporting Jackson's casket was soon dismissed. Instead, on Wednesday, March 3, the day that Jimmie Lee Jackson was buried in Marion, the SCLC announced that it would be holding a protest march from Selma all the way to Montgomery beginning on Sunday, March 7. The fifty-four-mile hike along Highway 80 would take five days, guaranteeing the marchers a full week of intense press coverage and plenty of opportunity to engage the national news media.

At least that was the theory. In reality, no preparations were being made for this enormous logistical undertaking because no one expected the marchers to get very far.

King's own focus that week was elsewhere. As the pace of protest in Selma accelerated, so did the tempo of politics in Washington, where more and more congressmen were lining up behind the SCLC on the voting rights issue. The president, too, was coming around. Johnson met with King for more than an hour on Friday, March 5, and afterward announced that the administration's bill was nearly ready.

The Selma-to-Montgomery march was now just two days away, but rather than return to Selma, King decided to fly home to Atlanta. He had been away from Ebenezer Baptist too much lately, he thought, and he felt the need to preach again from his own pulpit that Sunday. More to the point, he was also bone-tired. Three weeks earlier, he had been hospitalized briefly for exhaustion, and he still needed rest. The SCLC staff would have to handle the Selma march, King decided.

Meanwhile, in Montgomery, George Wallace and his staff discussed how the State of Alabama should respond. The governor hated the idea of

In a Marion funeral home, a group of mourners gather around the body of Jimmie Lee Jackson on March 2.

the march and initially wanted it stopped, but several of his aides pressed him to reconsider. The SCLC, they pointed out, was so ill prepared that the marchers had no realistic chance of reaching Montgomery. In fact, they would have to turn around the very first day, so why not let them march and look foolish? Wallace saw the point and agreed.

This was the plan: The governor would announce his intention to block the march. (Otherwise, the SCLC might begin making preparations.) Then, on Sunday, the state troopers at the Selma city limits would part like the Red Sea and allow the marchers to pass. With no provisions for food, water, or shelter, they couldn't get very far.

That arrangement stood until Friday, when State Representative Bill Edwards made an emergency phone call to the governor. Edwards represented rural Lowndes County, which straddled a lonely stretch of Highway 80 just east of Selma. His district was strong Klan territory— 81 percent black but without a single Negro voter.

An unflappable George C. Wallace sits at his desk inside the governor's office at the Alabama state capitol in Montgomery in March 1965.

Edwards had learned of the governor's plan to allow the march, and he was worried. If the marchers were allowed to reach Lowndes County, he warned, some would certainly be shot. Recognizing the severe political difficulties that such killings would engender, Wallace reluctantly changed his mind and ordered the state police to

"We was infuriated to the point that we wanted to carry Jimmie's body to George Wallace and dump it on the steps of the capitol. We had decided that we were going to get killed or we was going to be free."

MARION RESIDENT ALBERT TURNER

Alabama state troopers (left) swing their billy clubs at Negro marchers on Bloody Sunday. Meanwhile, another state trooper wearing a gas mask (right) plunges into the cloud of tear gas enveloping the Edmund Pettus Bridge.

stop the march. Publicly, he said that the march couldn't be allowed because it would obstruct traffic on the highway.

Ironically, SNCC also opposed the march. A few practical concerns were voiced—the drain on scarce movement resources, the likelihood of police brutality—but the real reason was emotional. With the notable exception of John Lewis, the SNCC leadership resented the SCLC deeply and believed that the march was being held for King, not for Selma. When Forman and others on the SNCC executive committee

learned that King himself would be taking a pass, they voted to keep SNCC out of the march as well. The organizations would "live up to those minimal commitments…to provide radios and cars, doctors and nurses," the executive committee wrote in a letter to King, sent under Lewis's signature, but "nothing beyond that."

BLOODY SUNDAY

March 7 dawned as a brisk, breezy spring day in Selma. The sun was out early as John Lewis arrived in town, having driven all night from Atlanta. But while he got a few hours' sleep, clouds began to gather, and by the time he rose,

dressed, and made his way over to Brown Chapel about half past noon, the sky was largely overcast. Although the SNCC executive committee had disavowed the march organizationally, it had nevertheless agreed that Lewis could march on his own if he wanted, representing only himself.

The suit and dress shoes that Lewis wore might have seemed inappropriate for a long march— but, again, no one expected the march to last very long. In fact, nearly all of the marchers were wearing their Sunday best, most having come straight from church. As they waited outside Brown Chapel, SCLC staffers demonstrated the proper way to protect one's body from a billy-club assault.

Lewis soon learned that late the previous night, King had decided to postpone the march until Monday so that he could take part himself. He had sent Andrew Young to Selma with this message, but Young, arriving at Brown Chapel, could see for himself that the six hundred

John Lewis (center, in a light-colored coat) bends over to protect himself as a state trooper swings at his head with a nightstick on Bloody Sunday. Lewis was later admitted to a local hospital with a skull fracture.

"This was a face-off in the most vivid terms between a dignified, composed, completely nonviolent multitude of silent protestors and the truly malevolent force of a heavily armed, hateful battalion of troopers."

JOHN LEWIS DESCRIBING BLOODY SUNDAY

people assembled there were going to march regardless. He was still discussing the situation with Bevel and Hosea Williams when Lewis joined their conversation.

Bevel and Williams were arguing that they would have to move ahead as planned or else risk losing the support of the local community. Young had to agree, and he used the church telephone to contact King in Atlanta. Hearing Young's report, King reversed himself and told Young that one of the SCLC men should join Lewis at the front of the line while the other two remained in the rear to manage the withdrawal should violence develop. Young, Bevel, and Williams then flipped quarters to see who would accompany Lewis; Williams was the odd man out.

No one expected anything worse than being arrested or perhaps getting roughed up a little, but the Medical Committee for Human Rights had nevertheless flown in a team of New York doctors and nurses to set up a makeshift clinic in the Brown Chapel parsonage. When word spread that tear gas had been issued to the state troopers, the medical personnel began instructing the marchers to walk low and avoid rubbing their eyes if the gas was used.

About four o'clock, the marchers finally lined up two abreast behind Lewis and Williams. Lewis read a brief statement for the benefit of the dozen or so reporters covering the event. Next, everyone kneeled as Young delivered a prayer; then they set off. The column stretched out, unbroken, for several blocks.

There were no police in sight as the marchers walked down Sylvan Street, turned right onto Water Avenue, and continued the five blocks to Broad, the Edmund Pettus Bridge, and the start of the road to Montgomery. The mood was somber, and the only sound, that of scuffling feet. Lewis wrote later that he was reminded of Gandhi's Salt March.

The sharp arch of the Edmund Pettus Bridge made it impossible to see one side from the other, but when Lewis and Williams reached the top, they stopped still for a moment because they

could see in front of them line after line of helmeted state police, gas masks hanging from their belts and billy clubs slapping in their palms. "Can you swim?" Williams asked Lewis. "No," Lewis replied. "Well," Williams said, "neither can I."

Waiting at the foot of the bridge was Maj. John Cloud, commander of the Alabama state highway patrol. Unexpectedly, Cloud's boss, Col. Al Lingo, had just arrived on the scene with Jim Clark. Clark had been away in Washington, appearing that morning on a television news program. Cloud had earlier assured a worried Wilson Baker that Lingo would keep Clark at the Montgomery airport until the march was over. Evidently, Lingo had other plans.

In a toneless drawl over a loudspeaker, Cloud ordered the marchers to turn around and gave them two minutes to comply. "May we have a word with you, Major?" Williams asked. "There is no word to be had," Cloud replied. A minute passed by Lewis's watch, then Cloud called out, "Troopers, advance!" The patrolmen moved forward in a wedge.

According to one reporter's account, "The first ten or twenty Negroes were swept to the ground screaming, arms and legs flying, and packs and bags went skittering across the grassy divider strip and onto the pavement on both sides. Those still on their feet retreated."

Behind the state troopers came a wave of Clark's possemen, mounted and riding at a run into the receding mass. "The Negroes cried out as they crowded together for protection, and the whites on the side whooped and cheered," the newspaper report continued.

Above the din, Sheriff Clark could be heard shouting, "Get those goddamned niggers!" Then the first tear gas was released. (According to some reports, Clark fired the first canister.) Soon, clouds of gas obscured the view of the reporters, who had been confined by police to

A fellow marcher suffering from tear-gas inhalation tries to comfort Amelia Boynton on Bloody Sunday after Boynton was beaten unconscious by state troopers.

the lot of a nearby Pontiac dealership—but not before their cameramen and photographers got all the images they would need.

The marchers fled back into Selma's black neighborhood with Clark's possemen in hot pursuit. Attempting to restore order and stop the beatings, Wilson Baker confronted Clark in the street, but the sheriff pushed him aside, growling, "I've already waited a month too damn long about moving in!" Angry young blacks who hadn't participated in the march now emerged from their homes to resist Clark's men with rocks and bottles—one of which nicked the sheriff, infuriating him further.

As ambulances provided by local black funeral homes relayed the seriously wounded—including John Lewis, with a fractured skull—to Good Samaritan Hospital, Andrew Young tried to talk others out of going home for their guns. "You had to talk them down," Young later explained. "'What kind of gun you got? A thirty-two?

A thirty-eight? You know how that's going to hold up against the automatic rifles and shotguns they've got? And how many you got? They have at least two hundred shotguns out there with buckshot in them. You ever see buckshot? You ever see what buckshot does to a deer?' You make people think about the specifics of violence, and then they realize how suicidal and nonsensical it is."

Eventually, Clark slowed down, at which point Baker reasserted himself and set up a cordon around the church. "All right now," he told Clark harshly, "get your cowboys the hell out of here." Clark complied.

That evening, shortly after nine thirty, ABC interrupted its Sunday night movie, the much-advertised television premiere of *Judgment at Nuremberg*, to air a special news bulletin. Anchorman Frank Reynolds reported the basic facts, then narrated fifteen minutes' worth of stunning film footage. Viewers saw images of clubs being raised and swiftly lowered onto the heads and bodies of peaceful, defenseless, well-dressed marchers; they saw shots of bleeding, broken bodies— some limping along together in mutual support, others being carried off on stretchers. Even the footage from Birmingham that had sent Mickey Schwerner into Mississippi couldn't compare to this.

"When that beating happened at the foot of the bridge," Mayor Smitherman remembered, "it looked like war. That went all over the country. And the people, the wrath of the nation, came down on us."

TURNAROUND TUESDAY

In Atlanta, Martin Luther King quickly prepared a telegram to be sent to prominent clergymen all over the nation, asking them to join him in Selma for a "ministers' march to Montgomery" on Tuesday, March 9. Subsequently, a public call was issued that brought even more people into Selma. In the meantime, King asked bus boycott lawyer Fred Gray to file papers with the federal district court in Montgomery, requesting that Judge Frank M. Johnson Jr. enjoin the State of Alabama from interfering with the Tuesday march.

Johnson, a forty-six-year-old Eisenhower appointee, had jurisdiction over Alabama's Middle District, which didn't include Selma (part of Judge Thomas's Southern District) but did include Lowndes County and the rest of the route

to Montgomery. King chose to petition Johnson, rather than Thomas, because earlier rulings— against segregated buses, for integrated schools— had indicated Johnson's willingness to buck the state's white establishment, if necessary, to protect Negro constitutional rights.

King expected Johnson to grant the injunction immediately, but early on Monday evening Fred Gray reported that the judge wanted more time. Johnson was reluctant to grant the injunction without first holding a hearing, and the earliest

Marchers leave Brown Chapel on Tuesday, March 9, headed for the Edmund Pettus Bridge. Seen in this photograph are (from left to right) James Farmer, Andrew Young, Martin Luther King, and James Forman.

he could schedule such a hearing was Thursday morning. According to Gray, Johnson wanted the march postponed until then; otherwise, he would ban it.

King, who hadn't disobeyed a federal court order yet, was inclined to go along, but he wasn't sure and thus invited debate. Hosea Williams argued that the SCLC had an obligation to the hundreds of people who had answered King's call and paid their own way to Selma to go ahead with the march. SNCC's position was also to go ahead. Calling Johnson's ultimatum "legal blackmail," Forman acknowledged that SNCC had opposed the Sunday march, but asserted that now, given the police violence that had resulted, the movement shouldn't back down.

Nevertheless, as the time approached for that night's mass meeting at Brown Chapel, King decided to postpone the march and told Gray to relay the news to Judge Johnson. At the mass meeting, however, the electric atmosphere got to King, and he began to waver. By the time he

stepped up to the pulpit shortly before midnight, he had changed his mind, and he announced to the crowd that there would indeed be a march the next day.

Well after midnight, when the leadership reconvened at the home of Abernathy family friends Jean and Sullivan Jackson (where King always stayed when he was in Selma), Gray and the other movement lawyers expressed their frustration with the minister. They had already told Judge Johnson that the deal was on and would now look foolish reneging. The argument continued until four in the morning, when King finally went to bed. The deal was still off.

Federal officials had also been lobbying King to postpone the march. On Monday afternoon, Louis Martin, now deputy chairman of the Democratic National Committee, had called King to discuss his plans. Learning that King might be willing to give up the Tuesday march in exchange for meaningful federal intervention, Martin passed this information along to the White House, which immediately sent John Doar and former Florida governor LeRoy Collins to meet with King. Collins had recently been appointed head of the new Community Relations Service, established under the Civil Rights Act of 1964 to mediate race-related disputes.

When Doar and Collins found King on Tuesday morning, he was still in his pajamas. Over the Jacksons' kitchen table, they pressed him again and again to postpone the march. King replied each time that his conscience told him to go ahead—and that even if it didn't, others, especially the SNCCers, were going to march anyway.

Eventually, Collins tried a different tack: What if King led the marchers across the Pettus Bridge to where the Bloody Sunday violence had taken place, said a prayer, and then turned around, marching back into Selma? King pointed out that Lingo and Clark would never allow such a performance, but Collins pressed the point: What if he could get Lingo and Clark to agree? King said he couldn't make any promises, but if Collins got the cooperation of Lingo and Clark, he would see what he could do. Shortly after Collins hustled off to find the Alabama lawmen, King received word that Judge Johnson had indeed enjoined that afternoon's march.

A **federal marshal** reads the text of Judge Johnson's order prohibiting the Selma-to-Montgomery march. The marshal then stood aside and allowed the marchers to pass.

Collins found Lingo and Clark out on Highway 80 at the Pontiac dealership they had made their field headquarters. Both men dismissed the deal at first, but the more Collins talked, the more they began to see its virtue for both sides. Soon Lingo left the room to make a telephone call, presumably to Governor Wallace. When he returned a few minutes later, he spoke privately with Clark and then told Collins that they would accept his offer on one condition: that the marchers follow a precise route to and from the Pettus Bridge, which Clark drew for Collins on a piece of paper. Collins then raced off in search of King.

At that moment, King was already leading fifteen hundred people, including four hundred out-of-state ministers, down Sylvan Street. Collins caught up with him there and pulled him aside, giving him the gist of his conversation with Lingo and handing him Clark's map. King said he would try to turn the column around and hurried back to the head of the line.

As King crossed the Pettus Bridge, Lingo described what was happening to Governor Wallace over an open telephone line to Montgomery, while John Doar did the same for Attorney General Katzenbach in Washington. The marchers advanced to within fifty yards of the state troopers, at which point Major Cloud ordered them to halt. King complied and informed the major that they would now be conducting prayers. Several clergymen stepped forward to recite homilies, after which all of the marchers sang "We Shall Overcome." Then King turned around and began leading the column back into Selma.

Martin Luther King Jr. addresses followers in Selma on March 9 after aborting their second attempt to march to Montgomery.

Unaware of King's intention to retreat, many marchers became confused and upset. But, as John Lewis recalled, "they followed Dr. King—what else could they do?"

BETRAYAL AND REDEMPTION

Back at Brown Chapel, King and members of the SCLC staff praised the marchers for standing up to the state police and hailed their great "symbolic" victory. But the ministers' body language was defensive, and their plaudits sounded hollow.

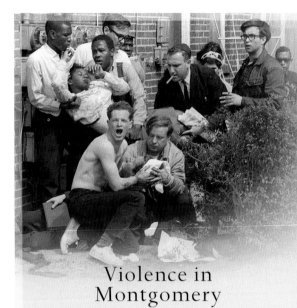

Violence in Montgomery

While moving the SNCC staff out of Selma on Wednesday, March 9, Jim Forman declared that there would be no more waiting for a judge's injunction. SNCC would march when it wanted, and it wanted to march *now*.

Supported by several hundred Tuskegee and Alabama State students, Forman took to the streets of Montgomery on Monday, March 15. The demonstration that he led was much more aggressive than anything yet seen in Selma and hardly nonviolent. When mounted police tried to disperse the taunting, provocative crowd, violence ensued, and the next day, the situation escalated. The students were even more defiant, and the police that much less reserved. Mounted once again, they charged the student demonstrators, brandishing ropes, whips, and cattle prods, while the students fought back with rocks and bottles.

An enraged Forman let his anger escape that night at a mass meeting held in the Beulah Baptist Church and attended by King, who was in town for the final day of Judge Johnson's hearing. "I said it today, and I'll say it again," the SNCC executive secretary shouted. "If we can't sit at the table, let's knock the fuckin' legs off—excuse me."

The fact that Forman quickly caught and excused himself was lost on the audience, most of whom felt shock at hearing such profanity in a church. Even King failed to revive them when he spoke a little later. Instead, it took the news, brought by Andrew Young, that Judge Johnson was granting the injunction and allowing the Selma-to-Montgomery march.

Groups of SNCC student protesters (above and below), including many from northern colleges, try to escape violent sheriff's deputies during a March 16 voting rights demonstration in Montgomery.

Later in the day, as reports of King's arrangement with Collins began to circulate, many more marchers began to feel betrayed, and SNCC accused the SCLC of "selling out."

King's less than forthright behavior had put him in a difficult position. If he disavowed the deal with Collins and insisted that he had intended to march beyond the bridge (thus ignoring Judge Johnson's order), he would be insulting the judge and possibly leaving himself open to a contempt-of-court citation. On the other hand, if he admitted the deal, he would be confirming SNCC's worst fear about his leadership. Faced with these two unattractive choices, King dodged and weaved, admitting in testimony before Judge Johnson the existence of a "tacit agreement" with Collins but also telling reporters untruthfully that "no prearranged agreement existed."

King's attempt to tell the story both ways fooled no one and served only to intensify SNCC antipathy. Forman was especially outraged that King would have made a deal without consulting (or even informing) SNCC first.

Denouncing King's behavior as "a classic example of trickery against the people," Forman let it be known that SNCC was pulling out of Selma because it could no longer work with the SCLC.

Meanwhile, there was another important development Tuesday night. At Brown Chapel after the turnaround, King had asked the out-of-town ministers to stay on in Selma until after Judge Johnson's hearing on Thursday—when, he was confident, the injunction would be granted and the march would proceed. Many did, including a group of three white Unitarian ministers: Orloff Miller, Clark Olsen, and James Reeb. That night, following SCLC's advice to keep clear of the city's white sections, Miller, Olsen, and Reeb ate dinner at a soul-food restaurant called Walker's Cafe.

"After dinner," Miller recalled, "as we started walking across the street, there appeared four or five white men, and they yelled at us, 'Hey, you niggers.' We did not look across at them, but we quickened our pace....One of them was carrying a club, and Clark said he turned around and saw the club just as it was swung. Jim Reeb, who was closest to the curb, caught the full impact of the blow on the side of his head."

Reeb's death two days later produced an even stronger national reaction against the violence in Selma. The increased attention certainly benefited the movement, but at the same time many blacks couldn't help feeling bitter that, once again, it had taken the death of a white man to move a nation so untroubled by the deaths of blacks like Jimmie Lee Jackson.

Judge Johnson's hearing lasted four days, but from the start his disgust at the behavior of Clark and Lingo made clear what his final ruling would be. George Wallace certainly got the message, and on Friday he wired President Johnson, asking for a meeting. The president granted the request, and on Saturday the governor flew up to Washington. He was feeling desperate and wanted Lyndon Johnson to pressure King into giving up the march. According to Assistant Attorney General Burke Marshall, who sat in on the meeting, "Governor Wallace didn't quite grovel, but he was pliant by the end of the two hours, with President Johnson putting his arm around him and squeezing him and telling him it's a moment of history, and how do we want to be remembered in history? Do we want to be remembered as petty little men, or do we want to be remembered as great figures who faced up to our moments of crisis?"

After the meeting, Johnson led Wallace into the Rose Garden so that he could observe the president's first press conference since Bloody Sunday. "What happened in Selma," Johnson told the assembled reporters and a national television audience, "was an American tragedy.

A Negro family watches Pres. Lyndon B. Johnson on television as he delivers his voting rights speech before a joint session of Congress on March 15.

The blows that were received, the blood that was shed, the life of the good man that was lost, must strengthen the determination of each of us to bring full equality and equal justice to all of our people. This is not just the policy of your government or your president. It is in the heart and the purpose and the meaning of America itself." He concluded by announcing that on Monday he would be sending a new voting rights bill to Congress.

In fact, Johnson did much more than simply send over the bill. On Monday night, he addressed a joint session of Congress. King, Lewis, C. T. Vivian, and others watched the speech in the Jacksons' Selma living room.

"Even if we pass this bill," Johnson told an audience of seventy million Americans, "the battle will not be over. What happened in Selma

Martin Luther King Jr. speaks at the memorial service held in Brown Chapel for slain white minister James Reeb.

is part of a far larger movement which reaches into every section and state of America. It is the effort of American Negroes to secure for themselves the full blessings of American life. Their cause must be our cause, too, because

"When LBJ said, 'And we shall overcome,' we all cheered. And I looked over...and Martin was very quietly sitting in the chair, and a tear ran down his cheek. It was a victory like none other."

C. T. VIVIAN

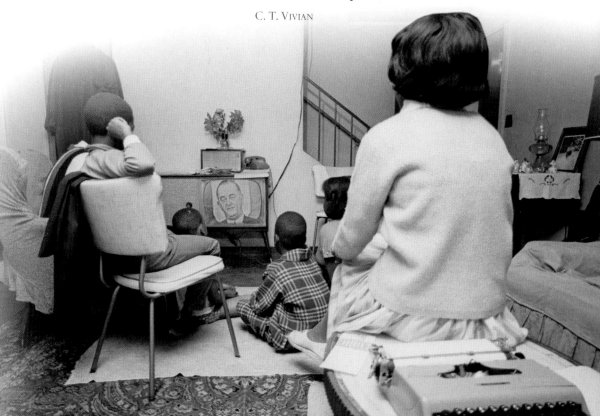

it is not just Negroes, but really it is all of us who must overcome the crippling legacy of bigotry and injustice. And we *shall* overcome."

Johnson's speech confirmed the emergence of a new relationship between the civil rights movement and the federal government, one foreshadowed by the passage of the 1964 Civil Rights Act but not consummated until now. Under President Kennedy, the federal government had certainly provided meaningful support to the movement, but only occasionally and always with great reluctance; now, President Johnson was positively embracing the movement and making its goals the centerpiece of his own domestic agenda.

Two days later—on Wednesday, March 17—Judge Johnson released the written text of his decision to grant the injunction. After reviewing the embarrassing record of state and county law enforcement, he presented his central finding. "It seems basic to our constitutional principles," Johnson reasoned, "that the extent of the right to assemble, demonstrate, and march peaceably along the highways and streets in an orderly manner should be commensurate with the enormity of the wrongs that are being protested and petitioned against. In this case, the wrongs

Five thousand marchers cross the Edmund Pettus Bridge on March 21 on their way to Montgomery.

are enormous. The extent of the right to demonstrate against these wrongs should be determined accordingly." The march was on.

THE MARCH THAT CHANGED THE SOUTH

Governor Wallace's reaction was to call the leaders of the march "Communist-trained anarchists" and to declare that Alabama couldn't afford to pay for any police protection. President Johnson responded by federalizing the Alabama National Guard and mobilizing eighteen hundred guardsmen. Along with two thousand more regular army troops, one hundred FBI agents, and another hundred U.S. marshals, these soldiers beat the bushes from Selma to Montgomery looking for snipers, explosives, and any other security threats they could find.

In the meantime, the SCLC staff scrambled to make arrangements for thousands of marchers,

National Guard helicopters keep the long line of civil rights marchers under continuous surveillance. Meanwhile, guardsmen on the ground line the entire route from Selma to Montgomery.

Marchers trudge along Route 80 on Wednesday, March 24. Their feet are encased in mud from their Tuesday night campsite, which had been soaked by Tuesday's rain.

who would need food, water, shelter, and medical care—mostly, as it turned out, for their aching, blistered feet. According to Judge Johnson's order, the westbound lanes of Highway 80 would be closed to traffic during the march, with westbound traffic diverted into one of the two eastbound lanes. In Lowndes County, however, there was a section of road with just one lane in each direction. There, the number of marchers would be limited to three hundred to ease the burden on the state highway patrol.

On Sunday, March 21, thirty-two hundred people gathered at Brown Chapel to begin the march to Montgomery. By nightfall, they had covered seven of the fifty-four miles, reaching the two-lane portion of Highway 80. At that point, twelve hundred marchers went home to Selma. The rest bedded down for the night in three enormous tents set up on am eighty-acre farm owned by the maintenance manager of Selma's largest black housing project. Still suffering from exhaustion, King spent the night in a mobile home.

The next morning, seventeen hundred more people returned to Selma, leaving just the three hundred permitted by Judge Johnson's order. These marchers walked briskly and a little nervously through Lowndes County, logging another sixteen miles and completing the entire two-lane section of highway, thus lifting the judge's limit. On Tuesday morning, the number of marchers swelled again to three thousand, cheering everyone, but then the sky darkened, and it

rained hard all day. Tuesday night and Wednesday passed uneventfully, with King taking Wednesday off to rest and prepare. On Wednesday night, the marchers reached the City of St. Jude, a Catholic enclave just outside the Montgomery city limits. The compound's church, hospital, and school all served the local black community, and this night its grounds were put to use as well. In addition to the campsite, a large stage was constructed on which national celebrities such as Tony Bennett and Sammy Davis Jr., recruited by Harry Belafonte, performed a four-hour concert for twenty thousand people.

U. S. Army troops called in by President Johnson watch as a long line of marchers passes their position on the second day of the Selma-to-Montgomery march.

PREVIOUS PAGES: **A line of helmeted** state troopers watches as the first of twenty-five thousand marchers arrive at the state capitol in Montgomery on March 25. **LEFT: An aerial view** of the crowd in front of the Alabama state capitol, atop whose dome flies a Confederate battle flag.

The next day—Thursday, March 25—twenty-five thousand people, most but not all of them black, completed the final six miles of the march to the Alabama state capitol. On their way, they passed the Dexter Avenue Baptist Church, the sight of which caused many in the crowd to ponder how far the movement had come since the start of the Montgomery bus boycott ten years earlier.

At the capitol, a podium had been set up on a flatbed truck rigged with a microphone and loudspeakers. Peter, Paul, & Mary performed. Then came speeches from diplomat Ralph Bunche, Roy Wilkins, James Farmer, Whitney

The Voting Rights Act of 1965

The voting rights bill that President Johnson submitted on March 15 followed a much easier course through Congress than the Civil Rights Act of 1964 had for two reasons. The first was that Johnson's landslide victory in 1964 carried with him into office a large number of liberal Democrats, all of whom supported the bill. The second was the enormous popular response to Bloody Sunday, which demonstrated beyond doubt the strength of support Americans felt for this issue.

During the bill's first House hearing—held on Thursday, March 18—Judiciary Committee chairman Emanuel Celler observed that the "outrages" in Selma had now made possible passage of "a bill that would have been inconceivable a year ago." Although Negro disfranchisement had been a problem for generations, movement leaders graciously refrained from pointing this out to the many congressmen now finally taking notice.

Appearing before Celler's committee that same day, Attorney General Katzenbach explained that the bill's key provision was a "trigger formula" that suspended literacy tests and other voter qualification devices in any state or county where fewer than 50 percent of the eligible voters were registered as of November 1964. Another important clause empowered the attorney general to appoint in "triggered" states and counties federal registrars to reexamine the cases of residents denied registration.

This time around, the southern filibuster was broken in days rather than months, permitting the

On August 6, 1965, President Johnson presents one of the pens he has just used to sign the Voting Rights Act of 1965 to CORE national director James Farmer.

bill to move along swiftly. The Senate approved it overwhelmingly on May 26 by a vote of 77–19, and six weeks later the House passed it as well. On August 6, Lyndon Johnson signed it into law in the President's Room off the Capitol Rotunda—where Abraham Lincoln had signed the Emancipation Proclamation 102 years earlier.

The impact of the new voting rights act was both immediate and revolutionary. In Mississippi, where only 7 percent of the black population was registered to vote in 1964, that figure shot up to 60 percent by 1968. In Alabama, there were similar, remarkable gains. During 1966, nine thousand of Dallas County's fifteen thousand eligible blacks joined the voter rolls, and in November of that year they enthusiastically voted Jim Clark out of office, electing Wilson Baker in his place.

In May 1966 (and for the first time since Reconstruction), Negroes line up in large numbers to vote in Wilcox County, Alabama, where they outnumber whites three to one.

Young, Rosa Parks, Ralph Abernathy, Fred Shuttlesworth, James Bevel, Bayard Rustin, and John Lewis. Finally, King closed the program with one of the most important orations of his life, televised live by all three networks. His dream— as always, but more pointedly articulated now— was of a class-based interracial alliance that could lift the poor and the oppressed of all races out of their misery.

I know you are asking today, "How long will it take?" I come to say to you this afternoon however difficult the moment, however frustrating the hour, it will not be long, because truth pressed to earth will rise again.

How long? Not long, because no lie can live forever.

How long? Not long, because you still reap what you sow.

How long? Not long, because the arm of the moral universe is long but it bends toward justice.

How long? Not long, 'cause mine eyes have seen the glory of the coming of the Lord, trampling out the vintage where the grapes of wrath are stored. He has loosed the fateful lightning of his terrible swift sword. His truth is marching on.

Martin Luther King delivers his speech at the climax of the Selma-to-Mongromery march.

Black Power

1965–1968

The Selma-to-Montgomery march, like the civil rights movement itself, is generally remembered for its nonviolent character. Yet the specter of violence was never far off. Threats against the life of Martin Luther King were so common that he rarely paid attention to them, but during the Selma campaign there came a telephone call on February 22 that unsettled both King and his staff. Attorney General Nicholas Katzenbach reported that the Justice Department had just uncovered a failed assassination attempt against King. According to Katzenbach, several Klansmen had been lying in ambush for the SCLC leader during his visit to Marion one week earlier. King was still alive, Katzenbach said, only because they had been unable to get a clear shot.

A crowd at a Black Panther rally gives the clenched-fist Black Power salute.

SCLC executive director Andrew Young was particularly worried about King's safety as the Selma marchers arrived in Montgomery on Thursday, March 25. Knowing that King would never agree to leave the march, Young searched out other ministers who shared King's build and were wearing similar blue suits. Then he escorted these ministers to the front of the line so that they could stand beside King. As Young recalled, "Since we couldn't stop him from marching, we just had to kind of believe that it was true when white folks said we all look alike.... There were some very important people who felt as though they were being pushed back, but all of the preachers loved the chance to get up in the front of the line with Martin Luther King. I don't think to this day most of them know why they were up there."

After the rally at the state capitol, aware of the continuing potential for violence, the SCLC staff advised the marchers to leave Montgomery as soon as possible. Volunteers driving private cars ferried many of the participants back to Selma that afternoon. One of these volunteers was a thirty-nine-year-old housewife and mother of five from Detroit named Viola Liuzzo. Like most Americans, she had been shocked by the images of Bloody Sunday she saw on her television set; like a few, she decided to heed King's call and travel south to Selma. "There are too many people who just stand around talking," she told her husband before leaving on the three-day drive.

She arrived in time for the march, walking herself on the first and last days and in between shuttling people in her car to and from the Montgomery airport. After listening to King's closing "How long will it take?" speech, she rendezvoused with teenager Leroy Moton, who had been assigned to drive her car while she was at the rally. Together, they drove five passengers to Selma. Then they turned Liuzzo's Oldsmobile around and headed back to Montgomery to pick up more marchers.

At a traffic light in Selma, a car containing four Klansmen spotted Liuzzo's Michigan license plates and followed her east along Highway 80, the route of the march. When Liuzzo noticed the tail about twenty miles later, she accelerated to outrun her pursuers—singing, according to Moton, "We Shall Overcome" at the top of her lungs. In the middle of rural Lowndes County, about halfway between Selma and Montgomery,

the Klansmen overtook the housewife. One of them shot her twice in the face as she drove. Liuzzo was killed instantly; her car ran off the road into a ditch. When the Klansmen pulled over to inspect the wreck, Moton saved himself by pretending to be dead.

As it turned out, one of those Klansmen was Gary Thomas Rowe, a paid FBI informant. Rowe was, in fact, the same informant who had tipped off the bureau in May 1961 that the Freedom Riders were going to be beaten on Mother's Day in Birmingham. With Rowe's cooperation, Pres. Lyndon Johnson was able to announce the day

ABOVE: The smashed window and bloodstained door of the car in which Viola Liuzzo (at right) was shot to death on Highway 80 near Lowndesboro. The Klansmen prosecuted for Liuzzo's murder were all found not guilty of murder in state court but were later convicted on federal civil rights charges in the Montgomery courtroom of Judge Frank M. Johnson Jr.

after Liuzzo's murder that her killers were already in custody. Later, on the basis of Rowe's testimony, the three others in the car were found guilty in federal court of participating in a criminal conspiracy. Rowe himself was never charged in the case.

Liuzzo's death was a chilling reminder to those in the movement that their struggle was far from over. It caused many to question—and not for the first time—whether nonviolence had finally reached its limit as an effective political strategy.

The SNCC leadership began addressing this question at a meeting held in Montgomery shortly after Liuzzo's death. The discussion, led

by James Forman, reached no conclusion, but it was decided that the SNCC response to Liuzzo's murder would be an organizing drive in Lowndes County, where she had been killed. Stokely Carmichael was soon named project director.

As the story goes, Carmichael was dropped off in Lowndes County the day after Liuzzo's murder with a sleeping bag, a few dollars in his pocket, and the name of a local resident willing to put him up for the night. That story, however, is myth, not fact. "Gimme a break," Carmichael complained in his autobiography. "That's romantic. It's also silly and as Fred [Hampton], the brother they murdered in Chicago, would say, 'Custeristic.'"

Carmichael went into Lowndes County neither alone nor unprepared. During the march to Montgomery, he and SNCC colleague Bob Mants had trailed the column, collecting the names and addresses of anyone brave enough to come out to the highway and cheer the marchers on. Carmichael and Mants also asked questions: What were the important churches in Lowndes? Who were the ministers? What other leadership existed in the community? By the time they returned to the county with Judy Richardson and Scott B. Smith in early April, they already had most of the information they would need to begin organizing the county.

Although active in SNCC since 1961, Carmichael generally spoke for the newer, younger, more militant SNCCers, who respected the courage shown by SNCC chairman John Lewis but considered his willingness to be beaten foolish—or, even worse, an anachronism. The growing rift between Carmichael's faction and Lewis's old guard had become obvious at the quarrelsome October 1964 staff meeting held in Atlanta while Lewis was still away in Africa. At that meeting, SNCC's northern intellectual wing (notably Carmichael, Courtland Cox, Ivanhoe Donaldson, and Charlie Cobb) had urged the disbanding of the executive committee and the closing of SNCC's headquarters in Atlanta.

Rather than seeking more formal structure, they wanted to transform SNCC into a loose confederation of activists with unlimited freedom of action. This never came to pass, but in Lowndes County, Carmichael operated as though it had, taking little direction and acting as he alone saw fit.

LOWNDES COUNTY

In April 1965, Lowndes County had fifteen thousand residents, twelve thousand of whom were black, yet it had only one black voter, John Hulett, who had only just registered. According to *Black Power*, the landmark 1967 study written by Carmichael and political scientist Charles V. Hamilton, "The history of the county shows that black people could come together to do only three things: sing, pray, dance. Any time they came together to do anything else, they were threatened and intimidated. For decades, black people had been taught to believe that voting, politics, is 'white folks' business.' And the white folks had indeed monopolized that business, by methods which ran the gamut from economic intimidation to murder."

In the usual SNCC fashion, Carmichael, Mants, Richardson, and Smith began by searching out indigenous leaders. Quickly they gravitated to Hulett, who worked construction jobs in Montgomery and knew people who had been active in the bus boycott. Prior to SNCC's arrival in Lowndes County, Hulett had worked with Andrew Young and James Bevel to establish the Lowndes County Christian Movement for Human Rights; however, when the SCLC failed to send a full-time organizer, Hulett chose to work with SNCC instead.

Initially, Carmichael's group produced few tangible results, registering just fifty voters during its first four months of work. Few residents were willing to enter the county courthouse in Hayneville because, according to Hulett, so many white men "walked around with a gun on them." Out of 800 adult white males in Lowndes County, the sheriff had deputized 550.

On August 10, however, just four days after President Johnson signed the Voting Rights Act, the first federal registrar appeared in Lowndes County. No longer would applicants be asked ridiculously complicated questions about the Alabama state constitution or rejected for

inadequately dotting their *i*'s or crossing their *t*'s. Hundreds of eligible blacks immediately began to register, substantially alarming the county's white power structure.

Meanwhile, Carmichael scheduled a demonstration for Saturday, August 14, in Fort Deposit, the largest town in Lowndes County and a notorious Klan stronghold. The protest didn't last long as Klansmen immediately surrounded the picketers. "That was one time," Carmichael admitted later, "I was not sorry to be arrested." Those taken into custody included—unusually—two whites, seminary student

Episcopalian seminary student Jonathan Daniels poses in his study with two unidentified black children in this 1965 photograph.

Stokely Carmichael
1941–1998

Stokely Carmichael was born in Trinidad, moving with his family to Harlem in 1952 and becoming a naturalized citizen two years later. That same year, 1954, his family moved to Morris Park, a predominantly Italian neighborhood in the Bronx, where Carmichael became the sole Negro member of the Morris Park Dukes street gang. His circle changed considerably in 1956, however, when he was admitted to the Bronx High School of Science, one of New York City's most elite public schools.

At Bronx Science, Carmichael associated with the children of left-wing Manhattan radicals, who introduced him to politics. Among his closest friends was Gene Dennis, the son of Eugene Dennis, then general secretary of the Communist Party USA. "I began making the Village scene and partied down on Park Avenue," Carmichael recalled. "I felt strange every time a black maid handed me something. My mother, May Charles, was also a maid, making thirty bucks a week."

During his senior year in high school, he traveled down to Washington, where he picketed hearings of the House Un-American Activities Committee and also took part in a few early sit-ins. "In 1960, when I first heard about the Negroes sitting in at lunch counters down South, I thought they were just a bunch of publicity hounds," Carmichael

wrote. "But one night when I saw those kids on TV, getting back up on the lunch counter stools after being knocked off them, sugar in their eyes, catsup in their hair—well, something happened to me. Suddenly I was burning."

Carmichael's experiences in Washington led him to enroll at Howard University, where he became a leader of the Nonviolent Action Group (NAG) and served as Howard's representative to SNCC. At the end of his freshman year, he hurried down south to join the Freedom Ride and served some time in Parchman. After completing his philosophy degree in 1964, Carmichael became a full-time organizer for SNCC.

During Freedom Summer, Carmichael was put in charge of Mississippi's Second Congressional District. Unlike SNCC's Nashville contingent, whose perspective was strongly spiritual and theological, Carmichael's NAG faction had a much more practical, political focus. Some of its members, Carmichael among them, embraced the challenge of organizing a new, independent black political party. But others in NAG continued to see voter registration as a diversion intended to blunt student militancy. What SNCC really needed, they thought, was a radical economic program.

Jonathan Daniels and Catholic priest Richard Morrisroe, who had both driven down from Selma to "observe" the protest.

Although SNCC had a few white organizers working in Selma and other neighboring counties, there were none with Carmichael in Lowndes. "This was not because we had a formal policy to exclude them," Carmichael explained; "we simply did not encourage them." Yet the absence of whites from Carmichael's project was not mere happenstance.

Ruby Sales was a local black teenager arrested with Carmichael, Daniels, and Morrisroe. As she recalled, "I had some serious concerns about what

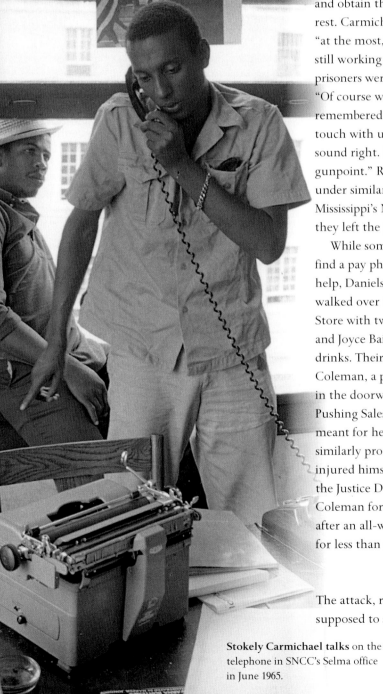

Stokely Carmichael talks on the telephone in SNCC's Selma office in June 1965.

it meant to allow white people to come into the county and what kind of relationship that set up in an area where black people had historically deferred to white people, and whether or not that was in some real way creating the very situation that we were struggling very hard to change.

"More fundamentally," Sales continued, "I was very afraid of unleashing uncontrolled violence because of Lowndes County's history…but ultimately it was decided that the movement was an open place and should provide an opportunity for anyone who wanted to come and struggle against racism."

There was only enough bail money for two people. Carmichael and Scott Smith were chosen because they could most easily raise the funds and obtain the legal counsel needed to free the rest. Carmichael promised to return in four days "at the most," but on Friday, August 20, he was still working out the arrangements when the prisoners were released on their own recognizance. "Of course we were suspicious," Gloria House remembered. "No one from SNCC had been in touch with us…and we thought, this doesn't sound right. But they forced us out of the jail at gunpoint." Remembering what had happened under similar circumstances in Mississippi's Neshoba County, they left the jail warily.

While some of them went to find a pay phone to call for help, Daniels and Morrisroe walked over to Varner's Cash Store with two teenagers, Sales and Joyce Bailey, to buy soft drinks. Their way inside was blocked by Thomas Coleman, a part-time deputy sheriff, who stood in the doorway with a shotgun leveled at Sales. Pushing Sales to the side, Daniels took the blast meant for her and was killed instantly. Morrisroe similarly protected Bailey and was critically injured himself. Later, under pressure from the Justice Department, the state prosecuted Coleman for Daniels's murder, but he went free after an all-white Hayneville jury, deliberating for less than an hour, found him not guilty.

THE LCFO

The attack, reportedly arranged by the Klan, was supposed to stop the registrations, but it had the opposite effect, strengthening the resolve of the movement to wrest political control from

This Alabama Democratic party handbill from the 1930s utilizes the party's traditional symbol of white supremacy, the White Cock.

Lowndes's despotic white minority. Shortly after Daniels's death, Carmichael contacted SNCC research director Jack Minnis and asked him to look into Alabama law concerning the formation of political parties. Minnis hit the books and a few days later found an obscure statute that allowed county residents to form their own political party (and thus gain ballot access) simply by holding a nominating convention.

> "To ask the Negroes to get in the Democratic party is like asking Jews to join the Nazi party."
>
> STOKELY CARMICHAEL

There had already been some debate within the movement about whether newly registered blacks should join the Democratic party or form their organization. The movement's more conservative elements argued that blacks should register as Democrats out of loyalty to President Johnson, who had made the Civil Rights and Voting Rights Acts possible. But the Democratic party in Alabama was not the party of Lyndon Johnson; it was the party of George Wallace, and it did not welcome blacks. (The party's official motto was "White Supremacy for the Right.")

Furthermore, national attention leading to federal intervention was no longer Carmichael's strategy. Legislation and troops weren't going to solve the problems that remained, he argued persuasively; the situation would only improve when local blacks possessed political power themselves. "All right," Carmichael wrote in his autobiography. "There it was. The primary was next May. Ten months off. In Mississippi, we'd had five months to organize an entire state [for the MFDP]. Here we had nearly a year to do a single county. We were psyched, Jack."

To carry out this work, Carmichael founded the Lowndes County Freedom Organization (LCFO). John Hulett became its first chair. Weekly mass meetings were held around the county, and workshops were organized to explain the duties of the seven offices up for election in 1966: sheriff, coroner, assessor, tax collector, and three seats on the board of education. SNCC also printed comic books to disseminate some of this information because many Lowndes County blacks were barely literate.

Lowndes) contacted a graphic designer in Atlanta for help. The first symbol she provided was a dove, which Cox thought too delicate. Her second offering was a snarling black panther.

About the same time, Cox gave a talk at the November 1965 SNCC staff meeting on the progress being made in Lowndes County. Since Robert Moses's resignation from SNCC nine months earlier (he left because he feared he was becoming a "creature of the media"), attrition, especially among whites, had

The headquarters of the Lowndes County Freedom Organization in an undated photograph.

> "This black panther is a vicious animal as you know. He never bothers anything, but when you start pushing him, he moves backwards, backwards, and backwards into his corner, and then he comes out to destroy everything that's before him."
>
> JOHN HULETT

Illiteracy was a serious enough problem statewide, in fact, that Alabama law required political parties to use ballot symbols so that voters could mark their choices without being able to read each party's name. Tasked with developing an LCFO symbol, Courtland Cox (who had recently joined Carmichael in

sharply reduced the size of the staff. Those who remained, according to Jim Forman, were more inclined to "think in long-range revolutionary terms." The "turning point" in their thinking, Forman said later, came when Cox wrote on a blackboard: "Get power for black people."

Meanwhile, white resistance in Lowndes County became even meaner. Just as in Mississippi, tenant farmers and sharecroppers who became involved

with SNCC were evicted from their homes. Many left the county, but some twenty families stayed on through the frigid winter, living in unheated tents set up by Carmichael on land donated by a local black farmer.

Relying on their Freedom Summer experiences, the SNCCers set up a Freedom School for those families in which volunteers taught literacy, politics, and African history. "I wish we could have kept everyone in Tent City," Carmichael mused later. "Once the people were out from under the oppressive plantation system, they just blossomed and developed confidence. Every day you could see it growing. When night riders started driving by, firing guns, the men and boys posted sentries along the road and returned fire. The night-riding stopped."

WEAPONS

As in Mississippi, most black farmers in rural Alabama owned guns and used them from time to time against whites in defense of their homes and families. Although this familiarity with violence had long disturbed Moses and other SNCCers working in Mississippi, it had never seriously challenged their own commitment to nonviolence. Yet this wasn't the case in Alabama—or, more accurately, it wasn't the case by 1965.

Like an ominous drumbeat, the killings of Goodman, Schwerner, Chaney, and Liuzzo had cast accumulating doubt upon the efficacy of nonviolence, and—for the SNCCers in Lowndes at least—the murder of Jonathan Daniels settled the matter. Afterward, according to Carmichael, "the project staff took the strong position,

LOWNDES COUNTY FREEDOM ORGANIZATION

Mass Meeting, May 3, 1966, to nominate candidates for the November 8, 1966 general election.

LOWNDES COUNTY

SHERIFF — put (x) before one name

ONE MAN · ONE VOTE

— —MR. JESSE 'NOTE' FAVORS
X—MR. SIDNEY LOGAN, JR.
— —OTHER (write in name)

A newly registered voter fills out a sample ballot listing the sheriff candidates in Lowndes County. On the right side of the ballot is the LCFO's black panther logo.

Three stores burn on Avalon Boulevard as Los Angeles firemen remain unable to reach the scene because of continued rioting in the Watts section of town.

Police drag a young man from the wreckage of a looted store in Watts. According to one report, "Looters, including women and children, ran wild throughout the day, grabbing everything in sight."

The Watts Riot

On Wednesday night, August 11, 1965, a white police officer made a routine traffic stop in the black neighborhood of South Central Los Angeles. As the officer interrogated the driver, who seemed to be drunk, a crowd gathered and began taunting the policeman, who called for backup. A second officer arrived and began intimidating the onlookers with his nightstick. The crowd became angry, and additional police were called in.

By ten o'clock, more than twenty squad cars had blocked off the intersection of Avalon Boulevard and Imperial Highway, not far from the Watts ghetto. Learning of the disturbance from radio and television reports, a large crowd gathered on the sidewalks, waiting to see what would happen.

According to one eyewitness, "Finally—it must have been close to midnight—someone threw a rock. It hit a squad car. A minute or two later, a bottle crashed in the street, and the

This sign warned away white motorists during the height of the rioting in Watts.

newsmen began to leave. From this point on, it becomes difficult to remember the sequence of events....I remember that the tempo of rock and bottle throwing gradually increased. There was also a lot of shouting....When the police left, the rock and bottle throwers began checking out passing cars, looking for whitey."

By two o'clock in the morning, roaming bands were pulling whites from their cars and beating them. "We been getting hit a long time," one rioter said. "Now we hitting back."

The next night, police set up barricades along the "riot perimeter," but within that perimeter, Watts was ravaged. Negro arsonists drove up and down the otherwise deserted streets, throwing Molotov cocktails into store windows and shouting a slogan borrowed from a local disc jockey: "Burn, baby, burn!" By Friday night, the *Los Angeles Times* reported, "a huge section of Los Angeles was virtually a city on fire as flames from the stores, industrial complexes and homes lit the skies."

The blazes reached from 41st Street all the way down to 108th. The fire department mobilized its reserves, but sniper fire and rock throwing limited the firefighters' effectiveness. At any one time, as many as fifty fires burned out of control. "The rioters were burning their city now, as the

insane sometimes mutilate themselves." Robert Richardson, a black *Times* reporter, wrote. "I had to do all of my telephoning from street-corner booths in gas stations," Richardson went on. "You have no idea how naked you can feel in an exposed, lighted telephone booth. But I was hep by that time. Whenever a group of Negroes approached to look me over I knew what to do. You open the door, stick your head out, and shout, 'Burn, baby, burn.' Then you are safe."

Late Friday afternoon, Lt. Gov. Glenn Anderson reluctantly called out the National Guard. The first of two thousand guardsmen reached Watts about 9:45 P.M., reinforcing five hundred overwhelmed police, deputy sheriffs, and state highway patrolmen. Order wasn't fully restored until Monday, August 16.

The Watts and South Central rioting was the great explosion that some militant blacks, notably Malcolm X, had been predicting for years. Certainly Los Angeles police chief William H. Parker wasn't surprised. "It's a result of the terrible conflicts building up with these people," he said that Friday. "You can't keep telling them that the Liberty Bell isn't ringing for them and not expect them to believe it."

nonnegotiable, that to allow whites in would be tantamount to inviting their deaths. That became our policy. And we armed ourselves."

The public reaction was, as one might expect, harsh. Speaking for the SCLC, Hosea Williams condemned the exclusion of whites as "reverse racism," while syndicated columnists Rowland Evans and Robert Novak used the new prevalence of firearms among its full-time organizers to

ridicule SNCC as the "Nonstudent Violent Coordinating Committee."

A few weeks after the May 1966 Alabama primary, in which all seven LCFO candidates qualified for the November general election, SNCC held a staff meeting at Kingston Springs, Tennessee. Atop the agenda was the organization's annual leadership election. Forman had already announced that he did not want to continue as

executive secretary, and he privately asked Lewis to join him in making way for new leadership. Lewis resisted, however, preferring to stay on as national chairman.

Ironically, Lewis's candidacy was hurt by his close identification with nonviolence and the idea of a "beloved community" redeemed by suffering. These religious principles had defined SNCC since its founding in 1960 but had lately fallen away to

The new SNCC leadership at a May 23, 1966, press conference in Atlanta. Beside Forman on the far left are (from left to right) Sellers, Robinson, and Carmichael.

the point at which most staff members felt that Lewis no longer represented them politically.

To replace Forman, the staff chose Ruby Doris Robinson, who had joined SNCC in 1960 as a seventeen-year-old Atlanta high school senior; it also reelected Cleveland Sellers, Moses's successor, as program secretary. The choice of chairman, however, proved much more contentious. Initially, Lewis ran unopposed, but then Robinson, Sellers, Ivanhoe Donaldson, and others approached Carmichael to run. "There's a clear question of direction and policy," he was told. "You represent our position. You know it. You're the logical person to run for chair." At first, Carmichael demurred, but then Donaldson said, "Man, that's irresponsible. There's a crisis in the organization. You gotta [run]. You're the obvious choice." Carmichael eventually agreed and let himself be drafted.

The election debate went on for hours. By the time a vote was finally taken at two in the morning, more than a few staffers had already gone to bed. Lewis won narrowly, but then Worth Long came back into the room and, learning what had happened, insisted that another vote be taken with all of the staff present. Those who had gone to bed were dutifully awakened, and the debate continued. During this second round, Lewis made a few impolitic statements that turned some erstwhile supporters against him. When another vote was taken several hours later, Carmichael won.

The national press reported the leadership change as a "coup" in which "moderates" Lewis and Forman had been ousted by violent black nationalists led by Carmichael and Robinson. In the *Los Angeles Times*, Jack Nelson wrote that

the election had "cast the student group further adrift from the mainstream of the civil rights movement" because Lewis had been SNCC's principal link to King and also because of "SNCC's emerging policy of deemphasizing involvement of whites." Integration was out; "black consciousness" was in.

"Black consciousness signaled the end of the use of the word *Negro*," Cleveland Sellers wrote later. "Black consciousness permitted us to relate our struggle to the one being waged by Third World revolutionaries in Africa, Asia, and Latin America. It helped us understand the imperialistic aspects of domestic racism. It helped us understand that the problems of this nation's oppressed minorities will not be solved without revolution."

Carmichael's new duties precluded his return to Lowndes County, but the LCFO continued its work with energy and optimism. On Election Day, however, its candidates came up about six hundred votes short out of four thousand cast. Although the LCFO charged fraud, including the stuffing of ballot boxes and the use of eviction threats to control the votes of sharecroppers, the results stood.

The disappointment was profound, but the organization held together and persevered. SNCC left, but Bob Mants and others stayed.

At the same time, more local leaders stepped forward. Four years later, John Hulett was elected sheriff of Lowndes County.

KING MOVES NORTH

As SNCC continued to focus on the South, King and his organization looked to the North. With his national legislative goals now largely met, King had been thinking less about legalities and more about economic exploitation and political powerlessness, especially as these concepts applied to urban ghettos.

In late 1965, King decided that Chicago would be the site of his major northern campaign. One reason was the city's large black population, which had shot up from 250,000 in 1940 to more than 1,000,000 by 1965. Another was the remarkable segregation of blacks in Chicago into strictly defined ghettos on the West and South Sides.

Because housing segregation in the birthplace of the restrictive covenant was so strict and pervasive, equal educational opportunity also became an important issue. The Chicago Board of Education, personified by Superintendent Benjamin C. Willis, had for years gerrymandered the attendance zones so that 84 percent of the city's black children attended what were essentially segregated schools. In those schools, as in southern black schools, the physical plant was inferior, the teaching standards were poor, and class sizes were out of control. A post-*Brown* report commissioned by the Urban League documented the need for ghetto schools to operate on double

shifts to ease overcrowding, while schools in white neighborhoods operated on a single shift with hundreds of classrooms empty.

In 1963, about forty local civil rights groups came together to form the Coordinating Council of Community Organizations (CCCO). In October of that year and again in February 1964, the interracial CCCO sponsored one-day school boycotts that received substantial support from black parents but failed to influence either Willis or his patron, Chicago mayor Richard Daley. After the second boycott, the CCCO suspended activity until May 1965, when the board of education renewed Willis's contract, provoking the CCCO to organize new demonstrations. Initially, six hundred people a day took part in the picketing of Daley's home. Hundreds were arrested. But Daley remained unyielding, and the picketing gradually declined.

CCCO demonstrators protesting racial segregation in the Chicago public schools sit down in the offices of schools superintendent Benjamin W. Willis in July 1963.

About this time, the CCCO leadership reached out to King for help. Its emissary was Jim Bevel.

Bevel first became acquainted with the CCCO in April 1965, when Bernard Lafayette invited him to Chicago to lead workshops on the southern movement. At the time, Lafayette was working for the American Friends Service Committee as its local urban affairs director. Lafayette suggested to Bevel that Chicago would be an ideal location

Members of the CCCO picket outside the home of Chicago mayor Richard J. Daley, demanding that Daley fire schools superintendent Benjamin Willis.

On July 26, 1965, Martin Luther King (center, foreground) leads a crowd estimated at more than ten thousand people through the streets of downtown Chicago to protest segregation in the city's public schools.

for SCLC's expansion into the North, and Bevel gradually came to agree. Taking temporary leave from the SCLC, he became program director at the West Side Christian Parish and began learning even more about the community.

What Bevel came to realize was that the Chicago ghettos existed because powerful white real estate interests had important economic stakes in them. By confining blacks to strictly defined neighborhoods, and thus limiting the *supply* of housing available to them, the slumlords were able to boost artificially the *demand* for their housing and thus the rents and mortgage interest rates they charged—no matter how squalid the housing itself. Absentee owners made out particularly well because of provisions in the tax law that encouraged them to let their properties decline, and compliant building inspectors rarely enforced the city code.

By the end of 1965, Bevel had brokered the deal that brought the SCLC to Chicago. Staff and money would be made available, as well as King

The SCLC leadership waves from a window of the ghetto apartment that Martin Luther King (center, standing beside his wife, Coretta) occupied while in Chicago.

for at least two days a week. For the propaganda value, King rented a slum apartment at 1550 South Hamlin Avenue in the middle of the West Side ghetto. Before he moved in, however, the SCLC sent over a small army of contractors to make repairs; even so, when King arrived in January 1966, he had to spent his first few nights in a downtown hotel because the apartment building's boiler wasn't working and his new residence had no heat.

THE CHICAGO PLAN

Meanwhile, Bevel worked with fourteen SCLC advance men on developing a strategy for the Chicago Freedom Movement (CFM). Initially, he envisioned a straightforward direct action campaign that would desegregate Chicago housing the same way that Project C had desegregated Birmingham's public facilities. But the more he learned about Chicago, the more he realized that southern tactics would not translate quite so easily to the North.

For instance, arranging interracial cooperation in Chicago proved problematic—not because of white racism, which was present in the South as well, but because of the strong antiwhite feelings shared by so many northern blacks. In addition, Richard Daley was no Bull Connor. The Chicago mayor was more powerful, more intelligent, and he knew how to pacify an opponent without actually giving him anything.

As Bevel thought more about the issue of economic exploitation, he began playing with the idea of tenant unions through which the residents of a building could bargain collectively with their landlord. But this conception was still too narrow; what Bevel really wanted to do was expand beyond housing to encompass a much wider range of ghetto issues. Eventually, he came up with the "union to end slums," which became the basis of his Chicago Plan.

Tactically, however, the Chicago Plan was textbook SCLC. First, there would be mass meetings to educate the public, then staff-led workshops to teach the theory and practice of nonviolence, and finally mass marches, led by King, designed to attract the attention of the national media. If all went well, these efforts would revive the open housing legislation currently stalled in Congress and bring change to all northern ghettos. "Our work will be aimed at Washington," King explained at the January 7 press conference kicking off the campaign.

As before, the SCLC organized its work through local churches, but this approach turned out to be much less effective in the North than it had been in the South. According to Linda Bryant Hall, a native Chicagoan working for CORE in 1966, the city's black community was "very diversified, and some people in Chicago didn't even believe in churches, didn't believe in God. I mean, they were avowed atheists, and for someone to come in now and ask them to come

An impoverished black family inside their run-down apartment on Chicago's South Side in February 1968.

Martin Luther King, who played a great deal of pool while at Crozer Theological Seminary, shows off to CCCO leader Al Raby (left, with cigarette in hand) during a tour of Chicago's West Side neighborhoods in February 1966.

into the church and follow his movement through that mechanism, it didn't wash so well with a lot of people.

"When King came through," Hall continued, "what he wanted to do was just work with that one umbrella group [CCCO], and then not understand that each group within that group had a program of its own, had leaders of its own, had its own kind of direction that it was going in….We needed somebody like King to lend us his strength, to lend us his name, and we wanted him to come and join our movement, not come in and lead it, because we already had leaders. So when he came in to try and discount what was already here, he offended quite a few people."

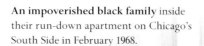

Young protesters take part in the July 10 Freedom Rally held at Soldier Field in Chicago and billed by the CCCO as a "massive workshop in nonviolence."

The Chicago Plan notwithstanding, King's desire to distill the issues led him to concentrate nearly exclusively on open housing. As a result, by early summer, the CFM had become a battle between King and Daley over housing segregation. Bevel still suggested innovations, such as a massive rent strike, but King increasingly fell back on his two mainstays: press conferences and mass marches.

On July 10, after a large rally at Soldier Field, King led several thousand marchers to City Hall, where he ostentatiously posted a list of demands on the mayor's door. Most related to racial discrimination in housing as practiced by the Chicago Real Estate Board, banks, and the municipal government, but others referenced police brutality, inadequate municipal services in the slums, the exclusion of blacks from local trade unions, and enactment of a two-dollar minimum wage.

King knew that the likelihood of any of these demands being met was negligible, but he was probing, searching for an opening—the sort of serendipitous opportunity that had presented itself in Birmingham and again in Selma. It would not appear in Chicago.

Instead, during the week after the Soldier Field rally, the temperature in Chicago climbed so high that children in the ghettos began opening fire hydrants to splash in the cool water. On Tuesday, July 12, city fire commissioner Robert Quinn ordered the hydrants turned off to conserve water pressure. Police enforced this order, but youths on the West Side turned the hydrants back on, claiming that others remained open in a nearby white neighborhood. When police began making arrests, localized rioting broke out. Each night, the violence got worse until, finally, it encompassed six hundred city blocks. At that point, on July 15, Illinois governor Otto Kerner called in the National Guard.

During the rioting, King and his staff worked around the clock to no effect. As the second night of violence began, Andrew Young and Bernard Lee insisted that King remain off the streets for his own

Ignoring the police beside them, youths on Chicago's West Side enjoy the spray being emitted from open fire hydrants on July 13. Seven people were injured in the rock throwing and police retaliation that followed.

protection. "The people we're working with are so much a part of the problem that we have as much fight to keep them from encouraging the riots," Young told Stanley Levison during a telephone conversation monitored by the FBI.

Two weeks later, hoping to regain the initiative, the CFM began staging marches in all-white neighborhoods. Their purpose was to demonstrate dramatically the lack of tolerance that whites had for blacks in Chicago, but the protests worked a little too well. On August 5 in Gage Park, a huge crowd of angry whites pelted eight hundred marchers with rocks and bottles, one of which struck King in the head.

Martin Luther King ducks his head after being hit by a rock thrown during an August 5 housing discrimination march in one of Chicago's white neighborhoods. Bottles and firecrackers were also thrown at the marchers.

Had it not been for the one thousand police assigned to protect the marchers, much worse might have occurred that day.

Clearly King was losing, but Daley didn't want violence any more than King did, so in early August, Daley began to send out peace feelers. Meanwhile, a young SCLC aide named Jesse Jackson announced on August 8, apparently without authorization, that the CFM would be staging a march in Cicero, a notoriously racist suburb on the western edge of the city with seventy thousand white residents and not a single black one. The prospect of a bloodbath in Cicero focused everyone's attention.

On August 17, the mayor and other prominent Chicagoans held a "summit meeting" with King and his CFM colleagues. Little progress was made, but a subcommittee was formed to continue the negotiations. A second plenary session was set for August 26. Meanwhile, to keep up the pressure, the CFM set a date for the Cicero march: Sunday, August 27. Governor Kerner readied the National Guard.

On August 26, however, King decided to fold, accepting the ten-point settlement drafted by the subcommittee even though it was flimsy at best and contained no real concessions from the realtors, who were the chief cause of the housing problem. On the other hand, the settlement did express enough of the proper

Whites in Chicago's Gage Park section respond negatively to the presence of blacks in their neighborhood during an August 15 protest march.

sentiments for the CFM to save face. (The document concluded, for instance. "Although all of the metropolitan areas of the country are confronted with the problem of segregated housing, only in Chicago have the top leaders of the religious faiths, commerce and industry, labor and government sat down together with leaders in the civil rights movement to seek practical solutions.") Afterward, it was with great relief that King, as part of the settlement, called off the Cicero march.

Remarkably, the Cicero march took place anyway. "When [King] called off the march, we were surprised; we were shocked," Linda Bryant Hall remembered. "This is the march we looked forward to." So she and other local activists led a group into Cicero without King. "Dr. King's marches in Chicago were usually made up of movement people," Hall continued. "This march was community people. These people had not attended any workshops on nonviolence; they had not listened to any lectures on love and loving your fellow man and all; they were just people who were angry about what was happening and wanted to do something."

The police and National Guard were able to prevent bloodshed, but not the rock and bottle throwing that had become a predictable part of these marches. In Cicero, however, the marchers, for the first time, threw some of the rocks and bottles *back*.

THE MEREDITH MARCH

Although King had promised the CCCO leaders that he would spend at least two days each week in Chicago, he was absent from the city during much of June because on Monday, June 6, James Meredith was shot outside Hernando, Mississippi.

Following his August 1963 graduation from Ole Miss, Meredith had spent a year studying in Nigeria before entering Columbia Law School in September 1965. Once that academic year ended, he announced that he would spend his summer walking through Mississippi on a March Against Fear. His purpose, he explained later, was "to talk to Negroes, to explain that the old order was passing, that they should stand up as men with nothing to fear." He especially wanted blacks in Mississippi to vote "because that was one of the keys to the future."

Meredith's announcement didn't generate much reaction from his peers within the civil rights movement, most of whom considered him a moody loner with great courage but also an exaggerated sense of self-importance. Privately, Cleveland Sellers called the idea "absurd."

It also seemed suicidal. Meredith's proposed 220-mile route, from Memphis to Jackson along Highway 51, took him through the heart of the Mississippi Delta, where he was perhaps the most hated Negro alive.

He began his march on Sunday, June 5. The next day, about an hour out of Hernando, he noticed that the small convoy of cars that had been following him (carrying local police, state highway patrolmen, FBI observers, and a few reporters) had leapfrogged ahead to reach a small roadside store selling soft drinks. Just then, a man jumped out of the bushes behind him carrying a shotgun.

"I wished suddenly that I had brought a gun," Meredith wrote later in the *Saturday Evening Post*. "Things were happening so fast that I had no time to fear. I threw myself on the ground, and the gun roared, and I was hit somewhere in the back. I'm still not sure of the sequence of events. I thought four shots were fired; other witnesses said three. I was hit again and then tried to get across the road and into the safety of a gully. But the last shot hit me in the head and knocked me flat." Meredith was

James Meredith grimaces in pain as he pulls himself across Highway 51 after being shot outside Hernando, Mississippi, on June 6, 1966.

later hospitalized in Memphis with about one hundred pellets of bird shot in his body.

News of the attack spread like wildfire through the civil rights community, and on June 7, the leaders of SNCC, CORE, the SCLC, the NAACP, and the Urban League all made pilgrimages to Meredith's hospital room in Memphis. The first dignitary to arrive was comedian Dick Gregory, who had stood with King in Birmingham and Selma and with SNCC in the Mississippi Delta. After speaking briefly with Meredith, Gregory left for the spot where Meredith had been shot to resume the march.

Soon after Gregory left, Carmichael, King, and Floyd McKissick (James Farmer's successor as national director of CORE) appeared. They also told Meredith that they wanted to continue his

Stokely Carmichael (left), Martin Luther King (center), and Floyd McKissick hold a press conference in Memphis on June 7 to discuss the Meredith March.

> "America is a rough country, and a man has to look out for his own, to be his own man."
>
> JAMES MEREDITH

march, and left to join Gregory out on Highway 51. After about three hours of trudging along, they all returned to Memphis.

That evening, King hosted a meeting at the black-owned Lorraine Motel, where he usually stayed when in Memphis. The purpose of the gathering was to discuss a more thorough

resumption of the Meredith March. By this time, Roy Wilkins and Whitney Young had also arrived in town, so they attended as well.

Wilkins and Young wanted to re-create the glories of the Selma march by issuing a nationwide call to whites of goodwill. This was King's inclination as well, but Carmichael had

Martin Luther King Jr. (center) and others walk along a red-dirt road in Mississippi during the Meredith March.

other plans. He wanted to deemphasize the participation of whites and instead promote the creation of independent black political organizations. The new SNCC chairman also wanted to entrust march security to the Deacons for Defense, a group of Louisianians whose members openly carried guns.

Finally, when Carmichael insisted on issuing a strident manifesto critical of President Johnson, Wilkins and Young threatened to walk out. "The two put on their coats, made an elaborate show of shuffling their papers and snapping their briefcases shut with dramatic finality," Carmichael wrote later. "Then they sat there glowering. I almost laughed out loud, I mean, they were like little kids waiting for someone to implore them to stay."

King could easily have stopped them, but instead he let them go. His own dislike for Wilkins, dating back to their fund-raising conflict during the Montgomery bus boycott, may have influenced his judgment. In any case, letting Wilkins and Young go was a mistake.

Carmichael had, of course, been baiting Wilkins, hoping that he would leave and take Whitney Young with him. Carmichael wanted SNCC to control the Meredith March, and Wilkins represented a threat to that ambition. However, Carmichael also coveted King's name and prestige, so once Wilkins and Young departed, he became much more accommodating to King. "We wanted to pull him to the left," Carmichael explained later. "We knew that if we got rid of Young and Wilkins, the march was ours."

"I believe in nonviolence not only as a religious and moral matter but also as a matter of tactics," King told Carmichael. "If you want a violent march, go have one,…but don't expect me to join in your march." Quickly Carmichael gave in: There would be no guns; also, whites would be allowed to participate. In fact, there was little Carmichael wasn't willing to concede because he knew that once the SCLC became involved in the march, extricating itself would be nearly impossible.

Meredith March button

MEREDITH MISSISSIPPI MARCH
FOR
FREEDOM
June - 1966

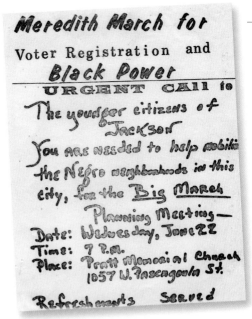

This mimeographed flyer encouraged the youth of Jackson to organize their community for the finale of the Meredith March.

It remains unclear why King didn't protect himself and his organization more adequately. Perhaps he was preoccupied with Chicago; perhaps he didn't fully apprehend the changes that had taken place within SNCC during the past few months. Previously—in Albany, in Selma—he had been able to control the few SNCC hotheads. Now, he must have believed that he could work this magic once again.

BLACK POWER

For several years, white politicians looking for a reason not to help had been warning movement leaders that white Americans were tiring of civil rights. Now, finally, they appeared to be right. When the March Against Fear resumed on June 9, it did so with just 150 marchers.

"So," journalist Paul Good wrote, "a march that should have been an epic emerged, in much of the nation's press, as an irritant, an ill-considered excursion by competing civil rights groups bent on organizational aggrandizement. But anyone who spent those weeks on Mississippi roads knows it was much more. The march lacked the clean lines of purpose, national backing, and surface unity of the Selma-to-Montgomery march. But the Negroes who led it were one year deeper into frustration and disillusion, and this created a desperate atmosphere that encouraged vindictiveness and distrust."

Despite SNCC's years of work in the Delta, many of the towns through which the Meredith March passed seemed untouched by *Brown*, the Civil Rights Act, and the Voting Rights Act. "Rural Negroes, most vulnerable to intimidation, remained at the mercy of white power exerting absolute dominion over their lives," Good reported. The climate of fear was so strong in Carroll County, for instance, that when federal registrars held open office hours on four consecutive days, not a single black resident dared to apply.

King was away in Chicago on June 16 when the march reached Greenwood. This was Carmichael's turf; he had spent his Freedom Summer there and knew many of the locals. Following their usual practice, the marchers began setting up their tents on the grounds of the local black high school. The police, however, intervened, insisting that the schoolyard couldn't be used without the permission of the school board. When Carmichael continued putting up tents regardless, he was arrested and held for six hours. The police released him just as that evening's rally was concluding. It was the opportunity for which Carmichael had been waiting.

Because of Carmichael's arrest, the rally that night had attracted nearly three thousand people, or five times the usual number. When he finally appeared, the charismatic SNCC leader was greeted with a huge roar, which he acknowledged with a clenched-fist salute. "This is the twenty-seventh time I have been arrested," he began,

> "We been saying freedom for six years, and we ain't got nothing. What we gonna start saying now is black power!"
>
> STOKELY CARMICHAEL

"and I ain't going to jail no more!" He had to wait for the explosion of cheers and clapping to subside before he continued, "The only way we're gonna stop them white men from whupping us is to take over. We been saying freedom for six years, and we ain't got nothing. What we gonna start saying now is black power!" At this point, SNCC advance man Willie Ricks shouted out, "What do you want?" "Black power!" the crowd yelled back in unison. According to Cleveland Sellers, "Everything that happened afterward was a response to that moment."

Carmichael's introduction of the phrase *black power* took his ideological struggle with King to an entirely new level. In Carmichael's mind, *black power* meant simply what Courtland Cox had written on the blackboard at the SNCC staff meeting seven months earlier: getting political power for black people. "Black power means black people coming together to form a political force and either electing representatives or forcing their representatives to speak their

Greenwood police handcuff Stokely Carmichael (rear) after arresting him on June 16 for trespassing. Bruce Baines of CORE was also taken into custody.

needs," he told photojournalist Gordon Parks. "It's an economic and physical bloc that can exercise its strength in the black community instead of letting the job go to the Democratic or Republican parties or a white-controlled black man set up as a puppet to represent black people. *We* pick the brother and make sure he fulfills *our* needs."

Nevertheless, hostile press reports relentlessly equated Carmichael's "black power" with black nationalism, racism, and violence, making King's position uncomfortable indeed. After Greenwood, the relationship between the SNCC and SCLC staffs became openly acrimonious; yet, as Carmichael had anticipated, the SCLC was far too deeply involved with the march to consider pulling out now.

King soldiered on as best he could, refusing to criticize SNCC publicly yet distancing himself from Carmichael's rhetoric. King knew that, upon close examination, the substance of what Carmichael was saying wasn't all that different from what Bob Moses had been saying for years. But Carmichael's *style* was something else entirely, and that was frightening whites.

The Meredith March ended in Jackson on Sunday, June 26, with an unconvincing display of unity. By that time, all the media could talk about was black power. *Time* magazine called it "the new racism." Even President Johnson used the issue to justify his sacrifice of domestic programs to the ever-expanding Vietnam War. King left the march dispirited, but the SNCCers were thrilled. It didn't matter that Carmichael's words were being twisted; Stokely had become a star.

THE BLACK PANTHERS

As the Meredith March demonstrated, the movement's "mass" nature was declining, and so was its commitment to nonviolence. Two forces were driving this trend. One was accumulating frustration, built up over years of stiff white resistance. The other was increasing factionalism. The smaller a group is, the more militant it must be to exert any influence at all. Sit-ins and marches are effective tools for large mass movements; small revolutionary vanguards tend to have guns.

Even after the Meredith March, SNCC remained committed to nonviolence, at least as a tactical

> "I don't use the term 'black power,' but I do know the Negro must have power if we're gonna gain freedom and human dignity."
>
> MARTIN LUTHER KING JR.

approach, but other young blacks, especially those in urban areas outside the South, moved quickly away from King's philosophy. In Oakland, for instance, two former Merritt College classmates, Bobby Seale and Huey P. Newton, organized a new community group— some called it a gang—to encourage black empowerment.

Like Newton, Seale had moved with his family to Oakland during World War II. Quitting high school when he failed to make the football and basketball teams— because of racial prejudice, he believed— Seale spent three years in the air force before receiving a bad-conduct discharge in 1958 for insubordination. He and Newton had been talking about the need for a revolutionary group to speak for ghetto residents when a September 1966 outbreak of violence in San Francisco's Hunters Point

neighborhood galvanized them into action.

The black rioters' haphazard efforts to fight off the police were a waste, Seale and Newton concluded; a more deliberate strategy was necessary. Having recently read a pamphlet "about how the people in Lowndes County had armed themselves," Seale and Newton appropriated the LCFO ballot symbol and in October 1966 founded the Black Panther Party for Self-Defense.

While two of their comrades lie wounded on the ground, residents of San Francisco's Hunters Point neighborhood shout obscenities at police during September 1966 rioting.

Huey P. Newton

1942–1989

Huey Newton's family left Louisiana in 1945, moving to Oakland so that his father could find work in the defense factories there. A rebellious child who repeatedly defied school authorities, Huey was suspended several times and finally arrested at age fourteen for vandalism and gun possession.

"During those long years in the Oakland public schools," Newton wrote in his 1973 autobiography, *Revolutionary Suicide*, "I did not have one teacher who taught me anything relevant to my own life or experience. Not one instructor ever awoke in me a desire to learn more or to question or to explore the worlds of literature, science, and history. All they did was try to rob me of the essence of my own uniqueness and worth."

Yet Newton persevered with his education, explaining (perhaps apocryphally) that he learned to read properly by listening to records of Vincent Price reciting poetry and reading along with a printed text. After high school, he began taking

classes at Merritt, a local junior college on the fringes of the Oakland ghetto, where he met Bobby Seale (six years his senior) in 1962. The more intellectual of the pair, Newton was particularly influenced by the writings of Malcolm X, Mao Tse-tung, and Frantz Fanon, anticolonial author of *The Wretched of the Earth*.

During this period, Newton supported himself by burglarizing homes in the Berkeley hills. In 1964, he was arrested for assault with a deadly weapon. Sentenced to six months in the Alameda County jail, he had his time there extended because of more defiant behavior. Newton organized food strikes and other protests, which earned him several months in solitary confinement. Other inmates called these cells "soul breakers."

Each was completely bare with no sink, no bed, no toilet. Naked prisoners were forced to sleep on cement floors in the middle of which were holes for defecation. They were allowed out for showers and exercise only once every fifteen days. "For Newton, as for Malcolm X," Sol Stern wrote in a 1967 *New York Times Magazine* profile, "the prison experience only confirmed his hostility to the white world and made him more militant."

The first task that Seale, the party's thirty-year-old chairman, and Newton, its twenty-four-year-old minister of defense, set for themselves was to produce a ten-point statement of demands. Some of these were familiar, such as calls for decent housing, full employment, and an end to economic exploitation. Others were decidedly fringe, including the exemption of blacks from military service and the freeing of black prisoners from federal, state, and local jails. The most significant demand, however, turned out to be Number Seven: "We want an immediate end to police brutality and murder of black people."

PICKING UP THE GUN

Police brutality had long been an important mobilizing issue in the black community, speaking directly to its sense of powerlessness. "The police have never been our protectors," Newton wrote in *Revolutionary Suicide*. "Instead, they act as the military arm of our oppressors and continually brutalize us." Understanding that it was pointless to expect the police to police themselves, Seale and Newton organized community patrols of armed men to monitor police activity in the ghetto.

"The dream of the black people in the ghetto is how to stop the police brutality on the street," Seale explained to journalist Sol Stern in 1967. "Can the people in the ghetto stand up to the cops? The ghetto black isn't afraid because he already lives with violence. He expects to die any day."

Seale began talking up the Panthers on the street, while Newton, who had taken a few classes at San Francisco Law School (to become a better burglar, he said), studied the relevant statutes. Together, they trained their new recruits in the finer points of Second Amendment law and then began the patrols, driving around the Oakland ghetto in groups of four, armed with shotguns. "Out on patrol," Newton wrote, "we stopped whenever we saw the police questioning a brother or a sister. We would walk over with our weapons and observe them from a 'safe' distance so that the police could not say we were interfering with the performance of their duty."

The bravado of the patrols soon caught the community's attention and elevated the Panthers to folk-hero status. The patrols also

This Black Panther Party poster from the early 1970s features armed leaders Bobby Seale (left) and Huey P. Newton.

attracted recruits to the party until it numbered between seventy-five and two hundred people throughout the Bay Area; not even Newton and Seale kept track of the exact numbers. Instead, the party was divided into "units," each of which had its own "captain." Together with Seale, Newton, and a treasurer, these captains formed the Panthers' executive committee, which set basic policy. Early in 1967, *Ramparts* staff writer

Eldridge Cleaver was invited to join as the party's minister of information.

The Panthers became a national sensation in May 1967, when they sent an armed delegation to the California statehouse in Sacramento. The ostensible purpose of this mission was to oppose

new gun-control legislation that prohibited the carrying of loaded firearms. (With good reason, the Panthers believed that this bill was aimed directly at them.) Their real purpose in traveling to Sacramento, however, was to attract attention to the party and thus spread awareness of the Panthers and their program to an audience far beyond the Bay Area.

Upon entering the statehouse, the Panthers, ostentatiously brandishing their weapons, were quickly surrounded by reporters. Seale wanted to reach the visitors' gallery of the assembly but had no idea how to get there. He asked for directions, but none were forthcoming, so he began walking down a randomly selected corridor. Eventually, he realized that the photographers who were walking backward in front of him (so that they could continue taking pictures) knew where they were going, so he simply followed them.

The photographers, however, led the Panthers not to the visitors' gallery but to the doors of the assembly chamber itself. Before anyone could stop them, or Seale realized what they were doing, the Panthers marched with their loaded shotguns onto the floor of the California state assembly.

Recovering itself, the security force followed them into the chamber and snatched away some (but not all) of the Panthers' guns. This provoked a loud outburst from the revolutionaries, who demanded that the guards either arrest them or return their weapons. Eventually, order was restored, and the Panthers were detained briefly. None were arrested, because they hadn't broken any laws. Instead, Seale was able to read the "executive mandate" that Newton had penned and Cleaver edited.

"The Black Panther Party for Self-Defense," Seale began, "calls upon the American people in general and the black people in particular to take careful note of the racist California legislature, which is now considering legislation aimed at keeping the black people disarmed and powerless at the very same time that racist police agencies throughout the country

Eldridge Cleaver readies himself for an audience of American University students in October 1968, the year that he ran for president as nominee of the Peace and Freedom party.

> "With weapons in our hands, we were no longer their subjects but their equals."
>
> HUEY P. NEWTON

Followed by reporters, Black Panthers Bobby Hutton (left) and Bobby Seale walk through the corridors of the California state capitol in Sacramento on May 2, 1967.

are intensifying the terror, brutality, murder, and repression of black people."

Passage of the new gun-control bill, assured by the Panthers' performance in Sacramento, brought an end to the armed patrols, but Newton was nonplussed. As he explained, they had been only a temporary measure. "Ninety percent of the reason we carried guns in the first place was education," he said. "We set the example. We made black people aware that they have the right to carry guns."

During late 1967 and early 1968, the party turned its energies instead to less violent means of community service. It sponsored a free breakfast program for black children and began offering free health-care services to ghetto residents. It opened schools that, like the Freedom Schools, taught politics and African-American history, and it also counseled welfare recipients on their rights. The Panthers even ran buses to distant state prisons so that families could visit their incarcerated relatives.

Nevertheless, the mass media continued to see only their guns. According to the prevalent view, the Panthers were the shock troops of the incipient youth rebellion, and as the party expanded its reach to other cities, the tone of the reporting grew ever more frantic. To some extent, the Panthers encouraged this with their revolutionary rhetoric, calls for armed struggle, and close alliances with other radical left-wing groups.

During late 1967 and early 1968, for example, the Panthers pursued a close alliance with SNCC—hoping, in fact, for a merger that would yield not only SNCC's organizational experience but also, more importantly, its mimeograph machines (the most widely used duplicating machines prior to the advent of xerographic

technology). Carmichael was the principal contact, although by this time he had been succeeded as chairman by Hubert "Rap" Brown.

An increasingly militant Jim Forman, still playing a leadership role in SNCC, was especially attracted to the rising Black Panther Party because he attributed SNCC's corresponding decline to the middle-class origins of most of its staffers. "The emphasis on recruiting street brothers, young people from the 'ghetto,' rather than college students," Forman wrote later, "gave it a large base and eliminated some of the class tensions which we had experienced."

Forman wasn't the only one to realize that the Panthers were quickly supplanting SNCC. So did FBI director J. Edgar Hoover, who wrote

in a September 1968 memo that the Panthers were "the greatest threat to the internal security of the country." In 1956, Hoover had established a counterintelligence program—known by its acronym, COINTELPRO—to disrupt covertly the political activities of suspected American Communists. During the 1960s, he gradually expanded the reach of the program to include the civil rights movement as well. COINTELPRO's methods, many of them illegal, emphasized disinformation but also included IRS harassment, anonymous letters of provocation, and even violence. According to the 1976 Senate report that exposed Hoover's abuses, the Panthers had become, by July 1969, "the primary focus of the program"

The First Black Mayors

In February 1965, Bayard Rustin published an influential essay in *Commentary*, in which he argued that the civil rights movement needed to evolve "from protest to politics." That same year, Ohio state assemblyman Carl B. Stokes ran his first campaign for mayor of Cleveland. Running as an independent against three white candidates and campaigning almost exclusively on the Negro East Side, Stokes received only 3 percent of the white vote but amazed political veterans by coming within two thousand votes of victory. In 1967, Stokes ran again.

"From the outset of the campaign," Calvin Trillin wrote in the *New Yorker*, "it was taken for granted that most white people in Cleveland would not vote for a Negro candidate for mayor under any circumstances, and that Cleveland's Negroes, who now make up more than a third

of the city's registered voters, would vote for a Negro candidate even if he were, in the words of one local politician, 'a Black Muslim, a black dog, or a black automobile.'"

The second time around, however, Stokes challenged incumbent mayor Ralph Locher for the Democratic nomination and went after liberal white voters disturbed by recent rioting in the Hough ghetto. One of Stokes's slogans was "Don't Vote for a Negro. Vote for a Man. Vote for Ability." Attracted to the smooth, articulate Stokes because they believed he could bring racial peace to the city, these voters provided his margin of victory in the fall election.

Also in 1967, City Councilman Richard C. Hatcher won an equally historic mayoral campaign in Gary, Indiana. Stokes and Hatcher thus became the first black mayors of major northern cities.

"In a sense," Trillin concluded, "the Stokes campaign…was a throwback—a kind of electoral March on Washington, a relic of the days when it was thought that well-meaning black people and well-meaning white people could work things out, and that the enemy was Bull Connor."

A jubilant Carl Stokes stands beside his wife, Shirley, as he greets supporters with news of his victory in the 1967 mayoral election in Cleveland.

A fan from 1969 celebrates recently elected blacks.

and were ultimately the target of 233 separate COINTELPRO "actions."

One of these actions led to the December 4, 1969, police raid on Panther headquarters in Chicago. The police arrived at four thirty in the morning, when most of the Panthers were sleeping. Twenty-year-old Fred Hampton, the local Panther chairman, was killed, along with fellow party member Mark Clark. They were just two of the twenty-eight party members killed by police during the late 1960s and early 1970s. Afterward, the Chicago police department claimed that the Panthers had started a gun battle, but a subsequent forensic investigation showed that of the ninety or so shots fired, only one could have come from a Panther's gun. Eventually, the city of Chicago was forced to settle wrongful-death lawsuits for close to two million dollars, but nothing could bring back the Panthers.

THE POOR PEOPLE'S CAMPAIGN

By late 1967, Martin Luther King Jr. was depressed. Devastating summertime riots in Newark and Detroit had made it clear that, since Watts, circumstances in the ghettos were getting

worse, not better. Nearly as troubling was the conservative political revival fueled by these disorders, which had cut deeply into President Johnson's Democratic majorities during the midterm elections of 1966. In the South, election victories by such outspoken segregationists as Lester Maddox, who ran for governor in King's home state of Georgia, seemed to reverse what little positive momentum there had been.

But, more than anything else, King was troubled by Vietnam. He had first spoken out against the war in early 1965, but his calls for a negotiated peace were met with harsh criticism. Both the president and the war were still popular, and conservative civil rights leaders of the Roy Wilkins–Whitney Young variety were concerned that neither the White House nor their white donors be offended.

King took heed and backed off, keeping his grim opinion of the war to himself throughout 1966. But the escalating violence in Vietnam continued to weigh heavily on his mind, and after the president announced in December 1966 that

Julian Bond at a February 1966 peace rally in New York City. The twenty-six-year-old won a seat in the Georgia assembly in 1965, then was barred from it by lawmakers who objected to his public stand against the Vietnam War.

he planned to divert funds from the War on Poverty to the war in Vietnam, King decided to remain silent no longer.

In a major speech delivered at Riverside Church in New York City on April 4, 1967, King said,

This August 1969 photograph hints at contradictions within the Black Panthers: the peacefulness of their community programs and the violence associated with their attachment to weapons. The bullet holes in this door were made by Chicago police during a predawn raid.

"It would be very inconsistent for me to teach and preach nonviolence in this situation and then applaud violence when thousands and thousands of people, both adults and children, are being maimed and mutilated and many killed in this war." Eleven days later, he led an antiwar rally in Central Park that attracted 125,000 protesters. Again the attacks came. In a September 1967 article in *Reader's Digest*, Carl Rowan wrote that King "has become *persona non grata* to Lyndon Johnson…alienated many of the Negro's friends and armed the Negro's foes." Still, the SCLC leader persevered in his criticism and, if anything, became more strident.

Meanwhile, King groped for a new nonviolent approach that could address not merely the needs of black America but also those of American society as a whole. He knew that nearly three years had passed since the last major SCLC victory, that the old tactics no longer produced the desired results, and that his own thinking somehow had to change.

"Quietly," historian Manning Marable has observed, "King was beginning to articulate a democratic socialist vision of American society: the nationalization of basic industries; massive federal expenditures to revive central cities and to provide jobs for ghetto residents; a guaranteed income for every adult American. King had concluded, like Malcolm X, that America's political economy of capitalism had to be transformed, that the civil rights movement's old goals of voter education, registration, and desegregated public facilities were only a beginning step down the long road towards biracial democracy."

On December 4, 1967, King announced the audacious Poor People's Campaign. Its purpose was to bring together the rural and urban poor of all races and ethnicities for a massive campaign of economic protest and civil disobedience. The focus of the effort would be a gathering in Washington of fifteen hundred protesters, whose job it would be to lobby a Vietnam-obsessed government for an "economic bill of rights," full employment, and thirty billion dollars in new antipoverty spending.

King thus moved beyond a narrow definition of civil rights to begin addressing the larger structural problems that restrained black advancement, such as militarism, materialism, and the government's anticommunist paranoia. Unfortunately, given all the competing demands on King's time and the SCLC's resources, the Poor People's Campaign wasn't well planned, and it suffered from insufficient staff. As late as February 1968, just two months before its projected start, the recruiting of volunteers was only barely under way. James Bevel and Jesse Jackson pleaded with King for a postponement, but none was forthcoming.

A 1960s antiwar button.

THE KING ASSASSINATION

Such was the situation in late February when King received a call from James Lawson in Memphis, inviting him to speak at a rally for striking sanitation workers there. King demurred, but Lawson kept after him, explaining that the strike had all the classic civil rights elements—daily mass marches, nightly mass meetings, the support of the city's ministers—but the issues, like that of the Poor People's Campaign, were *economic*.

Memphis's thirteen hundred garbagemen, nearly all of whom were black, had gone on strike February 12, Lawson reported, because they worked full-time jobs but remained poor because their wages were so low. They wanted to organize so that they could bargain collectively, but Memphis mayor Henry Loeb had consistently refused to recognize their union. "Even if garbage piles up over an apartment roof," Loeb declared on March 10, "I'm not going to budge."

Eventually, King agreed to add Memphis to his schedule but only for a single appearance on

A club-swinging Memphis policeman disrupts a crowd of youths looting downtown display windows during the March 28 garbage-strike march led by Martin Luther King.

March 18. His speech before fifteen thousand enthusiastic people in the Mason Temple went so well, however, that he spontaneously agreed to return four days later to lead a protest march and general strike. It would mark the beginning of the Poor People's Campaign, he told the jubilant audience.

King's staff was opposed to the venture. His own schedule was already overbooked, and no advance men could be spared to supervise the preparations in Memphis. Lawson had little experience in these logistical matters, and relying on amateurs was always unwise, they said. It didn't matter. King's mind was made up. It had been a long time since he had witnessed the sort

King speaks at the Mason Temple on March 18. As James Lawson suspected, once King put his prestige on the line for the garbage strikers, he found it difficult to walk away.

"in the turmoil of the moment" he might be killed, and just that morning his plane had been delayed leaving Atlanta by a bomb scare. But, he said, none of this mattered to him now because he had "been to the mountaintop."

And I don't mind. Like anybody, I would like to live a long life. Longevity has its place. But I'm not concerned about that now. I just want to do God's will. And He's allowed me to go up to the mountain, and I've looked over, and I've seen the Promised Land. I may not get there with you, but I want you to know tonight that we as a people will get to the Promised Land. So I'm happy tonight. I'm not worried about anything. I'm not fearing any man. Mine eyes have seen the glory of the coming of the Lord.

Martin Luther King addresses a Memphis audience of some two thousand people on April 3, the night before his assassination.

of energized, vital activity going on in Memphis, and he wanted badly to be a part of it.

Because of snow on March 22, the march and strike were postponed until Thursday, March 28. King still planned to attend the demonstration but arrived late when his morning fight from New Jersey was delayed. While Lawson held up the march for King's arrival, the large and undisciplined crowd grew restless, especially the several hundred teenagers congregating at the back of the line. A group of young militants who called themselves the Invaders, angry at being excluded from the planning of the march, used the delay to denounce nonviolence and exhort the teens to bolder action.

The march leadership was completely unaware of this development because there were no parade marshals around to witness it. All of the inexperienced volunteers recruited by Lawson's group, eager to accompany King at the head of the line, had abandoned the rear. None saw the bottles of wine being passed around in brown paper bags; none saw the teenagers arming themselves by ripping placards off sticks of two-by-two lumber. By the time King arrived about an hour late, the situation was already heading out of control.

As the front of the column turned right onto Main Street from Beale, the sound of breaking glass could be heard clearly as teenagers began breaking store windows and looting their contents. Borrowing a police bullhorn, Lawson quickly ordered the marchers to return to their assembly point at Clayborne Temple, but he was too late. The police surged into the crowd of marchers, swinging nightsticks and firing tear-gas canisters. Before order was restored, sixty-two people were injured, four with gunshot wounds, one of them fatal. Tennessee governor Buford Ellington called in the National Guard, which imposed a 7 P.M. curfew.

King was both embarrassed and traumatized. He wanted to cut and run and even considered calling off the Poor People's Campaign. But after three days of soul searching, he chose a different course. He decided to prove that nonviolence was not a spent force by leading another march in Memphis, this one fully peaceful. To ensure its success, he pulled staff off the Poor People's Campaign and sent them to Memphis.

King returned there himself on Wednesday, April 3, two days before the scheduled march. He checked into Room 306 at the Lorraine Motel and that night spoke before a relatively small audience at the Mason Temple. Remarkably, King's theme was his own mortality. Before coming to Memphis, he had been warned by the city attorney that

About six o'clock the next evening, King stepped out onto the balcony of the Lorraine Motel to get some air while Ralph Abernathy finished shaving. They were expected that night at the home of a local minister for dinner. About three minutes later, at 6:08 P.M., a single

rifle shot was fired from the rear bathroom window of a flophouse across the street. "He had just bent over [the railing]," Jesse Jackson recalled. "If he had been standing up, he wouldn't have been hit in the face."

The gunshot ripped off King's necktie and left a gaping hole at the base of his neck. Abernathy tried to stanch the flow of blood with a towel, but little could be done. Doctors at St. Joseph's Hospital pronounced King dead at 7:05 P.M. He was thirty-eight years old.

On April 19, FBI agents, working around the clock, identified his assassin as James Earl Ray, a forty-year-old thief who had recently escaped from the Missouri State Penitentiary. The ensuing manhunt ended on June 8, when Ray was arrested in London, trying to enter Great Britain under a false Canadian passport. He subsequently confessed to the crime in exchange for a ninety-nine-year sentence

WANTED BY THE **FBI**

CIVIL RIGHTS - CONSPIRACY
INTERSTATE FLIGHT - ROBBERY
JAMES EARL RAY   FBI No. 405,942 G

DESCRIPTION

Photographs taken 1960   Photograph taken 1968
(eyes drawn by artist)

Aliases: Eric Starvo Galt, W. C. Herron, Harvey Lowmyer, James McBride, James O'Connor, James
Walton, James Walyon, John Willard, "Jim,"

Age:	40, born March 10, 1928, at Quincy or Alton, Illinois (not supported by birth records)		
Height:	5'10"	Eyes:	Blue
Weight:	163 to 174 pounds	Complexion:	Medium
Build:	Medium	Race:	White
Hair:	Brown, possibly cut short	Nationality:	American

The FBI issued this flyer after its agents identified James Earl Ray as the likely assassin in the King case. Ray was captured, convicted, and sentenced to life in prison, where he died in 1998.

An unidentified man on the balcony of the Lorraine Motel kneels to cover the dying Martin Luther King with a blanket.

Flames pour from a building on Seventh Street in Washington, D.C., as troops patrol the city's black neighborhoods on April 6. Martin Luther King's April 4 assassination touched off rioting around the nation.

(in order to avoid the death penalty). But shortly after being sentenced, he recanted his confession and insisted that he had been framed.

The immediate reaction to King's death was more rioting, with racial violence erupting overnight in 125 cities across the nation. President Johnson quickly deployed nearly fifty thousand army troops and National Guardsmen to control the situation, but the disorders continued for nearly three weeks, leaving forty-six people dead and twenty-one hundred injured.

An intermediate consequence of King's death was the dooming of the Poor People's Campaign. New SCLC president Ralph Abernathy decided to cope with his and the staff's grief by pressing ahead; however, deprived of King's personal leadership, the campaign foundered. On May 12, the first contingent of protesters arrived in Washington, establishing a settlement of tents and shacks on the Mall called Resurrection City. Over the next six weeks, as the population of Resurrection City grew to an unmanageable seven thousand, the demonstrators spread out over the government, lobbying to no avail. Few officials listened, and the press was almost universally bad, focusing primarily on the tent city's miserable living conditions. The poor people left town empty-handed on June 19.

The long-term effect of King's assassination, of course, was the crippling of the civil rights movement, or at least that part of it committed

to nonviolence. King's path from Montgomery to Memphis had ultimately led him to recognize the true nature of the paradox that lay behind the movement's struggle—how to obtain freedom without power and power without freedom. But he was unable, in the short time granted, to resolve that paradox, and there has been no resolution since.

Members of a poor family from Mississippi make a temporary home for themselves in one of the plywood huts that comprised Resurrection City. The cot-lined quarters were illuminated by a clear plastic skylight and a single window cut out of the hut's rear wall.

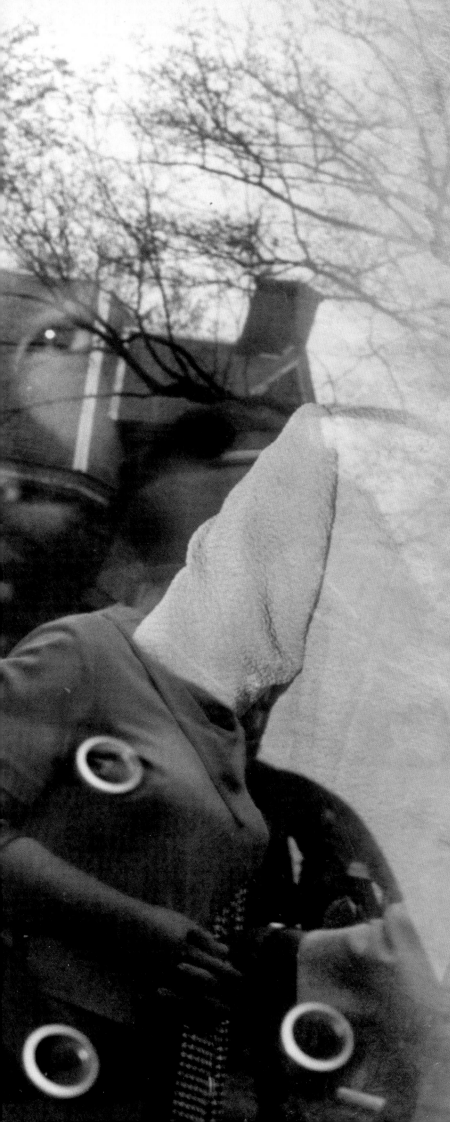

EPILOGUE
FREEDOM

To interpret history as it happens is a perilous undertaking. The larger forces that underlie significant events generally emerge only after some time has passed. In 1941, for example, when the Japanese bombed Pearl Harbor and the United States entered World War II, the fate of the world seemed uncertain. Yet historians have since argued rather persuasively that America's industrial superiority made that war's outcome inevitable, whether Americans realized it at the time or not.

An aspect of interpretation that certainly changes over time is that the individual actions come to seem less important. What would have happened, for example, if Rosa Parks had given up her seat on the Cleveland Avenue bus? Would the history of the civil rights movement have been changed? Certainly so, in some of its details, but the larger story told in this book would have remained essentially the same. The reason is that the historical forces driving the civil rights movement forward were far more profound than the will of any one person or group of people.

Yolanda King stares out of a car window as she leaves for the Atlanta funeral of her father, Martin Luther King Jr., on April 9, 1968. Seated beside her in the rear of the car is her mother, Coretta Scott King. A group of mourners can be seen reflected in the car's window.

Nineteenth-century German philosopher G. W. F. Hegel called the accumulation of these forces the Zeitgeist, or "the spirit of the time." In the case of the civil rights movement, these forces had been building for nearly a century—through Booker T. Washington and accommodationism; through W. E. B. Du Bois and the Niagara Movement; through the founding of the NAACP, the BSCP, the SCLC, and SNCC. Before Linda Brown was even born, Charles Hamilton Houston had already set in motion the legal campaign that eventually produced the *Brown* decision. If Rosa Parks hadn't channeled the Zeitgeist herself, someone else would have.

Nevertheless, it was Rosa Parks—and not Claudette Colvin or Mary Louise Smith—whose act of defiance spawned the Montgomery bus boycott. Like a reluctant match, the tinderbox that was postwar America had to be struck several times before it would light. In December 1955, Parks hit it just right, and Montgomery ignited. After that, events inexorably took their course.

The part played by Martin Luther King Jr., however, resists this analysis. Had King returned home to Atlanta instead of taking the Dexter Avenue job in Montgomery, a great many details of civil rights history would have been changed. How many, and to what degree? No one can say, but it is hard to imagine a national holiday honoring E. D. Nixon or L. Roy Bennett.

"Men make history but only so much history as it is possible for them to make."

HISTORIAN C. L. R. JAMES

A WORLD-HISTORICAL FIGURE

Another important aspect of Hegelian philosophy is the idea of the world-historical figure. According to Hegel, history moves in stages, with each stage offering a greater degree of freedom than the one preceding it. A world-historical person in Hegelian terms is an individual who—because he embodies the Zeitgeist— helps humanity transition from one stage of history to the next.

Hegel developed this theory to make sense of Napoleon, whose impact on the Western world during Hegel's lifetime was so far-reaching that it had to be explained. What Hegel came to see was that Napoleon, through his wars of conquest, spread the bourgeois creed of the French Revolution, which in turn swept away the remnants of European feudalism and ushered in the capitalism that took its place.

Martin Luther King might also be considered a world-historical figure in this sense because of the way he led America from one stage of history (the segregated, pre-*Brown* era) into the next (the integrated, more free, post-Selma world). For all of the work and influence of John Lewis, Robert Moses, Stokely Carmichael, and others, none challenged King's preeminence as the face and voice of the movement. If the idea of a central figure has merit, then King would have to be it.

Busing in Boston
September 1974

The *Brown* decision outlawed de jure segregation in southern public schools but not the de facto kind that was common in the North. In March 1972, a group of black parents in Boston filed suit in federal court, charging that the Boston School Committee was not providing equal educational opportunities for black children. The school committee responded that the segregation was caused by housing patterns over which it had no control.

In June 1974, district court judge Arthur Garrity ruled that the school committee had "intentionally brought about and maintained segregation." To remedy this situation, Garrity ordered the busing of white students to black schools and black students to white schools. In some neighborhoods, the integration took place without incident, but in white South Boston, buses carrying black students were met by angry, rock-throwing crowds.

Police hold back a crowd of angry whites as a school bus carrying the first black students arrives at South Boston High School on September 12, 1974.

Had King lived during another era, his ministerial career might have more closely resembled his father's. But he was born into a remarkable age, when the Zeitgeist moved into his neighborhood and became particularly active. Furthermore, King was no simple vessel. Beyond his remarkable oratorical skills, he had a strong faith, a shrewd political sense, the ability to inspire deep personal loyalty, and a unique capacity for engaging a wide range of people, from impoverished black sharecroppers to wealthy white philanthropists. Because of these attributes, he was able to take advantage of a situation in Montgomery and produce the first successful mass civil rights movement.

Nobody saw it coming. Of whites at the time, historian Taylor Branch has written, "Their superior status was relatively secure then; the notion of drastic change for the benefit of Negroes struck the average American as about on a par with creating a world government, which is to say visionary, slightly dangerous, and extremely remote. The race issue was little more than a human interest story in the mass public consciousness." But then—in just three years—*Brown* and Emmett Till and Montgomery and Little Rock changed everything.

Even more than *Brown*, Montgomery was the turning point, engaging the moral energy of the African-American masses in ways that were both unprecedented and highly effective. Quickly it became a force that couldn't be stopped. The first targets were the most egregious moral wrongs: segregation; inequality; the denial of the right to vote; physical intimidation, even to the point of murder. The initial leadership came from the clergy, but as the movement grew, it drew in all manner of blacks and whites, the only commonality among them being a shared belief that what they were doing was right and good and merited sacrifice.

For a decade, while the Zeitgeist tarried, this moral energy transformed American politics and society. The triumphs were epic; the remaking of hearts and minds, profound. But then, sometime after the Selma-to-Montgomery march, the Zeitgeist departed. The movement fractured. The moral energy dissipated. This, of course, wasn't obvious at the time.

BLACKS AND WHITES

King's leadership style had focused on white public opinion. He wanted whites to pay more attention to the oppression of blacks, so he chose "projects" that allowed him to frame

Trailed by news reporters, Allan Bakke leaves the UC Davis campus on September 25, 1978, after attending his first day of medical school classes.

The *Bakke* Case

June 1978

In 1973, thirty-three-year-old Allan Bakke applied for admission to the University of California, Davis, Medical School and was rejected. He applied again the following year and was rejected once more.

The medical school admitted one hundred students each year, reserving sixteen slots for minority students who weren't judged against the general applicant pool. Because of this affirmative action policy, designed to compensate for the lasting effects of racial discrimination, several of the minority students admitted in 1973 and 1974 had significantly lower grades and standardized test scores than the rejected Bakke.

Bakke subsequently filed suit in state court, charging that Davis's system of "reverse discrimination" violated his rights under the California state constitution, the Fourteenth Amendment to the U.S. Constitution, and the Civil Rights Act of 1964. His case eventually reached the Supreme Court, where it resulted in a divided June 1978 decision. Four justices opposed any use of race in university admissions; another four judged the medical school's consideration of race to be permissible. The deciding vote was cast by Lewis Powell, who believed that race could be one of many factors used by admissions officers conducting a "holistic review," but that quota systems and other set-asides went too far.

political issues in the strongest moral terms. In this way, he generated national attention that compelled the federal government to change the law so that African Americans would be treated more fairly.

Yet, as most people know, laws in and of themselves are insufficient to compel good behavior. They can be ignored or defied, especially when widely unpopular. "There is no discernible change in the racial climate of the city," journalist Haynes Johnson wrote after visiting Selma in July 1965. "The Negroes have scored no real advances in their areas of greatest need—employment, housing, and education. They are discovering that these goals are easier to express than to achieve."

National attention could force breakthroughs, but the nation's attention couldn't be held indefinitely. And then what? As King himself realized near the end of his life, lasting change required constant grassroots pressure. As Robert Moses had pointed out, blacks needed to be organized; as Stokely Carmichael had said, they needed power.

The field secretaries of SNCC had been pursuing this difficult, low-profile, largely thankless work for years. Unfortunately, by the time King finally came to appreciate its worth, SNCC was already falling apart. Always losing out to the SCLC and the NAACP in the fund-raising arena, SNCC had become a pressure cooker, asking its members to work harder with fewer resources than was bearable. Resentment grew, and radicalism took hold. When conditions are so bad that there seems to be nothing to lose, moderation has little appeal.

This was the mind-set in which Stokely Carmichael found himself in Lowndes County in 1965. In the course of being arrested more than two dozen times for exercising his basic constitutional rights, Carmichael had developed an understandable contempt for the civic virtue of most Americans. Who in his position would have felt otherwise? And with one's personal security threatened, as Carmichael's was in Lowndes County, who would have resisted the pressure to consolidate leadership within a loyal cadre of fellow activists and exclude those volunteers who perhaps couldn't be trusted?

As long as the civil rights movement emphasized its opposition to the egregious moral wrongs stemming from segregation, there existed a natural alliance between engaged blacks and liberal whites. But the goals of these two constituencies were not identical: Liberal whites wanted legal equality for blacks, and most considered the *Brown* decision, the Civil Rights Act of 1964, and the Voting Rights Act of 1965 the realization of that goal. Activist blacks, however, wanted legal equality not for its own sake but as a tool for improving the quality of their lives. As Amzie Moore pointed out to Robert Moses in 1960, what's the use of integrating a lunch counter if you can't afford to eat there?

When Carmichael began preaching "black power" in 1966, he alienated movement whites who, rightly or wrongly, didn't share his political program. Generally, liberal whites sought a colorless society in which all people were treated the same. Until that society came to pass, however, the whites would remain white, and Carmichael would remain black, with all the attendant problems of being black.

Not surprisingly, Carmichael didn't share the whites' millennial patience. Like his friends in the Black Panthers, he wanted security today, not promises for tomorrow.

This resurgence of black nationalism—expressed in a combative, violence-tinged rhetoric—swiftly devalued the movement's moral authority, much to King's dismay. Most white Americans could support sit-ins, freedom rides, and marches on Washington because these were nonviolent dramatizations of black oppression. On the other hand, the guns of the Black Panthers and the rioting in Watts were neither dramatizations nor nonviolent. White Americans were scared, and fear rarely inspires racial generosity.

At the same time, resistance to black advancement became more subtle and thus more difficult to overcome. Most white supremacists had learned by 1965 that their initial course of action had been counterproductive. Resorting to violence against blacks had only outraged northerners and forced the federal government to intervene on the side of the movement. Though perhaps not as emotionally satisfying, quiet discrimination and foot-dragging turned out to be much more effective. This was because, compared with beatings and murder, tactics of avoidance and delay were practically invulnerable to moral reproach.

Jesse Jackson Runs for President

November 1983

In November 1983, Jesse Jackson announced his intention to seek the Democratic nomination for president. He thus became only the second African American (after Shirley Chisholm in 1972) to run a major nationwide campaign for the White House.

Following Martin Luther King's assassination in 1968, Jackson had continued working for the SCLC on the economic issues in which he specialized. But his aggressiveness, impatience, and outspoken manner irritated the SCLC leadership, and in 1971, he resigned to found his own organization in Chicago, People United to Save Humanity (PUSH).

Jackson's 1984 platform supported affirmative action and called for social programs to help poor Americans badly hurt by the economic policies of incumbent president Ronald Reagan. Dismissed by most pundits as a fringe candidate, Jackson nevertheless attracted 3.3 million primary voters to his multi-ethnic "rainbow coalition."

Jackson ran again in 1988 and performed even better, winning primaries or caucuses in seven states, including five on Super Tuesday and the Michigan caucus on March 26.

Jesse Jackson steps off a plane in Alabama in January 1984.

Overall, he won 6.7 million votes, finishing second to Michael Dukakis and earning serious consideration for vice president.

The L.A. Riots

April 1992

On March 3, 1991, Rodney King led Los Angeles police in a high-speed chase after officers tried to pull him over for speeding. When King was finally stopped, according to the officers, he resisted arrest and had to be physically subdued. According to King, the police simply beat him.

Police brutality, long a problem in L.A., had been a cause of the 1965 Watts riot. What made this case special was a video of the beating shot by an amateur cameraman. The tape, shown over and over again on television, turned the King case into a national sensation. Because of all the publicity, the trial of the police officers was moved to the mostly white suburb of Simi Valley, where a jury acquitted the men on April 29, 1992.

The verdict set off the worst rioting in U.S. history. Over four days, fifty-five people were killed, eight thousand arrests were made, and eleven hundred buildings were destroyed.

A man walks past a burning building during the L.A. riots, which began after a Simi Valley jury set free the policemen accused of beating Rodney King (inset).

As a result, after Selma the civil rights movement lost focus, and by the time of King's death, it had ceased to function as a mass movement. There was still a great deal of civil rights consciousness, but no shared program or unity of purpose. The gap between the SCLC and SNCC had always been wider than most people understood, but that divide was nothing compared with the gulf that existed in 1968 between the Black Panthers and the NAACP.

THE LEGACY

Civil rights activity continued after 1968 but on an ad hoc basis, with different groups pressing different agendas. Among the extremists, SNCC continued its descent into radicalism, becoming so dysfunctional that, according to a May 1971 FBI report, the organization had "not staged or participated in any demonstration or disruptive activity, and it is believed incapable of accomplishing same in view of the limited membership, lack of funds, and internal dissension." Part of the problem was a lack of leadership, with Moses, Carmichael, and Eldridge Cleaver all having left the country to live in Africa—Cleaver to escape prosecution on charges stemming from a Black Panther shootout with police.

The SCLC survived the death of King and the debacle of the Poor People's Campaign but became nearly as impotent as SNCC, never regaining its former glory. Several King protégés did take up the master's baton—notably Jesse Jackson, who founded Operation PUSH to carry on the economic work of the Chicago Freedom Movement, and Andrew Young, who won election to Congress in 1972 before becoming Pres. Jimmy Carter's ambassador to the United Nations in 1977. But neither was King, and neither had the Zeitgeist in his pocket.

As Young, Jackson, and other black leaders turned increasingly to electoral politics for the achievement of their goals, the campaign for black equality became a political movement not unlike those of other organized minority groups, such as Hispanics, union members, or gays. Although black politicians typically wrapped themselves in the rhetoric of the civil rights movement, they lacked its remarkable moral energy and instead had to make do with blacks' neither noble nor ignoble desire for an equitable share of the commonwealth.

Even so, the status of blacks in American society remains unique. Because of slavery, the African-American experience is not comparable to the familiar immigrant experiences of Germans, Italians, Poles, and Latinos. Blacks in America have been forced to bear a particularly heavy cultural burden, accumulated over centuries of oppression. That is why the influence of Malcolm X has grown, even posthumously—because his passion, strength, and insight have helped ease this burden. Malcolm's fundamental message—that blacks needed to be proud of themselves, not envious of whites—became the basis for a positive racial identity that still serves struggling blacks today.

Although the Zeitgeist no longer animates the cause of racial equity, the thoughts and deeds of Malcolm and others nevertheless remain ennobling and instructive. For all Americans, the civil rights movement of the 1950s and 1960s presents a model of idealized political activity—of how wrongs can be made at least partially right and how good intentions can overcome institutionalized hate. The history of this period teaches us about what should (but not always does) matter in life and how a great cause can bestow purpose at the same time it dispenses pain, anger, and disappointment.

The legacy of the civil rights movement, however, is also experienced today in more practical terms. Beginning with Eisenhower, U.S. presidents chose to force integration on a reluctant South through the federal courts. This strategy absolved them of personal responsibility for the integration, but only up to a point. Even worse, it left the work of consensus-building unattempted.

Federal troops could force all-white public schools to admit blacks, but they couldn't force angry white parents to keep their children enrolled there, so many all-white schools quickly became all-black ones. Private white "academies" began to appear, stripping public schools of their middle- and upper-class white constituencies, and with those students went most of the public

Million Man March

October 1995

African-American men from all over the country gathered on the Mall in Washington, D.C., on October 16, 1995, for the Million Man March, organized by Nation of Islam leader Louis Farrakhan. The advertised goal of the march was "unity, atonement, and brotherhood." Although most crowd estimates fall short of the one million participants envisioned by Farrakhan, the rally nevertheless exceeded the quarter-million people who attended the 1963 March on Washington.

Although Farrakhan's leadership was controversial, in part because of his consistently negative statements about Jews, blacks from many different faiths and walks of life took part in the Million Man March because they wanted to heed Farrakhan's call for African-American men to "take responsibility for their lives and families and commit to stopping the scourges of drugs, violence, and unemployment." As one marcher told a reporter, "Minister Farrakhan has some very

Participants in the Million Man March carry a banner along the Mall.

strong viewpoints on certain issues. We may not agree with everything, but we thought this was larger than just Minister Farrakhan."

In addition to Farrakhan, the day's speakers included, among many others, Rosa Parks, Jesse Jackson, and D.C. mayor Marion Barry. Also, as part of the event, which sought to boost black participation in national politics, hundreds of thousands of new black voters were registered.

Killen Redux

June 2005

Because the jury deadlocked in Edgar Ray Killen's 1967 trial, he never served any time for his role in the murders of Andrew Goodman, Michael Schwerner, and James Chaney in June 1964. Four decades later, however, Mississippi attorney general Jim Hood reopened the investigation and began presenting evidence to a Neshoba County grand jury, which indicted Killen in January 2005. At his subsequent arraignment, the seventy-nine-year-old Killen pled not guilty.

Killen's second trial featured testimony from both living and dead witnesses. (The testimony of those witnesses no longer alive was read into the trial record using the transcript of the 1967 proceedings.) The testimony focused on his leadership role in the Neshoba County Klan.

Although the jury couldn't reach a verdict on the murder charges because Killen wasn't at the scene of the crime, he was nevertheless convicted on three counts of manslaughter and sentenced to consecutive twenty-year terms.

According to John Lewis, who was first elected to Congress from Georgia's Fifth District in 1986, the reopening of this and other notorious civil rights cases "will have a redeeming effect on the very soul of this region of our country."

RIGHT: Two sheriff's deputies lead Edgar Ray Killen into the Neshoba County courthouse on January 12, 2005, for his arraignment on murder charges. Killen, who is shown wearing handcuffs and a bulletproof vest, was held by Judge Marcus Gordon on $250,000 bail.

LEFT: Killen waves to friends as he enters the Meridian, Mississippi, federal courthouse on October 12, 1967, during his first trial on charges related to the 1964 murders of Andrew Goodman, Michael Schwerner, and James Chaney.

funding for education. As a result, southern public school systems, especially those in large urban areas, deteriorated to the point at which the *Brown* victory seemed nearly hollow.

During the 1970s, in the wake of "white flight," the federal judiciary tried again, ordering forced busing to remedy the growing disparities between affluent white schools in the suburbs and inferior black schools in the inner cities. Sadly, this strategy produced a great deal of violence but few educational improvements.

Wandering even farther into legislative areas, federal courts also mandated during the 1970s racial preferences in hiring and school admissions. The intent of these orders was to close the economic gap that has long existed between blacks and whites as a result of racial discrimination, but their legal basis was vague and their popular support nearly nonexistent. The political backlash from them is still being felt.

Which brings us back to Hegel and his grand ideas about world history. In Hegel's view, history is always moving forward, from less freedom to more freedom. Before the civil rights movement, African Americans lived in a state of legal oppression. This was the stage of their history in which Martin Luther King found them.

> "I don't know how many of you would be able to write a history book. But you are certainly making history, and you are experiencing history. And you will make it possible for the historians of the future to write a marvelous chapter."

MARTIN LUTHER KING AT A MASS MEETING IN BIRMINGHAM ON MAY 6, 1963

The stage to which he and others brought black America was not truly the "promised land" of which he often spoke. Many of the problems that he identified in Chicago in 1966—economic exploitation, political powerlessness, substandard housing, inferior education—still plague

African Americans today. But a new stage of history was reached before his death—a stage in which blacks can pursue economic and social opportunities without the legal barriers that had previously restricted them.

This is how history happens: No revolutions are complete; no victories are absolute. Slavery persisted in America for more than 250 years before it finally ended in 1865. Legal inequality lasted another century before it, too, passed away, leaving other hardships unresolved. Additional work still needs to be done. But, as Hegel assures us, more freedom is coming. History is merely taking its time.

Index

Picture Credits

AP/WWP   AP/Wide World Photos
BNA   Baltimore News American, Special Collections, University of Maryland Libraries
BPL   Birmingham Public Library Archives
JFK   John F. Kennedy Presidential Library
LBJ   Lyndon B. Johnson Presidential Library
MDAH   Mississippi Department of Archives and History
MSRC   Moorland-Spingarn Research Center, Howard University
UNC   University of North Carolina at Chapel Hill, Wilson Library, Manuscripts Department, Southern Historical Collection
USM   McCain Library and Archives, The University of Southern Mississippi
WHS   Wisconsin Historical Society
WP/DCPL   Copyright Washington Post, reprinted by permission of the DC Public Library

1: Montgomery County Archives; 2: LOC/ LC-U9-10358; 4: Corbis; 6: Corbis; 7: Corbis; 8: Corbis; 9: (t) Corbis, (b) AP/WWP

Part I
10: LOC/LC-B8171-3448

Chapter 1
12: (l) LOC/LC-USZC4-4608, (r) LOC/LC-USZC4-5341; 13: (t) LOC/LC-BH83-171, (b) LOC/LC-B8184-B1163; 14: (t) LOC/LC-USZ62-19234, (b) LOC/LC-USZ62-77086; 15: (t) LOC/LC-USZ62-49988, (b) LOC/LC-USZC4-2623; 16: (t) Agincourt Press, (b) LOC/LC-USZ62-126347; 17: (t) LOC, (b) Denver Public Library/GB-8463; 18: (t) Agincourt Press, (b) LOC/LC-USZ62-224478; 19: (t) LOC; 20: (t) LOC/LC-USZ62-66365, (b) National Park Service, Museum Management Program, Tuskegee Institute National Historic Site/TUIN 1800, TUIN 1249-1251; 21: (t) Special Collections, Tuskegee University, (b) NA/306-PSD-58-2517; 22: Harry Hayden Collection, New Hanover Public Library; 23: (tl) MSRC, (tr) University of Massachusetts—Amherst, (b) University of Massachusetts—Amherst

Chapter 2
24: (tl) LOC, (tr) University of Massachusetts—Amherst, (b) LOC/LC-USZC4-4734; 25: (t) Illinois State Historical Society, (bl) Agincourt Press, (br) Illinois State Historical Society; 26: (l) University of Massachusetts—Amherst, (r) LOC; 27: (t) LOC/LC-USZC4-1971, (b) Agincourt Press: 28: Agincourt Press; 30: (t) Yale Collection of American Literature, Beinecke Rare Book and Manuscript Library, Yale University, (b) Corbis; 31: LOC/LC-USZ62-33789; 32: (tl) LOC/LC-USZ62-36619, (tr) LOC/LC-USZ62-96154, (b) Marcus Garvey and UNIA Papers Project, UCLA, 33: (t) Agincourt Press, (b) Corbis; 34: (t) Morgan County

Archive, (bl) LOC/LC-USZ62-121575, (br) Corbis; 35: (t) LOC/LC-USZ62-35824, (b) Scottsboro Collection, Cornell Law Library; 36: (t) LOC/LC-USZ62-35363, (b) NA/47-GA-98-4220; 37: (t) Agincourt Press, (bl) LOC/LC-USW3-T01-015550-E, (br) LOC; 38: (t) LOC/NYWTS, (b) James Leonard Jr. and Lula Peterson Farmer Papers, Center for American History, The University of Texas at Austin/Box 2R637; 39: (t) LOC/LC-USF-33-20522-M2, (bl) LOC/LC-USZC4-10296, (br) LOC/LC-USZC4-10296; 40: LOC/NYWTS, 41: (t) LOC/NYWTS, (b) Special Collections Department, Georgia State University Library/Amsterdam News; 42: (tl) NA, (tr) NA/306-NT-355-S-22, (b) Agincourt Press; 43: (tl) LOC, (tr) Strom Thurmond Collections, Clemson University, (b) LOC/NYWTS

Part II
44: Corbis

Chapter 3
46: AP/WWP; 47: (l) MSRC, (r) MSRC; 48: (t) LOC/LC-USZ62-101029, (bl) LOC, (br) MSRC; 49: (t) LOC/LC-USF34-44089-D, (b) LOC/LC-USF34-46580-E, 50: LOC/LC-USZC4-4733; 51: (t) NA/306-PSD-67-1984, (b) LOC/LC-USZ62-118181; 52: Corbis; 54: (t) LOC/LC-USZ62-84494, (b) LOC/LC-USZ62-116927; 55: (l) Agincourt Press, (r) Agincourt Press; 56: (t) LOC, (cl) Agincourt Press, (cr) Agincourt Press, (b) Corbis; 57: (t) South Carolina Department of Archives and History, (b) South Carolina Department of Archives and History; 58: (t) LOC, (b) LOC/LC-USZC4-4866; 59: (tl) AP/WWP, (tr) Carl Iwasaki/Getty Images, (b) Corbis; 60: (t) LOC/LC-USZ62-113498, (b) LOC/LC-USZ62-126455; 61: (t) WP/DCPL, (bl) Collection of the Supreme Court of the United States/Urban Archives, Temple University Archives, (br) AP/WWP; 62: (t) LOC/LC-U9-183B-20, (b) LOC/LC-MS-52258-S79; 63: LOC/LC-U9-657B-14

Chapter 4
64: LOC; 65: (t) LOC, (bl) LOC/LC-USZ62-111239, (br) WP/DCPL; 66: (t) LOC/LC-USF33-030660-M2, (b) LOC/LC-USF33-030592-M1; 67: (t) LOC/LC-USZ62-124377, (b) AP/WWP; 68: (t) LOC/LC-USZC2-6304, (b) AP/WWP; 69: Memphis Commercial Appeal; 70: (tl) Memphis Commercial Appeal, (tr) LOC/NYWTS, (b) LOC/LC-USZ62-118182; 71: LOC/NYWTS, 72: (t) LOC/NYWTS, (b) LOC/NYWTS; 73: (t) LOC/NYWTS, (b) Corbis; 74: (l) LOC/NYWTS, (r) LOC; 75: LOC/LC-USZ62-131058

Chapter 5
76: BPL/30.47; 77: (t) Montgomery County Archives, (b) Peaceful Warriors Collection; 78: (t) Agincourt Press, (b) LOC/LC-USZ62-121754; 79: (t) NA/306-PSD-65-1882, (b) Collections of The Henry Ford/B.115838.1; 80: (t) LOC, (b) Alabama Department of Archives and History, Montgomery, Alabama; 81: (t) The Martin Luther King Jr.

Collection in The Howard Gotlieb Archival Research Center, Boston University, (b) Alabama Tourism; 82: (t) Agincourt Press, (b) AP/WWP; 83: (t) Agincourt Press, (b) LOC/LC-U9-11696 #14A; 84: (tl) Corbis, (tr) BNA, (b) Swarthmore College Peace Collection; 85: Don Cravens/Getty Images; 86: LOC/LC-USZ62-119165; 87: (t) Don Cravens/Getty Images, (b) LOC/NYWTS; 88: Don Cravens/Getty Images; 90: (t) NA/306-PSD-68-1120, (r) Alabama Department of Archives and History, Montgomery, Alabama, (b) Don Cravens/Getty Images; 91: (l) WHS/30654, (r) Don Cravens/Getty Images; 92: (t) Don Cravens/Getty Images, (b) Don Cravens/Getty Images; 93: (t) NA/306-PS-51-671, (bl) Agincourt Press, (br) LOC/NYWTS; 94: (l) Paul Robertson Sr., (r) Montgomery County Archives; 95: (t) WP/DCPL, (b) LOC/NYWTS; 96: (tl) Fellowship of Reconciliation, (tr) Fellowship of Reconciliation, (b) AP/WWP; 97: (t) LOC/NYWTS, (b) LOC/LC-USZ62-111235

Chapter 6
98: Corbis; 99: (t) Strom Thurmond Collection, Clemson University, (bl) NA/306-PSD-57-18300, (br) NA/306-PSD-57-1829; 100: (t) University of Arkansas, Fayetteville, (b) Central High Museum Collection, UALR Archives and Special Collections/B-12, I.298; 101: (tl) University of Arkansas, Fayetteville, (tr) LOC/LC-USZ62-115050, (b) Corbis; 102: (t) LOC, (b) LOC/LC-USZ62-126829; 103: (t) Corbis, (b) WP/DCPL; 104: (t) LOC/LC-USZ62-120258, (b) Central High Museum Collection, UALR Archives and Special Collections/B-12, I.251; 105: (t) Corbis, (b) Will Counts/Arkansas Democrat-Gazette; 106: A. Y. Owen/Getty Images; 108: (t) Stan Wayman/Getty Images, (r) Andy Kraushaar/Wisconsin Historical Society, (b) LOC/NYWTS; 109: (t) Corbis, (b) WP/DCPL; 110: (t) LOC/LC-USZ62-126828, (b) LOC/LC-U9-1525F-28; 111: (t) WP/DCPL, (b) Francis Miller/Getty Images

Chapter 7
112: © Eve Arnold/Magnum Photos; 113: (t) Robert W. Kelley/Getty Images, (c) Bruce Hartford, (b) Photographs and Prints Division, Schomburg Center for Research in Black Culture, The New York Public Library, Astor, Lenox and Tilden Foundations; 114: (t) California Department of Corrections, California State Archives/SQ 42314, (c) LOC, (b) LOC/LC-USZ62-116384; 115: (t) Afro-American Newspapers Archives and Research Center, (c) Corbis, (b) Commonwealth of Massachusetts, Department of Corrections; 116: (t) Agincourt Press, (c) Agincourt Press, (bl) Agincourt Press, (br) Agincourt Press; 117: © Leonard Freed/Magnum Photos; 118: (t) Corbis, (b) Lloyd Yearwood/Getty Images; 119: (tl) LOC/Lot 13100, No. 0041, (tr) LOC/LC-L9-61-9520-U, #11, (b) Peter Keegan/Getty Images; 120: (tl) FBI, (tr) LOC, (b) LOC/LC-USZ62-111169; 121: (tl) LOC/LC-U9-6355, #9, (tr) Corbis, (b) LOC/NYWTS; 122: (t) Agincourt Press, (b) LOC/LC-USZ6-1847; 123: (t) LOC/LC-USZ62-111431, (b) WP/DCPL; 124: Corbis

Part III
126: Corbis

Chapter 8
128: (t) Swarthmore College Peace Collection/Fellowship of Reconciliation, (b) LOC/NYWTS; 129: Corbis; 130: (tl) LOC/NYWTS, (tr) Corbis, (b) LOC/LC-USZ62-115078; 131: (t) WP/DCPL, (bl) LOC, (br) Corbis; 132: (t) Corbis, (b) Nashville Public Library, Nashville Room; 133: (t) Nashville Public Library, Nashville Room, (b) Lynn Pelham/Getty Images; 134: (t) Corbis, (c) Nashville Public Library, Nashville Room, (b) Nashville Public Library, Nashville Room: 135: (t) LOC/LC-USZ62-110575, (b) Donald Uhrbrock/Getty Images; 136: Donald Uhrbrock/Getty Images; 137: (tl) Horace Mann School, (tr) Jan Moore, (b) Donald Uhrbrock/Getty Images; 138: AP/WWP; 139: (t) AP/WWP, (b) AP/WWP; 140: (l) Donald Uhrbrock/Getty Images, (r) WP/DCPL; 141: (t) LOC/NYWTS, (c) Agincourt Press, (bl) Agincourt Press, (br) Corbis; 142: (t) JFK, (b) AP/WWP; 143: (t) Corbis, (b) NA/306-PSD-61-4520

Chapter 9
144: © Bruce Davidson/Magnum Photos; 145: (tl) WP/DCPL, (tr) LOC/LC-USZ62-119480, (c) Jo Freeman, (b) William Lovelace/Getty Images; 146: Swarthmore College Peace Collection; 147: (t) Corbis, (bl) Corbis, (br) Central Press/Getty Images; 148: (l) AP/WWP, (r) Corbis; 149: (l) LOC/NYWTS, (r) LOC/NYWTS; 150: (t) WP/DCPL, (b) LOC/NYWTS; 151: (t) AP/WWP, (b) Agincourt Press; 152: (l) AP/WWP, (r) NA/79-R-6372A; 153: (t) LOC/LC-USW38-003893-D, (b) WP/DCPL; 154: (tl) Tommy Giles, (tr) WP/DCPL, (b) WP/DCPL; 155: (t) LOC/LC-USZ62-117558, (b) LOC/NYWTS; 156: (t) WP/DCPL, (c) Paul Schutzer/Getty Images, (b) NA/306-PSD-62-484; 157: WP/DCPL; 158: Paul Schutzer/Getty Images; 160: (t) Lee Lockwood/Getty Images, (b) LOC/LC-USZ62-119919; 161: (t) Johnson (Paul B.) Family Papers, USM, (b) Agincourt Press

Chapter 10
162: (t) Corbis, (b) University Museums, University of Mississippi; 163: (tl) Jo Freeman, (tr) Jo Freeman, (b) Ed Clark/Getty Images; 164: (t) © Danny Lyon/Magnum Photos, (b) Hazelton (Margaret) Freedom Summer Collection/Frazer Thomason, USM; 165: (t) WHS/32236, (b) WHS/32237; 166: (t) Corbis, (bl) LOC/LC-USZ62-122432, (br) MDAH, Tougaloo College Archive/GM0025; 167: (l) MDAH, Tougaloo College Archive/GM0007-01, (r) LOC/LC-U9-8556-24; 168: (l) Corbis, (rt) MDAH/2-55-2-68-1-1-1, (rb) MDAH/2-55-2-70-1-1-1; 169: (l) WHS/32238, (r) Corbis; 170: (t) Field Foundation, Center for American History, The University of Texas at Austin/Box 2S451, (b) Campbell (Will D.) Papers/Al Clayton, USM; 171: (t) LOC/NYWTS, (b) LOC/LC-DIG-ppmsca-05544; 172: (t) Corbis, (b) Corbis; 173: (t) LOC/NYWTS, (b) WP/DCPL; 174: (t) LOC/LC-USZ62-133365, (b) Corbis; 175: (tl) JFK, (tr) LOC/NYWTS, (b) Corbis; 176: (tl) NA/306-PSD-62-5837, (tr) JFK, (b) LOC/NYWTS; 177: (tl) LOC/LC-USZ62-111240, (tr) LOC, (b) LOC/NYWTS

Chapter 11
178: WP/DCPL; 179: (tl) LOC/LC-U9-8339, #10, (tr) WHS/32235, (b) LOC/LC-U9-8340, #17; 180: (t) LOC/LC-U9-8342, #14, (b) LOC/LC-U9-8341, #16; 181: (t) LOC/NYWTS, (b) NA/306-PSA-63-4702; 182: (t) LOC/NYWTS, (b) Corbis; 183: (t) Corbis, (b) WP/DCPL; 184: (t) Donald Uhrbrock/Getty Images, (b) WP/DCPL; 185: Donald Uhrbrock/Getty Images; 186: (tl) LOC/LC-U9-9769, #7, (tr) BPL/829.1.1.62, (b) BPL/827.1.1.8.29; 187: (l) Corbis, (tr) LOC/LC-USZ62-128478, (br) BPL/45.1.1.1.23; 188: (t) LOC/LC-USZ62-121286, (b) AP/WWP; 189: BPL/1125.11.20A2; 190: (t) WP/DCPL, (b) Corbis; 191: (t) Fellowship of Reconciliation, (bl) American Friends Service Committee, (br) LOC/LC-USZ62-120213; 192: (t) AP/WWP, (b) WP/DCPL; 193: (t) AP/WWP, (b) AP/WWP; 194: AP/WWP; 196: (t) AP/WWP, (b) AP/WWP; 197: (t) WP/DCPL, (b) LOC/NYWTS; 198: (t) Corbis, (b) Corbis; 199: (t) LOC/LC-U9-9769, #9, (bl) WP/DCPL, zz(br) NA/306-PSD-67-3917

Chapter 12
200: Corbis; 201: (t) LOC/LC-U9-9930-20, (b) Corbis; 202: (l) LOC/LC-U9-9956-30, (r) JFK; 203: (t) Corbis, (bl) NA/306-PSD-63-4066, (br) John Loengard/Getty Images; 204: (t) FBI, (b) NA/306-PSC-63-4059; 205: NA/306-PS-63-3251; 206: (t) LOC/LC-USZ62-119524, (b) LOC/LC-USZ62-133366; 207: (t) LOC/NYWTS, (b) LOC/NYWTS; 208: (t) WP/DCPL, (bl) LOC/NYWTS, (br) Warshaw Collection of Business Americana–Afro-Americana, Archives Center, National Museum of American History, Behring Center, Smithsonian Institution; 209: (t) Robert W. Kelley/Getty Images, (b) NA/306-SSM-4A-53-26; 210: LOC/LC-L9-68-1495-X, #21; 211: Jo Freeman; 212: (t) LOC, (b) AP/WWP; 213: NA/306-SSM-4D86-3; 214: (t) BPL/85.1.20, (b) AP/WWP; 215: (t) Corbis, (b) LBJ/W425-21; 216: (t) LOC/NYWTS, (b) LOC/NYWTS; 217: Corbis; 218: LBJ/C522-2-WH64; 219: (t) LOC/NYWTS, (b) Hulton Archive/Getty Images

Part IV
220: LOC/LC-U9-12053-6

Chapter 13
222: (t) Randall (Herbert) Freedom Summer Photographs, USM, (b) Zeman (Zoya) Freedom Summer Collection, USM; 223: (l) LOC/LC-USZ62-126802, (r) UNC/4340, Box 1, Folder 2; 224: (tl) UNC/4340, Box 32, Folder 361, (tr) UNC/4340, Subseries 9.5, Box 194, Folder 366, (b) UNC/4340, Box 32, Folder 363; 225: (t) Jo Freeman, (b) LOC/NYWTS,; 226: (t) Agincourt Press, (b) Zeman (Zoya) Freedom Summer Collection, USM; 227: (t) Randall (Herbert) Freedom Summer Photographs, USM, (b) WP/DCPL; 228: (t) LOC/LC-U9-12065-8/9, (b) Grupper (Ira) and Beech (Bob) Civil Rights Collection, USM; 229: (t) WP/DCPL, (b) Randall (Herbert) Freedom Summer Photographs, USM; 230: (t) Ellin (Joseph and Nancy) Freedom Summer Collection, USM, (b) Ellin (Joseph and Nancy) Freedom Summer Collection, USM; 231: (tl) Corbis, (tr) Corbis, (b) LOC/LC-USZ62-114327; 232: (t) LOC/LC-USZ62-125504, (bl) WP/DCPL, (br) Randall (Herbert) Freedom Summer Photographs, USM;

Chapter 14
233: (t) Corbis, (b) AP/WWP; 234: LOC/NYWTS; 235: (tl) Zeman (Zoya) Freedom Summer Collection, USM, (tr) Hazelton (Margaret) Freedom Summer Collection/Frazer Thomason, USM, (b) NA/306-PSD-64-1246; 236: (t) LOC/LC-U9-12250M-13A, (c) Zeman (Zoya) Freedom Summer Collection, USM, (b) LOC/LC-U9-12470B-17; 237: (t) AP/WWP, (b) AP/WWP; 238: Corbis; 240: (t) LBJ/355-45-WH64, (b) LOC/NYWTS; 241: (t) Corbis, (b) AP/WWP

Chapter 15
242: LOC/NYWTS; 243: (t) Zwerling (Matthew) Freedom Summer Collection, USM, (b) AP/WWP; 244: WP/DCPL; 245: (t) AP/WWP, (b) AP/WWP; 246: (t) LOC-LC-USZ62-121757, (b) AP/WWP; 247: NA/306-PSD-68-1127; 248: (t) BNA, (b) Corbis; 249: (t) WP/DCPL, (b) LOC/NYWTS; 250: (t) LOC/LC-USZ62-118220, (b) WHS/32458; 251: (t) AP/WWP, (b) Corbis; 252: (t) LOC/NYWTS, (b) LOC/LC-USZ62-127732; 253: Corbis; 254: Corbis; 255: (t) LOC/NYWTS, (b) LOC/LC-USZ62-111158; 256: (t) AP/WWP, (b) BNA; 257: (t) Corbis, (b) Corbis; 258: (t) NA/306-PSD-65-1109, (b) NA/306-PSD-65-1112; 259: (t) AP/WWP, (b) WP/DCPL; 260: William Lovelace/Getty Images; 262: (t) LOC/NYWTS, (c) NA/306-PSD-65-3502, (b) NA/306-PSD-66-1887; 263: Corbis

Chapter 15
264: Corbis; 265: (t) LOC/NYWTS, (b) Corbis; 266: (t) Corbis, (b) Corbis; 267: (t) Agincourt Press, (b) LOC/LC-L9-65-2434-QQQ, #4; 268: (t) Agincourt Press, (b) Corbis; 269: (tl) Corbis, (tr) LOC/LC-USZ62-113636, (b) Corbis; 270: (t) AP/WWP, (b) AP/WWP; 271: (t) AP/WWP, (b) Art Shay/Getty Images; 272: (tl) AP/WWP, (tr) Corbis, (b) Corbis; 273: (t) Corbis, (b) AP/WWP; 274: (t) Corbis, (b) AP; 275: (t) AP/WWP, (b) AP/WWP; 276: (l) Jo Freeman, (r) Corbis; 278: (l) MDAH, Tougaloo College Archive/T-90.20, (r) WP/DCPL; 279: (t) LOC/NYWTS, (b) LOC/LC-USZ62-91158; 280: (t) LOC/LC-USZC4-6286, (b) LOC/LC-U9-20020-17A; 281: (t) Ward Sharrer, (c) Susie Paige Afro-American Greeting Card Collection, Archives Center, National Museum of American History, Behring Center, Smithsonian Institution, (b) NA/306-PSA-67-4501; 282: (t) AP/WWP, (b) Corbis; 283: (t) AP/WWP, (c) Agincourt Press, (b) Mississippi Valley Collection, University of Memphis; 284: (t) Corbis, (b) Joseph Louw/Getty Images; 285: (t) Corbis, (c) Corbis, (b) WP/DCPL

Epilogue
286: Santi Visalli Inc./Getty Images; 288: Corbis; 289: AP/WWP; 290: Corbis; 291: (l) Corbis, (r) Corbis; 292: Corbis; 293: (l) Corbis, (r) Corbis

Author's Acknowledgments

The quality and scope of the images in this book could not have been achieved without the diligent efforts of many people. Not the least of these were the archivists whose job it is to preserve these materials for future generations. Of particular help to us were the following, who endured many telephone calls and detailed questioning: Cynthia Luckie of the Alabama Department of Archives and History, Terry Foss and Barbara Montabana of the American Friends Service Committee, Don Veasey of the Birmingham Public Library, Charles Niles and Sean Noel of Boston University, Genevieve Troka of the California State Archives, Alan Burns and Susan Hiott of the Clemson University Libraries, Brian Eden and Jean Callihan of the Cornell Law Library, Peggy Appleman of the D.C. Public Library, Richard Deats and Stephanie Hughes of the Fellowship of Reconciliation, Barbara Connolly of the Horace Mann School, Stephen Plotkin and Laurie Austin of the John F. Kennedy Presidential Library, Anthony Yuen of the Marcus Garvey Papers Project at UCLA, Diane Wiffin of the Massachusetts Department of Corrections, Jim and Mary Anne Petty of the Middle Passage and African American Museum, Sarah Rowe-Sims and Clarence Hunter of the Mississippi Department of Archives and History, Clifford Muse and Donna Wells of the Moorland-Spingarn Research Center, Beth Odle of the Nashville Public Library, Beverly Tetterton of the New Hanover Public Library, Thomas Lisanti and Anthony Toussaint of the Schomburg Center for Research in Black Culture, Kay Peterson of the Smithsonian Institution, Bryan Collars of the South Carolina Department of Archives and History, Mary Beth Sigado and Wendy

Chmielewski of the Swarthmore College Peace Collection, Jim Orr of The Henry Ford, Cynthia Wilson of the Tuskegee Institute, Anne Prichard of the University of Arkansas–Fayetteville, Jillian Barnett of the University of Arkansas–Little Rock, Yvonne Arnold and Diane DeCesare Ross of The University of Southern Mississippi, Chris Ratliff of the University of Memphis, and Dee Grimsrud and Lisa Hinzman of the Wisconsin Historical Society.

Many other images reside in the collections of news agencies and stock photography houses. We would like to thank those who facilitated our access to these images: Christina Cruse of the Afro-American Newspapers, Barry Arthur of the *Arkansas Democrat-Gazette*, Barry Asman of Asman Photo, Christine Thompson Ferrero of Getty Images, Michael Shulman of Magnum Photos, Claude Jones of the *Memphis Commercial Appeal*, and Carolyn McGoldrick and Regalle Asuncion of Wide World Photos.

In some cases, the photographers themselves kindly agreed to allow us to reproduce their unique work. These included: Al Clayton, Tommy Giles, Herbert Randall, Paul Robertson Sr., and Ward Sharrer.

Likewise, these veterans of the civil rights movement granted us access to their collections of rarely seen memorabilia: Anne Braden, Will Campbell, Joseph and Nancy Ellin, Jo Freeman, Bruce Hartford, Margaret Hazelton, Bubby Johnston, Edwin King, John Maurer, Jan Moore, James and Ted Otis, Wally Roberts, R. L. T. Smith, Loris Thomason, Zoya Zeman, and Matthew Zwerling.

The following on-site image researchers made it possible for us to search archives whose collections would otherwise have been beyond our reach: Laura Anderson, Joshua Bearden, Diana Claitor, Donna Coates, Sally Jacobs, Ken Johnson, John Nondorf, Laura Puaca, and Brent Riffel.

Finally, we would like to offer a few extraordinary thanks: to Jim Kates of Zephyr Press, for his generous guidance in pointing us in the right directions; to Charles Dunagin of the *McComb Enterprise-Journal*, who took the time to help us find out more about the McComb project, an underappreciated aspect of civil rights history; to Will and Phelan McGreal, who pitched in when we most needed their help; and to our legal counsel, Alan J. Kaufman, who made this book possible.